# TOTEMISM
# IN INDIA

# TOTEMISM
# IN INDIA

JOHN V. FERREIRA
*Reader in Cultural Anthropology*
*University of Bombay*

OXFORD UNIVERSITY PRESS
1965

*Oxford University Press, Amen House, London E.C. 4*
GLASGOW  NEW YORK  TORONTO  MELBOURNE  WELLINGTON
BOMBAY  CALCUTTA  MADRAS  KARACHI  LAHORE  DACCA
CAPE TOWN  SALISBURY  NAIROBI  IBADAN
KUALA LUMPUR  HONG KONG

PRINTED IN INDIA BY V. D. LIMAYE AT THE INDIA PRINTING WORKS,
FORT, BOMBAY AND PUBLISHED BY JOHN BROWN
OXFORD UNIVERSITY PRESS, OXFORD HOUSE, APOLLO BUNDER, BOMBAY 1

IN MEMORIAM
EMERITUS PROFESSOR DOKTOR
WILHELM KOPPERS
S.V.D.

# PREFACE

THIS WORK is a somewhat modified version of a dissertation presented in the University of Vienna for the Ph.D. degree. The modifications consist mainly in the redrafting of the terminal section in Chapter II and in a few additions, subtractions and rephrasings in the other chapters.

The extent of interest in the phenomenon of totemism may be partly gauged from the fact that Christian Chulliat's *Bibliographie critique du totémisme* (Paris, 1936) is a book of 204 pages, that ethnologists in the German-speaking countries continue steadily to examine the phenomenon from the historical standpoint, and that John Beattie in his recent work *Other Cultures* (London, 1964) deals with the subject at fair length, recognizing the variability of its forms but hesitating to dismiss it as an illusion, as had C. Lévi-Strauss somewhat earlier (Paris, 1962). A re-examination of the phenomenon in India has given me the opportunity of reconsidering its psychological roots, of re-affirming its sociological significance without Durkheimian exaggerations, and of taking a more moderate stand towards its diffusionist aspect. As an aberrant but widely distributed form of the craving for wholeness (complementarity as I call it), totemism is both colourful and fascinating. I have therefore no doubt that this work will interest both the specialist and the general reader.

I am indebted to Professor J. Haekel, Director of the Ethnological Institute, Vienna, under whose guidance I wrote this study, for a number of valuable suggestions, most of which have been embodied in the text in the course of my revisions. It goes without saying that the responsibility for whatever faults of a factual or interpretative nature which remain in the work is mine alone. Ethnological interpretations on a scale as large as the Indian subcontinent confront the risk of being dubbed ' too speculative ', particularly when they are based on ethnographic material which in many directions is still extremely limited. Despite these limitations, however, large-scale works of this kind serve a useful, almost indispensable purpose, when undertaken from time to time. They offer a comprehensive picture which facilitates the task of researchers with narrower or broader interests.

In presenting the evidence on Indian totemism directly, that is to say, as it appears in the old and new sources, I have been actuated by two reasons: first, that Niggemeyer's study (Wien-Mödling, 1933), in which the material has been condensed in the form of an analytical and classificatory digest, obviates in some measure the necessity of following in his footsteps; and, second, that anthropologists interested in the totemic phenomenon in India can thus observe more easily the nature of the material with which the interpreter is faced. In reporting the views of, or presenting the material supplied by, the older pre-independence writers, I have generally retained the names of the states and provinces given by them. This has been done because the state boundaries in post-independence India do not coincide with those of the states, provinces and presidencies of pre-independence India. Therefore, a translation of the old names into the new ones—if undertaken in this connexion—would raise considerable difficulties and would perhaps not represent the views and reports of the older writers quite accurately.

I should like to take this opportunity of recording my cordial thanks to Dr Stephen Fuchs, S.V.D., of the Indian Anthropos Institute, to Dr Anna Hohenwart-Gerlachstein and the other staff-members of the Ethnological Institute in Vienna, and to P. C. Thoma, S.V.D., for various kindnesses of which I was the happy recipient.

                                                                    J.V.F.

# CONTENTS

# I

## *INTRODUCTION*

IN THE YEAR 1933 there appeared in the pages of *Anthropos*
(*Internationale Zeitschrift für Völker- und Sprachenkunde*—
Founder: P. W. Schmidt) Hermann Niggemeyer's study of totemism in India.[1] In this study, remarkable for its thoroughness and
compactness, Niggemeyer undertook a survey of the phenomenon
in India based on the then available written sources and in terms
of the then current ethnological standpoint in Vienna and its
spheres of influence. In other words, he attempted (*a*) a description and analysis of the sociological and religious forms of
totemism in India, and (*b*) a culture-historical interpretation—in
so far as that was then possible—of the available evidence.

According to Niggemeyer, totemism is present where a definite
group of human beings is set in certain relations to an animal,
a plant, a heavenly phenomenon or an object, after which they
are named, and in connexion with which the views prevail that
the members of this group as such may not marry among one
another, and that the object after which the group is named must
be respected in some way by the members of the group.[2]

On the basis of his study, Niggemeyer arrived at the following conclusions, summarized by himself into thirteen points:

1. India is a country in which totemism occurs clearly
formed in wide areas.

2. With the exception of the extremest southern point
of the peninsula where it is lacking, totemism in India has
spread southwards from the line Gujarat-Allahabad-Benares.
Central India and the entire east from Chota Nagpur to
the Telugu country in the south are specially intensive
totemic regions.

3. Indian totemism was organized originally and predominantly along patrilineal lines; two matrilineal-totemic
regions—Southwest India and Assam—are secondary, local
contact-phenomena between totemless motherright and patrilineal totemism.

4. Characteristic is the strong emphasis on the exogamy

[1] For notes to this chapter see pp. 6-7.

of the totem clans which are in all cases again combined into strictly endogamous castes and tribes. The tribe or caste frequently breaks up into many sub-tribes or sub-castes with a number of exogamous totem clans; yet this type of division seems to be younger than the ' atomic ' tribes and castes.

5. Sex totemism is lacking in India. Individual totemism has been proved in one single case; it occurs, however, in the tribe concerned, next to the usual group totemism. Its culture-historical position in India is not clear.

6. The religious side of totemism in India is distinctly formed. The avoidance rules are universally spread and constitute indeed the oldest element. Mourning for the totem occurs as a characteristically local development in Central India and further eastward. Worship of the totem is widely spread and took on a greater range only under the influence of the advanced culture.

7. The worship of the totem at marriages developed in the Maratha area and spread with the modelled representation of the totem to Central India.

8. The inner relation of the totem clans to the totem is apprehended as a kind of relationship. Among many tribes and castes the idea of descent is recognizable; other tribes identify the totem clan or single members of the clan with the totem.

9. Indian totemism can be classified into five districts, two matrilineal—Southwest India and Assam—and three patrilineal: Maratha totemism, Southeast group and North-east group. From these groups the northeastern primitive tribes appear to represent the oldest state of things.

10. The probable original bearers of totemism are von Eickstedt's Gondid racial group. The distinctly formed totemism of the Munda peoples and of the Grazil-Indid Telugu is to be traced back to Gondid influences.

11. If one claims the Gondid as bearers of totemism, one must adopt a relatively great age for Indian totemism; for in India, the Gondid are older than the Indid, perhaps also older than the Melanid.

12. The thousand-year-old influence of the advanced culture in India is essentially determinant in regard to the existence and forms of totemism. Totemism has contributed an essential factor—group exogamy—to the development of the advanced culture, but has ever more been broken up, reshaped and displaced by the advance of that culture.

13. The forms of Indian totemism prove that it is not a special product of Indian culture; but that it must have

once stood in an historical connexion with totemism in other parts of the world.[3]

Earlier works dealing with totemism in India contrast adversely in range and depth with Niggemeyer's. These may be classified as follows: (a) works by foreign scholars, and (b) works by British officials and missionaries in India, and by Indian scholars. Of those by foreign scholars, Sir James Frazer's in his monumental *Totemism and Exogamy*[4] takes its rightful place at the head. In the first and fourth volumes of this five-volumed achievement, Frazer outlines his theories of totemic origins, and in these and the rest of the five volumes gives us a world-wide survey of totemic phenomena as extensive empirical base. Although he allots relatively considerable space to the compilation of the Indian material, Frazer's theoretical attention was concentrated on Australia. He has, therefore, comparatively little to add of a theoretically significant nature on Indian totemism. But his influence on British officials and others in India was considerable; and the publication of his *Totemism and Exogamy* in 1910 served to strengthen interest in the totemic phenomenon all over the world. Other scholars like Graebner,[5] Schmidt,[6] and Przyluski put forward interpretations which may be characterized as hasty, sweeping or more or less incorrect. Of the references, ethnographic compilations and interpretations by British officials and missionaries in India and by Indian scholars, all are marred by inadequacies in range or depth and by other shortcomings. The earlier works like those of Macpherson, Dalton and P. B. Bose make occasional and incidental references to totemism. They were followed by the great ethnographic compilations begun by Sir Herbert Risley[7]—doyen of Indian anthropology, and the first to call attention to the wide prevalence of totemism combined with exogamy in India.[8] Risley's work of compilation was carried further by others for other provinces of India.[9] As pioneer works these vast, often many-volumed compilations suffer from inaccuracies and shortcomings of various kinds; their inaccuracies have been time and again unveiled through the researches of later field-investigators like Roy, Elwin and others; and their other shortcomings have been exposed by ethnologists and sociologists seeking comparative or background material for their studies. So far as totemism is concerned, Niggemeyer has well indicated some of these defects.[10] Despite these inaccuracies and shortcomings, however, these works constitute an indispensable source for scholars of various categories. Other sources like the gazetteers, census reports, manuals and encyclopaedias compiled by officials, missionaries or Indian scholars have the usual advantages and

disadvantages of their kind. When interpretations are offered
they are often sweeping, as is, for example, evidenced by J. H.
Hutton's remark's on totemism in the Census Report of 1931;[11]
when information is supplied it is often incomplete on points
of basic interest. Nevertheless, as with the ethnographic compilations by Risley and his successors, so with these: they constitute valuable sources despite their shortcomings, exemplified—
to quote but one instance—by Hoffmann and van Emelen's
*Encyclopaedia Mundarica*.[12] Of the Indian scholars, two merit
mention here: these are Sarat Chandra Roy and D. N. Majumdar. As founder of the journal *Man in India* and as author of
excellently executed monographs, Roy has rendered priceless
service to Indian ethnology. Characterized by depth of field-
research, some of his monographs have unfolded aspects of
totemism[13] till then utterly undreamed of. In large-scale interpretation, however, Roy too leaves much to be desired.[14] This
applies also to D. N. Majumdar so far as totemism is concerned.[15]
But Majumdar's main services to Indian ethnology were to come
later.[16]

Considering its culture-historical standpoint and its comparative excellence for its time, it is no wonder, then, that Niggemeyer's study should have been accepted as authoritative and
utilized as such partly or wholly by a number of ethnologists on
the continent of Europe, and by a few resident elsewhere but
with affiliations to the Culture-Historical School. Ehrenfels, for
instance, points out in his study on *Motherright in India* that
Niggemeyer's attempt at proving that matrilineal descent in
totemic tribes and castes is not original but a kind of assimilation of matriarchal elements, and that patrilineal descent combined with totemism in India is the older and more original
form, are in conformity with the results of his own investigations into motherright in India.[17] So likewise W. Schmidt in his
re-study of totemism in Asia and Oceania [18] uses Niggemeyer's
study as a basic text for Indian totemism, accepts Niggemeyer's
conclusion that the Gondid in north-central Deccan are the old
bearers of totemism in India; and, going a step further than
him, maintains with certitude the existence of a totemic culture
circle among the Gondid, a culture circle of patrilineal higher
hunters.[19]

If now, with the passage of time, critical revaluations of Niggemeyer's study have not grown apace, the primary reason is
very likely that it was written and published in German. Thus,
Indian and other English-speaking scholars who might well be
regarded as occupying a position of vantage for the purpose of
evaluating such studies, had no direct access to it. One finds, for

instance, scarcely any reference to Niggemeyer in works by such scholars. G. J. Held, who regards the conception of motherright culture circles as problematic, and who dismisses some of Niggemeyer's explanations elucidating the connexion between dualism and patrilineal organization in India as 'a wild guess, hopelessly at war with the facts', is a Dutchman;[20] and Stephen Fuchs, who aims his shafts more centrally, is an Austrian. Fuchs' remarks are interesting. In 1957 he wrote: 'A problem of a more general nature is that of the origin and function of totem- ism in Indian aboriginal tribes. H. Niggemeyer, who dealt with this subject about 25 years ago, saw in the Gond the real repre- sentatives of Indian totemism. Since his study was published, much new material has come to light and his conclusions require a revision'.[21] Returning to the charge in 1960, Fuchs is more specific. He writes: 'I cannot agree with H. Niggemeyer who thinks that the Gond (with Bhil, Baiga, Korku, Oraon, Maria, Kui, etc.) are the true representatives of totemism in India'.[22]

Since the publication, then, of Niggemeyer's study in 1933, much new material, as Fuchs rightly points out, has come into existence. In his bibliography Niggemeyer cites approximately ten monographs—that is, full-length ethnographic works.[23] For the Gond, the Bhil and the Baiga whom he regards as primary bearers of totemism in India he had at his disposal scarcely one full-length field-study; for the Munda-speaking tribes he relies chiefly on Roy (the Birhor, the Asur), Driver, Ghosh, Gurdon, Hoffmann, Monfrini, and the general, official ethnographic surveys. Today, however, there are at hand six full-length and all-round ethnographic works on the Gond (including the Pardhan) [24] four (excluding Luard) on the Bhil,[25] two on the Baiga,[26] and several more on the Munda-speaking and other tribes. On topics of a more general or more limited nature, too, several studies have been published since 1933.

But a relatively large addition to the relevant literature is not the only reason calling for a re-survey of totemism in India. Since the publication of Niggemeyer's study, new orientations have crystallized in Vienna, and new emphases and interests have developed there and elsewhere in the ethnological and related worlds. While still working within a historical frame and still adhering to the principles of the historical method as estab- lished and developed by Graebner, van Bulck, Schmidt and Koppers,[27] the Viennese ethnologists have jettisoned the culture circle concept and the culture circle scheme for methodological and factual reasons.[28] In their attempt at a critical re-examina- tion of the older culture-historical standpoint, they seek to refine methodological principles, to apply them with greater finesse, and to surmount their inadequacies by concentrating temporarily on geographically limited areas and by extending interest to non-historical approaches. In the field of totemic studies, Haekel's re-examinations [29]—viewed against the background of Schmidt's patriarchal culture circle of totemic higher hunters—has rendered the situation in some of its more important aspects considerably and contrastingly fluid. For instance, on the question of the single origin of clan totemism and its diffusion from one centre as against its multiple origin in different regions and different times, Haekel finds a series of indications pointing to the second possibility.[30] The new orientations and the general fluidity of the ethnological situation today, therefore, are an added justification for a re-examination of totemism in India.

There is another element, however, which adds to this fluidity in both a more basic and more general sense. The march of ' civilization ' into the remotest reaches of the tribal world has broken down its isolation, and speeded up its disintegration, transformation and assimilation. Anthropological attention, therefore, has of late years been increasingly concentrated on problems of acculturation, and particularly so in America.[31] In India D. N. Majumdar was one of the pioneers in this field.[32] Niggemeyer, too, registers many of the consequences of acculturation on the totemic tribes and castes of India, although of course he does not mention the word. But much still remains to be done in this direction.

In short, then, the aim of the present study is a re-appraisal of totemism in India:

(a) in the light of the new material—ethnographic and other—that has become available since 1933;

(b) in the light of the new orientations that have arisen in Vienna (and elsewhere);

(c) and in the light of relatively new interests like acculturation and the dynamics of culture change.

## NOTES AND REFERENCES

[1] xxviii, 407-61, 579-619.
[2] Niggemeyer, 1933, 412-13.
[3] Niggemeyer, 1933, 600-1.
[4] 1910, four volumes. Volume ii, 218-335, contains excerpts bearing on totemism in India. An additional volume entitled *Totemica: A Supplement to Totemism and Exogamy*, with the Indian material recorded between pp. 365 and 402, appeared in 1937.
[5] 1923, 511.

6 1915-16, 593-610, especially 598-9. See also Schmidt & Koppers, 1924, 225-54.

7 1891-2, 1915. Earlier of course Dalton had also made a compilation.

8 1886. See also Frazer, ii, 218.

9 Crooke, 1896; Thurston & Rangachari, 1909; L. K. Anantha Krishna Iyer, 1909-12; Rose, 1911-19; Russell & Hiralal, 1916; Hassan, 1920; Enthoven, 1920-22; Nanjundayya & Iyer, 1928-35; and later L. A. K. Iyer, 1937-41.

10 1933, 411 and elsewhere in the study.

11 Published in 1933.

12 1930-41.

13 1912, 1915a, 1915b, 1925b, 1928, and his two articles on the Asur, 1917, 1926.

14 1925a.

15 1930, 1944.

16 Majumdar was founder of the journal *The Eastern Anthropologist* and author of several ethnographic and other works.

17 1941, 100. See also Rahmann, 1936, 54.

18 *Totemismus in Asien und Ozeanien* (Micro-Bibliotheca Anthropos, Vol. xvi, 1955).

19 Bornemann, 1956, 615-40.

20 1935, 64-5.

21 1957, 129.

22 1960a, 153.

23 This figure includes smaller works like those of Dehon, 1906, and Luard, 1909a.

24 Grigson, 1938; Singh, 1944; Elwin, 1947; Fürer-Haimendorf, 1948; Fuchs, 1960a; and Hivale, 1946.

25 Konrad, 1939; Koppers, 1948; Naik, 1956; Nath, 1961. A thesis on the Bhil submitted by Uma Bose in the University of Cornell has not yet been published. Shah, 1959, is a small work on a related group. So likewise I. Karve has a small work on one section of the Bhil.

26 Elwin, 1939; Fuchs, 1960a. Nag, 1958, concentrates on the economic side, but also gives a chapter on the other aspects of the Baiga culture.

27 Graebner, 1911; Bulck, 1931; Schmidt & Koppers, 1937. See also Kluckhohn, 1936.

28 Haekel, 1956, 17-90; 1959a, 127-47; 1958b; 1961; Koppers, 1959, 110-26.

29 1952; 1956, 56-7; 1958.

30 1952, 43.

31 Beals, 1953.

32 1937, 1939, 1950a.

# II

## THE NATURE OF TOTEMISM

A RE-ASSESSMENT of totemism in India necessitates as a precondition a re-assessment of the ways in which totemism has been conceived and defined and its distribution explained. Such attempts at re-assessment (if one includes interpretations of origin and nature more speculative than empirical) have been prolific ever since J. F. McLennan brought the phenomenon to the attention of the intellectual world in his articles ' Totemism ' (*Chambers's Encyclopaedia* for 1867) and ' The Worship of Animals and Plants ' (*Fortnightly Review* for 1869).[1] A roll-call of the more distinguished of these assessors would comprise J. G. Frazer, A. A. Goldenweiser, W. Schmidt, E. Durkheim, Sigmund Freud and A. R. Radcliffe-Brown. In recent years, however, J. Haekel of Vienna has examined the existence of totemism in various parts of the world, and has also attempted more than once to assess its nature, its origin, its variation and distribution.[2] In this chapter we shall, therefore, first undertake to present as succinctly as possible the views on totemism of the more prominent of its interpreters, and next attempt an integral approach to the problem on the basis of the more valid aspects of the various interpretations.

### J. G. Frazer

Sir James Frazer's views on totemism merit attention here not only because the vastness of his evidence and the beauty of his style succeeded in winning the interest of scholars to the phenomenon, but also because some aspects of his thought continue to find acceptance among contemporary thinkers and others persist in existence in more or less modified forms. In the four volumes of his *Totemism and Exogamy* published in 1910 and the supplementary volume, *Totemica*, published in 1937, Frazer brought together much material which is often otherwise not so easily accessible.

Defining a totem as ' a class of material objects which a savage regards with superstitious respect, believing that there exists

---

[1] For notes to this chapter see pp. 57-60.

between him and every member of the class an intimate and altogether special relation ',[3] Frazer outlined three theories of totemism, two of which he later discarded. The theory that totemism originated in the doctrine of the external soul or the supposed possibility of depositing the souls of living people for safety in external objects such as animals and plants, Frazer confesses, was not confirmed by subsequent research. Using Spencer and Gillen's discoveries in Central Australia, Frazer next suggested that totemism originated as a system of magic designed to supply a community with the necessaries of life. He abandoned this theory also because the motive underlying it was too rational and the social organization associated with it was too complex to be really primitive. The third theory which he developed, he regarded as probably true. According to this theory, totemism originated in the primitive explanation of conception and childbirth. In other words the ultimate source of totemism was the ' savage ' ignorance of paternity which Frazer, believing in an early stage of sexual communism and group marriage, assumed to be at one time universal. The fancies and longings of pregnant women might have had, as Frazer sees it, a preponderant influence in the emergence of totemism, which is therefore the product of the feminine rather than the masculine mind.[4]

Frazer lists the varieties of totem as follows: *Individual totem* which is not transmitted by inheritance; *sex totem* which distinguishes the women as a group from the men; *clan totem* which is the most important of all types, other types of group totems being variations of it; *split totem* or a part of an animal of a specific species, arising through the segmentation of a single original clan which had a whole animal as its totem, into a number of clans, each taking the name of a part of the original animal or of a subspecies of it; *cross totem*, a part of all animals or a number of species; *phratry totem* or the totem of an exogamous division intermediate between tribe and clan (evidence indicates that in many instances it was a totem clan which underwent subdivision; *sub-totem, pseudo-totem* or *multiplex totem*, that is, natural objects classed under the totem and sharing the respect due to it. Following Howitt, Frazer regards the last type as totems in a state of development.[5]

At the outset Frazer followed McLennan and Robertson Smith in regarding the religious side of totemism as fundamental, and dissociated himself from the views of Spencer and Lubbock who stressed the primacy of the social side. The religious side of totemism comprised the relations of mutual respect and protection between man and totem; the social side the relations of clansmen to one another and to members of other clans. In the history of totemism the religious and social sides tend to part company, the social side sometimes surviving the religious, and religion sometimes bearing traces of totemism even when the social side has disappeared. But the two sides were originally inseparable, and the further backwards that one goes, the more one finds that the clansman regards himself and his totem as beings of the same species. Pure totemism, however, is democratic; it is a religion of equality and fraternity. It is only when one individual of the totem species is elevated as elder brother or guardian spirit to a position of superiority over the rest that totemism declines and religion advances to its monarchical stage, that is, totems become tribal gods. Restrictions on killing and eating the totem demonstrate the religious side of totemism, and on marrying or cohabiting with a woman of the same totem the social side. Later, however, Frazer emphatically denied that totemism is a religion. In practice it is allied with democracy, and in theory with magic. But magic progresses towards religion; and although totemism is a system of brotherhood it might develop into a worship of animals and plants under favourable conditions. Such worship, it is noted, is not found among the lowest savages who have totemism in its purest form; it occurs only among peoples who have considerably advanced in culture, and is hence a product of the disruption and decay of totemism.[6]

Totemism and exogamy, says Frazer, are fundamentally distinct in origin and nature, although they have accidentally crossed and blended in many tribes. Totemism is older than exogamy, the latter being introduced when the totem stocks were bisected into two or four classes in order to prevent intermarriage first of brothers and sisters, and next of parents with children. Totemism without exogamy is pure totemism, and with exogamy exogamous totemism. The classificatory system of relationship which is associated with totemism is younger because it is founded on exogamy. Totemism became hereditary before exogamy came into existence, and so the totemic clans became exogamous by being distributed among the exogamous classes. It is possible, and appears actually to have happened, that the exogamous-totemic clans were once grouped in exogamous classes or phratries, which then tended to disappear, leaving behind the exogamous-totemic clans; for exogamous classes were more burdensome than exogamous clans. The exogamy of the totemic clans is exogamy in decay.[7]

The totem bond weakens in proportion to its extension. Thus, sub-phratric and phratric totems are successively weakened representations of the clan totem. As sub-totems, totemism is in the stage of growth; as clan totems, it is full-grown; and as sub-phratric and phratric totems it is in a state of decay. In America and Australia the totems seem always in a state of flux. The conceptual or local totemism of the Central Australian tribes is only one remove from absolutely primitive totemism, which is a theory to account for pregnancy and childbirth at a time when the true causes of these occurrences were unknown. Among the Central Australian tribes (Arunta, Kaitish) a person takes his totem not from his father or mother, but from the place where his mother first felt that she was with child. This is a very primitive form, since it dates from a time when blood-relationship was not recognized and the idea of paternity un-known. Next, local totemism grows into hereditary totemism. The hereditary totem clans occupy each its own separate area. Thus, among the Umbaia and Ganji tribes, the spirits are sup-posed to live in totem centres where they enter a woman and cause conception; but the child is given the father's totem. The *Intichiuma* ceremonies are a natural development from the original germ of totemism. Hence these magical practices are a later, although still early, outgrowth of totemism rather than its original root. Conceptual totemism in its hereditary phase can combine either with male or female descent; for the paternal and maternal forms of totemism can be derived from the local, and not vice versa. In tribes with maternal descent a tendency would grow to prefer male descent as a result of the recognition of individual fatherhood and the desire of the father to pass his belongings to his own children rather than to those of his sister. Tribes with male descent are not impelled by any desire to change it. The eating of some portions of the totem is older than not eating it at all; for in the native myths the ancestors are represented as eating the totems freely. The taboo against killing and eating the totem was meant to conciliate it, and thus ensure a supply of it for the rest of the community. If any one of the three factors—totemism, democracy or magic—decays, so will the others. Totem clans pass later into local clans.[8]

Totemism, says Frazer, is not coeval with absolutely primitive man. At present it exists and flourishes among races at very different levels of culture, among pure hunters, simple cultiva-tors, herders and peoples with mixed economies. Therefore, while it originated in the hunting stage, there is nothing in-compatible in it with the pastoral, agricultural, commercial or industrial modes of life. Totemism, however, was not practised by the Aryan, Semitic and Turanian families. It appears to have originated independently in several areas as the result of certain general laws of intellectual and social development

common to all races of men. In fact, both totemism and
exogamy are better explained by independent origin than by
inheritance from primeval ancestors. But diffusion from tribe to
tribe has also occurred. The theory of conception accounts for
the wide distribution of totemism in many parts of the world.[9]

The relation between man and totem is one of mutual help
and respect, of friendship and kinship; and the identification
with the totem is the object of various ceremonies at birth,
initiation, marriage, death and other occasions. The great
majority of the totems are animals and plants. Totemism has
done much to knit men together in society. It may have given
rise to agriculture, domestication of animals and the use of
metals. It stimulated the growth of art. One or two powerful
men, Frazer believes, could have initiated the changes which
have marked the course of totemic and other socio-cultural
development.[10]

In thus theorizing mainly from the Australian evidence,
Frazer tended to ignore the variability of the totemic phenomenon—a fact which Goldenweiser clearly perceived but over-
stressed. To the extent to which he clung to conceptions rooted
in the doctrine of unilinear evolutionism, Frazer's interpretations are out-of-date. Some of his insights, however, as the views
of Haekel, Petri, Hutton and others demonstrate, still exercise
a hold on the minds of ethnologists.

## A. A. Goldenweiser

Goldenweiser's analytical approach to totemism was published
in 1910, the year in which Frazer's voluminous work, *Totemism
and Exogamy*, also made its appearance. His theories on the subject were dismissed by W. Schmidt as being of a negative
character;[11] and more recently his definitions of the phenomenon
have been characterized by Ralph Piddington as too wide.[12] His
influence in America, however, has been considerable. Thus,
R. H. Lowie was greatly influenced by his analysis;[13] and G. P.
Murdock cites his study as a basic text.[14] The merit of Goldenweiser's approach lies in the fact that he underscored the variability of totemic complexes. But if totemic complexes are variable, a crucial question is: What are the processes which give
rise to this variability? Goldenweiser stresses the process of
convergence.

In his article of 1910 Goldenweiser undertook a systematic
analysis of totemic phenomena in Australia and British Colum-
bia, and then sought to confirm his conclusions by extending
his survey somewhat less rigorously to other areas. From this

survey he came to the conclusion that totemism with its several features was not historically and psychologically an integral phenomenon, as Frazer, Haddon, Rivers, Spencer & Gillen, Howitt, Lang, Hartland and so many others more or less regarded it. Exogamy, taboo, religious regard, totemic names and descent from the totem fail as invariable characteristics of totemism. ' Each of these traits, moreover, displays more or less striking independence in its distribution, and most of them can be shown to be widely-spread ethnic phenomena, diverse in origin, not necessarily coordinated in development, and displaying a rich variability of psychological make-up ' (p. 88). Their diversity of origin and psychological variability render null and void all attempts at assigning a correlated historical development to the various factors in totemism or their psychological derivation from one another. As they are widely distributed ethnic features, it is no wonder that they are so frequently found together in totemic complexes. In all continents one finds marriage regula-tions, food and other taboos, religious regard paid to animals, plants and inanimate objects, assumption of animal names by social groups, and belief of social groups in a common descent. As, however, the totemic complex is variable, no particular set of features can be taken as characteristic of totemism. Nor can any single feature be regarded as basic or primary.

What, then, is totemism? It is a relation, a type of intimate association of various elements with social units like clans, accomplished by means of descent and a product of convergent evolution. Dynamically defined, ' Totemism is the tendency of definite social units to become associated with objects and symbols of emotional value ' (p. 97). Alternatively: ' Totemism is the process of specific socialization of objects and symbols of emotional value ' (p. 97). The totemic process gives rise to totemic complexes. Individual totem and sex totem are contradic-tions in terms.

In his later articles on the subject Goldenweiser clarifies his views a little more.[15] Some features of the totemic complex are more constant than others. They vary in their emotional value, and one of them often predominates over the others, lending its impress to the entire complex. A totemic complex ' represents a highly complex aggregate of cultural features of varied psycho-logical and historical derivation which become associated into a closely integrated psycho-sociological system '.[16] Although diverse in origin, totemic complexes are in many ways comparable through the working of certain psycho-sociological factors; in other words, totemization through assimilation is a convergent process. But parallelism and diffusion are also relevant principles;

for isolated totemic processes must have recurred numerous times, and diffusion of totemic features and perhaps of entire systems must have certainly occurred over wide and continuous geographical areas. Genetically speaking, however, independent totemic complexes must be ascribed to multiple processes of convergence.

As essential descriptive characteristics of a totemic complex Goldenweiser mentions the following: (1) Cultural features, ceremonial, artistic, mythological, etc., centring about beliefs relating to animals, plants or inanimate objects; (2) subdivisions of the tribe into definite social units, or clans; (3) socialization of equivalent features within the limits of the clans.

A totemic complex grows through a series of cycles of diffusion of totemic features which permeate the system. The totemic features appear one by one or in small groups. They spread from clan to clan, become socialized in the clans and absorbed in the complex. As each new feature appears in the clan it becomes a pattern, followed shortly thereafter by other clans, until the wave of diffusion has swept over all of them.

Totemic clan names, though not universal in totemic complexes, must have provided in many instances the link between the mystical and the social elements in totemism; for a community subdivided into clans must have required some kind of classifiers or names, preferably taken from the animal or plant worlds, by which they could be identified as separate units. Their sense of clan solidarity and common interest tends to project itself into some concrete thing which represents the unity of the group and thus acquires a halo of sanctity.

As background Goldenweiser accepts a certain *Denkart* (Thurnwald), a way of looking at things which makes possible the emergence of totemism. Traces of this attitude may also be seen in modern times—in the tendency, for instance, to romanticize about animals, to ascribe to them qualities of reason or emotion peculiar to human beings, to name individuals and groups after animals, to adopt mascots, and so on. ' All this is not totemism, but in these odds and ends of customs, notions and values there may be discerned bits of culture which, in a setting of sibs, might have coalesced and flourished as totemism '.[17]

Goldenweiser's influence, as we have already pointed out, has been considerable in America. But more often than not its effect has been markedly negative, resulting in the break-up of the problem into other specific ones, in the denial of its reality, or in its reduction in significance. Thus, in his otherwise justly celebrated book, *Primitive Society*, R. H. Lowie quotes Golden-

weiser at length and with hearty approval and then asserts: ' I
am not convinced that all the acumen and erudition lavished
upon the subject has established the reality of the totemic
phenomenon '.[18] Lowie thinks that the problem of totemism can
be broken up into a series of specific problems not related to
one another.[19] G. P. Murdock, too, regards the bearing of totemism on the formal structuring of social relations as comparatively
slight. The explanation, he believes, may be quite simple; for
totemic names can identify a member of a group of kindred
who resides apart from his relatives, thus helping to keep alive
the consciousness of group membership.[20] These views seem to
have had an effect in India too; for Majumdar and Madan rely
heavily on Goldenweiser, Lowie and Murdock in their more
recent treatment of the problem.[21]

## E. Durkheim

Emile Durkheim's interpretation of totemism as presented in his
*Les formes élémentaires de la vie religieuse* (Paris, 1912) is an
elaborate and eloquent argument in favour of the propositions
that totemism is a genuine religion of the most archaic form,
and that the realm of the sacred is a reflection of the emotions
underlying the social. In its extreme aspects this interpretation
has been rightly criticized on ethnological and other grounds by
W. Schmidt,[22] A. A. Goldenweiser and R. H. Lowie.[23] Thus,
the Australian tribes to which Durkheim confined his main
attention are not the most primitive, nor do the simplest tribes
in the world have a clan organization or totemism. Hence the
origin of religion cannot be traced back to totemism, as Durkheim traces it. But in clan totemism the totem is basically a
symbol of clan solidarity; and it lies to the credit of Durkheim
that he saw in the totem a reflection of group consciousness.

According to Durkheim all religions assume a division of the
universe into a realm of the sacred and a realm of the profane.
To go back to the roots of this division, it is therefore necessary
to study the most primitive tribes existing. Now the Australian
tribes have a social organization based on clans, which is the
most primitive known. The Australian clan is a group of kindred
with a clan name which is its totem, derived from species of
material things. The totem is, however, not merely a name, but
an emblem or badge, which is often represented in art or tattooed
on the body. It plays a role in sacred ceremonies and is the object
of religious concern. Indeed it is the very type of the sacred
thing. Therefore, individuals who bear its name are associated
with it and share in its sacredness.

Totemism is not animal worship; for man belongs also to the sacred realm, and the relationship between man and totem is one of kinship. The source of sacredness in this relationship stems from what is common to the totemic objects—the names, the members of the clan and the animal species. It is a secret and impersonal power which dwells in all of these, without being identified with them. This is the totemic principle, and it represents the early prototype of *mana, wakanda, orenda* and so on; but the totemic principle is not generalized, for it remains associated with the specific characteristics of the clan. The totemic representation symbolizes the totemic principle and also the clan. In fact the totemic principle is the clan itself—the atmosphere of sanctity which pervades the totemic realm emanates from the clan.

In the life of the Australian tribes there are two sharply contrasted periods: one, the colourless, daily life involving dispersal in the food quest or the profane period; and two, the assembling for ceremonial purposes or the sacred period. The spirit of religion arises amidst the frenzied experiences of the ceremonial life. But the savage does not perceive the social source of his transformation in the ceremonial life; he is only aware of the totemic symbols around him, to which he attributes the cause of his condition and the transformations in his consciousness effected by social pressures. Religion, however, reflects the way in which the collective consciousness affects the consciousness of individuals. It is associated with morality; for the powers of religion are moral powers aroused by the moral being, society, and impinging on other moral beings, the individuals who constitute it.

All social life tends towards symbolism; for symbols being concrete and definite permit the social organism to become conscious of itself and assure the continuance of social solidarity. The symbols are saturated with social associations, which are revived when the group is in the presence of its totems. Animals and plants are chosen as totems because they are important to primitive man; and each clan selects those animals and plants which are common in the locality where it holds its gatherings.

The tribal gods are ancestral spirits which were originally individual souls; and individual souls are individualized forms of the impersonal power which lies at the base of totemism. The exclusiveness of the sacred, its contagious character or tendency to expand and the inner contradiction in which it stands to the profane demand safeguards; hence taboos, sacred places and sacred times. The sacred is a projection of the religious consciousness or emotion.

Totemic sacrifices are meant to rejuvenate man physically and socially, as nature rejuvenates animals and plants. Mimetic performances raise the social consciousness; and this subjective effect is projected into nature, where it finds its actual success in the multiplication of animals and plants at certain seasons. The real significance, however, of these rituals is the periodic self-assertion of the social group.

When individuals united by blood or by a community of interests or traditions become aware of their moral solidarity, they seek objective expression of this fact by believing that they share in the nature of some animal or plant, that is, the collective consciousness asserts itself by identifying itself with some animal or plant species. Arising in the depths of consciousness, this conviction expresses itself in external acts or taboos and rituals relating to animals and plants with which the participants have identified themselves.

Individual totemism is a derivative of clan totemism, and sex totemism combines in itself the nature of both individual and clan totemism.

Totemism, therefore, is a genuine religion consisting of a division of beings, things and activities into the sacred and the profane; it produces a belief in souls, spirits and gods; it has its cosmology and its rituals. The root of this religion is the totemic principle, a belief which expresses the reaction of the individual consciousness to the social control exercised by the clan. The totemic principle is the clan, the social is the sacred.[24]

## A. Lang

In recent years both Murdock [25] and Haekel [26] have imparted a new lease of life to the nominalist hypothesis of totemic origin; the former thinks that the use of animal names for the purpose of identifying social groups is a basic causative factor in the emergence of totemism, and the latter that it could be one among several possibilities. The nominalist explanation, as Andrew Lang points out, is a very old one. It reaches back into the seventeenth century when Garcilasso de la Vega, an Inca on the maternal side, stated in his history of the Incas that totems arose in the early efforts of human groups to differentiate themselves from one another. In one form or another this explanation has had several supporters such as A. H. Keane, Max Müller, J. Pikler, Herbert Spencer, Lord Avebury and Andrew Lang himself. Starting from the fact that the clans or groups needed differentiation by names, Lang maintains that the sobriquet chosen for the purpose had to be such as could be easily expressed in pictographs and easily signalled in gesture language. When the origin of the names had been forgotten, they suggested a relationship between the objects from which the names were derived and the groups which bore them. The relationship was then explained by a series of myths which converted the animals, plants and other objects into mystic kinsmen, patrons or ancestors of the groups concerned. Reflection on this mystic relationship gave rise in course of time to the taboos and prohibitions which characterize totemism.[27] Lang's hypothesis was in part endorsed by Sigmund Freud, who stressed the fact that the origin of the names had been forgotten.[28] On the whole, however, the nominalist explanations have been found wanting on various counts.

## Sigmund Freud, R. Thurnwald— Psychological Interpretations

Sigmund Freud's psychoanalytical hypothesis, first published in 1912-13 in the journal *Imago*, has not found much favour among ethnologists. With Darwin and Atkinson, Freud assumes the existence of a primitive horde dominated by an old man who accordingly monopolizes all the females of the group. The young males, therefore, conspire together and kill and eat the father. The feelings of guilt arising from this act of parricide become displaced in the unconscious and take the overt form of the totem which is a substitute of the murdered father. The feelings of ambivalence and the series of taboos accompanying the totem are logical derivations from the foregoing events. Freud's hypothesis was later refined and elaborated by Geza Roheim who defines totemism as the ' self-projection of a social unit in a natural unit '.[29] Ethnologically speaking, however, Freud's hypothesis and his attempt at tracing the origins of religion and society to it have been demonstrated—in particular by A. L. Kroeber and W. Schmidt—as lacking in factual foundation. Thus, Schmidt points out that totemism is a later stage of development and does not occur at the ethnologically earliest level; that it is not universal, nor have all peoples passed through it; that the totem sacrifice is an extremely rare occurrence; that pre-totemic peoples have no knowledge of cannibalism or patricide; and that sexual promiscuity and group marriage do not exist at all as institutionalized forms of behaviour.[30] But the falsity of Freud's totemic hypothesis does not detract from the validity of concepts such as the unconscious, ambivalence, displacement, projection, flight from reality and so on, considered in a general sense. J. L. Fischer, for instance, studying totemism on Truk and

Ponape, uses these concepts to advantage in evaluating differences in the phenomenon in the two areas.[31] If totemism is in large part a symbolic phenomenon, the roots of this symbolism must needs extend to some extent at least into the unconscious parts of the mind. The nature of this extension requires re-clarification.

To Richard Thurnwald, who devoted a lengthy article in *Anthropos* to the psychology of totemism,[32] the feeling of unity between the group and its totem is the fundamental feature of totemism. The unity and equality of the logical processes among all mankind is a fact; but primitive men, like the mass of the population in civilized societies, show certain differences in modes of thinking from those who are more accustomed to analytic thought. The primitive mentality uses the concept of descent to stress what is specially important in the inner world of feelings and relations, projects its processes outwardly, and views them as real or concrete. Primitive thought is collective; and community feeling is closely related to religious feeling. Further, to primitive man what precedes is often regarded as the cause of what follows. In other words, the primitive *Denkart* is not so much analytical as integral. From a strict community of views springs the idea of descent from a common ancestor. But suffering and misery condition a good deal of primitive thought and action; and suffering flows out of nature and man, and particularly from animals and plants and everything that moves. Dangerous animals and plants are the first to cause anxiety, then others, and finally everything else without distinction. In primitive societies the feeling of passive dependence on the community controls the life of the individual; and through this control the group acquires a superhuman form. Its power is transferred to animals; and respect shown to the animals concerned is worship of this power which lies in the community life itself. Hence, totemism is a kind of self-veneration of the group, a *sinnliche Religion*; the religious attitude becomes localized and concretized in totemism. The observation of associations in nature and between nature and life influences the growth of totemism; and these associations in turn are conditioned by a process of ' philosophizing ' and socialization. The taboos which surround the totem arise out of anxiety and fear and an envy of the power which is presumed to reside in the totem; hence, identification with the totem is a means of securing this power. The totem is protected because the protectors expect protection from it in turn. Thurnwald points out that there is an interaction between the religious and social aspects of totemism, and that the historical side of totemism results from the differing spiritual capabilities and cultural possibilities which influence totemism among different peoples. But in different places phenomena of a similar kind are due to a similar *Denkart*. Ancestor cults, soul concepts, animatism and nature myths may sometimes mix with totemism, but are not directly connected with its essential nature. Demons, oracles, omens and magic are further ways in which totemism is led astray.

## W. Schmidt

In dealing with Schmidt's views on totemism, it is necessary also to give an account of the ethnological system to the erection and elaboration of which he contributed so much. There are three reasons for doing so. First, Schmidt's views on totemism constitute an integral part of his culture-historical system, and this system consists of a procedural aspect, the methodology, and a structural aspect, a series of related but differing culture circles. Second, it is this system which underlies the study that Niggemeyer made of totemism in India. Third, the revisions of the older culture-historical system which have been going on in Vienna for some time now cannot be fully understood without a fairly rounded account of that system.

The culture-historical system was in its essence the result of a reaction against the materialism and naive simplifications of the doctrine of unilinear evolution. Agreeing with Bernheim [33] that human nature is everywhere basically identical, that there are no peoples without a history, that history is full of regularities but not of immutable laws, and that historical causation is extremely complex, and following in the footsteps of the pioneers F. Ratzel and L. Frobenius and above all of the early culture-historically oriented ethnologists, F. Graebner, B. Ankermann and W. Foy, Schmidt erected an impressive system of universal culture history extending from the oldest, non-literate cultures to the invention of writing and the birth of high cultures. But this was only possible on the basis of a method in keeping with the nature of historical ethnology. Historical ethnology, or the historical study of non-literate peoples and their cultures, has no written documents at its disposal, as does history; hence the culture-historical method. Both method and concepts were laid down and elaborated by Graebner, following cues contained in preceding studies. The method consisted essentially of two primary criteria, two secondary ones, and an array of other guides, rules and suggestions. The two primary criteria were that of quality or form (' a formal resemblance neither inherent in the nature of the phenomena compared nor due to geographical causes ') and that of quantity (' the chance association of a whole series of elements in two or more regions ');[34] and the two secondary ones were that of continuity and that of the degree of relationship. The concepts were the culture circle and the culture stratum. Graebner's methodological principles [35] were taken up, refined and somewhat extended by Schmidt & Koppers.[36] A little before Schmidt & Koppers the Dutch Jesuit, G. van Bulck, had also made a contribution to the culture-historical method.[37] So likewise Graebner's concepts—the culture circle and the culture stratum—were adopted with enthusiasm and developed into a vast system by Schmidt & Koppers in their book *Völker und Kulturen* [38] and other writings. The key figure in this development and the main contributor to it was, of course, W. Schmidt.

Schmidt conceived the culture circle as a culture complex which comprises all the essential categories of human culture— ergology, economy, society, morals and religion; as such it is self-sufficient and leads an independent existence. If important human needs remain unconsidered and unsatisfied, the gaps will be filled by other cultures. The more this happens, the more the culture circle ceases from being an independent one. Geo-graphically considered, such a culture circle consists of a large group of tribes and peoples; and it is this fact which generates the necessary stability, enabling the culture circle to survive down the ages, and to migrate in its entirety to other areas and influence other peoples.[39] A culture circle is ' a living organism like life itself which it serves '. Its various parts—ergology, society, economy, morals and religion—are organically con-nected with one another, so that one can infer from one of its parts the existence of the others. This fact is all the more strengthened when one remembers that one of its parts usually dominates and lends its colour and impress to all the other parts.[40]

The culture strata are cultures or culture complexes looked at from the time-dimension. Schmidt suggested the following criteria for the purpose of determining and delimiting them: (1) The criterion of geographical location: Simple cultures in marginal or inaccessible areas are older than more complex ones in more accessible areas. (2) The criterion of geographical distribution: A wide, inter-continental distribution of culture elements indicates considerable age. (3) The criterion of super-imposition: In general, the culture overlaid is older than the overlying culture.[41]

On this basis of method and concept, therefore, and of the pre-ceding characterizations of culture circles by Graebner, Anker-mann and a few others, Schmidt sketched his system of culture history. The so-called old (or early), primitive culture circles are the exogamous-monogamous culture circle; the exogamous, sex-totemic culture circle; and the exogamous, bilateral culture circle. Economically, hunting and food-gathering are the sole means of subsistence at this level. To the exogamous-monogamous culture circle belong the Pygmies of Central Africa, the Andamanese, the Semang of Malacca and the Negritos of the Philippines; and then the Asiatic, pygmoid peoples (the Vedda of Ceylon, the Senoi of Malacca, the Kubu of Sumatra and the Toala of the Celebes). The other characteristics of this culture circle are monogamy, stability of the marriage bond, equal status of husband and wife, local exogamy, predominance of wooden, bone and shell tools, bows and arrows in their earliest form, wind screens and half or full-formed beehive huts, the recognition of a Supreme Being worshipped through primitive sacrifices, a weak development of animism, ancestor cult, naturism and magic, and burial of the dead in the earth. The exogamous, sex-totemic culture circle comprises the Tasmanians and the Kurnai of South-east Australia. Polygamy has already begun to creep into this culture circle, but sex-totemism maintains the balance between man and wife among the Kurnai and other tribes in the south-east of Australia. Other features of this culture circle are local exogamy, primitive stone tools, pointed spears, throwing-clubs, wind screens, beehive huts, a type of basketry, scarification, initiation rites (perhaps), boring of the nose, worship of a Supreme Being, no cult of the dead, not much magic, little animism and naturism, and both earth burial and cremation among the Tasmanians and earth burial alone among the Kurnai. The exogamous, bilateral culture circle called Boomerang culture by Foy and Graebner and Nigritic by Ankermann shows considerable influence from later culture circles, particularly perhaps in the matter of polygamy. Sex totemism prevails here also. Local exogamy co-exists with clan and class exogamy which have intruded from later culture circles. Other characteristics are the boomerang, the sickle club, an early form of the shield, deformation of the teeth as an initiation rite pointing to a lunar mythology, the first musical instrument in the shape of sounding sticks, and the first man and tribal father as a kind of lunar being with whom the Supreme Being is sometimes blended.

From these primitive culture circles emerged the primary culture circles—that is, the patrilineal, joint-family culture circle, the exogamous-patrilineal or totemic culture circle, and the matrilineal culture circle.

The patrilineal, joint-family culture circle of pastoral nomads took its rise in the steppes of the northern parts of Central Asia

sometime in the Mesolithic. From there it spread to West and
Middle Europe, Arabia and Africa. The first domesticated animal
was the reindeer; the centre of domestication was the northern
steppelands of Central Asia. The domestication of the horse and
the camel to the south of this area followed next; and still further southward occurred the domestication of cattle. The donkey
was domesticated in the south-west, perhaps in Arabia and
Africa; and goats and sheep in all the remaining areas except
the extreme north. The peoples involved in this culture circle
might be classified into three groups: the north-eastern group
representing the core and the exit-point of this culture circle,
the middle group and the south-west group. The main features
of this culture circle are the joint (or extended) family with an
emphasis on the patriarchal principle and on primogeniture,
monogamy with a tendency towards polygamy, bride-price, joint-
family exogamy, virginity tests, an aristocratic sense of blood
purity, low position of women, individualism, no initiation rites,
care of domesticated animals as the main task of men, and
so in keeping with the principal economic activity—pastoralism.

In the exogamous-patrilineal or totemic culture circle of higher
hunters a reverential awe towards animals and abstention from
killing, eating or hurting them with a view to securing a kind
of mystic support becomes a prominent feature. This attitude
is manifested not by all the human beings towards all the animals equally, but by certain groups among them towards certain
species of animals. As a result of this attitude and the accompanying belief that the human beings constituting this group are
related to the species of animal, and therefore to one another,
the solidarity of the human group is nurtured and strengthened.
Thus, the totemic attitude subserves a sociological requirement.

The group concerned is the totem clan. The nature of the
relationship to the animal species is of two kinds: (1) Relationship of descent or the belief in descent from the totem animals
and (2) parallel relationship or the belief that the ancestor of the
human group had experiences with the totem of a pleasant or
unpleasant kind, the totem animal appearing as friend or helper
or as enemy.

Plant and object totems arose later than animal totems through
the contact and intermixture of the totemic culture circle with
the matrilineal, cultivating culture circle. The fact that these
plant and object totems are often matrilineally inherited or that
they are divided into two, four or eight classes, a system which
arose in the matrilineal culture circle, is a proof of their later
emergence. In Oceania animal totems prevail in the older, marginal areas; whereas in the other areas such as Central Australia

there is a rich development of plant totems. In almost the entire area of New Guinea, Melanesia and India where totemism exists, it is of this younger type. Moreover, India has several groups of people among whom the greater number or even all the totems are plant totems. In Africa, too, the greater number of the totemic areas show the existence of animal totems side by side with plant and object totems. In North America areas of plant and animal totems are sharply separated from one another.

In general there is not so much a religious worship of the totems as a certain reverential awe towards them which expresses itself in the following rules: The totem must not be hurt, killed or eaten; if the totem is an inanimate object it must not be touched or used. These rules do not always co-exist in all tribes. There are tribes, for instance, which are permitted to kill the totem, but only those groups whose totem it is may not eat it.

When a part of an animal or plant is the totem, one speaks of partial totems. Frazer pointed out that such animals and plants are specially used as food; but his term ' split totems ' is better confined to varieties such as red cow, black cow and so on of the animal species concerned. Indirect totems (as among several tribes in India) are plants, animals and objects which come into some contact or other with the main totems or are rendered conspicuous in some way or other in relation to the main totems. The term ' multiplex totems ' implies the existence in a human group of several totems without any underlying order; when such order or regularity prevails, the term ' linked totems ' is more advisable.

All totems were originally localized, that is, the groups in which they occurred had their place of residence in a definite area. Two factors promoted the localization of the totems: the cone-roofed house as a stable dwelling-place of this culture circle and the patrilineal inheritance of the totem. But contact and intermixture with the matrilineal culture circle, resulting in some cases in the matrilineal inheritance of the totems and the transfer of the children to the mother's place of residence, dis- located the localization of the totems. The absence of localization in totemic groups is, therefore, a secondary phenomenon.

Exogamy had nothing to do with totemism as such when it first arose. As, however, the totem clans were originally localized, clan exogamy coincided with local exogamy in the totemic cul- ture circle. But the totemic psychology, that is, the belief in kin- ship with animals, strengthened the sense of clan solidarity, and this in turn strengthened clan exogamy. Clan exogamy thus con- tinued in existence, while the localization of the totems dis- appeared through contact with the matrilineal culture circle.

Totemic clan exogamy sets group totemism apart from individual and sex totemism. Individual totemism lacks the social factor; and sex totemism belongs to an earlier culture circle. Sex totemism has of course a social function, but this occurs within the already existing social group, the family; whereas totemism proper creates and sustains a new social group. Hence, group totemism is totemism in the exact sense of the term.

Geographically considered, there are six chief areas of totemism: (1) Oceania (Australia, Melanesia and New Guinea) and Indonesia (Moluccas and a part of Sumatra); (2) India; (3) Africa; (4) Prehistoric Southwest Europe; (5) North America; (6) South America. From the Oceanian-Indonesian area where it first arose some time in the Upper Palaeolithic, the totemic culture circle spread to the other parts of the world where it is found today. As Graebner demonstrated with respect to Australia and the South Seas, totemism and motherright had nothing to do with each other in their essential nature and first emergence.

In India the pure, patrilineal totemic tribes to which belong the Telugu-speaking Dravidian tribes and a part of those in Kanara have been pushed back towards the east coast by other Dravidian tribes (defined by the terms Tamil, Tulu and Kanarese remnants). The latter located in the west and extreme south have motherright or totemism with motherright and a predominance of plant totems. In the northeast totemism has influenced the Munda tribes which show Dravidian traces even in their Austroasiatic languages. Traces of motherright once characteristic of these tribes are still perceptible among them. Where an Austroasiatic language appears unmixed, as among the Khasi, exogamous motherright with hoe-cultivation only lightly touched by totemism reveals a fuller development. The same is true of some Tibeto-Burman tribes such as the Garo and the Lalung and also of the Nicobarese. Other tribes of the area also show traces of motherright. Therefore, these tribes can be regarded as the bearers of motherright, and the East Dravidians as the bearers of patrilineal totemism. The West Dravidians, on the other hand, have retained free motherright with plough cultivation and totemism. Originally, however, they must have had no motherright. So far as the geographical continuity of the totemic culture circle is concerned, India constitutes the pivot with the Oceanian-Indonesian area on one side and East Africa on the other.

Other characteristic features of the totemic culture circle are: sun worship and sun mythology, circumcision, growth of the tribe, totem clan names, initiation of boys into the clan, age classes, youth dormitories, lowered position of women, magic, high development of the arts and crafts, daggers and spear-throwers, bamboo flutes, dug-outs and skin canoes, cone-shaped huts, the penis case, embalming of the corpse and platform burial, and higher hunting and its accompaniments.

The third primary culture circle—the exogamous-matrilineal culture circle of horticulturists—appears unmixed in the South Seas, from where it spread to other areas. The characteristic traits of this culture circle lie in the sociological sector. The tribe is split into two halves or marriage classes based on class exogamy or the rule that members of one class must seek marriage partners from the other class. There is no local exogamy as the two classes co-exist in the same locality. Motherright is the dominant principle here; the children belong to the mother's group. There was no totemism in this culture circle at the start; but as many contacts between totemism and motherright have occurred, various mixed forms have arisen, specially in the matter of the grouping of totem clans between the two moieties or phratries. Further intermixture produced the four and eight class systems. In unmixed, dually-organized motherright cultures initiation rites decline in significance or disappear altogether. Their place is taken by rites and practices connected with the first menstruation. As for the men, they organize themselves into secret societies. The chief economic activity in this culture circle is hoe-cultivation which arises naturally out of the earlier plant collection undertaken by the women. Cultivation renders the land valuable, giving rise to property in land; and this in turn constitutes the economic cause of motherright. Indeed, all the valuable and stable property of the family belongs to the wife and is handed down from mother to daughters. The characteristic dwelling-place is the rectangular house with a gabled roof; and the characteristic boat, the plank boat without outriggers. Visit marriage defines the first stage, matrilocality the second, and the avunculate the third in the development of this culture circle. Some of its other elements are clubs and shields, advanced basketry techniques, pan pipes, musical bows and slit drums, round forms and concentric circles as ornamental devices, masks, cult of skulls, decline of the Supreme Being concept, and the moon as tribal mother and a moon mythology.

In India the western and southern Dravidian area (Tamil, Tulu, South Kanara area) belongs to the younger form of the motherright culture circle. But two Telugu tribes, the Muka-Dora and the Tottiyan, show traces of dual organization, a feature of the older form, which also occurs among the Garo, the Bodo and the Naga of Assam. In other tribes of Further India (Khasi, Manipuri, Lalung, Koch, Kachari) and among the

Nicobarese, there are matrilineal formations which antedate the dual system. In Ceylon the Tamils are matrilineal, and the Vedda are strongly influenced in the same direction.

The three primary culture circles mingle and fuse and so produce the secondary culture circles of which the following are outstanding: (1) the culture circle of free matriarchy in Southern China, Indo-China, Melanesia, north-eastern South America, and other places; (2) the culture circle of totemism and motherright in the older cultures of Peru, Egypt, Further India and North and South America; and (3) the culture circle of free patriarchy standing at the dawn of history and at its highest in Polynesia, Sudan, India, Western Asia, Southern Europe and other areas. Lastly, arose the tertiary or high cultures of Asia, Europe and America as known to us from classical history.[42]

The system of culture circles (sketched above briefly and broadly) might well be described, in the words of R. H. Lowie, as 'empiricism largely diluted with *a priori* speculation '.[43] As pioneers reacting against the oversimplifications of the unilinear evolutionists, Graebner and Schmidt rightly recognized the complexity of cultural causation, rightly underlined the significance of contact metamorphosis or diffusion, and rightly established a method in keeping with the nature of the data analysed and compared. But spurred on by a method and concept which appeared to suffice for the purpose of reconstructing the phases of culture history, Schmidt and his followers tended to allow enthusiasm to outrun caution. Thus the method was often subjectively applied; and the culture circle concept (regarded by Graebner as a conceptual aid) became with Schmidt an entity in the order of reality,[44] and grew in his hands into an elaborate system. This system was no doubt a more sophisticated approximation to the complexity of cultural development than the naive constructions of the unilinear evolutionists; but its clean and ordered lines betrayed its inappropriateness so far as the untidy reality of cultural causation was concerned. In other words, cultural development was more complex than even Graebner and Schmidt had realized.[45] It is, therefore, not to be wondered at that in Vienna, where the culture-historical school was most at home, some dissenting voices did not fail to make themselves heard at an early date,[46] and that in other than the German-speaking countries the system made but little headway. In the meanwhile the accumulation of ethnographic and archaeological facts has impelled reconsiderations of the culture-historical system in recent years even among the leading ethnologists in Vienna. Thus in a number of articles both Koppers and Haekel have recently attempted to define the extent of their deviations from the older standpoint. While Koppers tended more towards the task of salvaging what required to be retained —the historical basis of ethnology, the method, the concept of diffusion, Haekel has surveyed the entire field anew, cleared the paths of rubble, and suggested ways and means by which further progress can be achieved. Both Koppers and Haekel regard the older culture-historical system as a phase in the development of historical ethnology.[47]

The present standpoint in Vienna may be, therefore, described in brief as follows: Ethnology remains a basically historical discipline in keeping with Bernheim's postulates. Accordingly, the contributions made by Graebner, van Bulck, Schmidt and Koppers to its methodology retain their fundamental validity. But for methodological and factual reasons the culture circle concept and the culture circle system have been cast overboard.

As Haekel points out in his justly lauded article *Zum heutigen Forschungsstand der historischen Ethnologie* (Vienna, 1956), the methodological reasons calling for the rejection of the culture circle concept and the culture circle system lay in some of its presuppositions and in the manner in which the method was often applied in the past. As a result of its subjective and formalistic applications, the method gave rise to erroneous conclusions and to a rigid, oversimplified system which did not do sufficient justice to the extreme complexity of cultural development. For instance, totemism, motherright and nomadic cattle-breeding were considered central features of three independent primary culture circles. But a closer examination shows that there are many differences and cross-connexions among the middle cultures (that is, cultures which lie between those of the simple hunters and food-collectors and the early high cultures), and this even within the same economic type. Furthermore, not enough attention was paid to the relative flexibility of the cultural process and the extreme complexity of cultural development. The culture circle concept, for example, was based on the assumption of the constancy of a cultural totality, a complex covering all the major aspects of human life, persisting as such to a great extent in space and time, and spreading through diffusion and transmission. When identities in form established through the criterion of quality were further reinforced by identities among a great number of elements established through the criterion of quantity, a single place of origin was presumed for the cultural phenomena in question. But despite the formally correct application of these criteria of cultural relations the conclusion of a historical connexion between cultural phenomena or of their unique origin seems questionable. Comparisons of elements in the social and spiritual sphere of cultures and deductions of historical relations among them are much more difficult then in the material and ergological sphere; furthermore, evidence is not lacking that borrowing and invention play somewhat different roles in social structures or that social forms like sibs and clans can arise more than once from joint families. Nor is it any longer justified to identify culture types and complexes along sociological lines. Economic, demographic, psychological and emotional factors also play substantial roles in social phenomena; and marriage and the family are expressions of elementary human urges. Structural and functional studies, further, demonstrate that social organization is a semi-independent system characterized by internal dynamics of its own. Diffusion, too, may be of various types.

Again, the establishment of time relations and culture strata through time criteria such as those laid down by W. Schmidt was always a weak aspect of the culture-historical method. Therefore it is all the more necessary, when defining time relations, to utilize all other subsidiary aids such as reliance on prehistory, written history, the carbon-14 method, dendrochronology, and a thorough analysis of the components of complex institutions structurally and functionally as totalities.

The older view held that culture elements must be first traced back to the culture unities in which they arose, and only after that can the study of causation be taken in hand. But in most cases the identification of place of origin and culture of origin is no longer possible. What can, however, be proved from the standpoint of modern research is the close attachment of various elements in certain cultural forms or phases and the approximate centre of formation of certain cultures. But in this task it is necessary to distinguish between different grades of causal and final influences, from those arising through local interpretation to those included on a broader basis of culture types, culture strata and culture provinces or areas. From an analysis of cultural phenomena which have a global spread such as shamanism, dual organization and so on, one can secure footholds from which the causes of their rise can be traced; but here, too, the type of cultural phenomena or cultures is a relevant factor. The complexity of cultural causation, therefore, requires dependence on related disciplines like anthropogeography, ecology, climatology, physical anthropology, history in the narrower sense, and psychology.

From the standpoint of the new results of research, Haekel limns the following picture of cultural development: In the early period of cultural growth stand the old or basic cultures of relatively simple hunters and food-gatherers represented by certain Australian tribes, Pygmies, Negritos, Bushmen, certain Californian tribes, Fuegians and others. In essential matters these peoples have retained very old features; and in spite of numerous differences, they possess in common a series of fundamental elements. W. Schmidt's general outline of their society and spiritual culture is still partly valid in essential points, as, for instance, in the matter of their belief in a high god. From these old cultures arose the middle cultures; but instead of three primary culture circles one finds in reality only major tendencies in cultural attitudes, in which certain sociological, religious and ideological proclivities combine with the economic type concerned. In themselves these middle cultures display many differences and cross-connexions. To a certain extent it is true that primitive cultivation arose from the collecting work of women and that the domestication of animals arose from the activity of men as hunters. But the results of recent research show that the beginnings of cultivation and animal domestication have lain together in a certain spatial and temporal connexion. The latest prehistoric finds locate the earliest area in which this mixed economy arose in the Middle East.

Thus, the picture of the middle cultures, as Haekel shows, has increased in complexity and diminished in schematized rigidity. What this entails specifically in regard to totemism will be depicted later; but what it entails in regard to motherright and animal domestication will be briefly indicated below.

As Haekel demonstrates, motherright forms a complex unity among very few peoples. It is, therefore, necessary, he adds, to distinguish between matrilineal elements and matrilineal complexes. The various elements which raise the status of the wife as mother and of woman as such may appear separately or cumulatively. The maternal uncle plays a special role not only in matrilineal cultures, but also in some instances in patrilineal ones; in the latter case it is not always right to speak of matrilineal influences or after-effects. The same applies to cross-cousin and service marriages. As regards matrilocality W. Schmidt considered it a distinctive element of motherright; but post-nuptial residence may take many forms depending on various factors of an economic or social or other nature. The existence of a higher being conceived in female terms in religion and mythology does not always justify the inference that sociological motherright once prevailed in the cultures concerned. In some cases, however, as in that of the Shiva-Shakti ideology in Bengal, the former existence of such a sociological background can be legitimately accepted. Then again, there are societies which are masculine in their orientation, but in which the women enjoy considerable prestige, as for example among the Saora in India. In such cases, however, one must distinguish between formal motherright and a factual elevation of the position of women. The view held by W. Schmidt that visit marriage as among the Sinteng-Khasi and the Nayar is the oldest form of marriage in motherright can no longer be upheld as valid.

It is not correct to speak of an entire matrilineal phase in the cultural development of mankind. Nor is it justified to talk of an antithesis between matrilineal and patrilineal societies, since the factors involved are so complicated. There are also no sound proofs for the view that all matrilineal phenomena are historically connected and go back to a single origin. It is of course true that in some areas matrilineal structures or single elements are in fact historically connected; on the other hand, a series of indications point to the fact that in different areas matrilineal features evoked by various factors represent independent formations. The view once held by the Viennese School that motherright arose through the cultivating activities of women and their resulting economic supremacy still holds true, but not as an exclusive explanation. Finally, the opinion that the dual system was in its origin connected with specific matrilineal cultures does not appear today to be a proven fact. In the formation of such systems the emphasis lies primarily on an ideological plane, that is, on a bi-polar view of the world and on diverse dualities in nature and the cosmos. An ideology of this nature has nothing directly to do with motherright or fatherright. In fact, dual organization, sociologically considered, has as its basis smaller, unilateral, exogamous kinship groups in which matriliny or patriliny are fairly inessential. Other factors in the formation of dual systems may lie in ways of behaviour between affineal relations (reciprocity), in adjustments of contrasting tensions in society, in certain measures of marriage, and in the fusion of two different population elements.

The older hypothesis of the Viennese School relating to the emergence of animal domestication, of the animal-breeding culture circle, and of high cultures through the domination of agricultural communities by nomadic warriors (represented in later times in a modified form by W. Schmidt) can no longer be sustained in important directions. Animal breeding, as the results of recent research demonstrate, took its rise in the Middle East mainly in connexion with early cultivation in the sixth millennium B.C. This decisive step was taken by mesolithic or early neolithic hunters and food-collectors; wheat and barley were the first cultivated plants, and sheep, goats, pigs and cattle the first domesticated animals apart from the dog. Reindeer domestication in its development as a full-fledged economic type seems to have arisen in much later times. Elsewhere, as in Inner Asia, Africa and Europe, pastoralism was to all appearances a secondary phenomenon.

On the question of the origin of high cultures, Haekel holds the view of a single centre of emergence, and dispersion from there in other directions. In the light of modern knowledge that centre was the Middle East. In the Mesopotamian foothill regions and in Palestine there were village cultures extending back to the fifth millennium B.C., which were characterized by a considerable demographic continuity. Diverse cultural forms and ethnic groups flourished in the area; and a series of inventions like metallurgy, the plough, the wheel and so on occurred here. And so, through a unique combination of these and various other factors, the first high culture (or cultures) came into existence in the Middle East.

Thus, in keeping with the complexity of cultural development, Haekel calls for a refinement of methodology and an extension of interest to non-historical approaches and other neighbouring disciplines. The principal task of ethnology is the historical study of non-literate peoples through comparative cultural research, or, in other words, through comparisons of similarities and the establishment of relations between single elements and groups of them. But in the adequate fulfilment of this task, historical ethnology has to give due recognition to studies dealing with structure and function, culture pattern and integration, cultural axiology, culture and personality and so on. It must also utilize for its purposes—in so far as that is possible—the evidence garnered by neighbouring sciences like prehistory, documentary history, physical anthropology, folk-lore, Indology, Egyptology, Sinology, and linguistics. Aspects of the cultural problem like the internal dynamics of cultures, cultures as totalities and acculturation have a sufficiently close bearing on the immediate interests of historically oriented ethnologists to justify their inclusion in the formulation of ethnological problems. As an antithesis to this extension of interests, Haekel suggests the prime importance of local interpretations and the working out of culture complexes within geographically limited areas. Where the facts are inadequate, the question of world-wide connexions must be left open.

The critical re-examination of methodological principles and the attempt at extending the formulation of problems is still in process in Vienna.[48]

## A. R. Radcliffe-Brown

Historical ethnology, as Haekel has pointed out, can gain by an extension of interest to non-historical approaches like those relating to structure and function. But if concepts like structure and function have struck deep roots in social anthropology in England, that is primarily due to the advocacy of A. R. Radcliffe-Brown. Radcliffe-Brown's studies of certain institutions, earlier regarded as survivals and utilized as such to prop up evolutionistic interpretations, have thrown much new light on them. What he has to say about totemism, therefore, must needs be of interest to students of the phenomenon. Although influenced by Durkheim who regarded the totem as a symbol of the clan, and totemism as primitive religion expressive of emotions and sentiments underlying the sense of clan solidarity, Radcliffe-Brown considered the French scholar's hypothesis as too narrow, and hence extended the range of his own interpretation to give us a revised version of what he calls the ' sociological theory of totemism '. In an early article Radcliffe-Brown preferred to think of totemism as a class of magico-religious phenomena rather than to identify it with clans, because in Australia the Aranda and other tribes do not have clan totemism.[49] His main thoughts on the subject, however, were published in 1929 as an article in the ' Proceedings of the Fourth Pacific Science Congress ' (Java), and later republished together with some of his other writings in the book *Structure and Function in Primitive Society*.[50]

Radcliffe-Brown uses the term totemism to apply ' wherever a society is divided into groups and there is a special relation between each group and one or more classes of objects that are usually natural species of animals or plants but may occasionally be artificial objects or parts of animals '. From this it follows that clan totemism is a variety of totemism in the wider sense. In Australia totemism takes a wide variety of forms. There are, first, tribes like the Bad of Dampier Land with no totemism at all. There are next tribes like the Melville Islanders among whom a simple form of totemism exists but plays a relatively unimportant role in the life of the tribe. There are thirdly tribes like the Dieri among whom the totemic system is a highly complex one consisting of matrilineal clans, patrilineal hordes, and a highly elaborate totemic ritual and mythology. The only feature common to these totemic systems is the general tendency to associate the groups into which the society is divided with some natural species or some part of nature. The association itself may vary in form among the different tribes. Individual totemism is closely related to totemism in the wider sense, and must be taken into account in the formulation of a theory of totemism.

The problem of totemism, however, is a partial problem of the general problem of ritual relations, and the primary object of the ritual attitude is social order. In every human society there inevitably exist two different conceptions of nature, one naturalistic and the other mythological or spiritualistic. The former is implicit in science and technology; the latter in myth, religion and philosophy. In twentieth-century European culture the former has become explicit and preponderant; but to primitive man the universe as a whole is a moral or social order governed not by natural law but by moral or ritual law. ' Any object or event,' says Radcliffe-Brown (speaking of this as a law), ' which has important effects upon the well-being (material or spiritual) of a society, or anything which stands for or repre-sents any such object or event tends to become the object of the ritual attitude.'

As the ritual attitude in totemism expresses itself in terms of animals, plants and sometimes other objects, to understand totemism it is necessary to relate it to a wider group of pheno-mena or the general relation between man and natural species. In a great number or perhaps all of the societies in which men eke out an existence by hunting or food-collecting, whether they are totemic or not, the animals or plants are made the objects of the ritual attitude. They are personified in myths and regarded as ancestors or culture heroes; or again, the ritual attitude expresses itself in a mass of customs. Among non-totemic peoples like the Eskimo or the Andaman Islanders all the most impor-tant animals and plants are treated as sacred in some way or other. They are, however, sacred to every member of the whole community. Totemism is a special development of this general ritual relation between man and natural species. For, when the society differentiates into groups or segments such as clans, a process of ritual specialization occurs, and each group or clan acquires a special or particular relation to some one or more natural species. A tendency in this direction is, for instance, manifest among the Eskimo of parts of North America, who are segmented into two groups, one of which is connected with summer animals and the other with winter animals.

The special relation to the totem emphasizes the unity and individuality of the clan. Thus an important function of the ritual attitude towards the totem is the expression and mainten-ance of the identity and solidarity of the social group concerned. The ritual attitude of necessity crystallizes into a concrete object, such as an animal or plant, and blossoms into occasional collective expression.

It has been customary to view totemism as having two sides— religious and social; and to identify the social side with the clan organization. But the clan organization as such is not the social aspect of totemism. For exogamous clans similar in all essentials to totemic clans can exist without totemism. Hence the so-called social aspect of clan totemism is simply the social aspect of the clans.

On the subject of the multiple origins of totemism or its diffusion from one centre, Radcliffe-Brown inclines to the view that the very diverse forms of totemism in the world must have had diverse origins. He believes that evidence is lacking for the assumption that the diverse totemic institutions have been derived by successive modifications from a single form; and therefore regards speculations about the original form of totemism and the exceedingly complex series of events which have led to the various totemic systems as valueless. He has nevertheless no objections if anyone wants to believe that ' all the existing forms of totemism have come into existence by a process of what is rather unsatisfactorily called " diffusion " from a single centre . . .'. In that case he would point out that totemism has not spread everywhere or evenly and has not survived equally in all regions. He would further point out that ' it is only where certain other features of culture are present that totemism is likely to be accepted by a people when it is brought to them from outside, or is likely to remain in active existence after it has been introduced '.[51]

These, then, are the views of Radcliffe-Brown on totemism as stated in 1929 and reproduced unchanged in 1952 in the above-mentioned book. According to Claude Lévi-Strauss, however, Radcliffe-Brown, in an article on the comparative method in social anthropology published in 1952, changed his views on the subject radically, although he himself was not fully aware of the change in relation to his earlier theory. In his second theory, as Lévi-Strauss claims, Radcliffe-Brown's views supply the means of liquidating the totemic problem by demonstrating through a structural analysis that totemism is a particular illustration of certain modes of reflection. With these views of Radcliffe-Brown, Lévi-Strauss is in full agreement, as they reflect in the main his own standpoint on the subject.[52]

In his attempt at understanding totemism by relating it to a wider group of phenomena or the general relation between man and natural species, Radcliffe-Brown seems to have anticipated, albeit in less systematic terms, what H. Baumann later described as 'proto-totemism', and what J. Haekel, following Baumann and Friedrich, regards as the background for the emergence of group totemism. In his proclivity, however, to interpret tendencies as laws, Radcliffe-Brown confuses two differing areas of reality and thus perpetrates the fallacy of reductionism or the identification of the socio-cultural with the natural, the more complex with the less, the historical with the law-governed. In relating the problem of totemism to the general problem of ritual relations, he focuses attention on an approach to the problem which seems to be very meaningful.

## *J. Haekel*

Associated with the Viennese School from an early date, J. Haekel, as we have seen, has outgrown its rigidities and its less satisfactory presuppositions. Today he stands at the van of an eclectic movement which aims at a newer and broader synthesis more in keeping with the complex nature of cultural development. Haekel's views on totemism have crystallized over the years in numerous articles,[53] of which two—*Der heutige Stand des Totemismusproblems* (1952) and *Zum heutigen Forschungsstand der historischen Ethnologie* (1956)—attempt a general survey.

In the first of the two above-mentioned articles, Haekel defines totemism as specific ideological and reverential ties of kinship groups or single persons with animals, plants or natural phenomena, out of which a series of rules and usages functionally follow.[54] In his later article, however, there is within the ambit of his definition a shift in emphasis in three directions. In this article Haekel defines totemism as an ideology which expresses itself in mystical, kinship-engendering,[55] and reverential connexions of a durable nature of social groups or single persons with animals, plants or natural phenomena, out of which result in relation to these objects, the totems, variable systems of rules, usages and attitudes such as names, symbols, identification, respect, taboos and so on.[56] Thus, 'ties' (or relationship) in his first definition is replaced by 'ideology' as genus in his second; 'a series of rules and usages' in the first is replaced by 'variable systems of rules, usages and attitudes' in the second; and the word 'functionally' in the first is eliminated from the second.

Under the over-all term totemism, Haekel includes the following types:

1. Group totemism (in other words, social or collective totemism)
   (a) Clan totemism.

(b) Totemism in families, smaller blood-relationship groups (lineages) and local groups and settlements.

(c) Totemism in dually-organized tribes (moieties, phratries.)

2. Individual totemism (or personal totemism)

(a) Individual totemism of a general kind.

(b) Alter-ego beliefs (super-ego, animal or plant as mystical double or soul-bearer).

3. Sex totemism.[57]

But the above is regarded as a mere classification, not necessarily signifying a genetic or historical connexion among the types.

A basic difficulty is that of defining the totemic complex in general. This difficulty arises from the fact that the various features generally associated with totemism do not always appear together in each and every group of people. Therefore, Haekel believes that the absence of characteristic elements does not always imply a decay of totemism.[58]

In his article of 1952 Haekel enumerates the features common to all the above-listed types of totemism as follows:

1. Emotional, mystical, reverential, magical, mythical and kinship relations of a durable nature between an intratribal social unit like clans and local groups or a person to animals or natural objects as totems. As a rule the group is related to an entire species of animal or plant, a person to a single animal or plant.

2. On the one hand the totem is regarded as a protector, helper, companion or relative, and on the other it is regarded with awe and fear.

3. Names and emblems based on the totem.

4. Identification with the totem or approximations to it.

5. Taboos and rules of avoidance in regard to the totem (the totem must not be touched, killed or eaten).

6. Rituals in connexion with the totem.

7. Mourning for the totem.

In addition group totemism has the following features:

1. Myths and legends on the origin of the totem.

(a) Descent from the totem: the group derives itself directly or indirectly from the totem. If the human group and the animal species have the same ancestors, one speaks of twin totemism.

(b) Adventures and experiences of the ancestor of the human group with the totem, in which the totem appears as a helper or friend or in which the ancestor suffers hurt or damage from it.

2. Exogamy and certain marriage connexions of the group.

3.  Inheritance of the totem within the group (patrilineal, matrilineal).
4.  Collective character of totem names, emblems, symbols and taboos.
5.  Associations and coordinations of totems on the basis of real or fictional analogies or other grounds. Examples are multiple totems (several totems in one group) and linked totems (principal and subordinate totems).[59]

Haekel, however, no longer accepts exogamy as a distinguishing mark of clan totemism. The reason he gives for this change of opinion is that clan exogamy is in most cases a natural development from the factual blood-relationship exogamy of smaller unilineal groups (lineages, family groups). This applies to both totemic and non-totemic clans and sibs, even in cases where clan exogamy is given a totemic interpretation by the tribal peoples themselves. Furthermore, the older view once current in Vienna that the belief in descent from the totem or relationship of the group with the totem had produced the feeling of an (artificial) blood-relationship has not been empirically confirmed. Such a motivation in the emergence of fictional blood-relationship occurs rarely among primitive peoples. It is none the less true that the totem can lend a special sanction and strength to the feeling of relationship and group solidarity within the clan.[60] In taking this stand Haekel therefore confirms, as F. Herrmann points out, Frazer's opinion that there is no direct connexion between totemism and exogamy.[61]

The most widely spread form of group totemism, says Haekel, is clan totemism. In clan totemism the general tendency is for the ideological, semi-religious aspect to yield place to the secular-social; and what lends a totemic colour here are such factors as names, myths, insignia and formal taboos. In some cases, however, clan totemism tends to blend with other religious and ceremonial forms like ancestor cults, belief in spirits, power concepts, notions relating to the dead and to souls, initiation ceremonies, fertility feasts and the like, which contribute to a further alteration and development of the system. But clan totemism is not the only possibility in the coordination of beliefs and social groups; the same can also take place through the communal ownership of cult objects, shrines, traditions, ancestor cults and heroic legends. Sometimes social groups may be named after animals or natural objects, but may not possess other elements normally associated with totemism. In such cases it is doubtful if one can speak of group totemism, whether in its initial or end phases. Only a comparative analysis of such cases in a definite area can demonstrate if it is a matter of totemism in its initial phase or in its decline. Clan totemism occurs among all the basic economically defined groups—hunters, herders and cultivators.[62]

Totemism in families and local groups occurs more rarely. In Australia, Africa and America it appears to constitute the basis of clan totemism. In most instances it is either an earlier form of group totemism or a local formation of a special kind, the components of which are sometimes not clearly recognizable. Some light on the question of the origin of clan totemism can be secured through a study of these forms.[63]

In some tribes and villages totem clans are divided into exogamous, antagonistic dual divisions or moieties, connected more with matrilineal than with patrilineal descent and exhibiting totemism of a weaker variety. A dual system with totemic and other features but without a subdivision into clans can also occur. The tendency to coordinate animals and other natural objects in certain ways already existent in clan totemism acquires an extension in dual systems with totem clans. All the important natural objects and forces, the heavenly bodies, the world sections, colours and so on are shared out between the moieties and their clans; and the tribal organization comes in this way to represent the cosmos, while every clan stands magically and symbolically for a part of nature. In Australia this system often develops further into one of four and eight classes. Totemic dual systems of this nature with their classification of natural objects and phenomena may in part be ascribed to influences from more advanced peoples, and in part to local specializations.[64]

Sex totemism occurs predominantly in Southeast and East Australia. Men and women have separate totems which are mostly birds. Above all the totems play a part in the initiation ceremonies and in antagonistic demonstrations between the two sexes. A certain relation appears to exist between sex and individual totemism and the spirit-child idea. A variety of sex totemism (perhaps representing a point of origin) occurs among the Semang (Negritos of Malacca).[65]

Individual totemism consists in general of a durable relationship of protection and friendship between a person and a single animal (or a natural object, more seldom a species of animal). This relationship is of an emotional, mystic and magical character. As a rule the individual totem imparts special powers and abilities to its owner. Individual totemism displays an intensification in association with certain concepts of the soul in alter-ego and super-ego beliefs; the interrelationship between the lives and fates of the human being and the totem concerned is so intimate that, when injury, sickness or death overtakes one partner,

4

the same is suffered by the other. That is why such totems are very strictly tabooed. They are owned mainly by heads of families and other groups, by chiefs, medicine-men and other socially important persons. Sometimes, when that is possible, they are tamed and looked after with care.

Haekel suggests that the term 'Nagualism' (from the Aztec *nualli*, somewhat hidden), sometimes used to designate alter-ego beliefs, should be discarded, and the more appropriate 'tonalism' (from the Aztec *tonalli*, referring to a person's fate or soul) should be used in this connexion.

A belief related to the alter-ego concept is the belief in wer-wolves and other wer-animals, that is, the belief that sorcerors and witches can assume the shape of certain animals with a view to causing hurt or damage to others. So likewise the totem animals of rulers of certain East-African Negro kingdoms and the animals worshipped in the districts of the old Egyptian civilization might have perhaps been derived from individual totems. An individual-totemic component is also found in shamanism.

Individual totemism sometimes reveals a tendency to develop in the direction of group totemism. Thus, individual totems sometimes tend to pass by inheritance to others. Occasional instances of a tendency to taboo the entire species of animal to which the individual totem belongs also exist (Iban or Sea-Dyak of Borneo). Then, again, there are certain myths which narrate the experiences of the ancestors of the human group with the totem. In these experiences the totem appears as a helper or friend or as the agent of some untoward act; the members of the group concerned are, therefore, as a result of their presumed descent from these ancestors, obliged ever after to treat the totem with respect and veneration and to fence it around with taboos and other similar practices. Hence these factors seem to show that individual totemism could have been one of the sources from which group totemism took its rise.

Individual totemism is widely spread. It occurs among simple hunting as well as herding and cultivating tribes. Here and there the alter-ego belief has found entry into advanced cultures such as those of the Andean area and Middle America. In parts of Australia, especially among the older tribes, individual totemism and alter-ego beliefs are strongly accentuated. They also occur in some areas of Africa, Siberia and North America. But to ascribe the guardian-spirit belief of the North American Indians to individual totemism does not seem to be always justi-fied. A phenomenon which appears to occupy a place between individual totemism and the guardian-spirit belief is the 'Ngarong' beliefs of the Sea-Dyak of Borneo.

To what extent individual totemism, alter-ego and guardian-spirit beliefs can be historically traced to a common starting-point is a question which cannot at present be answered with certainty. The difficulty is particularly great in regard to the alter-ego concept, which to a certain extent is an expression of elementary, unconscious tendencies. Much light can accordingly be cast on this phenomenon by depth-psychology and parapsychology.

Individual totemism in its alter-ego form rests above all on a particular view of the human soul. As shadow or outer soul it can mystically merge with an animal or natural object; hence the close bond between a man and a single animal. These soul concepts of various tribes offer an indication of the manner in which alter-ego beliefs can arise.[66]

Considering the problem of totemism from a culture-historical standpoint, Haekel adds: The earlier findings of historical ethnology that group totemism does not occur among the most archaic culture types of forest gatherers and that it is not a stage (in the evolutionary sense of the term) in cultural development hold good even today. On the other hand, the view that totemism is the basis of religion and society (exogamy), as held by Robertson Smith, Durkheim and Freud, has been proved incorrect by W. Schmidt, F. Boas, R. H. Lowie, and others.

The first emergence of clan totemism must be consigned to a very distant past. Its setting was probably among tribes in which the men devoted themselves mainly to hunting and the women to simple cultivation. These conditions offered a measure of stability; thus making possible the rise of unilinear kinship groups (sibs, clans) from the families and local groups of primitive hunters and food-collectors, which then received a totemic impress. It can be stated with certainty that the clan totems were originally animals; plants and other totems arose later.

The question whether clan totemism goes back to a single origin in the sense of a totemic culture circle (Graebner, Schmidt) or whether it has arisen independently in different regions and at different times cannot be answered with definiteness. There are, however, a series of indications which favour the second possibility. Just as, for instance, non-totemic animal worship, diverse taboos, and clans and sibs with other orientations can arise several times, so can such a process affect group totemism here and there. This fact does not militate against historical connexions or the spread of group totemism over wide areas. But it is often very difficult to provide a satisfactory proof of the historical relationship of totem clan systems, specially when they occur in widely separated areas. To infer historical connexions from the presence of exogamous, patrilineal clans, animal totems, taboos, totemic names and emblems does not appear always to be justified; for these points of identity (in terms of the criteria of quality and quantity) are not clear enough. Then again, while it is easier under certain circumstances for the totemic ideology to spread from one area to another, the clan principle can be taken over only under specific conditions. Nevertheless, in specific areas such as Australia and Melanesia, East and Central North America, East Africa, and India, historical connexions between forms of group totemism appear highly probable.

As clan totemism occurs in basically different cultures, it is today often scarcely possible to state with what elements the forms of totemism were originally combined. The concept of the totemic culture circle as established by Graebner and elaborated by Schmidt, which was formerly presumed to be a tribal culture and in which clan totemism is supposed to have arisen for the first time conjoint with a large array of traits extending to most aspects of human life, cannot to a large extent be sustained today.

Although the earlier view of historical ethnologists to the effect that motherright as such had originally nothing to do with totemism can still be retained as generally true, it is possible to presuppose a polygenetic origin for clan totemism, and therefore to conclude that matrilineal tendencies can here and there be bound up with totem clans. Considered on the whole, however, most tribes with clan totemism exhibit an emphasis in the direction of patriliny.

Clan totemism displays its richest formations predominantly among the so-called middle cultures. These cultures are based on hunting (fishing) and cultivation, and sometimes also on cattle-breeding, and stand between the ancient cultures of simple hunters and food-collectors and the early high cultures. As early as 1910 Frazer also held the opinion that clan totemism was at its strongest among such tribes. In the herding cultures there is a weaker tendency towards clan totemism; and in the early high cultures it disintegrates to the vanishing point or is otherwise largely transformed. In the middle cultures, and perhaps more in those with matrilineal tendencies, the dual systems also took their rise. It is possible (as even W. Schmidt later came to believe) that in the development of these polar, exogamous, tribal moieties with animal affinities, group totemism was also to a certain degree involved. Totemic family and local groups had already been formed in hunting cultures; but a totemization of small kinship units and settlements can also enter into cultivating cultures.

Individual totemism (inclusive of alter-ego beliefs and partly of guardian-spirit concepts) seems in view of its occurrence among simple hunting tribes to be older than group totemism. Its relative homogeneity suggests a single origin, but here too full evidence is lacking.[67]

Following H. Baumann, Hackel outlines the background of totemism as follows: The ideological and religious background of totemism lies undoubtedly in an animalistic world-view (Baumann's proto-totemism), which was and still is characteristic of peoples with more specialized hunting such as the Bushmen, the Pygmies, the Australians, the Siberian hunting tribes, the Algonquin, the Eskimo and others. These tribes have no group totemism or else have developed it only later. Their interest, however, is clearly concentrated on animals which stand in various emotional, religious and ideological relations to them. These relations express themselves in the following ideas and practices: the animal as a helper and companion, relationship between animal and man, endeavours to appropriate particular powers of animals, transformation into animals, entry of the dead person's soul into an animal, reincarnation in animals, various animal myths and hunting stories, patron of animals, controlling spirits of the animals (a later development from the conception of lord of the animals as a hypostasis of the Supreme Being), the tribal father thought of in animal terms, attempts at reconciliation with and requests for pardon from the killed animals, preservation of the animal bones to enable them to return anew to life, animal pantomimes, sacrifices to the animal spirits, and hunting magic in different forms.

These ideas and practices do not form a system at this level. They vary in value and significance from tribe to tribe. Nevertheless they show several identities in distant areas (and even in cultivating cultures with a hunting substratum), so that one can scarcely doubt the existence of an entire ideological complex. This complex can presumably be traced back to the Upper Palaeolithic in Eurasia and Africa (Aurignacian, Magdalenian); and is also evident in the rock paintings of realistic animal and hunting scenes in Western Europe and South Africa. It must, however, be stressed that this 'animalism' does not constitute the entire religion of the higher hunters. It belongs more in the 'lower sphere' of religious activity in the daily life of the hunters, and is strongly magically oriented. Side by side with it there exists a belief in a Supreme Being as first cause and creator or in the form of lord and donor of food animals (to a large extent a hypostasis of the Supreme Being), and also in a tribal father and culture-bringer. But the strong emphasis on animalism renders the Supreme Being concept otiose. The belief in an omnipresent and efficacious power (dynamism), often as an emanation from the Supreme Being and concentrated in wild animals, certain natural objects and human beings, can also play a role here.

These religious and magical beliefs of a differentiated hunting type form the basis of the various types of totemism. Individual totemism in particular belongs in part to this ancient hunting religion; and in the older forms of group totemism one can still recognize the after-effects of this animalistic, dynamic and in part animistic religion of 'higher hunting'. As, however, the social factor rises to the foreground, these magical and religious beliefs tend to decline, and clan totemism solidifies into a formal pattern.[68]

On the problem of the origin of group totemism, Haekel lists several possibilities as likely starting-points:

1. Individual totemism (H. Baumann).
2. The notion that in early times men were transformed into animals or showed animal features.
3. The notion of the first tribal father in animal form.
4. The notion of a number of mythical heroes and culture-bringers (transformers), from whose bodies the animals and plants issue forth.
5. The notion of spirits that control animals.
6. Intensive hunting activities in family hunting territories.
7. The necessity of distinguishing clans from one another through names and symbols preferably taken from the animal and plant worlds.

The decisive factor in all these cases, however, is that the totem, whatever its derivation, was inherited within the group, and that respect towards it was required of all its members. Thus a further possibility of the independent development of group totemism in different areas and at different times is the fact that from the factual material many possibilities of explanation arise.[69]

\*                    \*                    \*

At the end of this review of the interpretations of totemism by the more prominent of its assessors, it would be fitting to size up the situation by a concise delimitation of periods in the history of these interpretations. This task has been attempted by J. Henninger in a recent article entitled *Uber das Problem des*

*Totemismus bei den Semiten.*[70] Henninger delimits the following periods: (1) From 1870 to 1900, a period during which totemism was regarded as a universal stage in the cultural history of mankind. (2) From 1900 to 1940 approximately, a period characterized by the emergence of the culture-historical approach in ethnology and the resulting view that totemism did not represent a stage in culture history, but a special phenomenon standing in point of time next to other types of cultural phenomena. (3) From 1940 onwards. This period is characterized in general by an attempt at a greater precision within the culture-historical approach, by a recognition of the complexity of cultural development, and by a many-sided loosening of the older standpoint. This has resulted in: (*a*) A distinction between 'totemic complex' and 'totemic culture circle'. The totemic complex as a social and ideological phenomenon is acknowledged as firmly grounded, but the totemic culture circle with its economic, ergological, social and religious characteristics appears more and more to be a strongly disputable construction. (*b*) The acceptance of an animalistic or proto-totemic ideology of the higher hunters as background of the different forms of totemism (A. Friedrich, H. Baumann, J. Haekel and K. J. Narr). (*c*) The question of the historical relationship between the various forms of totemism being left open. (*d*) The recognition that the concept of totemism as also its subdivisions is only a classificatory designation for phenomena which show a certain similarity among one another, but which do not necessarily go back to a single origin. However, a number of American scholars, as also L. Adam, H. Baumann and J. Haekel, incline towards the priority of individual totemism.

Henninger grants some recognition to the trend of thought which tends to deny the reality of the totemic phenomenon by pointing out that, while a number of phenomena or groups of phenomena are regarded as totemic, all of them never occur everywhere together. He therefore adds that it is difficult to say today what is genuine totemism, and that the proper question in totemic research is not 'Does totemism exist among a specific group of people like the Semites?' but 'What totemic phenomena can be proved as existing among them?' Henninger himself inclines to the view that group rather than individual phenomena fall under the term totemism, and that one can speak of genuine totemism when a belief in descent or relationship is present.

If, therefore, we turn now to an attempt at an integral approach to the totemic phenomenon, we are confronted at the outset with the standpoint of those who deny or tend to deny its reality. As representatives of this negative standpoint we may single out R. H. Lowie and C. Lévi-Strauss. As we have noted earlier, Lowie derives his inspiration from Goldenweiser, but goes further than that author in casting doubt on the reality of the phenomenon. He suggests that the problem can be broken up into a series of more specific problems not related to one another; but, curiously enough, although he does not give much attention to it in his book *Social Organization* first published in 1948, he speaks of the phenomenon of ' totemism ' as follows: '. . . the connexion of a descent group with an animal species, more rarely a plant species, still more rarely a cosmic phenomenon or other object. The emotional significance of the totem varies enormously. Sometimes it shrinks into a heraldic emblem distinguishing one kin from the rest, but almost always the totemites are prohibited from eating, killing or touching the totem; and in a few areas there is a truly religious aura investing it '.[71] Thus, in spite of his inclination to the contrary, Lowie is compelled to recognize the reality of the phenomenon by conceding the connexion of descent groups with animals and plants and the existence of taboos as essential elements in his attempt at defining or describing it. C. Lévi-Strauss also derives his inspiration—at any rate partly—from the views of Goldenweiser and Lowie; but he does not hesitate to describe the problem as the totemic illusion. In his book *Le Totémisme Aujourd'hui* (Paris, 1962) he surveys the views of a number of American, English and French scholars, and comes to the conclusion that the totemic problem is an illusory one. He adopts this conclusion because totemism is a particular illustration of certain modes of reflection[72] (in particular, binary opposition), as the structural approach to the problem (which Lévi-Strauss upholds) demonstrates. In dealing with the problem, however, Lévi-Strauss ignores developments in the German-speaking countries. A part of the *Anthropos* symposium on the problem of totemism, which was published in that journal between the years 1914 and 1924, receives a fleeting reference in his pages. But Baumann's carefully worked-out concept of the proto-totemic ideology, and the balanced surveys of the subject by J. Haekel, F. Herrmann and others, are not even mentioned. In so far as the modes of reflection to which Lévi-Strauss tracks down totemism are concerned, two points may be made against them: first, that it would be difficult to reduce the entire range of totemic phenomena to a series of analyses of this nature; and, second, that it is not at all clear why general modes of thought should not give rise to cultural forms which are phenomenally related.

What, then, is the reality behind totemism? When scholars,

whose number is legion, subsume certain phenomena under the term totemism, they are registering observed similarities which, in their opinion, constitute a unitary thing, a phenomenon of which the word totemism or the phrase totemic concept is a shorthand description. In the widest terms (and excluding consideration of the individual variety for the moment) totemism consists of a relationship between social units on the one hand and species of animals and plants, and more rarely inanimate objects, on the other hand. This fact is evident in the definitions of the totemic phenomenon by Schmidt,[73] Radcliffe-Brown,[74] Haekel[75] and many others. Frazer speaks of species of natural and artificial objects;[76] and Roheim, following Frazer, does the same.[77] *Notes and Queries in Anthropology* uses the phrase 'certain classes of animate and inanimate things',[78] and Goldenweiser 'objects and symbols of emotional value'.[79] In all these definitions, however, animals and plants are specifically stated or clearly implied; and so are social units and a relationship between the two basic terms of the definitions. In describing the nature of the relationship Frazer uses the word 'intimate', Goldenweiser 'emotional', Schmidt 'mysterious', Radcliffe-Brown 'special' and Haekel 'ideological, mystical, reverential and kinship-engendering'. The difficulty encountered in defining the nature of this relationship precisely arises from the fact that, as Baumann points out, the passage from the proto-totemic phase to the phase of group totemism involves the displacement of a distinctly ritual relationship by an increasingly social one. Durkheim would prefer the word 'sacred', and Radcliffe-Brown the word 'ritual'; but both authors extend the meanings of their terms in ways which are questionable. Goldenweiser's term 'emotional' covers both the proto-totemic and totemic phases, but is perhaps too wide in reference to both. Schmidt's term 'mysterious' is too vague; and Frazer's not specific enough. Haekel is more specific, but his definitions bring both individual and group totemism together, and therefore do not sufficiently differentiate between the nature of the relationship in the two cases which the socialization of the totem objects brings about. A way out of this difficulty, then, is to view the phenomenon in the first instance somewhat dynamically, and accordingly to define it as the development of ritual relations between human beings and animals, plants and inanimate objects into emotional relations with ritual undertones and social overtones between social units and species of animals and plants and other classes of objects.

By itself of course the above relationship is still rather too wide to do full justice to the totemic phenomenon. It is therefore

necessary to consider the totemic validity of other characteristics usually associated with it. In listing these characteristics Haekel is more specific than Koppers,[80] and distinguishes
between features common to all the types of totemism as enumerated and classified by himself and features common to group
totemism. Another distinction, however, can be made into primary and secondary characteristics. Primary characteristics would
be those which are most closely associated with the totemic
relationship, arise logically from it, and have a more or less wide
distribution. The primary characteristics would then be an ambivalent attitude towards the totem, identification with the totem
or approximations to it, taboos and rules of avoidance (that
is, the totem concerned must not be killed, eaten or touched),
names and emblems based on the totem, rituals of a relevant
nature in the proto-totemic phase and exogamy in the more
socialized one, myths and legends relating to animals and plants
and other objects which in group totemism are of two kinds:
myths of descent and parallel relationship myths (or experiences
and adventures of the ancestor of the human group with the
totem), and in group totemism the inheritance of the totem
patrilineally or matrilineally (with an emphasis on the patrilineal aspect). The secondary characteristics would then consist
of such extraneous ones as the belief in a pervasive power
(dynamism), ancestor cults and the belief in spirits which occasionally flow into a totemic complex and become functionally
integrated with it, and thus form a totemic system. A totemic
complex can, therefore, be defined as a series of totemic traits
functionally integrated with one another and located in a culture or cultures spread over a more or less geographically continuous area. This definition of a totemic complex agrees with
the definitions of a culture complex by Haekel,[81] Heine-
Geldern,[82] Winick [83] and Jacobs & Stern.[84] But both Haekel and
Heine-Geldern stress historical interconnectedness, which is however implied in our definition of a totemic complex. From this
it follows that a totemic system would consist of a series of characteristically totemic traits functionally conjoint with one or
more non-totemic ones in a culture or cultures spread over a
more or less geographically continuous area.

In delineating these characteristics which have been usually
associated with totemism, we are, however, confronted with the
problem of their variability in totemic complexes, to which
Goldenweiser drew conspicuous attention, and to which both
Haekel and Henninger refer. This problem can only be solved
from an integral standpoint, which implies considering the

phenomenon in its totality—that is, in its entire range both psychologically and dynamically.

Psychologically speaking, the totemic phenomenon can be traced to two fundamental urges in human nature which are closely related to each other—the urge towards complementarity and the urge towards dependence. That these urges are fundamental can be proved by a reference to two current philosophies —Marxism and Existentialism.

According to modern Marxists like Lukacs [85] and E. Fischer,[86] man is dissatisfied with himself and his surroundings, and therefore wishes to complete himself, to become ' a whole man '. But there is an organic, indissoluble connexion between man as a private individual and man as a social being. Therefore man can fulfil himself and become whole only in and through society. As Fischer puts it, ' He rebels against having to consume himself within the confines of his own life, within the transient, chance limits of his own personality. He wants to refer to something that is more than " I ", something outside himself and yet essential to himself. He longs to absorb the surrounding world and make it his own; to extend his inquisitive, world-hungry " I " in science and technology as far as the remotest constellations and as deep as the innermost secrets of the atoms; to unite his limited " I " in art with a communal existence, to make his individuality *social* '.[87] Fischer regards not only science and art, but also primitive magic and totemism, as illustrations of this urge towards wholeness. Although an illusion, primitive magic is a technique of controlling nature, and therefore illustrates the urge towards wholeness. The same can be said of totemism because after all it is a form of magic. In justification, Fischer quotes George Thomson's theory of totemism which affirms that the totem animal on which the horde originally fed produced, when eaten, a surge of vitality which was interpreted as the transmission of the life-force of the animal or plant to the eater concerned, involving a union of the two lives and an identification of the eater with the living organism he had eaten. When, however, improved hunting techniques made the tribe's preferred food scarce, taboos were raised in such a manner that the clans into which the tribe was now divided had each to abstain from killing and eating a particular species of animal or plant, thus reasonably assuring the food-supply of the entire tribe. Hence the violation of the taboo imperilled the existence of the collective. With the development of production relations and the discovery of new sources of nourishment, the totems and taboos lost their original economic meaning, but the forms were retained since they had become so deeply rooted. They were, however, given in part a new content, and now played the role of magic rules for safeguarding the traditional structure of society and thus protecting the tribes and their social property, and therefore also regulating sexual relations. But Fischer differs from Thomson in believing that the totem and taboo had a sexual as well as an economic significance from the start; for the primitive collective regards sexuality, food and work as an indivisible whole identical with life itself, a life not yet differentiated by the division of labour.[88]

In thus stressing the urge towards wholeness ingrained in human nature, the Marxists focus attention on a fundamental factor. But, as has been time and again pointed out by others in other contexts, they err in limiting their interpretation to the social and economic aspects of human life. It is true that man is by nature a social being, depending to a great measure on the facts and relations of social economics for his welfare, and that he can integrate himself in and through society by integrating himself with it. But this does not exhaust his existential needs, as the entire range of his religious cravings and experiences demonstrate. In fact, an overemphasis on the social side can generate the phenomena of self-estrangement and anxiety to which Kierkegaard and other non-atheistic existential thinkers bear witness.

As the Viennese existentialist, Leo Gabriel, points out, there is need today for a new mode of thought which may be called integral. This need arises from the transcendence of the self as a totality in a final relation to being considered as the basic totality. In this relation the individual self not only retains the personal integrity of its existence, but also brings it to the point of its highest development in the creative activity of a comprehensive world-structure.[89] Through the concept of self-transcendence, however, this view associates itself in its roots with an old tradition in philosophical and religious thought both in the East and the West.[90] Therefore, one is further justified in regarding the urge towards wholeness or complementarity as a fundamental factor in human nature.

If we turn now to the manifestations of the twin urges—complementarity and dependence—in early cultures, we have as a starting-point the assured conclusion of modern ethnologists that both proto-totemism considered as an organized, ideological form and group totemism in its clan variety do not occur in the main in the most primitive cultures known to them, and that in the few cases in which they do they have been borrowed from some more advanced groups or are the result of advance in certain directions but not in others. As the facts generally indicate, the proto-totemic ideology occurs most frequently in societies of more or less specialized hunters, and clan totemism most frequently in those in which hunting flourishes side by side with early forms of cultivation. In those early cultures then, in which totemism is generally absent, the two urges express themselves largely in a world of spirits or deities, and find satisfaction, as Schmidt has demonstrated at great length, in the prevailing belief in a high god (or Supreme Being). Magic is also present, but is less intense as compared with later cultures. Beliefs and practices relating to animals and plants of a proto-totemic colouring are scattered and floating, and do not give the impression of an organized ideology as in specialized hunting communities. J. Maringer's picture of prehistoric religion appears to support these facts.[91]

The next phase in the expression of the two urges in the context of totemic development occurs in societies of more or less specialized hunters, and takes the form of the proto-totemic ideology which was hinted at by Radcliffe-Brown,[92] more systematically studied by A. Friedrich,[93] H. Baumann,[94] and O. Zerries,[95] and supported by K. J. Narr[96] and J. Haekel.[97] As Haekel points out, however, the belief in a Supreme Being does not disappear at this level, but tends to grow otiose as a result of the strong emphasis on animalism. In other words, we are facing a process of gradual displacement in ritual conceptions occurring in a framework of developing hunting techniques, a displacement of conceptions in which the factor of transcendental personality predominates by conceptions of a largely impersonal kind like magic and mana within the limits of which the idea of transcendental personality now functions. The displacement exemplifies a shift in emphasis from dependence on spiritual beings to dependence on oneself, and was caused (since these are fundamental in human nature) by the urges towards complementarity and dependence under conditions of demographic increase and developing hunting techniques. That is to say, there is at all times a close interaction between the psychological side of human nature and the economic facts and relations by which man is surrounded, but, as Aristotle would say, man is the efficient cause in this interaction. Therefore, Thomson's theory of totemism is one-sided, and is based moreover on facts which are mainly confined to Australia. Furthermore, as we have seen, Frazer himself, who had earlier outlined a hypothesis of a similar nature, quickly discarded it as untenable. But to return to the shift in emphasis from dependence on spiritual beings to dependence on the human beings concerned, one can say that it was probably attended by something like an existential crisis accompanied by a sense of anxiety, which are to some degree illustrated by the ambivalent attitudes towards animals and an atmosphere surcharged by morbidity and disproportion and electric with magic. Both individual totemism, which is a component of the proto-totemic phase, and the other ritual beliefs and practices of an animalistic kind, secrete this aura. A great part of this existential drama, however, must have taken place in the unconscious in which the sense of personal inadequacy, of human finitude, must have found psychic compensations reflected outwardly in rituals towards animals and plants embodying a desire for a world of plenty as a substitute for psychic plenitude. Therefore Freud's interpretation of the totem as a symbol of the murdered father and of the ritual of consuming the totem as a means of assuaging the attendant sense of guilt falls far short of the mark not only ethnologically but also psychically.

The next high-water mark of totemic development is patrilineal clan totemism. In this phase there is an overemphasis on a social unit lying intermediate between the family and the tribe. Clan solidarity may serve economic ends, but much more so it serves to extend and strengthen the sense of kinship or consciousness of kind. The clan thus becomes a centre and symbol of power, in which the individual tends to merge himself but becomes submerged, in which he attempts to become whole but loses his identity in the process. As both Durkheim and Thurnwald point out, the clan totem is the symbol of the clan as a centre of power. When the clan members, therefore, identify themselves with their totem, do not kill, eat or touch it, regard it as kin, and do not marry persons with the same clan name, they strengthen the sense of clan kinship, and thus of clan solidarity, and so fulfil their cravings for complementarity in and through the clan by an act of dependence and surrender. There is once again a shift of emphasis in this phase as there was in the earlier: the clan becomes more powerful than the individual, the family or the lineage; and the social displaces the ritual in relation to the totem. Durkheim's attempt at seeing in the clan and its totem an elementary and early form of the religious life is based on the fallacy that reduces the religious to the social by adopting a limited conception of man's existential needs. Again, Andrew Lang's nominalist interpretation of totem clan names which regards them as a mere means of differentiating one group from another is by itself an inadequate one. In comparison with the proto-totemic ideology, its validity as a starting-point is extremely limited; and in connexion with clan totemism clan names are merely an additional means of reinforcing clan solidarity.

From the above analysis it follows that, in the polar relationship between man and his environment, man seeks to exploit his environment in order to satisfy his needs—his economic needs, his social needs, but most basically of all, his craving for wholeness. His environment lays down the conditions under which he must live and express himself; his exploitation of his environment is the measure of his creative freedom; and both the environment and its exploitation are shot through by a pervading, never-ending change. ' Change ', says MacIver, ' is insistent in all our experience, change in ourselves, change in our condition and in our relationships. Man's unrestingness is tuned to a changing society and a changing environment '.[98] It is under this circumstance of change from which only the ' primary infinitesimals ' escape, that man endeavours to set up his ideological and socio-cultural forms in his quest for certainty and complementarity, and through the four modes of existence—duration, continuity, succession and recurrence.[99]

There are, then, two peaks in the course of totemic development—the proto-totemic ideology and patrilineal clan totemism. These are upsurges which arise in a continuum which might be said to begin in beliefs and practices of an unorganized and floating nature relating to animals and plants in simple societies of food-gatherers and hunters. Later, perhaps in the Upper Palaeolithic, in societies of more or less specialized hunters, these beliefs and practices tend to become more organized and grow into what has been called the proto-totemic ideology. Baumann places sex totemism, which is an extremely rare occurrence found only in Australia and Malaya, in the proto-totemic phase. A more important component, however, is individual totemism, since it illustrates the underlying motivation behind the phenomenon very distinctly, and reveals the manner in which an individual totem can grow into a clan totem. According to Baumann, the rise of individual totemism and alter-ego beliefs can be ascribed to the quest which comes into existence in hunting cultures for a way of acquiring the natural and supernatural power presumed to inhere in animals. But once an individual has acquired a totem, it can pass through inheritance to the family and lineage, and so ultimately to the clan. Baumann quotes concrete evidence in favour of this view. Since, however, individual totems are found in societies in which no clan totemism exists, one must make allowances for a bilinear development of individual totemism—one line continuing in its individual course, and the other growing into clan totemism. The proto-totemic ideology must have been widely spread at one time, and had no doubt existed on all the continents, as either the ethnographic or the prehistoric evidence indicates. Therefore its recognition in the German-speaking countries as the background of group totemism is all the more justified.

Totemism in families and lineages is not a stable form, since the power and spread of the clan causes its displacement and therefore the evidence of its existence is meagre. Clan totemism is group totemism at its apex; and clan solidarity grows into a kind of social ' mysticism ' which expresses itself among other things in a feeling of brotherhood or kinship. As a symbol of clan solidarity the totem is absorbed into this consciousness of kind, is accordingly tabooed, and myths of descent and parallel relationship are invented to justify the relationship. Totem names and emblems reflect and strengthen the sense of clan solidarity; and so, as Roheim says, the social unit projects itself into a natural unit. With the decline of clan totemism, totemism itself begins to decline. There is a weakening of totemic attitudes and a scattering of totemic traits. The tribe grows into a nation, and may occasionally retain traces of its totemic past, as perhaps in Ancient Egypt, in the animal deities that it worships.

But there are instances of clans without totemism and of totem groups without exogamy; and, as Goldenweiser demonstrated, there are totemic complexes in which one or more of the traits usually associated with totemism are absent. Goldenweiser himself explains this variability by pointing out that divisions into groups such as clans, forms of descent and exogamy, naming of individuals and groups, various taboos, religious regard paid to animals, plants and inanimate objects and the like are widely distributed phenomena, and that totemic complexes are formed through the processes of diffusion, independent invention and convergence. If one adopts the standpoint that clan totemism has arisen independently in different areas, for which there is some evidence, as Haekel says, we may conclude that this happened a few times in geographically limited areas through the convergence of proto-totemic elements and the concomitants of a clan organization under the impulsion of the two urges—complementarity and dependence. The probable time when this occurred was the period between the end-phase of the Upper Palaeolithic and the beginnings of the Neolithic, since clan totemism is found most frequently in mixed cultures of hunting and early forms of cultivation,[1] where conditions of greater stability prevail. Australia, however, is an exception to this fact. These were, therefore, the first totemic complexes of a clan variety, and from them must have emerged the other complexes in each limited area through the processes of stimulus or trait diffusion combined with varying degrees of innovation and selection. Geographical contiguity would then be a sufficient explanation of the similarities of these complexes, while the varying degrees of innovation and selection would explain their variations. A complicating factor, however, is that forms prior to clan totemism such as cult totemism in Australia may persist in existence and spread to some extent in that arrested form, or that clan totemism in various stages of decline and disintegration may diffuse itself in surrounding areas. These complexities can be ascertained and disentangled by means of a local interpretation. But totem groups without exogamy are not as widely spread as clan totemism, and can be explained as a minor phenomenon in the totemic continuum of variant forms. Since clans without totemism are also fairly widespread, there must have been an absence of conjuncture between these clans and the proto-totemic ideology, despite the wide distribution of the latter.

In some respects Australia stands by itself as a totemic area. Here, as Elkin shows, the varieties and functions of totemism are multiple. There are moiety, clan, section, individual, sex and multiple totems; and in north-eastern South Australia matrilineal social totemism, patrilineal cult totemism, matrilineal cult totemism, dream totemism and sex totemism exist side by side and function together in maintaining the social and religious unity of the tribe. From the viewpoint of functions, the totem acts as a guardian, as an assistant or additional source of strength, and as an emblem or name in daily life or in dreams; and totemism acts as a method of social and religious grouping, as a means of expressing man's relations to nature, of preserving continuity with the past and providing assurance for the future.[2] Furthermore, although historical connexions have been proved with the Melanesian area, the Australian aborigines are all hunters. Whatever be the explanation of this fact, the rich efflorescence of their totemism can at any rate be interpreted as the result of the relative isolation of the continent and the consequent action and reaction of the totemic forms on one another and on the other aspects of their life.

Hence the problem of defining totemism is rendered difficult because the totemic phenomenon emerges in two upsurges on the totemic continuum, and because the variability of totemic complexes and systems is greater than was earlier believed. The following definitions can be regarded as representative of the various approaches to the subject:

1. J. G. Frazer: '. . . totemism is an intimate relation which is supposed to exist between a group of kindred people on the one side and a species of natural or artificial objects on the other side, which objects are called the totem.'[3]

5

2.   A. A. Goldenweiser: (a) 'Totemism is the tendency of definite social units to become associated with objects and symbols
of an emotional value.' (b) 'Totemism is the process of specific
socialization of objects and symbols of emotional value.' [4]

3.   W. Schmidt: 'Totemism is the practice of a social group
without regard to age or sex, of entertaining a mysterious relationship as a group to a class of animals, plants, or other material
objects.' [5]

4.   Geza Roheim: 'By totemism I mean, with Frazer, an intimate relation supposed to exist between a group of kindred
people on the one side and species of natural or artificial objects
on the other side, or, expressed more psychologically, the self-
projection of a social unit in a natural unit.' [6]

5.   A. R. Radcliffe-Brown: 'I shall use the term in the wider
sense to apply wherever a society is divided into groups and
there is a special relation between each group and one or more
classes of objects that are usually natural species or plants but
may occasionally be artificial objects or parts of an animal.' [7]

6.   *Notes and Queries in Anthropology*: 'The term totemism is
used for a form of social organization and magico-religious practice, of which the central feature is the association of certain
groups (usually clans and lineages) within a tribe with certain
classes of animate or inanimate things, the several groups being
associated with distinct classes.' [8]

7.   J. Haekel: (a) 'Totemism consists in specific ideological and
reverential connexions of kinship groups or single persons with
animals, plants or natural phenomena, out of which a series
of rules and usages follow.' [9] (b) Totemism can be generally
defined as an ideology which expresses itself in mystical, kinship
and reverential relationships of a durable nature between social
groups or single persons and animals, plants or natural phenomena, out of which result in relation to these objects of nature,
the totems, variable systems of rules, usages and attitudes such
as names, identification, respect, symbols, taboos and so on.[10]

Among all these definitions, it is only Haekel's which takes
cognizance of both the results of modern research—the proto-
totemic ideology which precedes clan totemism on the totemic
continuum and the variability of totemic complexes. But
Haekel's definition does not sufficiently distinguish between the
ritual nature of the totemic relationship in the proto-totemic
phase and the increasingly secularized nature of that relationship in the phase of clan totemism, or between complexes and
systems. Therefore, if we bear these distinctions in mind and
also accept a genetic connexion between individual totemism
and group totemism, we may define totemism as a ritual rela-

tionship between individual persons and animals, plants or other
objects, which grows into an emotional relationship with ritual
undertones and social overtones between social units such as
clans and classes of animals, plants and other objects, and which
expresses itself in variable complexes of attitudes such as ambivalence, identification, kinship and respect and usages such as
taboos, exogamy and the like, and in systems of these and other
less characteristic traits.[11]

\*                    \*                    \*

In the analysis of totemism in India we shall use the following
terms:
1. *Proto-totemism*: This will consist of (*a*) beliefs and practices
relating to animals and plants of a loose and floating nature,
and (*b*) the proto-totemic ideology proper, where these beliefs
and practices take on a more organized form.
2. *Quasi-totemism*: This is clan totemism in its early stages,
and consists of two varieties: (*a*) Primary quasi-totemism or clan
totemism in its early stages, which has arisen without outside
influence in the area in which it is found; (*b*) Secondary quasi-
totemism or clan totemism which has just begun to come into
existence as a result of diffusion.
3. *Apical group totemism*: This is clan totemism in which clan-
and-totem identification is very strong.
4. *Formal social totemism*: This is characterized by various
totemic traits which mainly serve social ends. But there is no
strong clan-and-totem identification.
5. *Totemism in decline*: Here the inner core of totemism has
almost or entirely disappeared, and the totemic traits lose their
cohesion or semblance of unity.

## NOTES AND REFERENCES

[1] Penniman, 1952, 158.  According to John T. Driscoll, 1913, the existence
of totemism was brought to the notice of the civilized world by the
Jesuit missionaries to North America.  But the earliest account of it in
English came from an Indian interpreter, J. Long (*Voyages and Travels
of an Indian Interpreter*, London, 1791).  The word itself is derived
from *ote*, root *ot*, possessive form *otem*, in the Ojibway dialect of the
Algonquin stock of American Indians.  Some authorities spell it *dodeme*
(Father de Smet), *todem* (Father Petitot) or *totam* (J. Long).  Others,
as Frazer points out (1910, I, 1-3), spell it *toodaim* (Rev. P. Jones, an
Ojibway), *dodaim* (Warren), and *ododam* (F. Assikinack, an Ottawa
Indian).  The word originally meant family or tribe.  But it was J. F.
McLennan who, through his writings on the subject, helped to focus

scientific attention on it, and thus deserves to rank in the full sense of the term as discoverer of the phenomenon.

[2] 1952, 33; 1956; 1962, and other articles.

[3] 1910, i, 3.

[4] 1910, iv, 41-64.

[5] 1910, i, 4, 10, 14, 55, 56, 58, 78-80, 133-4.

[6] 1910, i, 5, 81-3, 101-3, 105; iv, 5, 6, 28, 153, 154.

[7] 1910, i, 157, 165; iv, 9-10, 16, 73, 128, 133-5.

[8] 1910, i, 78, 80-1, 83, 156-8, 160, 238, 290; iv, 28, 130-1.

[9] 1910, i, 160; iv, 12, 14, 16-17, 18, 136.

[10] 1910, i, 20, 31, 43, 138; iv, 4, 19-20, 24, 38.

[11] 1921-2, 492.

[12] 1950, 203.

[13] 1949, 130-8.

[14] 1949, 49.

[15] 1915-16, 1918, 1931, 1951.

[16] 1915-16, 259.

[17] 1951, 660.

[18] 1949, 137.

[19] ibid., 137.

[20] 1949, 49-51.

[21] 1956, 122-6.

[22] 1931, 116-17.

[23] 1948, 157-8. Lowie incorporates Goldenweiser's criticisms in his own review of Durkheim's interpretation.

[24] For the above summary of Durkheim's views, I am considerably indebted to an article of Goldenweiser's which appeared in an early number of *Anthropos*.

[25] 1949, 50.

[26] 1952, 47.

[27] 1905, vii-viii.

[28] 1960, 111-13.

[29] 1925, 35.

[30] 1931, 113-15.

[31] 1957, 250-65.

[32] 1917-18, 1094-113; 1919-20, 496-531.

[33] 1908.

[34] Koppers, 1952, 24.

[35] 1911.

[36] 1937.

[37] 1931.

[38] 1924.

[39] 1937, 164-5.

[40] ibid., 165.

[41] ibid., 173-6.

[42] Schmidt & Koppers, 1924. Koppers, however, had early doubts about the general validity of the culture circle concept (1959, 119-22). A modified version of the culture circle system was rendered into English by Sieber & Mueller, 1950. In his later works Schmidt made modifications and extensions in his system. See, for instance, *Vorarbeiten zu einer Neuauflage von 'Völker und Kulturen'* (1955, Micro-Bibliotheca Anthropos, Vol. xxiii), *Totemismus in Asien und Ozeanien* (1955, Micro-Bibliotheca Anthropos, Vol. xv), and A. Randa, 1954. But the modifications and extensions, as Koppers and Haekel point out, do not involve any significant deviations from the old system.

43 1938, 181.
44 Koppers, 1959, 118.
45 Haekel, 1956, 20.
46 Heine-Geldern, 1921, and a few others.
47 Koppers, 1954, 1955, 1959; Haekel, 1956, 1959a, 1959b.
48 The above outline of Haekel's views is based largely on his lengthy article published in 1956 to commemorate the Silver Jubilee of the Viennese School. See also Koppers, 1954, 1955, 1959, and Haekel, 1959a and 1959b.
49 1914, 629.
50 1952, 117-32.
51 ibid., 117-32.
52 Lévi-Strauss, 1962, 84-9, 119-31.
53 For a list of some of Haekel's articles on the subject see the bibliography at the end of this book.
54 1952, 33.
55 Haekel uses the word ' *verwandtschaftlich* '.
56 1956, 56.
57 1952, 33.
58 ibid., 34.
59 ibid., 33-4.
60 1952, 34; 1956, 59.
61 Herrmann, 1961, 44.
62 Haekel, 1952, 9, 34-5.
63 ibid., 36.
64 Haekel, 1952, 35-6; 1956, 61-2, 63-6.
65 Haekel, 1952, 37. Compare Herrmann, 1961, 58-9.
66 Haekel, 1952, 18-25, 36-7, 46; 1956, 56, 57, 66-7.
67 Haekel, 1952, 43-4; 1956, 60-1.
68 Haekel, 1952, 44-5; 1956, 62-3.
69 Haekel, 1952, 45-7.
70 Seen in typescript.
71 Lowie, 1960, 178.
72 1962, 149.
73 Quoted by Sieber & Mueller, 1950, 123.
74 1952, 117.
75 1952, 33; 1956, 56.
76 1910, iv, 3-4.
77 1925, 35.
78 1951, 192.
79 1910, 97.
80 Koppers, 1936, 164-5.
81 1961, 275.
82 1959, 166.
83 1956, 127.
84 1947, 300.
85 1950.
86 1963.
87 1963, 8.
88 ibid., 154-5. Fischer's reference is to George Thomson's *Studies in Ancient Greek Society* (London, 1949).
89 1961, 10.
90 Gabriel, 1954.
91 1956.
92 1952.

[93] 1941-3.
[94] 1938, 1952a, 1952b.
[95] 1954.
[96] 1952, 1961.
[97] 1951, 1952, 1956.
[98] 1963, 16.
[99] MacIver, 1963, 26.
[1] Haekel, 1952; Dittmer, 1951; 1954, 89-98.
[2] 1933, iii, 258.
[3] 1910, iv, 3-4.
[4] 1910, 97.
[5] Sieber & Mueller, 1950, 123.
[6] 1925, 35.
[7] 1952, 117.
[8] 1951, 192
[9] 1952, 33.
[10] 1956, 56.
[11] I am aware that certain aspects of my interpretation in the terminal section of this chapter have been rather summarily dealt with. But this is a shortcoming which, it seemed to me, could only have been avoided at the cost of proportion in treatment from the standpoint of the work as a whole.

# III

# INDIAN TOTEMISM AS OTHERS HAVE SEEN IT

A  REVIEW  of the earlier interpretations of Indian totemism is an excellent starting-point for a study which seeks to evaluate the totemic facts in India afresh. Through such a review a vista into false trails is acquired, and errors of interpretation which tend to recur can the more easily be avoided. Theoretically, most of these earlier attempts at assessing Indian totemism were too sweeping or were too strongly influenced by general notions which were then current coin. Forced also to depend on material which was sometimes unreliable and often inadequate, these assessments can today be considered largely out-of-date.

## J. G. Frazer

One of the early assessors of Indian totemism was J. G. Frazer. He was of the view that totemism was widespread among the black race called Dravidian who formed the aboriginal population of India, and that totemism and exogamy were practised by all the branches of this race. Later some branches came to speak Kolarian or Munda languages, but were still totemic and exogamous. At the time of writing, however, totemism was more prevalent among the Telugu-speaking than among the Tamil-speaking or Kanarese-speaking branches of the Dravidian family. Frazer adds: It is doubtful whether totemism proper was ever practised by any race of India except the Dravidian. There are resemblances to it in combination with exogamy among the Mongoloid peoples of Assam, but it is not certain that these resemblances are proof of the actual existence of the institution. Furthermore, the Dravidians have the classificatory system of relationship, which is essentially associated with the bisection of society into two exogamous moieties and through it with totemism. So far as the Aryan race in India is concerned, exogamy but not totemism is practised by it. Can it therefore be, Frazer asks, that the ancestors of the Hindus borrowed gotra exogamy from the aborigines? In India the range of occupations followed by the totemic tribes and castes is very great, extending from hunting to the herding of cattle, agriculture, commerce and the mechanical arts like weaving, leather-making, stone-cutting and so forth. But exogamy divorced from totemism is also widespread in India. While totemism tends in general to develop into monarchical religion, the natural development in India was checked and obscured by contact with non-totemic races. Hence it is wholly unsafe to take Dravidian totemism into account in order to arrange the totemic society of the world into a series corresponding to the natural order of evolution. While totemism combined with exogamy is widely spread among the aboriginal tribes of India, no single indubitable case of it has been recorded for all the rest of the vast continent of Asia. Lastly, in the respect which the Bhil pay to the totem at marriages, Frazer sees a probable trace of conceptual totemism.[1]

The most obvious error in this series of comments on Indian totemism is Frazer's lumping together of the aboriginal population under the term Dravidian. The lack of discrimination which this reveals was an erroneous tendency of the times.

## *H. H. Risley*

In initiating the Ethnographic Survey of India and in attempting a classification of its racial types, Risley stimulated scientific interest in these hitherto rather neglected aspects of Indian anthropology. He was followed by a number of official and non-official investigators who contributed in varying degrees to the elucidation of the ethnic and ethnological problems of India.

Risley regarded totemism in India as essentially a form of exogamy. There are, he points out, five types of exogamy in India: (i) *Totemic*: confined largely to tribes and castes of Dravidian descent. (ii) *Eponymous*: Vedic saints as eponyms among the Brahmins and others. (iii) *Territorial*: This refers to a very early settlement of a section or the birth-place of its founder, and prevails among the Rajputs and trading castes supposed to be allied with them, but is also found among some tribal groups in a very primitive form as, for instance, among the Kandhs of Orissa. (iv) *Local, communal* or *family* sections of small size and relatively recent origin. (v) *Titular* or nickname groups referring to some personal adventure of the founder or to some office which he is supposed to have held. The titular type is found in castes in a state of transition from animism to Hinduism; the totems have been discarded, but full-blown eponyms have not yet been adopted. The totem is, therefore,

[1] For notes to this chapter see p. 94.

but one type out of a number of different types of sept names which serve the same purpose—that of supplying the machinery for giving effect to the rule of exogamy.[2]

Risley defines the totem as found in India ' as an ancient nickname, usually derived from some animal, of the supposed founder of an exogamous sept, now stripped of its personal associations and remembered solely in virtue of the part it plays in giving effect to the rule of exogamy '. Savages easily believe, says Risley, that they can transform themselves into animals at will or through the agency of witchcraft. It is therefore natural to them to call a man by the name of the animal which he is supposed to resemble. If the man so named happened to be the head of a sept (clan), the name would be perpetuated in connexion with the rule of exogamy, even when the man who had originally borne it had lapsed from memory. In large tribes in which new septs were being continually formed, the practice of naming them after animals would continue in existence by fiction or the force of habit. In course of time the names would become mere symbols to identify groups for the purpose of exogamy, and the tendency would then manifest itself to adopt any kind of distinctive designation as well as animal names. Thus among the Mundas there are queer names which could hardly ever have been personal names.[3]

The social side of totemism is more prominent than the religious side in India. In fact totemic exogamy is widespread, whereas the religious side has fallen into decay. The retention of the effective social side of totemism and the decline of the ineffective religious side is a further proof that totemism is essentially connected with exogamy. The not very prominent religious aspects of totemism in India, that is, reverence towards the totem and occasional divine honours offered to it, can be accounted for in terms of the hypothesis that the totems were originally nicknames. For a man who was named after a tiger, owing to some fancied resemblance to it, would be likely to be worshipped as a tiger after his death. The worship would constitute a form of appeasement of the spirits of the dead ancestors, lest they should enter the bodies of wild animals and thus cause trouble and misfortune to the living.[4]

Exogamy is traced to the general law of natural selection. Individuals tend to vary their habits, and useful variations would tend to be preserved. In a primitive community like the Naga *khel* or Kandh *gochi*, the men, it may be supposed, happened to vary their practices by taking wives from other communities. The infusion of fresh blood resulting from this innovation would prove advantageous to the group concerned, and would be stimulated by heredity. An element of sexual selection would also come into play in the course of time. The exogamous groups would thus have a larger choice of women than the endogamous ones, and would acquire finer women who would be appropriated by the strongest and most warlike men. The exogamous groups would thus eat up their endogamous neighbours or at any rate deprive them of the best of their marriageable girls. The rule of exogamy would then spread by imitation and partly by the extinction of the endogamous groups.[5]

Risley regarded the subject of totemism and exogamy in India as being of special interest because ' the Indian evidence seems not only to point to conclusions different from those arrived at by Mr Frazer on the basis of the Australian data published by Messrs Spencer and Gillen, but to suggest a new canon for determining the historical value of ethnographic evidence in general '.[6]

Risley classified the people of India into seven types as follows: Turko-Iranian, Indo-Aryan, Scytho-Dravidian, Aryo-Dravidian, Mongolo-Dravidian, Mongoloid and Dravidian. The Dravidians, represented at best by the Paniyan of South India and the Santal of Chota Nagpur, constitute the original type of population in India. But in the course of time the ' Brahmanization ' of the aboriginal tribes produced various transformations in the totemic-exogamous tribes, engendering a spectrum ranging from tribes with totemic clans on the one side to those which have been almost entirely Hinduized on the other. Risley enumerates four types of processes in the gradual Brahmanization of the aborigines.[7]

In speculating on the origin of totemism Risley follows in the footsteps of Spencer, Lubbock and Lang, and thus exaggerates the role of nicknames. His application of Darwinism to the problem of exogamy is a simplification of a complex question, as recent studies of the subject have shown. He places the aboriginal population of India under the designation Dravidian, and thus perpetrates the error of confusing linguistic and ethnic categories. As we have seen, Frazer also was thus led astray.

## R. V. Russell

In his four-volumed work *The Tribes and Castes of the Central Provinces of India* (London, 1916), Russell, aided by Rai Bahadur Hiralal, brought together a vast deal of ethnographic material on the tribes and castes of the area which fell under his jurisdiction. Totemic elements of a social and religious nature form a significant portion of this evidence. In an attempt at a general interpretation of these totemic facts, Russell offers the following views.

Totemic exogamy is almost universal among the non-Aryan, primitive tribes of India, but is also found among most of the Hindu castes, including some of the highest. Within the clan the idea of kinship occurs first, and then the idea of descent from an animal, plant, god, hero or nicknamed ancestor. Following Robertson Smith, Russell maintains that the groups called themselves after the animals and plants from which they derived their livelihood. In the later stage of domestication and cultivation the tribesmen speculated about their totem names, traced descent to them, and the totems ceased to be means of sustenance. It was at this time that tribal groups arose; and the totem clans, while still persisting in existence, no longer constituted the main forms of social organization. Belief in clan kinship was next traced to the bond of consanguinity in the family which now came into existence.

Totemism in India is a late and secondary form, since it is found among tribes which have long passed the migratory and hunting stage. When the Indian evidence is examined, one often perceives that in the same community, and sometimes in the same caste, there are exogamous clans which trace their descent to animals, plants, gods, heroes and titular ancestors. Many are named after villages, and others have names without meanings. All these exogamous clans arose from the earliest form of the totem clan. Therefore one may conclude that the exogamous clans with unintelligible names or those tracing descent from a common ancestor were probably everywhere derived from the totem clan. If one, therefore, takes the Indian example as a base, it would follow that even in Europe, America, Africa and Australia the totem clan was the original unit of society. Russell believes that female descent preceded male descent everywhere; and that the Indian exogamous clan with male descent acquired its special character because the members usually lived in one or more villages.[8]

Russell's theorizing reveals the antiquated character of its fundamental points even at the first glance. The precedence of the clan over the family and of matriliny over patriliny are beliefs which belong to the long outmoded, evolutionary phase of cultural studies. His view that the totems were derived from animals and plants from which the clan members got their sustenance is at best a simplification of the problem of totemic origins by a reduction of its causal side to a single material relationship.

## F. Graebner

Graebner's contributions to ethnology as an early protagonist
of the historical approach, as a major contributor to its methodology, and as a leading influence on W. Schmidt and other
European ethnologists, have been adumbrated in the preceding
chapters of this work. His main practical achievement, however,
as distinguished from his contributions towards the elucidation
of the basic character of the science and towards its method,
was the eduction of a number of culture complexes or circles
from the ethnographic data on the South Seas.

One of these complexes is the totemic culture named after the
form of its social organization. Some of its characteristic elements, according to Graebner, are the penis sheath, the leather
belt, the cone-roofed house, the dugout and skin-boat, leather
and wooden utensils, the bench with a head-rest, the spear with
a stone point, the spear-thrower, the patrilineal, exogamous local
group which stands in a relationship of a genealogically varied,
religious nature or of mere friendship to natural objects among
which animals predominate, and astral mythology in which the
sun, the moon and the planet Venus are personified but with
an emphasis on the sun, platform burial, initiation of boys,
circumcision perhaps, and a specific art-style.[9]

Another is the culture of the matrilineal dual system to which
the dispersal of the older totemic culture circle is attributed. It
is the first South Seas culture which is no longer nomadic. Its
principal elements are the cultivation of root crops like yam,
fishing with nets, plank boats, gable-roofed houses, the fire-
saw, a specific basketry technique, butted clubs, broad shields,
the division of society into two matrilineal, exogamous classes,
men's secret societies with masked dances serving religious ends
and holding the leadership of the community in their hands,
cults of the dead and of spirits, exhumed skulls of dead relatives
as cult objects, a moon mythology, pan pipes and one-stringed
musical instruments, signal drums and sounding-boards.
Significant mixed forms have arisen from the contact of the two
above-mentioned cultures. Examples of these mixed forms are
matrilineal totemism, totemic dual systems, the four-class and
eight-class system with totemic sub-groups, a totemic system
divorced from the regulation of marriage and conjoint to the
aim of a magical multiplication of the totem object or separated
from the factor of inheritance under the influence of ideas about
the origin of children from rocks, trees and so on.[10]

Referring to India Graebner points out that a far-reaching
cultural exchange has spread a uniform veneer over a large part

of the subcontinent, making it difficult to unravel the strands of its culture history. There are, for instance, within the same language group like the Dravidian very primitive tribes as well as peoples of an advanced culture. The Vedda of Ceylon, however, with their vegetation and hunting magic constitute the remnants of an old stratum of population. Among other influences they show traces of a matrilineal culture of which several elements are found in South India. A conspicuous component of Indian culture in the South, Northeast and Assam is totemism. It is strong and widespread in India, and so does not correspond in point of age with totemism in other parts of the world. In addition, many elements which accompany totemism in other parts of the world do not play an essential role in it in India. The division of large endogamous groups into exogamous-totemic sub-groups seems to connect Indian totemism with the animal breeders of Inner Asia. It is therefore not improbable that totemism in India owes its existence mainly to an invasion of animal-breeding peoples like the Toda who have penetrated deep into the south. The Toda, it is true, have no totemism; but they have endogamous divisions broken up further into exogamous local sub-groups. They have also cone-roofed huts and a ritual of a magical nature centring in cattle.[11]

While Graebner was more cautious than Schmidt in handling the culture circle concept, he none the less included in the totemic complex elements which do not seem to have a bearing on totemism as such. His view that totemism in India is a relatively recent phenomenon has been called in question by Niggemeyer on the ground that totemism in India is still strong and living because its bearers, inhabiting inaccessible hilly and jungle tracts, have remained comparatively free from more recent cultural influences. Graebner's attempt to connect Indian totemism with the animal-breeding peoples of Inner Asia is also untenable. For, as Niggemeyer points out, it is strange that of the alleged pre-Aryan invasion of animal breeders into India only a small group of approximately 700 persons like the Toda (who moreover do not have any totemism) should have survived, whereas totemism is fairly widespread on the subcontinent.[12]

## J. Przyluski

In his article ' Totémisme et Végétalisme dans l'Inde ' (1927) Przyluski attempts a study of the religions of the pre-Aryan population of India. There are, he says, two types of these religions: (i) the religion of the Kolarians with its human sacrifice, and (ii) the religion of the Dravidians characterized by the *puja*, a ritual involving the smearing of trees and stone-blocks with oil, red ochre and so on, and the offering of flowers. He then attempts to explain the so-called Kolarian religion with its human sacrifice by connecting it with the ritual eating of the totem in Australia through the cannibalism of the Kolarians as exemplified by the human sacrifices of the Khond. The Dravidian puja religion is likewise connected with the so-called ' vegetalism ' of the Semang, which he regards as a type of plant totemism. Vegetalism, Przyluski maintains, represents an older stage than the other types of totemism. Vegetalism flourishes principally in the tropical forests with their abundance of fruits and vegetables; and totemism in the steppes where there is an excess of wild animals.

The methodological and factual errors in Przyluski's interpretation are many. As Niggemeyer points out, an attempt to connect phenomena widely separated from one another historically (*Ferninterpretation*) must be preceded by an extensive, culture-historical investigation, which in this case has not been done. Furthermore, the Khond speak a Dravidian language, the geographical classification to which Przyluski refers is not so certain or clear-cut as he makes out, animal totemism is older than plant totemism, human sacrifice and the puja have nothing to do with totemism in India, and Przyluski's main error in his totemic interpretation of the pre-Aryan religions is that he did not try to examine the nature of Indian totemism in itself.[13]

## S. C. Roy

The services of Sarat Chandra Roy to Indian ethnology were considerable. Inspired by the humanitarian and scientific urges, he championed the cause of the tribal peoples of India and dedicated his life to the collection of ethnographic material on them. His chief field of activity was Chota Nagpur and the immediately adjoining areas. But through the journal *Man in India* which he founded he was responsible for focusing attention on all aspects of the tribal problem throughout India and to a lesser extent elsewhere. In his ethnographic investigations of the Birhor, the Oraon and the Asur, he was able to unfold aspects of totemism in India which had till then remained unknown and unregarded. In 1925 Roy ventured to speculate in an article entitled ' Totemism and Religion ' on the inner nature of totemism on the basis of his findings relating to the Birhor and some other Chota Nagpur tribes.

Roy points out that among the Birhor and some other tribes in Chota Nagpur the bond between clan and totem is a very close one. The Birhor believe that a diminution in the number of the totem species will lead to a corresponding diminution of the clan and vice versa. The Birhor do not believe in the actual descent of the clan from the totem, but find, as do other tribes in India, a certain resemblance in temperament or physical appearance between the clan members and the totem animal or plant. This fancied resemblance, however, does not stop at temperament or physical appearance, but extends to the spiritual substance or soul stuff; and this intuitive recognition of a spiritual identity of clan, totem and clan god expresses itself in thought and ritual. This mystic force or power is of the nature of the ' Melanesian ' mana, which forms the basis of their world view, science and religion. The *Buru Bonga* or hill cradle of each Birhor clan came naturally to be regarded as a perennial reservoir of energy or spiritual grace which warded off the evil influence of harmful powers, and brought good fortune in the food quest, health, progeny and general well-being. The clan was also the embodiment of this energy. Totemism, says Roy, is thus one of the forms in which the religious feeling expressed itself in a sociological setting among certain tribes at an early stage of culture. It is an aspect of animism or rather animatism, and as such of early religion, though neither the source nor the whole of it. The two aspects of totemism—the religious and the sociological—appear to be twins born of the same primitive world view. In another context Roy holds out the possibility and probability of a multiple origin of totemism in India.[14]

So far as Indian totemism is concerned Roy would appear to be right, as we shall see, in selecting the Birhor for special attention. The weakness of his interpretation, however, lies mainly in the slenderness of his evidence. In an attempt dedicated to the study of the origin and nature of totemism, one would expect a broader comparative basis than that offered by the tribes of Chota Nagpur alone. Nor can the totemic mystique be identified so undiscriminatingly with animism or animatism, although both might be rooted in the same basic psychological propensity— the urge towards complementarity as an expression of human inadequacy or finitude.

## L. K. Ananthakrishna Iyer

L. K. Ananthakrishna Iyer's contributions to Indian ethnology lay mainly in the collection of ethnographic material on the Cochin tribes and castes, the Syrian Christians, and, together with H. V. Nanjundayya, on the Mysore tribes and castes. Among the Mysore tribes and castes he unearthed a good deal of totemic

evidence, and in the first volume (1935) of his four-volumed
work *The Mysore Tribes and Castes* he gives us his views on
totemism in general.

Totemism is closely connected with exogamy, the clan organization, magic and animism. Originally it went hand in hand with
matriarchy. Among primitive tribes there are strict rules regulating the choice of food, its preparation and the mode of eating.
In fact an undue importance is attached to the sanctity of food.
Then again, the knowledge of the reproductive process is of
recent date; and so reproduction was often connected with food,
and conception was ascribed to supernatural agencies. It was
also believed that eating the flesh of an animal imparted the
physical and psychic qualities of the animal concerned to its
consumer. The animal on which the hunter's existence depended
was his totem. But in the course of migrations and altered
economic conditions this was changed. Many theories on the
origin of totemism have been offered, but none have acquired
wide acceptance. Totemism in Mysore is in a state of decadence
as a result of the process by which tribes are being transformed
into castes.[15]

This is an odd mixture of ideas and ethnographic facts reflect-
ing in part the views of Frazer, Briffault, Haddon, Hutton and
others. As an interpretation, it is superficial and sweeping and
bears the character of a series of borrowed ideas ill-coordinated
with one another.

## J. H. Hutton

Hutton has contributed excellent monographs based on long
and painstaking field-work to the ethnography of the Naga
tribes, and has devoted much attention to the elucidation of
the caste problem and in general to Indian ethnology and anthropology. His classification of the people of India was based on
racial, linguistic and cultural criteria. He enumerates the following ethnic groups: Negritos, Proto-Australoids, Early Mediterraneans, Advanced Mediterraneans, Armenoids, Alpines and
Mongoloids; and attributes totemism, or at least its basis, to
the Proto-Australoids who, he claims, came from the eastern
Mediterranean.

There are totemic traces, says Hutton, among all the primitive
tribes in all parts of India, and even among a number of castes
that have reached or retained a high status. Totemic traces survive in a vast area ranging from the Bhil in the west to the Wa
of Eastern Burma, and from the Kanet of the Simla Hills to the
Telugu castes of South India.

Totemism may have originally started with Frazer's conception theory based on the ignorance of the fact of fatherhood, and has been kept alive and extended by ideas of life-matter, a separable soul, transmigration and other connected beliefs. A number of these ideas have contributed to totemism as it is still found in India. Totemic manifestations exhibit an extreme variety, ranging from the sacramental consumption of the totem or its use for the magical increase of the food supply to the merest peg for exogamy to hang upon. In India it is commonest in this latter form, having decayed into a mere totemic clan name. There are, however, traces of beliefs and taboos which are essential to it at an earlier stage. Exogamy originated probably at an early stage of totemism, and is therefore naturally found where totemism survives either in some semblance of its earlier form as the conception theory or in a developed form into which other beliefs have entered. If Frazer's view of conception is assumed as the origin of totemism, the other explanations, perhaps not adequate in themselves to start it, may have contributed to support and extend it. This view would also explain the extreme variety of totemic manifestations.

If one presumes the existence of the soul-matter theory of life and death and inclusion in it of plants and fruits, the source of new life in the womb could then be easily ascribed to the soul-matter imbibed in food. In the conception theory, however, belief in life-matter seems scarcely to enter. On the other hand, the external soul idea which seems to be a development of the life-matter belief appears to be connected with totemism in India. Thus it is believed that the after-birth or placenta is closely associated with the external soul or sometimes actually contains it. In this belief lies a possible source of totemism. For the placenta might be devoured by some scavenging animal or bird or could be associated with the tree on which it was placed for security or with some plant which sprang on the spot where it was buried. The totem would then be transferred from the individual concerned to the exogamous clan descended from him or her. The placenta theory accounts for the purely social form of totemism and perhaps the soul-transmigration form. Another possible source of ideas leading to vegetable totems could be food restrictions or peculiarities of diet. The quest for vegetable food must have played an important part in the early economy; and new vegetables discovered together with their sources would be concealed, in order to prevent others from taking advantage of them. Among the Naga of Assam, for instance, certain wild vegetables are important in the clan ceremonial, probably because of their discovery, communication to kindred

6

and concealment from other clans. The test of whether a clan
is related or not is the vegetable used in the clan ceremonial.
Not all these plants, however, are used as food; though all,
Hutton believes, are edible. Nevertheless, he confesses that not
all totems are accounted for directly by the ideas suggested above;
and that it is likely from every point of view that totemism in
general has received accretions from a number of sources.[16]

Hutton does well in noting the variety of totemic manifestations and in pointing out that totemism in general has received
accretions from a number of sources. But his dependence on
Frazer's conception theory as the original root of totemism, and
his attribution of totemism in India to the Proto-Australoids in
general are prime weaknesses in his interpretation. The Central
Australian tribes on whom Frazer mainly based his theory do
not culture-historically constitute the most primitive tribes; and
the most primitive tribes do not show an ignorance of paternity.
Further, to ascribe totemism in India to the Proto-Australoids in
general is to shut one's eyes to the possibility of identifying its
actual bearers along narrower lines. Hutton's placenta and
vegetable-food theories would appear to be too slim to be taken
as sources of totemism in India; and even their partial validity
seems questionable.

## J. Hoffmann

The Jesuit missionary, J. Hoffmann, whose assiduous labours
among the Munda-speaking tribes gave him a first-hand knowledge of their culture, rendered valuable service to Indian ethnology with the publication of his *Encyclopaedia Mundarica* (1930-
1941) in thirteen volumes.

Hoffmann's views on totemism run as follows: Totemism
existed long before exogamy, and so totemism and exogamy are
often found in separate existence. Totemism tends to be naturally endogamous; for, on the principle that like seeks like, the
members of a totem group would tend to seek wives in their
own group. When, therefore, a totem clan is exogamous, it is
so in spite of totemism. In totemic clans totemism is an addition
to the pre-existing clans, and their origin cannot be ascribed to
it. Taboos are not essential to totemism, since in Australia there
are admittedly totemic clans which eat their totems. As the
Munda plainly state, the purpose of clans is exogamy or the
prevention of incest. The clan and tribe system must have sprung
up quite naturally amongst many primitive groups. The gotra
system of the Aryans in India and the clans of the aborigines
were independently formed; so perhaps also the clans of the

Munda and the Dravidians. When once formed, it was also natural for these clans to receive some distinctive designation—a name or a nickname—taken perhaps from some trivial circumstance connected with one or several members of the family or clan in question. Such names could of course be those of animals, plants or other objects without involving the worship of the entire species or respect towards it or protection by it. In other words a name need not be totemic.[17]

In offering these remarks on totemism, Hoffmann was primarily actuated by the intention of explaining away the totemic elements found in the Munda tribe, as appears from his analysis of the phenomenon among the Munda. His assertion that totemism is naturally endogamous goes against the observed fact that in its inner nature social totemism exhibits a sense of kinship between the clan and the totem species, thus strengthening exogamy and hindering marriage relations within the clan. The most widely distributed form of totemism is clan totemism; and while clans and totems are in their origin the products of varying impulses and forces, there is evidently a strong affinity between the two. Clan names need not be totemic in all instances; but one of the basic totemic elements is precisely animal and plant names; and when these are found as clan names together with other elements commonly regarded as totemic, the existence of totemism among the Munda or any other tribes can scarcely be denied. Hoffmann's basic weakness is that he lacks a clear conceptualization of totemism.

## D. N. Majumdar

Majumdar was one of India's leading anthropologists in the wider sense of that term. His anthropometric, ethnographic and other investigations added vastly to the quantum of anthropological information on the ethnic groups of India, and served to throw fresh light on some obscure problems. He was founder of the journal *The Eastern Anthropologist*.

Although all totemic tribes in India are exogamous, says Majumdar, totemism has nothing to do fundamentally with exogamy. In India, for instance, as evidenced by the Naga khels and Hindu gotras, exogamy exists without totemism. Further, geographical isolation weakens the possibility of diffusion; and although diffusionists have sought to explain certain cultural similarities between India and Australia in terms of culture contact, there is another possibility—independent development. In other words, regional influences play a significant role in moulding social forms, and every part of the world may have its own story to tell. Hence the functional analysis of totemic practices will lead to a reshuffling of totemic traits on the basis of their cultural significance. The worship of various animals, plants and other objects exists among the higher castes without totemic features; therefore religious reverence towards them is inessential to totemism and may arise independently of it. There are many food restrictions too which have nothing to do with totemism; hence Hopkins's hypothesis that the totemic bond is connected with dietary restrictions does not hold water. Myths relating to the origin of totemic clans are widespread in India. Many of them, as with those of the Ho, explain how the totem relationship came into existence at a time of extreme necessity when human help was not possible or was of little avail. The spirit of totemism is, therefore, to be sought ' in a simple adjustment of social order which could bring about a sympathetic relationship between man and his environment. Such a relation subserves the needs of human adjustment to the habitat, and might be the result of an age-long process of trial and error or of an accidental discovery in the course of human migration occasioned by the exigency of unfavourable conditions in the parent zones '. In Indian totemism an accidental connexion between a group and an animal or vegetable seems to have been the rule. Although traces of totemism are found in all parts of India (and even among the castes), the primary totemic region is the Middle Indian belt consisting in the main of Proto-Australoid people. Therefore, totemism was probably brought into India by the Proto-Australoids. It is now found in a mild form also among the Mongoloid Naga tribes of Assam, and has penetrated into the more advanced sections of the Indian population.[18]

In some of its aspects Majumdar's standpoint coincides with that of present-day students of totemism. But general statements are not adequate substitutes for close comparative and analytic studies. Further, myths may point to origins of institutions, but may also be later explanations to justify customs, the origins of which might have been forgotten for one reason or another. Majumdar's over-all weakness was a certain inability for exact theoretical construction.

## H. Niggemeyer

In the introductory chapter of this work reference has already been made to the comparative excellence of Niggemeyer's study of totemism in India, and the conclusions at which he arrived have been duly recorded there. But the task of sketching the results of his investigation in somewhat greater detail still remains.

After Australia and North America, says Niggemeyer, India is one of the regions of the world in which totemism is strongly formed. But what is characteristic of India is that totemism has over the millennia come under the influence of a high culture, a fact which has imparted a specific impress on totemic relations on the subcontinent. There are of course primitive peoples who still retain totemism as the basis of their social organization, and among whom totemic institutions have not been shrouded by more recent cultural forms. In the coastal areas, however, and in the more accessible parts of the inner areas where the advanced culture has made its effect felt, and the European influence has still further undermined the old relations, a decline of totemism has set in. Under the impact of the Indian high culture, the ideological core of totemism has all but disappeared and totemism has degenerated into pure externals; and new forms and secondary metamorphoses have come into existence.

The population of India is in the main divided into tribes and castes. The castes, again, are divided into subcastes which in turn break up into *gotras* (Sanskrit: family, family name, originally cowshed). The castes and subcastes are endogamous, but the gotras are exogamous. The gotras are generally named after real or mythical ancestors, localities, titles and the like; among some castes, however, they are all or in great part totemic, that is, they bear the names of animals, plants or other objects which are revered and tabooed. Two-thirds of the total population of India are Hindus and, therefore, come under the caste system. Those who do not are the primitive tribes of Northeastern, Central and South India. Nevertheless, the tribes and castes have influenced one another from early times; and so a middle group has arisen manifesting tribal and caste characteristics in varying forms and degrees. Just as the castes have exogamous gotras, so also the tribes have exogamous sub-groups or clans. Some of these tribal sub-groups resemble the gotras in their geographical and titular designations. But for the most part they bear the names of animals, plants and other objects, and have myths to justify their mystic attitude towards their totems. Thus it is evident that a series of tribes and castes possess totemic elements. But of the exogamous gotras and the tribal clans, the clans are in the narrower sense the bearers of totemism in India.

The tribes and castes may be classified into atomic, polytomous and dichotomous ones. Atomic tribes and castes are divided

directly into exogamous totem clans; polytomous ones are divided
first into endogamous sub-groups and then into exogamous clans;
and dichotomous ones have a division into two sub-groups.
There is an entire series of tribes and castes with exogamous
sub-groups, but without intervening endogamous sub-groups.
This is specially so in the northeastern parts of the Deccan
(that is, Chota Nagpur, Eastern United Provinces and Eastern
Central Provinces up to Northern Hyderabad) among a number
of small tribes, tribal castes, and smaller castes whose tribal ante-
cedents can no longer be recognized. These groups are small and
have a rigid organization resulting from their geographical compactness. On the other hand, the tribes and castes with intermediate endogamous sub-groups are widely spread and very
populous, and hence have no rigid organization. Judging from
their names the sub-tribes and subcastes are of quite modern
origin, and hence of no importance to totemism. They have
either geographical names or those of other tribes, and have
spread with the growth and expansion of the caste system. The
atomic tribes, however, represent an older condition than the
polytomous ones; in fact, they are the most primitive tribes and
are least influenced by the advanced culture.

Dichotomous tribes in India may be classified into endogamous-
dichotomous    and    exogamous-dichotomous    ones.    Graebner
showed that the dual system was connected with the older
motherright culture circle. Therefore, if traces of the dual system
exist in India, the fact would be of importance in arriving at a
cultural stratification and as proof of a totemic-matrilineal mixed
culture. There are two principal criteria in determining the
existence of a dual system—exogamy and matriliny. But some
tribes and castes which have two endogamous groups named big
and small, superior and inferior, genuine and non-genuine and
the like are patrilineal. They are therefore not examples of the
dual system, but have arisen as a result of mixed marriages and
the influence of the caste system, and constitute like the other
endogamous sub-groups a relatively recent phenomenon. There
are however two or three dichotomous castes in South India in
which the two phratries are exogamous. W. Schmidt interpreted
these facts as traces of the dual system. But the evidence is not
conclusive, and the question of a dual system in India must
therefore remain an open one.

In a number of tribes and castes the exogamous totem clans
are divided into exogamous sub-groups, some of which are
totemic and others not. The exogamy of the sub-clans hinges
on the chief clan and is hence non-genuine. The sub-clans which
are non-totemic are probably secondary.

Excluding tribes like the Naga which belong more to Further
India than to India, there are tribes in Assam which have totemic
elements in varying degrees. Two of these, the Khasi and the
Garo, are also distinctly matrilineal. Fürer-Haimendorf opines
that a culture complex similar to the totemic culture of the
South Seas once existed in Further India, and that tribes of this
area probably took their totemic elements from a common substratum of a pure totemic culture or a matrilineal-totemic, mixed
culture. While agreeing with Fürer-Haimendorf that a relatively
recent transmission of totemism from India to this area is scarcely acceptable, Niggemeyer suggests the possibility that the totemic
substratum of Assam might have been connected with totemism
in India at one time, if it was not quite identical with it. Totemism in Assam, judging from the poverty of the material, is very
much weaker than in India.

The exogamous groups have various names like gotra, kula,
intiperulu, vamsa, bali, devak, baink, kili, pari, barga and so on.
Of these names the most widely spread is the word gotra which
is of Aryan-Indian origin. Information on the localization of
the clans and their number is scanty. The localization may have
disappeared with the growth of Hindu influence. In general the
number of clans is fairly high.

All tribes and castes, with a few exceptions, have some animal
totems. The area, however, in which animal totems predominate
is Chota Nagpur, Bengal, and the adjoining part of the country
extending southwards to the northern districts of the Madras
Presidency. No tribes have animal totems exclusively. In the
Bombay Presidency excluding Gujarat and Sind, that is, the
region south of the Narbada, most of the devaks are plants.
The bearers of devak totems are the Marathas, Kunbis and
related castes. The Maravar, a Tamil caste in Madura, is the only
group with plant totems only. The object totems are relatively
few, and hence constitute a recent element. Non-genuine totems
like garland, ocean, pearl, rifle, sovereign and so on are found
mainly in the East and South-Central Deccan. Split totems occur
among the Oraon, Munda and Majhwar; and multiplex totems
among the Oraon and the Basor. Almost the entire flora and
fauna of India occur as totems, and not only the economically
useful ones. For about fifty totemic tribes and castes, or about
one-fourth of the total number, there are no statements on the
kinds of totems, and for others only a selection is offered. Complete lists are available for a few tribes only.

Totemic clan exogamy is not confined to any language, race
or culture. It is present everywhere in the totemic area, and
survives as a form of marriage regulation even when the other

elements like totem taboos and the consciousness of the totemic relation have disappeared, and totemism itself has considerably degenerated. But in many places totem exogamy too has weakened, one reason being the shrinkage of the totemic society through contact with the advanced culture. Some tribes have taken to agriculture and the caste system, and have thus lost totemism and totem exogamy. Others, again, have family and sib exogamy together with totem clan exogamy; and in some cases clan exogamy is being replaced by blood-relationship exogamy. The gotra exogamy of the higher castes was borrowed from the group exogamy of the tribal population, and retained together with blood-relationship exogamy, as S. V. Karandikar has amply demonstrated. Blood-relationship exogamy among the totemic groups in the northeast, centre and west of India has been borrowed from the Hindu castes. It is an old Aryan custom, but a young element among the totemic groups. Among the Dhunniya of the United Provinces the endogamous subcastes are named after trees which are regarded with awe. It may be presumed that either totemism or endogamy is a secondary element in this caste. There are different types of exogamy; and each has a different sense and a different range. So, for instance, there are blood-relationship exogamy, local exogamy, dual system exogamy and clan exogamy. Karandikar distinguishes two types in India—blood-relationship and group exogamy—which are different in meaning and origin. Hence, D. N. Majumdar errs when he maintains that totemism has nothing to do with exogamy, since exogamy exists without totemism in India. The only form of exogamy which is bound up with totemism in India is totemic clan exogamy.

In the main the totem is inherited patrilineally in totemic India. There are however two areas which are exceptions. These are Assam and the Southwest Deccan (or South and North Kanara). In Assam the Khasi and the Garo are matrilineal, and the Lalung and the Kachari show matrilineal traces. South and North Kanara are separated from Assam by the entire extent of the Indian peninsula. In South Kanara the language is Tulu, and in the northern parts of South Kanara and North Kanara it is Kanarese. In the Tulu areas the bali is inherited matrilineally, and so also is property among many castes there; but in Kanarese-speaking North Kanara the bali and property are patrilineally inherited. In between these two areas the totem is inherited matrilineally and property patrilineally. The reverse— patrilineal inheritance of the totem and matrilineal inheritance of property—does not occur. It therefore follows that patrilineal inheritance of property intruded later, perhaps only under the influence of the high culture, into the full matrilineal relations of inheritance. The matrilineal inheritance of the totem remained because the high culture had no corresponding institution to replace it. Beyond this matrilineal-totemic area in Kanara, there is only one caste in the extreme south, the Maravar of Madura, which has matrilineal inheritance of totems and patrilineal inheritance of property.

There is only one instance of individual totemism. The Birjia Asur of Ranchi and Palamau (Chota Nagpur) have individual totemism together with group totemism, and the clan totem is changed in every third or fourth generation. Hence every individual has two totems—his own and that of the clan. As against the strict patrilineal totemism of the Munda, the change of the clan totem among the Asur is a young and special development. Once the strict inheritance of the totem in the clan was broken, the idea was probably extended to the individual. But, as more research on the question is necessary, this is not a final solution. There is no sex totemism in India.

Only half the number of totemic tribes and castes have totem taboos; but this may be partly due to the inadequacy of the reports. The totemic taboos are of many types in India. Reverence towards the totem is of a general and a more specific kind. Thus the reports mention in a general way the existence of attitudes of respect, reverence and worship. There are also greeting customs among the Bhil and some northern tribes and castes. The more specific kind is the worship at marriages of the totem itself or its modelled representation—a practice found chiefly in the northwestern parts of the Deccan among the Marathas and related castes. The Marathas have exogamous kuls or family groups with devaks (gods) which are mainly trees. In former times the devaks were certainly totems. Traces of a former devak exogamy are also present; though today devak exogamy has been largely replaced by kul or family group exogamy. The devaks coincide with the balis of the south, which are regularly worshipped, carefully treated, and regulate marriage relations. In Kanara the totem is not only worshipped, but also protected against harm; among the Marathas, however, it is mainly worshipped at marriages and other important occasions. Although among the Marathas totem exogamy has been replaced by kul or family exogamy, the totemic meaning of plants, animals and other objects has not been lost, but retained at marriages. For the totem is everywhere a marriage regulator, and marriage is dependent on the difference of totems of the marriage partners. This latter custom is a further proof of the totemic character of the devaks. Other occasions when the devaks are worshipped are the occupation of a new house, the laying down of the threshing-floor at harvest time, and the bestowal of the sacred thread on boys. This custom is widespread in the Bombay Presidency and the western parts of the Deccan far into Central India. From there it has spread to the south and the north-east. The totems are mainly plants, but among some animal totems predominate. Various types of sacrifices are offered to the totem or representations of it at marriages.

Totem cults exist among the Oraon and the Birhor. Among the Oraon there are certain marriage usages and also a direct worship of the totem animal with sacrifices, which do not seem to proceed distinctly from the rules of avoidance. Divine honours are paid to wooden crocodiles and other animal figures kept in a kind of totemic shrine. Other usages also point towards totem worship. At any rate the worship of these animals as divinities seems to indicate a totemic root. But the totemic meaning has been almost lost, while totem exogamy and the avoidance taboo are strictly followed. Hence the totem worship of the Oraon with its attendant sacrifices is a young, deviant formation. Among the Birhor of Chota Nagpur every clan believes that it has come from a specific hill; and every year a sacrifice is offered to the spirit of the hill. A part of the clan totem procured by members of other clans who are not forbidden to kill the totem animal plays a role in these ceremonies. It is supposed to represent the entire clan. The ceremony not only identifies the clan with the totem, but also with the spirit of the hill. In the absence, however, of adequate material, it is not possible to determine the age of these phenomena.

In the eastern parts of the Central Provinces the members of the clans mourn for the totem when they hear of its death or happen to see its dead body. Earthen vessels in the house are thrown away or destroyed, a purification bath is taken, the beard and the hair of the head are shaved away, and new clothes are worn. The practices are the same as when a member of the family dies. Mourning practices centring in the totem also occur among the Kachari in Assam. Perhaps further research will uncover other examples of such usages in the intervening areas and thus connect Assam with the Central Provinces.

Avoidance rules are widely distributed in the entire totemic area in India. These rules forbid the members of the clan to wound, kill or eat the animal or to touch, uproot, cut down or use the totem plant. Many believe that the violation of these rules will result in physical disadvantages like sickness, blindness and the like. The absence of taboos as among the Kharia of Chota Nagpur implies the decadence of totemism. When the totems have an economic value, the taboos are circumvented or grow weak. Since the rule of avoidance occurs in the entire totemic region, and moreover among tribal groups whose primitive culture is still uninfluenced by the high culture, it is the oldest of all existing taboo rules in India. It occurs however only among one-third of the totemic groups—a fact which may be ascribed to inadequate research and the destructive impact of the high culture. In earlier times it must have been more widely spread than today.

The other rules and usages show a local expansion only. The mourning for the totem, confined as it is to a specific area in Central India, probably had a uniform origin. Lacking uniformity the worship of the totem is therefore a younger, local development, as is evidenced by the totem ceremonies of the Oraon and the Birhor. The worship of the totem among the Marathas is a younger element than the rule of avoidance, and was probably formed with the intrusion of Hindu ideas and in imitation of them.

The representation of the totem in sculpture and painting is not widely spread in India, but limits itself to a small area of the totemic region. It occurs where the totem is worshipped specially at marriages and other occasions, and is therefore connected with religious purposes. But the worship of the totem at marriages, predominantly a Maratha phenomenon, which has spread eastwards from the west, is a comparatively recent development. Hence the representation of the totem in sculpture and wall-painting is a young element in Indian totemism. The Oraon totem figures, however, constitute another problem.

There are only two tribes which appear to have totem tattooing —the Bhil and the Bhaina of Bilaspur. The age of the phenomenon cannot, therefore, be determined.

The destructive impact of the high culture and the inadequacy of the source material make it difficult to determine the exact nature of the spiritual core of totemism in India. The outward elements of totemism have survived, but the inner have almost disappeared. The rule of avoidance has been transformed into worship, and totem exogamy into blood-relationship exogamy in many areas. Hence the only general statement possible is that a special relation between the human groups and the totem exists; but it is not possible to say whether a belief in totem descent was generally connected with the kinship relation towards the totem found in large parts of India. Some groups (the Khasi, the Halepaik, the Kawar) believe in totem descent; but others reject it and explain their totemic nomenclature by connecting it with incidents supposed to have occurred in the lives of their ancestors. These myths however are of a younger origin, and must have been formed, as J. Hoffmann also believes, when the original meaning of totemism was lost and it was in a state of decay. Therefore these myths cannot be used to explain the original contents of totemism. Among the Asur and the Birhor the clan and the totem are identified together, and there is no difference between the two. Although this is known to prevail only among these two tribes, it seems to constitute a root of totemism. Among the Oraon it is believed that the tiger desists from killing members of the tiger clan. There are in India no food multiplication rites of the type common in Australia. All that can, therefore, be said of the inner side of totemism in India is that there is a relationship, which cannot be more closely defined, between the clan and the totem, with an inclination to identify the clan with the totem.

Apart from Assam, totemism in India is largely confined to the greater part of the Deccan. There is no trace of totemism north of a line that runs from Gujarat to Allahabad and along the Ganges till its estuary. From these upper areas totemism spread downwards in a more or less compact mass throughout the entire peninsula to the south, excluding the extreme southern point. A line drawn from Mahe to Madras constitutes the southern boundary. There are nine castes to the south of this line which are totemic, but they have migrated from the north in recent times. In this more closely defined totemic area the forms and intensity of totemism vary. All the tribes and castes of the area are not totemic. But anthropologically and culturally the totemic tribes and castes stand essentially nearer to the old population of India than the non-totemic castes. Totemism is particularly intensive where the primitive culture is relatively free and uninfluenced as in Chota Nagpur and large parts of Central India. In the northern parts of the east coast, that is specially among the Telugu castes, totemism is still distinct but has already been overlaid by the caste system. In the northwestern and southcentral areas of the Deccan the rule of avoidance is scarcely observed, totem exogamy is on the decline, and the totemic core of the devak has been partly covered over by younger forms and institutions.

The two areas in which the totem is inherited matrilineally— South Kanara and Madura on the one side and Assam on the other—are separated from each other by an extensive area in which pure patrilineal totemism prevails. The area with a distinct and predominant motherright is the totem-free south in which the language is Malayalam. In the adjoining Tamil area motherright is less distinct but clear. Whether motherright existed originally in the Tamil area or has been borrowed from the Malayalam area cannot be definitely answered. So also in the western parts of Further India there are clear matrilineal features. Thus, the matrilineal-totemic Tulu castes in South Kanara and the Maravar of Madura and the matrilineal-totemic tribes of Assam live on the frontier between the pure motherright and pure patrilineal-totemic areas. It is only in these contact areas that there is a matrilineal descent of the totems; and never in Central India and the Eastern Deccan where totemism is deeply entrenched. Therefore it follows that matrilineal totemism in South India and Assam is a contact phenomenon resulting from the encounter between pure motherright and patrilineal totemism, that totemism in India had nothing to do originally with motherright, that the matrilineal descent of the totem is a secondary phenomenon, and that patrilineal totemism is the older and more original form in India.

Niggemeyer classifies the totemic areas of India as follows: *Matrilineal totemism*: (1) Matrilineal southwest group, (2) matrilineal group in Assam. *Patrilineal totemism*: (3) Maratha totemism, (4) Northeast group, (5) Southeast group. The areas with matrilineal totemism, says Niggemeyer, are easy to define, but not so those with patrilineal totemism. Of the latter the area of Maratha totemism with its predominating plant totems and their worship at marriages stands out distinctly. Comprising the Maratha country proper or the middle parts of the Bombay Presidency, northwestern Hyderabad and the southwest of the Central Provinces, it spread from there into the south and further north and east. The other areas of patrilineal totemism may be distinguished by the character of the totems and their importance to the social organization. In the northeastern area (Central India and Chota Nagpur) animal and plant totems predominate; but in the southeast of the Deccan non-genuine totems increase in number, and totemism yields ground to the caste system. Some totemic elements are common to all the groups, and thus constitute the oldest form of totemism in India; others are secondary formations. For instance, the matrilineal inheritance of the totem is secondary; so likewise Maratha totemism, which has greatly degenerated, has a large number of younger elements. In the northeast and specially in the southeast the non-genuine totems are secondary formations. Totemism at its best is represented by the tribes of Chota Nagpur and Central India. The totemism of the northeastern group is, therefore, the original form of Indian totemism.

The problem of locating the bearers of Indian totemism is a difficult one because the course of cultural development has obscured totemic relations. The views of both Risley and Frazer are based on the linguistic principle and are, therefore, not valid. They ascribe totemism to the Dravidians. Frazer is somewhat more specific and speaks of the Telugus as participating in a stronger measure in Indian totemism. But he also believes in a relationship of the Munda peoples with the Dravidians, and so includes the Munda peoples too among the bearers of totemism. The term Dravidian, however, is a linguistic one, and embraces peoples of varying ethnic stocks and cultures.

A more precise classification of the Indian races is that of Eickstedt. There are first the Weddids who comprise the Malids, a small dark-skinned people in the southern parts of the Western Ghats up to the estuary of the Kistna, and the taller and brighter Gondids in the hills and jungles of the northcentral areas of the Deccan. The latter constitute the principal mass of the tribal population. There are next the Melanids who are dark-skinned but are not primitives. They occupy the plains of the southeast and the extreme northeast (Bihar, Orissa and West Bengal). The northeastern Melanids are the Munda peoples and are known as the Kolid type. The Melanid groups were once connected. Lastly come the Indids with a Keralid type on the Malabar coast and the Telugus on the east coast, and the North Indids to the north of Delhi.

The Malids have no totemism. The Indids are also not its bearers, as the northern and northwestern parts of India which are mainly their habitat have largely no totemism. There is also no totemism among the Indids of Malabar. Totemism is strong, however, among the Indids of the Western Deccan and specially among the Telugu population. The extreme south is free of totemism and this is precisely the domain of the Melanids. The Melanid Tamil in Ceylon also have no totemism. Hence, it is not true, as Fürer-Haimendorf believes, that the Melanids are the bearers of totemism in India. The original bearers of totemism in India are the north Weddids or Gondids. The habitat of the Gondids coincides with the main area of totemism, that is, Central India; and the most important Gondid tribes (the Bhil, Baiga, Korku, Gond, Oraon, Maria, Kui and others) still possess a living totemism which forms the basis of their social organization. The Munda tribes among whom totemism is strong must have got it from the Gondids. For the Munda, as Eickstedt shows, are a mixed group consisting of at least three ethnic strains of which the principal is the Mongolid which came from the east and brought the Austroasiatic languages. The other two components are the Melanid and the Gondid. The course of development was probably as follows: the Mongolids, bringing with them the Austroasiatic languages from the east, intruded into an area with a mixed Melanid-Gondid population, imparting their language but taking over totemism and adapting themselves to the new culture. The result of this mixture is the Munda peoples of today. The totemism of the Austroasiatic Khasi seems to indicate that Gondid totemism once extended over the Ganges far towards the east. But the corresponding anthropological investigations for Assam are lacking. On the other hand, it is possible that the Austroasiatic Mongolids had themselves brought a kind of totemism which was not so distinctly formed as the totemism in India, and which can scarcely constitute an explanation of the living totemism of the Munda tribes. The totemism of the Telugus and the Indids of the West Deccan could have been taken from the Gondids; for, as Eickstedt points out, the Telugus formed an Indid block which broke through to the east, and in the Middle Deccan came in contact with and disturbed the Malids and Gondids. A further proof of this is that totemism among the Telugus with its non-genuine totems is a secondary form. It is totemism in decay. The same applies to the Indids of the west and southcentral Deccan, that is, Maratha totemism and the southwest group.

If the Gondids were the original bearers of totemism in India, totemism must be very old on the subcontinent. Judging from the general situation and the entire culture of the Gondids, they are obviously older than the Indid group. But the age of the Gondids in relation to the Melanids is not clear. Eickstedt holds that the Gondids in the eastern areas of Central India bordering on the north Melanids are relatively younger than the latter. This of course does not imply that the Gondids considered as a whole are younger in India than the Melanids. The question calls for more anthropological and ethnographic research.

The older view that the Indian high culture was a product exclusively of the Aryans and that the primitives made no contribution to its development is no longer widely held today. The Aryans came to India in the second millennium before Christ, and there followed a mixture of race and culture. The end product of this mixture was Hinduism and the Indian culture. Totemism has contributed to the development of the Indian high culture on its sociological side. When the Aryans entered India they had no group exogamy but only blood-relationship exogamy, as Karandikar clearly demonstrates. On the other hand, the primitive peoples possessed group exogamy in the form of totem clan exogamy. Hence the group exogamy of the Aryans was adopted from the primitives, but the accompanying totemism was left out as it was foreign to the Aryans.

An exception to this are the Shivalli Brahmins of Kanara who also possess totemism. Since totemism was excluded, the gotras were named after ancestors, localities, titles and the like. R. V. Russell was also of the same opinion. Hierarchical order and strict endogamy were contributions of the animal-breeding nomads to the development of the caste system. Once formed, the caste system spread from the north over the whole of India and forced itself upon the primitive population. As a result totemism declined; some totemic tribes were organized into endogamous groups; the original equality of the totem clans was replaced by the hierarchical order of the caste system; and hypergamous clans and other social forms emerged. The religious side of totemism represented by the totem taboos decayed fast; its place was taken by types of totem worship. Totem names were either replaced by those of mythical saints, localities, titles and so on, or survived side by side with them. The gotras, owing their origin to primitive totem exogamy, are now sought after by the tribal peoples. Totemism, which contributed to some extent to the formation of the Indian high culture, has been condemned to decay and destruction through its impact.

Totemism in India exists at different levels—among peoples belonging to the high culture, to certain middle cultures (hoe cultivation), and sometimes among hunters and food-collectors. Unfortunately, the culture of the Central Indian tribes who were probably the original totemists is still to a great extent unknown. It is therefore not possible to work out a totemic culture circle for India.

Niggemeyer concludes: To attempt to explain totemism in general from the standpoint of Indian totemism is not feasible. For, as Graebner points out, every phenomenon may only be derived from the culture and natural relations under which it has arisen. That totemism arose in India has not been proved. On the contrary all the criteria speak in favour of the fact that Indian totemism is historically connected with other totemic regions of the world. Thus, Indian totemism has forms of phenomena which are common to the other parts of the world—the naming of a human group after an animal, plant and the like bound up with the feeling of an inner relationship to the totem, and the rule of exogamy which forbids marriage between members of the same totem clan (form and quantity criteria).[19]

A critical evaluation of Niggemeyer's study can be conveniently divided into two parts, the first dealing with his theoretical presuppositions, and the second with his specifically Indian conclusions. The validity of his Indian conclusions will be tested in the course of this work. His theoretical presuppositions stand or fall to the extent to which the old culture-historical stand-point stands or falls today. That extent has been admirably measured by W. Koppers and J. Haekel in a series of recent articles, a condensed version of which has been presented in the preceding chapter. There are, however, some aspects of the old culture-historical standpoint to which Niggemeyer specifically refers. These call for a specific commentary here.

Niggemeyer describes totemism as a group phenomenon in which group exogamy is a leading characteristic, and in which the attitude of respect towards animals, plants and other objects expresses itself above all in certain rules of avoidance. Apart from the fact that he fails to give due recognition to the relative variability of totemic manifestations, Niggemeyer's description or definition falls short in that it too exclusively identifies totem-ism as a group phenomenon and connects it too emphatically with group exogamy. There is now at our disposal sufficient evidence to justify the conclusion that individual totemism is a significant component, at least in some large areas, of the corpus of beliefs and practices called animalism or proto-totemism which is characteristic of the more differentiated hunting cultures. When totemism is dynamically conceived, its conceptualization must therefore logically embrace this component, particularly when, as Baumann demonstrates, some evidence is available of the growth of group totemism from its individual forms. In so far as exogamy is concerned, Haekel, reverting to Frazer's view on the subject, holds that clan exogamy is in most cases a natural extension of the factual blood-relationship exogamy of smaller, unilateral groups like family agglomerates and lineages, and that the presumed course of development from belief in totem descent or relationship to the totem to a feeling of artificial blood-relationship and hence to exogamy rarely occurs among primi-tives. It is true that the bond between the totem and the clan serves to strengthen clan exogamy, and by association imparts to it a totemic colour. But by emphasizing the connexion Nig-gemeyer implies an original relationship, and thus ignores the likelihood of a convergence of two phenomena with different origins.

In referring to the dual system Niggemeyer follows Graebner and thus identifies it with the old motherright culture circle. He uses motherright and exogamy as criteria in determining the existence of a genuine dual system, and regards the existence of such a system or traces of it as a valuable aid in establishing cultural strata and mixed matrilineal-totemic cultures. But the facts are not as simple as this old schematization of ethnological relations would have us believe. Although the dual system is

7

often associated with matrilineal cultures, and in some areas like Northwest America and Melanesia seems to be historically connected with matrilineal tendencies, the view held by Graebner and Schmidt that it was originally connected with specific matrilineal cultures is no longer valid as a general standpoint. As Haekel points out, the roots of the system lie in a particular ideological plane, in a polar world view and various dualities in nature and the cosmos. The system rests on an ideological and social order similar in many respects to certain forms of clan totemism. Even the exogamy of the dual system depends on its characteristic world view, and has nothing to do as such with patriliny or matriliny. The sociological background of the system consists of small, unilateral kinship groups; and it is inessential if these groups are matrilineal or patrilineal. Other factors which contribute to the development of the system are certain behavioural tendencies between affineal relations, the settlement of contrasting tensions in society, and the blending of two different populations.

Niggemeyer falls further into the error of using the criteria of quality and quantity too broadly and loosely. He thus sees historical connexions between the totemic phenomena in his specific area of study and other widely separated regions of the world. But, as Haekel rightly points out, the presence of exogamous patrilineal clans, animal totems, taboos and totemic names and emblems do not in themselves justify the assertion of historical connexions. For these factors are not sufficiently clear in terms of the criteria of quality and quantity. Then again some elements are more easily diffused than others.

Finally, Niggemeyer accepts by implication the concept of a totemic culture circle. But this concept is, as has been earlier indicated, the least tenable side of the old culture-historical standpoint.

## W. Schmidt

One of Schmidt's more recent studies was an extensive work on totemism in Asia and Oceania (*Totemismus in Asien und Ozeanien*, pp. xxviii + 1408, 1955, Micro-Bibliotheca Anthropos, Volume 15). In this work Schmidt attempted to vindicate his position and extend his conclusions by an examination of the new material that had accumulated since his earlier writings on the subject.

In his study of Indian totemism, to which he devotes about 200 pages of the above-mentioned work, he relies mainly on O.

Menghin, S. Piggott, H. Niggemeyer and the relevant ethnographic compilations and monographs.

The miolithic blade cultures of India, says Schmidt, are found
just in the areas occupied by the Gondids who have the oldest
totemic culture. These blade cultures represent the later stages
of the cultural series extending from the Aurignacian to the
Capsian, and have a strong microlithic character which Menghin
views as a mixture of the Aurignacian and Pygmy cultures, connecting them with the strongly microlithic Shabarakh culture
of Mongolia. Schmidt adduces some further evidence in order
to lend strength to the connexion.

The oldest forms of Indian totemism are met with among the
four tribes of the Gondids—the Gond, Muria, Khond and Oraon.
Animal totems preponderate among them, and there are even a
few cases of pure animal totems. All these tribes have taken to
agriculture and no longer eke out an existence by hunting alone.
The existence of some plant totems among them need not necessarily be attributed to a matrilineal culture, since the most
primitive or old cultures had private property in trees. Except
for one case of totem descent among the Gond, the others are
instances of parallel relationship, that is, the human and animal
ancestors are supposed to have had in early times a special relation to each other. Totem descent is not necessarily older than
parallel relationship; and parallel relationship also engenders a
feeling of solidarity which expresses itself in the first instance
in totem clan exogamy. There are, however, among all the Gond
tribes (except the Oraon and the Betul Gond) phratries also,
which are totemic and which have their own exogamy. The
phratries have been chiefly formed by an association of totem
clans. There is no dual or multiple class system among the
Gondids. Where the influence of Hinduism is not great, the
totem taboos are still strong, and have in some places been
strengthened by mourning customs, and in others, as among the
Muria, weakened by an excess of sexual activity. The totems
among the Gondids are everywhere patrilineally inherited. All
reports indicate that the totem clans of the Gondids were originally localized, and the localization was disturbed by migrations
and the modern tendency to take up residence where and when
the inclination impelled. Nevertheless, they still possess a localized shrine with a hereditary priest, which geographically and
religiously strengthens the sense of clan continuity. All in all,
therefore, it can be said that among the Gondids classical totemism still exists to its full extent. But while Niggemeyer leaves
the question of a totemic culture circle in India undecided, the

existence of such a circle of higher hunters among the Gondids can be affirmed with certainty.

Although the Gondids have taken to agriculture, they have retained the consciousness of having once been mere higher hunters, which expresses itself through a high evaluation of hunting and assumes ritualistic forms. Hunting and fishing have still an economic importance among them, are pursued with enthusiasm by the men, and among the Muria and the Oraon a good harvest depends on the success of the ceremonial hunt. There are economic-religious hunting feasts with a series of cultic features among the Muria and the Oraon. In the dormitories the young men are taught hunting, while agriculture receives no attention. Bows and arrows, daggers and spears, swords and axes and various types of nets and traps are used in hunting. The shield, however, is lacking. There is a cult of hunting weapons, and among the Gond the weapons and the tree out of which they were produced in the 'age of wood' have grown into the highest divinity. The high position of the god of the hunt further demonstrates the importance ascribed to hunting among the Muria and the Khond. Higher hunting makes possible a fixed dwelling-place. Thus, before their adoption of agriculture, the Gondids had the round hut with a cone-shaped roof which was supplanted by the rectangular house with a gabled roof typical of agricultural communities.

Totemism is not the basis but a consequence of the higher hunting culture which busies itself more intensively with animals than the primitive or old cultures had done. This was so because plant food retreated to its place of origin, and because improvements in hunting weapons and methods produced better results. As a consequence, the bond between men and animals became so close that both were considered as standing on the same footing, involving a kind of pact forbidding the killing or harming of one another, to which their descendants were also obliged.

The social organization of totemic higher hunting transcended the blood-relationship of the natural joint family and created the clan in which the members were presumed to be related, and therefore incapable of marrying one another on the ground of common relationships to a specific animal. The clan is everything in this culture circle; for totemism as such is unacquainted with phratries because of clan localization and the bond with a particular animal. This condition of the existence of mere clans is still found among the Gond, and it must have been so also among the other Gondids as an original condition in India. The social organization of higher hunting with its totemism rests on men because hunting is a male activity. This aspect of Gondid society was further strengthened by the adoption of plough cultivation and the domesticated animals that it required. A typical feature of the totemic culture is a quest for organization through individual men with definite functions, or, in other words, through chiefs and priests and their assistants. Among the Oraon, for instance, there are a series of functionaries who satisfy this quest for organization.

The self-education of youth occupies a more prominent place in the higher hunting cultures than in the primitive or old cultures or in the other two primary cultures of patriarchal herders or matriarchal cultivators. In the patriarchal herding cultures the father takes the management of cultural affairs in hand, and in the matriarchal cultivating cultures the mother. But among the higher hunters the male youth strive to win influence and to make themselves effective. This comes about because the parents resign their duty to educate their children particularly in the years when they are most in need of it. The boys therefore take their education in their own hands. The centre of education is the dormitory, which exists in various phases of development among the Oraon, certain Gond sub-tribes and the Muria.

In the totemic higher hunting cultures the economic position of men is strong; therefore the position of women sinks in the social order. This begins in the period of youth; for in the process of self-education the young men convert the young women into objects for the exercise of loose sexual relations, as is evidenced by various practices and orgies in and outside the dormitories among the Gondids.

The elevation of their weapons into a cult by the Gond follows not only from their importance in hunting but also in war. Thus among some tribes the god of the hunt is also a god of war. The warring nature of the Gondids expressed itself not only against foreign tribes such as the Munda against whom they appeared in the role of attackers and conquerors, but also against one another, as is testified by reports on the Khond.

The entire religion of the Gondids agrees with the character of their totemic higher hunting culture. The hunting weapons are regarded as the highest deity among the Gond, the god of the hunt is the husband of the earth goddess among the Muria and the Oraon, the sun god as supreme deity is at enmity with the earth goddess and her human sacrifices among the Khond, and the Supreme Being is interpenetrated and surrounded by concepts related to the sun among the Oraon and the Maria. The sun acquires its high position in the religion of the higher hunters as they move out of the woods into sunlit areas, particularly rivers and brooks where the animals gather in numbers to quench their thirst, and are thus easy prey to the hunters. Among the Oraon the most important feast of the year is the *Darhul* feast in honour of the sun, which is identified with the Supreme Being. There is some evidence that the Gondids treat their gods with both fear and familiarity, seeking more to force them to accede to their wishes rather than to supplicate them. This attitude lies very close to magic, which flourishes in full strength among the Gond.

The totemic higher hunting culture of the Gondids is independent of the culture of the Munda tribes on the one side and the original culture of the Dravidian peoples on the other. While the culture of the Munda tribes is closely connected with the matrilineal cultivating culture of the Austroasiatic peoples of Further India, the exact nature of the Dravidian culture is difficult to establish. When the Gondids came into contact with the Dravidians, a great part of the Dravidian peoples had already taken over matrilineal cultivation from the Munda peoples. These Dravidians were the Tamil, Malayalam, Tulu, and a part of the Kanarese-speaking groups. The rest (Kanarese, Telugu) were probably on the way to a matrilineal town culture. As the Gondids entered India from the northwest, they came first into collision with the Dravidians; but their traces in the north have been effaced by the later Aryans. In the Central Provinces the Gondids came into contact with the bulk of the Dravidians, adopted their language, but gave them patrilineal totemism in such strength that from the matrilineal culture which the Dravidians had taken over from the Munda not even mixed forms have survived. Mixed forms did not develop in general on the east coast. They arose only later in the southwest. More towards the east of the Central Provinces the Gondids came into contact with the Munda peoples and influenced them much more than they did the Dravidians, as they were less populous and culturally lower than the latter. They gave them patrilineal totemism and some elements of their language and culture.

Linguistically the Gondids stand apart from the Munda; and although they speak Dravidian languages today, they have been borrowed from the Dravidians. Racially also the Gondids differ from both the Munda and the Dravidians. As Niggemeyer shows, from among Eickstedt's racial groups only the Gondids could have been the bearers of the oldest and full form of totemism in India. This applies also to the totemic higher hunting culture itself.

In India the totemic higher hunting culture is younger than the matrilineal cultivating culture of the Munda tribes. The

Gondids took primitive hoe cultivation from the Munda and plough cultivation from the later Indids. They got the bow and arrow from the primitive or old culture, but they themselves contributed spears, daggers and axes. Among the Munda plant cultivation is fundamental; but the Hinduized Dravidians and Middle Dravidians of the Telugu and North Kanara areas have no uniform economic foundations. At any rate higher hunting and fishing and hoe cultivation are not basic to the Dravidians.

In none of the three totemic regions of India is totemism so living and so much the foundation of the entire social order as among the Gondids. Totem taboos and totem clan exogamy are still strongly observed, where Hinduism does not exercise an overwhelming influence. The Gondids have the oldest form of totemism, which is characterized by a strong predominance of animal totems, an earlier or still existing localization of the totem clans, and patriliny. The Munda have the patrilineal inheritance of the totems and a preponderance of animal totems, but the rule of avoidance and exogamy are uncertain, and the localization of the clans is not so clear as among the Gondids. The Birhor and the Bhumij have a full and strong totemism because they live next to the Gondids and are partly surrounded by them. The totemism of the Middle and Hinduized Dravidians is still weaker than that of the Munda, as is evidenced by the following facts: the prevalence of the matrilineal inheritance of the totems in a part of the Southwest, the preponderance of plant totems, the existence of object totems among many castes and the supersession of clan exogamy by family group exogamy in a great part of the area.

The individuality of the totemic higher hunting culture of the Gondids is at its strongest and most characteristic in relation to the youth dormitories which have the following features: they belong entirely to the youth, who are obliged to take their education into their own hands; they are economically autonomous; and there is a free exercise of sex in them. As far as the Munda are concerned, they have either no dormitories or their characteristics differ from those of the Gondids. The five Munda tribes —the Birhor, the Juang, the Bhuiya, the Gadaba and the Bondo —which have youth dormitories are close neighbours of the Gondids or are surrounded by them. In the area of the Middle Dravidians (Telugu, Kanarese) and the Hinduized Dravidians there are no dormitories. The matrilineal tribes of Travancore in Southwest India have no true youth dormitories. Though two Kurumba tribes have them, their culture-historical position is not clear. Although they are separated by great distance, they could have got them from the Gondids.

The religion of the Gondids has grown organically from their total culture of totemic higher hunting. Neither of the two other totemic areas lends the same importance to hunting and to the sun as does the Gondid religion. Among the Munda the moon plays a more important role, and even the words *Sing Bonga* mean ' day moon '. The sun cult of the Munda peoples does not merge organically with the character of their cultivation. Lastly, among the Middle and Hinduized Dravidians, hunting and the sun are either not given the significance that they have among the Gondids or at any rate are given it in a very weakened form.[20]

From the above summary of Schmidt's views on totemism in India, it is clear that he clung in essentials to the last to the culture-historical system which he was chiefly responsible in establishing and elaborating. The specific validity of his views on totemism in India will be tested in the course of this work.

## NOTES AND REFERENCES

[1] 1910, i, 228, 291, 329, 330, 336; iv, 10-11, 18, 30, 294.
[2] Risley, 1891-2, i, liii-liv, lx-lxi, lxvii-lxix.
[3] ibid., i, lxix-lxx.
[4] ibid., lxx-lxxi; Risley & Gait, 1903, 534-6.
[5] Risley & Gait, 1903, 537.
[6] ibid., 534-5.
[7] Risley, 1891-2, i, xl-li; 1915, 33-4, 95-108.
[8] Russell & Hiralal, 1916, i, 90-7, 136, 152.
[9] Graebner, 1923, 451-2.
[10] ibid., 452-4.
[11] ibid., 510-12.
[12] Niggemeyer, 1933, 593, 596.
[13] ibid., 598-9.
[14] Roy, 1925a; Elwin, 1942, Roy's foreword, ix.
[15] 1935, i, 245-62 in Nanjundayya & Iyer, 1928-35.
[16] Hutton, 1933, 411-14; 1961, 255-8.
[17] Hoffmann & Emelen, 1933, viii, 2406-31; Hoffmann, 1915.
[18] Majumdar, 1930; 1961, 345-66; Majumdar & Madan, 1956, 112-26.
[19] Niggemeyer, 1933.
[20] For Schmidt's views I have had to fall back on Bornemann's summary, 1956, 615-40, as Schmidt's larger microfilmed work was not easily accessible.

# IV

## THE MUNDA-SPEAKING TRIBES

IT WAS Max Müller who in 1854 established for the first time
the existence of a Munda family of languages as an independent
group from the Dravidian and gave it the name Munda.[1] Since
then various efforts have been made to connect the Munda languages with others such as the Australian, the Mon-Khmer, the
Maori and the Finno-Ugrian. Although some scholars had earlier
affirmed a relationship between the Mon-Khmer and the Munda
languages, it was W. Schmidt who was primarily responsible for
examining the connexion more elaborately than his predecessors.
According to Schmidt, the Austric family of languages has two
sub-families—the Austronesian (Malayo-Polynesian) and the Austroasiatic. The Austronesian is not represented in India. The
Austroasiatic has two branches—the Mon-Khmer and the Munda.
Of the Austroasiatic languages in India, the Khasi and Synteng
resemble the Mon-Khmer branch very closely.[2]

The principal home of the Munda languages is the Chota
Nagpur plateau and adjoining areas. The most southern Munda-
speaking tribes are the Gadaba and the Savara who have been
identified with the Suari of Pliny and the Sabarae of Ptolemy.[3]
As the Linguistic Survey of India is still incomplete, it is not
known if any other tribes of South India ever spoke a Munda
language. Excluding the Bhil who have sometimes been connected with the Munda-speaking tribes, the most westward
Munda speakers are the Korku in Madhya Pradesh, who are
isolated from the main body of the Munda tribes. It is believed
that the Munda languages probably once occupied the greater
part of Upper India,[4] and that a Mundaization of neighbouring
tribes also took place.[5] The main Munda-speaking tribes are the
Khasi, the Santal, the Munda, the Ho, the Bhumij, the Birhor,
the Korwa, the Kharia, the Asur, the Juang, the Korku, the Kol,
the Gadaba, the Savara and the Bondo.[6]

The Munda problem was next tackled by R. Heine-Geldern.
In a series of articles he attempted to show that the Munda-
speaking tribes were racially and culturally mixed, but that the

predominant type was Mongoloid, that this component was
brought by the neolithic Austroasiatics who came from the east,
that the Austroasiatics were the bearers of the shouldered celt,
and that the Austronesians influenced the Austroasiatics, thus
producing in India the megalithic elements of the eastern variety
and a blend between the two characteristic forms of adzes—the
shouldered adze of the Austroasiatics and the quadrangular adze
of the Austronesians.[7]

The views of W. Schmidt and R. Heine-Geldern have been
called into question by several critics. For instance, W. F. Hevesy
challenged the validity of Schmidt's Munda-Mon-Khmer comparisons, and endeavoured to show that the Munda languages
belonged to the Ugrian subdivision of the Finno-Ugrian branch
of the Uralian stock of languages.[8] On the question of the racial
character of the Munda-speaking tribes, D. N. Majumdar affirmed
that the general physical make-up of the tribes of Chota Nagpur
did not suggest a Mongolian infusion, that it was hard to maintain the ascription of a few stray cases of Mongoloid features
to a general miscegenation, and that the various tribes of India
like the Munda, the Santal, the Juang, the Korwa, the Saora,
the Parja, the Khond, the Chenchu, the Irula, the Paniyan and
others could be affiliated to the same Proto-Australoid racial
stock and might not be independent races or even types.[9] A
more recent attack on the Mon-Khmer-Munda identifications
was that of Gordon T. Bowles. Bowles calls into question
Schmidt's linguistic and racial comparisons, Heine-Geldern's and
Eickstedt's Mongoloid identifications and Hevesy's linguistic
hypothesis and concludes: ' A great deal more comparative work,
not only in language but also in material and social culture as
well as in racial studies, must be undertaken before Pater
Schmidt's or v. Hevesy's or anyone else's pronouncements can
be accepted '.[10] Lastly, A. H. Dani asserts that the archaeological
evidence available in India scarcely justifies the connexion which
Heine-Geldern attempts to establish between certain adze forms
and the Austroasiatics or the megaliths of the eastern type.[11]

In taking note of Hevesy's criticism, Schmidt conceded the
probability that the Finno-Ugrian languages might have exerted
some later influence on the Munda languages;[12] but so far as
Bowles' criticism was concerned, he found no reason to change
his position.[13] Heine-Geldern, too, adheres in the main to his
original standpoint. He says: '. . . even if the Munda languages
should not be basically related to the Mon-Khmer languages,
there can be little doubt that at least some of the eastern Munda
languages have been influenced by the latter. It is precisely in
the region where these eastern Munda languages occur, that

even today relatively strong traces of a Mongoloid racial strain
are to be found. In the first century A.D. the Munda tribes of
Orissa were called Kirata by their Aryan-speaking neighbours,
that is, with the Sanskrit term used to designate the Mongoloid
mountain tribes of the Himalayas, Assam and Further India.
We may infer from this that at that time the Mongoloid element
must have been considerably stronger than today. Again, it is
only in Orissa, Chutya Nagpur, and the northeastern Dekkan,
as far south as the Godavari River and as far west as the region
of Allahabad, that tanged adzes and other neolithic adze types
peculiar to Southwest Asia have been found.' [14]

## The Asur

Among the Munda-speaking tribes, the Birjia Asur have come
to occupy a somewhat unusual position through S. C. Roy's
discovery of a variety of individual totemism among some of
them. The Birjia of the Tumbadag Hill near the Netarhat
Plateau on the borders between the Ranchi and Palamau districts believe that a child receives its totem from the spirit of
some relative or neighbour, dead or living, which casts its
shadow on the child at birth. Thus the child's totem differs
from those of its parents. At the name-giving ceremony the *mati*
or spirit-doctor reveals the name of the relative or neighbour
whose spirit overshadowed the child at the moment of its birth,
and the child thus acquires the name and the totem of the said
relative or neighbour. Roy reports further that the clan totem
is sometimes changed in the third or fourth generation, and
with this change of totem the *mua* or ancestor spirits are also
changed. Consequently the bar to intermarriage within other
branches of the clan is also lifted. In some places the clan totem
was regularly changed in every fourth generation.[15] J. Hoffmann
accepts and seems to confirm Roy's findings on individual totemism among the Asur.[16] But Walter Ruben asserts that in spite
of close questioning he could not establish the existence of such
a phenomenon.[17] Ruben's negative results might have been due
in part to the rapid decay of totemism among the Asur, in part
to the reluctance of the people to talk about their peculiar
customs, and in part to the brevity of his stay among them.[18]

Risley reports the existence of thirteen totemic clans among
the Asur. Of these, ten are animal and three vegetable.[19] Roy
on the other hand mentions thirty-four totems, all of which are
animal. He reports further that totemism is fast decaying among
the Birjia Asur and other tribes in those parts. Nevertheless,
those Birjia groups which still knew their gotras abstained from

beating, domesticating, killing or eating their totems, or those of
their parents, brothers, children or wives. The totem is regarded
as a relation and the Birjia salutes it when he meets it. He weeps
over the carcase of his totem if he should come across it, takes
it up in his hands, buries or cremates it, and then after making
his final obeisance to its spirit goes away. Totem exogamy prevails, but there is no bar to marriage between persons belonging
to two subdivisions of the same gotra. Among the settled Asur,
however, totem exogamy is rapidly breaking down.[20] While Roy
classifies the Asur of Chota Nagpur into three divisions (Thania
or settled, Soeka or nomadic and Birjia, almost a separate tribe),
W. Ruben divides them into four endogamous groups as follows: the Birjia-Asur, the Bir-Asur, the Agaria or Senkha and
the Kodha or Thuppo. The Bir-Asur in Kujam have ten totems,
all of which are animals. They know nothing about the origin
of their totems and no traditions about it exist any more. They
have totem taboos and are stricken with grief when they see the
totem lying wounded or dead in the woods. But they do not
bury it and have no rites connected with it. In one place, Kera-
kair, however, it was related that their grandparents buried the
dead totems, but the parents had ceased from doing so. There
are no house animals as totems, and no monkeys or snakes as
among the Gond.[21] K. K. Leuva mentions three divisions among
the Asur—the Bir, the Birjia and the Agaria. Of the Bir clans
mentioned, eight are named after animals (mostly birds), one
after a tree, and two after rice and salt respectively. The Bir
do not now remember the origin of their totems, but clan
exogamy prevails.[22]

The individual totemism of the Birjia Asur is the only
example of its kind in India. It has been interpreted as follows:
(a) Roy thinks that it appears to be an early form of totemism.[23]
(b) J. Hoffmann offers three explanations, but regards the first
two as improbable:
(i) As the Asur resemble the Munda in race, language and culture, it is possible that the Munda once possessed individual
totemism but lost it in course of time. Since the Asur, however,
were not physically isolated, this explanation is unsatisfactory.
(ii) The Asur might have invented individual totemism in the
course of time; but this is also unlikely in normal times for
theoretical reasons. (iii) Some individuals were cast out of their
groups and so invented individual totemism.[24]
(c) H. Niggemeyer notes that among the Birjia Asur the clan
totems are either sometimes or regularly changed in every fourth
generation, and that this phenomenon is certainly a recent development as against the strict patrilineal totem inheritance among

the other Munda peoples. He therefore suggests that after the principle of inheritance was once violated and the acquisition of the totem became possible, the idea was extended to the individual. Niggemeyer does not regard his solution as a final one.[25]

Both Hoffmann and Niggemeyer, then, incline to the view that the individual totemism of the Birjia Asur is a relatively recent phenomenon. There are, however, some reasons to think that it is the isolated remnant of a proto-totemic mentality, and hence an earlier form of belief and practice than group totemism. The reasons for this view are as follows:

(a) The Birjia Asur are a primitive tribe with a very ancient racial component. Thus, W. Ruben points out that they are the darkest of the four endogamous groups of Asur and that they might have acquired their clan totemism from the Birhor.[26] Later they acquired the language and related customs of their Munda neighbours. They share their iron-working activities with a number of primitive groups. In fact, as Verrier Elwin demonstrates, there is an Agaria belt across the centre of India. The Agaria are racially short, have broad heavy noses, thick lips, coarse features and are very dark in colour. Their totemism and mythology are still strong elements in their socio-religious organization, and were probably highly developed in antiquity. But they tend to adapt themselves to the customs of the tribes in the area in which they are located.[27] Their iron-working activities, now their main occupation, were obviously acquired at a later date than their totemism.

(b) There are in this, as in other tribal areas of India, the scattered and attenuated remnants of beliefs and practices connected with animals and plants which can well be described as proto-totemic. A few instances are here indicated. J. Hoffmann tells us that the belief in the power of certain men to transform themselves into various animals is universal and deep-rooted among the Munda.[28] S. C. Roy, while pointing out that individual totemism does not exist among the Birhor, describes a belief which is somewhat analogous to it. When a Birhor dreams of a bird, beast, worm, reptile or other thing in the night and the following morning receives a visit from some friend or relative, he concludes that the object of his dream must be the *rais* (daemon or genius) of his guest.[29] Further afield, in the northeast, the Lakher believe that every person possesses a tutelary spirit or guardian angel called *zang*. They also have other beliefs and practices of a proto-totemic nature.[30] Again, among the Ho and related tribes there is a belief in *Bonga* which is conceived as an impersonal power. 'It is by virtue of this power', says D. N. Majumdar, 'that the totemic animal, plant or material

object gains its effectiveness and even its religious sanction.'
Bonga thus regulates social conduct and individual behaviour
towards the animal or plant kingdoms.[31] The belief in such a
power is an old and widely spread one and associates itself with
totemism at a very early stage.

(c) The reluctance which the Birjia Asur displayed in talking
about their individual totemism is perhaps also an indication
of its antiquity—the survival of an old belief in an atmosphere
of general adaptation to later customs would acquire an aura
of esotericism. A sense of awe and shame combined would thus
prevent its practitioners from talking about the belief.

(d) The absence of a social value, or for the matter of that
individual value, in the belief is a further pointer to the fact
that it is a chance survival from a remote past. In this case, however, the inadequacy of Roy's report may be at fault.

## The Birhor

In point of cultural height D. N. Majumdar places the Birhor
at the bottom of the scale, the Santal at the top, and the Ho,
the Munda, the Tamaria, the Kharia and the Korwa in that
order in between.[32] Extending the frame of reference, C. Fürer-
Haimendorf makes the following classification of cultural strata:
to the oldest layer belong the Birhor, the Chenchu and the
Malapantaram; next come the Baiga, the Reddi and the Kamar;
and lastly the Gond, the Oraon and the Munda.[33] In 1928 R.
Heine-Geldern suggested that the Birhor could hardly be called
Munda although they speak a Munda language;[34] and more
recently that the archaic type of Birhor totemism had various
points in common with that of certain Australian and Melanesian tribes.[35]

For a detailed account of the Birhor and their totemism, however, we are indebted to S. C. Roy. The Birhor are the rudest
of the jungle tribes of Chota Nagpur. They are divided into
two sections—the Uthli or wanderers and the Jaghi or settlers.
They are dark-skinned, short and broad-nosed. They are in the
main food-gatherers and hunters, and are organized into local
groups or *tandas* and exogamous totemic clans or gotras. In a
list (which is not exhaustive) of thirty-seven clan names collected
by Roy, twelve are those of animals, ten of plants, eight of
other castes, tribes and localities, and the rest are names of
other objects. The Birhor totems are inherited and not acquired.
There is no belief in descent from the totem. All that the few
Birhor legends indicate is that the totem had had some accidental connexion with the birth of the clan ancestor. Neverthe-

less, the Birhor appear to find some resemblance in the temperament or physical appearance of the clan members to that of
their totem. Totem taboos exist, and are sometimes carried to
extremes, as by the men of the Murum clan who cover their
eyes when they chance to come across a murum stag. Eating,
killing or destroying the clan totem is regarded as equivalent
to killing a human member of the clan. It is further believed
that a diminution in the number of the totem animals, plants
or other objects caused by their destruction or killing will
engender a corresponding decrease in the size of the clan. There
are, however, no magical multiplication rites of the type of the
*Intichiuma* among the Australian tribes. Totem inheritance is
patrilineal. Violation of the totem taboo entails payment of a
fine and the provision of a feast to the clan members. An encounter with the totem animal is generally not supposed to affect
the Birhor in any way; nor does he salute the totem when he
meets it. If, however, he should happen to come across the carcase of his totem animal, he must anoint its forehead with oil
or vermilion, although he has not actually to mourn for it or
bury it.

The intimate and vital connexion between the totem and the
clan is evidenced further by another practice—the annual sacrifice to the presiding spirit of the ancestral hill. Every Birhor
clan has a tradition of its ancient settlement having been located
in some hill or other within Chota Nagpur; and once a year
the men of each clan assemble in an open space to offer sacrifices
to the *Ora-bonga* or *Buru-bonga* of the ancestral hill. Members
of other clans do not participate in these sacrifices; and the
oldest member present of the clan officiates as sacrificer. A mystic
diagram with four compartments is drawn on the ground with
rice flour and in one of these compartments the sacrificer sits
down with his face turned in the direction of the ancestral hill.
In another compartment of the diagram the emblem of his totem
(a flower, a bit of horn or skin, a twig or a wing) is placed. The
emblem is regarded as representing the clan as a whole. If it
is a part of a bird or beast, it is obtained by members of other
clans to whom it is not taboo. The Birhor look upon the spirits
of their ancestral hills with great dread and as far as possible
avoid going to the hill or jungle presumed to be their homes.
A few of the clans claim that the situation of their traditional
homes has endowed them with magical powers. So, for instance,
the Here Hembrom and the Khudi Hembrom clans are said to
have power over the weather; and tigers, it is said, serve the
Kawan clan on certain occasions as friends and servants. Respect
for the totem has not developed into worship of the totem

animal or plant. The totem is not so much a god as a fellow clansman.

Roy offers two explanations of the origin and significance of Birhor totemism:

(*a*) In its origin the totem might have been the guardian spirit of the ancestor of the clan acquired by him perhaps in a vision. The evidence which seems to favour this view is as follows: (i) The importance which the Birhor attaches to his clan spirit or hill god which is regarded somewhat in the light of the guardian spirit of the clan. (ii) The prominent place given to the emblem of the clan totem which each ' family ' carefully treasures in its spirit-box and carries about with it in its wanderings. (iii) The Birhor spirit-doctor sometimes acquires his individual guardian spirit in a dream or vision. (iv) The rais or daemon of a guest may appear to the host in a dream as an animal or other object. But Roy believes that the facts that the guardian spirit of the Birhor spirit-doctor is always personal and never takes the form of an animal and that a very insignificant number of the Birhor population are known to acquire tutelary or guardian spirits in a dream or vision militates against the above hypothesis. (*b*) Roy therefore supposes that Birhor totemism results from a belief in a totemic principle, mystic force or mana, which is immanent in the clan, the hill or jungle and the totem species. The totem emblem placed reverently in a mystic diagram at the annual sacrifices might symbolize this totemic principle. The Birhor of course do not formulate their ideas in this fashion; but Roy believes that this interpretation is in consonance with the power-cult which appears to be of the essence of the Birhor religion.

Between the tribe and the clan the Birhor have no other intermediate dual or phratry system. Tribal sentiment is not strong. Totemism, exogamy and patriliny are the three main factors of Birhor kinship organization.[36]

Niggemeyer's unwillingness to date the totemic cult of the Birhor in the absence of parallel practices among the surrounding tribes [37] is based on an excessive dependence on the older culture-historical viewpoint. He ignores the possibility of using internal evidence, and this evidence seems to point to the great antiquity of the cult. In the cult the totem emblem is the symbol of the clan, and is therefore expressive of the intimate identification between the clan and the totem. This clan-and-totem identification is the central element of totemism at one of its peak points; for in this case the clan becomes the object of complementarity and dependence to its members and the totem is the symbol of this fact or relationship. Furthermore, the cult suggests a former localization of the clans. Therefore the spirits of the hills where the clans were formerly localized could be interpreted as a projection of the social power inherent in clan solidarity. If one adds to this the fact that the Birhor are basically hunters and food-gatherers, the view that their totemic cult is very old would seem to be justified. This implies that their present language and some other cultural elements were borrowed from their Munda-speaking neighbours in a relatively recent period of time. Could it be that the Birhor belong to the tribal group in India in whose ranks group totemism perhaps first emerged in the distant past, and then spread to adjoining tribes? If certain features of their totemism bear some resemblance to those of Australian totemism, other proofs are lacking to justify maintaining a direct connexion at the level of clan totemism.

## The Ho

The Ho are concentrated in the Singhbhum district, an important part of the lower plateau of Chota Nagpur. They are closely related to the Munda tribe and speak Mundari.[38] Like most other Munda-speaking tribes they are mainly cultivators and trace descent in the male line.

Dalton mentions eighteen Ho *kilis* or clans, but adds that the list is not exhaustive and that with one exception there are no names of animals among the Ho clans.[39] Risley lists forty-six septs or clans and says that their number is very numerous, that many appear to be totemic, and that six of the names are also shared by the Santal.[40] Chatterjee & Das, referring to the Ho of Seraikella, give sixty-five kilis and also state that the list is not exhaustive. They found that the meanings of most kili names were unknown to the tribals, but that the meanings of the sub-kili names had been better preserved. Hence they conclude that ' the Ho sub-kilis have preserved a greater amount of totemic character than the kilis '. They noticed further that the names of some of the Ho kilis are the same as those of neighbouring tribes such as the Santal, the Munda, the Birhor, and the Bhumija.[41] D. N. Majumdar, who devoted two monographs to the Ho (1937, 1950), says that Ho society is divided into a large number of kilis, many of which derive their names from some animal, plant or material object. A few of the names like *Kudedah* (the juice of the blackberry) appear to be partial totems. From an analysis of their totemic myths, Majumdar concludes that the totemic beliefs of the Ho can be traced to a recognition of assistance received at times of dire necessity from

the totemic animal or plant in the distant past. He points out
that 'the totemic object is still regarded as guardian angel of
the clan'. Totem descent, and with it veneration of the totem,
might have been added later when the Ho and other tribes
changed over from a hunting to a cultivating economy. But at
present there is no trace of any such veneration or belief in
descent from these animals or plants among the Ho. 'These
sept names are nothing to them beyond names designating a
consanguineous group of persons, and the only taboo that is
obeyed by the Hos is that members belonging to the same sept
do not marry among themselves.'[42]

## The Munda

The Tribal Map of India (Department of Anthropology, Government of India) differentiates between Mundari and Munda, and
locates the former in Orissa and the latter in Bihar, West Bengal,
Orissa and Madhya Pradesh. The term Munda is of Sanskrit
origin and means the headman of the village.[43] The Tamaria,
who are sometimes listed separately, are a section of the Munda
and have separated from the main body a few generations ago.[44]

Dalton, who has generally not much to report about totemism,
satisfies himself with the remark that the Mundari like the Oraon
have names of animals for their kilis and that the flesh of these
animals is tabooed.[45] Risley says that their kilis are very numerous, that many are totemic, and that totem taboos exist. In an
appendix he enumerates 339 sept names of which 142 are those
of birds and beasts, 83 those of trees, fruits and flowers, the
meanings of 42 are unknown, and the rest are the names of
various objects.[46] Roy reports that they have a large number
of exogamous kilis which are patrilineal and totemic, that when
they entered Chota Nagpur the number of their kilis was very
small, and that their respect for their totem is very great. The
totemic myths which Roy records trace the origin of the totems
in the main to incidents in which the ancestors of the clans
were assisted in one way or another by the animal, plant or
other object which they then adopted as their totem. The myth
relating how the subdivisions of the Soe kili acquired their names
is interesting as there are parallels of a basically similar nature
among various other tribes in India. The myth runs as follows:
A Munda once grew cotton near a river, which was damaged
every night by a Soe or Soel fish. One night he kept watch and
when the fish approached, killed it with an arrow. The fish was
then chopped and distributed. The man who killed the fish
came to be called Tuing-Soe, and his descendants formed the

Tuing-Soe kili. The man who chopped the bones was founder of the Jang-Soe kili; the man who divided the flesh was founder of the Til-Soe kili; the man who distributed the shares was founder of the Or-Soe kili; the man who brought leaves on which the meat was placed was founder of the Patra-Soe kili; and so on with all the other subdivisions. It is instructive to note that Hoffmann relates a slightly different version of this Munda myth in his account of Munda totemism. From Roy's evidence it is clear that totem taboos exist, but no myths of descent.[47]

J. Hoffmann reports the existence of 106 clans. The names of 60 have a known meaning and of 13 a doubtful meaning. The meanings of 33 are unknown. Of the names with known meanings, 11 are those of quadrupeds, 11 of birds, 3 of fishes, 2 of reptiles, 2 of insects, 4 of trees of which nothing is eaten, 4 of trees of which the fruit is eaten, 3 of food grains and one of a pulse, 2 of pot-herbs, 2 of edible tubers, one of a plant with edible oil, one of a condiment, one of a drink, 4 of inanimate objects and 2 are adjectives. Hoffmann adds that exogamy is the essential feature of their clans (as the Munda themselves affirm), and that there is no sufficient reason to call the Munda clans totemic as Roy does. Hoffmann adduces the following facts in justification of his view: (a) Half the number of the clans have names which do not appear to have a totemic significance. (b) The majority of the clans have no myths of origin, and the existing myths trace the origin of the names to various encounters rather than to descent from the animal, plant or other object. (c) No Munda believes that he is descended from the so-called totem or that he has any kind of kinship with it. There is no feeling of any kind whatsoever with the said animal, plant or object. The Hunipurti clan (*purti*, rat) regard rats as their brothers, but this is understood by all Munda in a metaphorical sense. (d) There are no sacrifices or ceremonies connected with the animals, plants and other objects, and no marks of respect or reverence such as saluting the totem when it is encountered, or burying its carcase when one is discovered. Nor does the folklore indicate such respect. On the contrary members of the Tuti clan uproot the plant or pluck out some of its leaves and throw them away when they happen to see some of these plants. (e) The ease with which Munda who form new clans (a frequent occurrence) abandon their old totems and taboos is not compatible with a deep-rooted respect towards the totem. (f) There is a good deal of evidence (Hoffmann goes into particulars, pp. 2418-30) to show that the taboos are not as strong or widespread as to indicate great respect for the totem. Hoffmann therefore concludes that it cannot be proved that the Munda clans were ever totemic or that they never were. He inclines however to the view that their totemic elements might have been borrowed from some of their neighbours, or that as the clans sprang up into existence naturally in the past, names were adopted for them from animals, plants and other objects as a result of some circumstance, however trivial, connected with some or several members of the families concerned.[48]

Hoffmann's view that it is not possible to prove or disprove the existence of totemism among the Munda is based on a much too narrow conception of that term. The evidence which he marshalls may be interpreted to indicate a much more considerable decline of totemism among the Munda than Roy was inclined to believe.

## The Kharia

In his alphabetical list of the totemic tribes and castes of India Niggemeyer, basing himself on Risley and Russell, summarizes their information on the Kharia as follows: In Chota Nagpur there are four endogamous sub-tribes divided into totemic clans, but totemic clan exogamy is no longer strictly observed. In the Central Provinces there are exogamous totemic clans. While the rule of avoidance is strictly observed in the Central Provinces, in Chota Nagpur it has considerably weakened.[49] In 1937, however, Sarat Chandra Roy and Ramesh Chandra Roy published a two-volumed monograph on the Kharia which, based on more extensive and intensive field-work, serves as an adequate test of earlier sources of information. The Roys, for instance, make specific reference to the inaccuracies and inadequacies of two earlier sources—Risley and T. C. Das. According to the Roys the relevant facts concerning the Kharia are as follows: they are divided into three groups or sub-tribes: the Erenga or Hill Kharia in the Mayurbhanj State of Orissa, the Dudh Kharia in the Ranchi district of Chota Nagpur, and the Delki Kharia in the Jashpur State of the Central Provinces. They are also found in adjoining areas. The Hill or Wild Kharia are hunters and food-gatherers with occasional shifting cultivation; the Delki Kharia practise plough cultivation and have a more advanced socio-economic system than the Hill Kharia; and the Dudh Kharia are the most advanced of all, ranking in this respect with the Munda, the Ho and the Santal. Physically also the Delki Kharia stand midway between the other two sub-tribes. The Hill Kharia of Mayurbhanj have practically no clan organization or totemism; the Hill Kharia of Manbhum and Singh-

bhum show some evidence of both; and among the Delki and
Dudh Kharia they are in full vigour. Those sections of the Hill
Kharia of Mayurbhanj who have totemic clan names also have
totem taboos, but generally no clan exogamy. The Roys, therefore, surmise that they might have had no clan system when
they separated from the main body of the tribe, or, what is
more probable, might have lost their original totemic organization and later acquired certain totemic names anew from their
neighbours, the Munda, the Ho and the Santal. Unlike the Hill
Kharia of Mayurbhanj, the Hill Kharia of Manbhum and Singhbhum recognize and practise clan exogamy; but their clan names
are different from those of the Delki and Dudh Kharia. Among
the Delki and Dudh Kharia there is a strong sense of social
solidarity and clan exogamy. The sense of clan solidarity is
strengthened by the possession of a common totem. The Delki
Kharia name eight totemic clans as their original ones, and
these have further subdivisions. The Dudh Kharia recognize nine
clans as their original ones, the others being considered as offshoots. The Roys mention nine totem clans for the Hill Kharia,
twenty-four clan names for the Delki Kharia, most of which
seem to have a totemic character and some of which are dupli-
cates, and thirty-one clan names for the Dudh Kharia, most of
which again have a totemic character. Animal totems exceed the
other kinds in all groups. The eight original clans of the Delki
Kharia are also found among the Dudh Kharia who regard two
of them as not being original and add three others. The Hill
Kharia do not have any of these eleven original clan names.

The Kharia have very few traditions about the origin of their
totems. Both Delki and Dudh Kharia have a vague idea of a
sympathetic relation between themselves and their totems, but
they do not claim any of the qualities of their totems for themselves, or claim to exercise any influence upon the totem species.
Nor do they trace descent from the totems, but ascribe their
acquisition, as a legend of their original clan has it, to accidental
encounters or other similar circumstances. Beyond their totem
taboos the Kharia do not appear to maintain a religious or
quasi-religious attitude towards the totem species. Some clans,
it is said, venerated their totems in the past by making an
obeisance when they came across them. But today this practice
has gone out of fashion. The infringement of their totem taboos
is believed to bring misfortune, but does not render the offender
liable to any social penalty.

Referring to the two major motives of a Kharia's life, the Roys
say: 'These are, first, his hankering for *social solidarity* and
union among his own tribe, clan and community as a bulwark

against the manifold risks and dangers of individual and tribal
life, particularly against the hostile influences or activities of
alien communities and the anti-social activities of individuals
of his own or some other community, and, secondly, the equally
supreme need and yearning for security and protection against
the incalculable and invisible hostile forces of Nature and of
the spirit-world.' [50]

Russell describes the Kharia as the most backward of the
Kolarian tribes and relates them to the Munda and the Savara.[51]
Dalton connects them linguistically with the Juang but reports
no totemism.[52] Risley points out that all the septs of the Kharia
of Chota Nagpur are totemic, but that the totem taboos are not
generally observed.[53] Frazer, on the other hand, believes that
the totem taboos must have been at one time in force;[54] and
Russell reports that among the Kharia of the Central Provinces
totem taboos prevail, that when abstention from eating the totem
is not wholly possible as in the case of the Baa or Rice clan,
they make a compromise, that veneration of the totem also
consists in folding the hands in obeisance when the totem is
met, and in taking some dust from the animal's track and placing
it on one's head, and that the tribe do not think these days
that they are descended from their totems, but tell stories
accounting for the connexion.[55] The Roys, however, show that
totem taboos exist among both groups of Kharia, the Delki and
the Dudh. They point out that physically the Hill Kharia are
the coarsest in features, that in general a slight tendency towards
the epicanthic fold exists, but that the nasal root is depressed
and the lips thick.[56] T. C. Das affirms that the Wild Kharia
possess all the characteristic features of typical Pre-Dravidians;[57]
and J. Hoffmann asserts: ' It takes an eye trained by years of
observation to distinguish at sight a Kharia from an Oraon or a
Munda; for there is little in their build, features, complexion
and dress, to single them out from their aboriginal neighbours '.[58]

## The Korwa

The Korwa are mainly found in Sarguja, Jashpur and Palamau,
and claim to be the original inhabitants of the country they
occupy. The fact that the priests who propitiate the local spirits
are chosen from among them seems to bear out their claims.[59]
Dalton says that they have mixed with the Asura and are not
greatly different from them except that they are more cultivators
than smelters. He does not report the existence of totemic clans
among them.[60] Risley states that the Korwa are divided into
four sub-tribes, and, quoting W. H. P. Driver, gives a list of

twenty clans, fifteen of which have 'totemic' names. He adds
further that there is no certain information on totem taboos,
that the taboos are falling into disuse, leaving behind only
exogamy, which exemplifies a general trend.[61] W. Crooke connects them with the Kol and states that there are no exogamous
divisions among the Mirzapur Korwa.[62] D. N. Majumdar describes them as the most primitive element in the United Provinces, a declining people with a disintegrating culture. Physically they are very dark, have no Mongoloid fold or obliquity
of the eyes, have heavy flat noses depressed at the roots, thick
lips, heavy jaws and some measure of prognathism. Majumdar
also reports the existence of five exogamous clans, but qualifies
his finding with the remark that the Korwa are an inbred
group and so traditional rules of marriage are not observed.[63]

## The Santal

The Santal are found in Bihar, Bengal, Orissa and Uttar Pradesh, and are among the most easternly of the compact mass of
Munda-speaking tribes. L. O. Skrefsrud maintained that they
entered India from the northwest; but P. O. Bodding on the contrary believes that they came from the northeast.[64] Racially, however, they possess very primitive components. Thus Frazer points
out that the proportions of the nose approach those of the
Negro, and the lips are thick and protruding.[65] Culshaw says
that they have short, broad flat noses sunken at the ridges;[66]
and Bodding states: 'The theory of Mongolian descent is not
tenable, but there cannot be any doubt that Mongoloid blood
has been introduced, either by the Santal taking Mongolian
wives, or the Santal women having illegitimate children by
Mongolian men.' [67] Culshaw relates the Santal racially, culturally
and linguistically to the Munda, the Ho, the Korku, the Savara
and the Gadaba;[68] and Russell points out identities in some
clan names between the Santal on the one hand and the Munda
and the Ho on the other.[69] Some writers speak of them as being
originally hunters and dwellers in the jungles;[70] and others point
out that they still take an absorbing interest in hunting, even
having annual hunts and a special functionary for the purpose.[71]

With a population of 2,732,266 in 1941, the Santal are the
second largest tribal community in India. The Gond (3,264,322)
exceed them in population strength, and the Bhil (2,346,570)
and the Oraon (1,122,926) come immediately after them.[72] It is
therefore not surprising that the authorities on Santal ethnography and ethnology should differ in some measure from one
another in their statements on the number of Santal clans (*paris*)

and sub-clans (*khunts, khuts*), and the extent of their totemic character.

Dalton speaks of twelve 'tribes' but lists only eleven: Murmu, Marli, Kisku, Besera, Hansda, Tudi, Baski, Hemrow, Karwar, Chorai and Saran. He says nothing, as is usual with him, about totemism; but states that they adore the tiger and that their most solemn oath is swearing on the skin of a tiger.[73] Risley mentions twelve exogamous septs as follows: Hasdak, Murmu, Kisku, Hembrom, Marndi, Saren, Tudu, Baske, Besra, Pauria, Chore and Bedea. The first seven in this list are the original clans, and the other five were added later. The Baske clan belonged at first to the original seven but its ancestors offered breakfast (*baske*) to the gods while the Santal were still in Champa, an unidentified tract or country; hence they had to form a separate sept. The immoral behaviour of their ancestor, Besra, the licentious one, caused the separation of the Besras. The Paurias (Pigeon) and Chores (Lizard) failed to kill anything but pigeons and lizards during the tribal hunt, and hence formed new septs. The Bedea were left behind and lost. Risley also draws attention to the Santal tradition which traces the origin of the tribe to a wild goose (*hasdak*) that laid two eggs from which the first parents of the tribe sprang. Each sept has passwords for purposes of recognition. These passwords are supposed to be the names of their original homes. They preserve and strengthen the memory of the blood-tie which connects the members of the septs, and suggest that the septs were in their earliest form groups of a purely local character.[74] Frazer points out that the Santal have twelve septs and seventy-six sub-septs; both are exogamous and appear to be totemic. The twelve septs are Hasdak (Wild Goose), Murmu (Nilgai, a species of antelope), Kisku, Hembrom (Betel Palm), Marndi (Grass), Saren (constellation Pleiades), Tudu, Baske (Hawk), Pauria (Pigeon), Chore (Lizard), and Bedea (Sheep). There are traces of totem taboos as, for instance, in the Murmu clan and the Jihu sub-clan. The latter may not kill or eat the babbler bird after which it is named because a babbler is said to have guided their ancestor to water when he was dying of thirst. The other sub-clans observe certain peculiar traditional usages the significance of which is not clear.[75] From P. C. Biswas's findings it would appear that of 115 sub-clans 18 are totemic. Although there is some evidence that totem taboos exist and that there is a feeling of kinship towards the totem, Biswas believes that totemism in its 'truest form' is not present among the Santal. This is so because there is no belief in descent from the totems, and the legends merely indicate an accidental connexion of the totems with the birth of the ancestor.

Biswas further believes that the sub-clans are not exogamous units, but mark family distinctions and traditions, and that they are not so much a vital part of the Santal social organization.[76] W. J. Culshaw has no doubts that the tribal organization of the Santal is totemic. He relates the following creation myth: Thakur made two birds out of siroin grass seeds. The two birds laid two eggs from which two human beings, Pilcu Haram and Pilcu Budhi, were born. They had twelve sons. During a food shortage they planted millet in the forest clearings. A female murum (deer) came to eat the millet and was killed with bows and arrows by the brothers who divided its flesh among themselves. At that time, while they were on their way home, Pilcu Haram and Pilcu Budhi divided them into clans as follows: (1) the original Hasdak or Nij Hasdak, (2) the one who ground down the horn: Marndi, (3) the one who killed a sunbird: Soren Sipahi, (4) the one who carried a deer: Hembrom, (5) the one who killed an owl: Tudu, (6) the one who killed a kingfisher: Kisku, (7) the one who made a bundle of stale rice: Baske, (8) the one who carried an umbrella over his head: Besra, (9) the one who killed a rough-necked iguana: Core, (10) the one who killed a dove: Pauriya, (11) the one who killed a bushy-haired monkey: Donka or Bhaduli, (12) the one who restores us to tribal status: Murmu. While there is little agreement about the names of the clans, Santal tradition is unanimous in talking of twelve clans. ' The totemistic basis ', says Culshaw, ' is very clearly marked, and in certain directions it still exercises a powerful influence on the habits of the Santals.' Thus, the Hasdak, who are always named first, are called after the goose of the creation myth, and do not eat geese or ducks because they are their brothers. In their case it is clear that descent from the totem is envisaged. The other Santal, however, although likewise supposedly descended from the same pair, are not prohibited from eating goose or duck flesh. Some of the other clan names are either the same as the totem, or are very closely related to it: Marndi (name of a weed common in the rice-fields), Soren (constellation Pleiades), Tudu (suggests the sound made by drums), Hembrom (suggests *hotrin* for deer), Kisku (like *kikir*, a generic name for kingfishers), Baske (stale rice), Murum (the buck of the traditions whose flesh the Murmi do not eat). The clan system of the Santal regulates their behaviour within the tribe and their dealings with the spirits. They accept its rule without question; and both it and the myths which form its background are a key to the understanding of nearly everything that is distinctive in their way of life.[77]

Statements on the number of sub-clans do not agree with one

another. Frazer puts them down at 76; Biswas at approximately
115; and Datta-Majumdar at from 13 to 28 for every *paris*.[78]
W. J. Culshaw says that tradition allots 12 sub-clans or *khuts*
to each of the 12 clans or paris, but in the Santal Parganas there
are 277 different sub-clans among the eleven known clans, and
many are found under more than one clan. Each sub-clan owns
a distinctive myth and customs that differentiate it from the
others. The customs or taboos determine the kind of ornaments
which may be worn, the type of houses that may be built and
the kinds of food which must be eaten. They are also linked
with marriages and the worship of the spirits. In each clan
there is one sub-clan which is taken to have been the original
one; it has the word *nij* prefixed to its name. A number of sub-
clans are known as *sada* or white, and may represent the reform-
ing element as they go against the use of vermilion.[79] Johannes
Gausdal, basing himself on Campbell, Skrefsrud, Bodding and
Culshaw and on his own researches, lists 405 sub-clans distributed as follows among the clans: Hasdak 41, Murmu 65, Kisku
32, Hembrom 32, Marndi 49, Soren 46, Tudu 48, Baske 31,
Besra 27, Core 18, Pauria 16, Bedea nil. Judging from the nature
of the names and statements on the existence of totem taboos,
very few of the sub-clans in Gausdal's lists seem to be totemic.[80]

About the totemism of the Santal, Ghurye, evaluating the pro-
ferred evidence, concludes that their septs or clans were totemic
in origin.[81] But this does not seem to be the case with a fairly
large number of their sub-clans. Majumdar's assertion that they
have more than a hundred clans named after animals, plants
and material objects indicates that he regards sub-clans as clans.[82]
But many of the sub-clans are probably of a comparatively recent
origin, emerging perhaps at a time when the totemic ethos had
already begun to pale under external influences. All things considered, however, there is no denying that the Santal are totemic,
and were very likely much more so in the more distant past.
Totem descent except for one instance is absent among the
Santal, but is not very frequent in India as a whole.

## The Bhumij

Located in Bihar, Orissa and Bengal, the Bhumij are a considerably Hinduized tribe who, however, still retain a totemic organization with totem taboos and occasional instances of a greater
degree of identification with their totems. They are closely related
to the Munda, the Santal and allied tribes. Risley says that
they have six sub-tribes, and enumerates 20 clans of which 15
seem to be totemic (11 animal names, 4 trees or vegetable ones).

According to him, they have begun to forget the totems which the names of their subdivisions denote, and have commenced to change from a tribe to a caste.[83] T. C. Ray Chowdhury states that the Bhumij of Mayurbhanj (Orissa) have four endogamous groups, each with exogamous clans. He lists 15 clans, of which 10 have evidently totemic names (5 animal names, 3 vegetable and 2 of inanimate objects). There are totem taboos, but no elaborate ritual in honour of the totem. They have also local groups called *thaka* named after villages.[84] T. C. Das mentions three main tribal divisions and 16 exogamous *gotras*. The word *gotra* has begun to replace the word *kili*, thus supplying a further instance of Hindu influence. The 16 gotras are totemic in nature (6 have animal names, one that of a flower, and one that of an inanimate object). There are totem taboos, but no worship of the totem or obeisance to it. However, the totem is considered a *bhayad* or agnate and is treated as such. Members of the Nag gotra believe that cobras will not harm them; and members of the Rui gotra bury their dead in the sand of the river so that they may join their bhayads, the rohit fish, under the water. Many of the Bhumij gotra names are also found among the other surrounding Munda-speaking tribes and also among some Hindu castes like the Mahli, the Kurmi, the Lohar, the Pan and the Pator, which have probably been recruited from these tribes. Each gotra has a traditional or ancestral village, the name of which it bears along with the name of the gotra. Marriage is prohibited among persons of the same gotra and also of the same ancestral village. Informants affirm that the ancestral villages were the original homes of the gotras.[85]

## The Kol

Another term for the Munda-speaking tribes which was once in greater use was Kolarian. Thus Russell speaks of the Kol as a great tribe of Chota Nagpur and includes under that head the Ho and the Munda.[86] There are tribes or sections of a tribe in Madhya Pradesh called Kol; and further westward in various parts of what was the old Bombay Presidency dwell groups called Koli, which have been linked by various writers (Ibbetson, Cunningham, Grierson, Baines and Russell) with the Kolarian or Munda-speaking tribes. Referring to the Koli of Bombay, Ghurye prefers to consider them by themselves as the history of their wanderings is unknown;[87] but Koppers is of the opinion that the Koli were originally an independent people racially not very far removed from the Bhil.[88] There is no clear evidence of a linguistic and cultural connexion between the Koli of the

West Coast and the Munda-speaking tribes. On the other hand, the Kol of Madhya Pradesh and Uttar Pradesh belong clearly to the Munda-speaking block, as both Russell [89] and Griffiths [90] bear witness.

Of the Kol of the Northwestern Provinces (Uttar Pradesh), W. Crooke says that they have shed the elaborate totem system of the Munda.[91] Of the Mandla Kol of the Central Provinces (Madhya Pradesh), however, Russell says that they have a number of exogamous, totemic septs: (i) The Bargaiyan sept is called after the village Bargaon, but the members of the sept connect their name with the *bar* or banyan tree and revere it. A branch of the tree is placed on the roof of the marriage-shed at weddings, and the wedding-cakes are cooked in a fire made from the wood of the same tree, and served to all the relations of the sept on its leaves. At other times they do not pluck a leaf or cut a branch from the banyan tree, nor even go beneath its shade. (ii) The Kathotia sept is named after *kathotia*, a bowl, but the members of this sept revere the tiger. The tiger god lives on a platform on their verandas. They may not join in a tiger-beat, and if a tiger is killed within the limits of his village, a Kathotia Kol will throw away his earthen pots, shave his head and feed a few men of his sept, as if in mourning for a relative. (iii) The Katharia sept is called after a *kathri* or mattress. Members of the sept are forbidden to keep a mattress in the house and to wear clothes sewn in cross pieces as are mattresses. They believe that if the word *kathri* is mentioned in their presence, a great misfortune will befall their families. (iv) The Mudia or Mudrundia sept (Shaven Head) revere the white *kumhra* or gourd. (v) The Kumraya sept revere the brown kumhra or gourd. (vi) The Bhuwar sept are named after *bhu* or *bhumi*, the earth, and must always sleep on the earth and not on cots. (vii) Other septs: Nathunia or Nosering; Karpatia, a kind of grass; and Binjhwar from the tribe of that name. In Raigarh the Kol have another group of septs, indicating that they are a mixed group. Violations of sept exogamy occur frequently.[92] W. G. Griffiths, however, studying the Kol tribe anew and reviewing the evidence supplied by Russell & Hiralal, comes to the conclusion that ' totemism as such is apparently a negligible factor in the lives of the Kols of Central India. There are, it may be, certain traces of it kept by tradition, but its real significance has been lost. The unit of social organization turns out to be the family within the endogamous kurhi '. Griffiths could find no traces of several beliefs and practices reported by Russell & Hiralal, no totemic rites

or taboos, and regards the veneration of the tiger as protective
rather than totemic. Likewise, he points out, there are no traces
of exogamous clans, and marriages are regulated on the basis
of genealogical relationships. The Kol, however, believe that
trees (including the banyan and the neem) and animals can be
the habitations of spirits, and therefore respect many trees and
animals.[93]

## The Korku

The Korku are the most western of the Munda-speaking tribes,
live in middle Madhya Pradesh, and are widely separated from
the main block of linguistically related tribes. W. H. P. Driver
lists thirteen gots or septs, of which six have names of plants or
trees, and the others of inanimate objects and distinctly non-
totemic designations.[94] Russell & Hiralal state that each of their
subcastes has traditionally 36 exogamous septs, but that the number has increased. The names of the septs are generally taken
from those of plants and animals, were no doubt originally
totemic, but are now explained by the Korku as having arisen
through their ancestors taking refuge behind trees and other
objects after a great battle in which they were defeated. There
are no totemic usages.[95] S. Fuchs, who visited the Korku in the
Melghat and the Nimar districts in 1939 and thereafter, but
has not yet published the results of his field investigations, has
kindly supplied the following information. In the villages around
Chikalda (Melghat district) thirteen clan names were located
and identified. Of these thirteen, seven referred to bushes,
trees or their products, four to inanimate objects, one meant
a pass between two hills, and the meaning of one was not
known. In the Kalibhit tract (Nimar district) also the Korku
have thirteen clan names, of which eight refer to plants, trees
or their products, two to animals, two to inanimate objects and
the meaning of one is not known. In the two districts about
eight names resemble one another, but the meanings applied
to them often do not coincide. Three names have been traced
to the Marathi language. In the Melghat district two clans have
two sub-clans each. The sub-clans have names which refer to
shrubs or trees. In the Nimar district there is in addition another
clan also with two sub-clans bearing names referring to two
different types of grain. No totem taboos or distinctly totemic
usages other than these clan names and clan exogamy were
found. The clans are dispersed and not localized. The myth of
clan origins narrated to Fuchs bears close resemblance to the
version related by Russell & Hiralal. Both Driver and Russell

point out that the Korku are closely related to the Korwa.
Although many of their beliefs and practices are evidently of a
different origin, they regard themselves as Hindus.

## The Juang

Located in Orissa, the Juang still retain an exceedingly primitive
cultural substratum as witnessed by their strong addiction to
hunting and food-gathering. They have a number of exogamous,
totemic clans (*ba, bak, bok*). Risley lists 24, of which 12 are
named after animals and 10 after plants. One is named after
hailstones, and the meaning of the other is not stated.[96] N. K.
Bose mentions two subdivisions of the tribe, and adds that they
have a number of patrilineal, exogamous 'sibs'. He was able to
trace the meanings of only three of the sept or clan names. Two
of them were those of trees which were tabooed and regarded
as kinsmen by the respective clan members. The third was named
after the bear. Its members were supposed to be very hairy;
and bears, it was said, did no harm to them, they in turn avoiding doing harm to bears.[97] A more detailed account of the Juang
than those of Risley and Bose is Elwin's monograph published
in 1948 in *Man in India*. Elwin states that the Juang have 'the
usual bewildering variety of septs', and that every village has a
somewhat different list. He thinks that the cause of this confusing variety lies in the fact that the Juang were once divided on
the basis of village, rather than sept exogamy, and that they
acquired their septs partly through imitation and partly through
actual historical happenings. Thus, a man kills a pigeon and
shortly afterwards goes blind. The medicine-man connects the
blindness with the pigeon. The sufferer decides that the pigeon
must be worshipped and protected, and so in course of time a
Pigeon clan arises.[98] In villages in which there are more than
one clan, it is not considered proper for marriages to take place
between them. Nevertheless, a certain percentage of marriages
do take place between members of the same village. The belief
that each clan had its own village or *mati* exists, but in actuality
today the practices connected with the belief have all but died
away. 'The septs', says Elwin, 'are patrilineal, strongly totemistic, and are governed by the usual rules.' Some septs are linked together as *bhai*-septs and marriages between them are not permitted. The Juang explain their emergence by saying that
quarrels took place among those clans and they thus refused to
give their daughters in marriage to one another. Elwin is inclined
to accept this explanation. The origin of the septs is traced to
various causes. At one place, Bali, a myth somewhat similar to

the story related by the Gond and other tribes narrates how
the twelve sons of their deified tribal ancestors, Rusi and Rusain,
acquired their sept names in an effort to save themselves in a
flood. The totems consist of eight plants or trees, two animals
and two inanimate objects. At another place, Jamara, there was
a different list and a different story. Of the 12 septs, 7 or 8
appear to have a totemic significance. At Kariapani and Dhenkanal the septs are assigned a geographical basis. Another and
almost entirely different list from Dhenkanal attributes the origin
of most of the clans to incidents of the nature of 'parallel
relationship'. The totems are the fig tree, the squirrel, the satin-
wood tree, the wood-pigeon, the semur tree and the toddy palm.
On the borders of Pal Lahara and Keonjhar Elwin uncovered
20 septs, with 11 tree totems, 5 animal totems, two types of
grain, the sand of a river, and the leaves of a certain tree. The
clans with tree totems in this list are said to go back to the time
when the first brothers divided the forest clearings. The trees are
tabooed. The clans fall into four *kutumb* or agnatic groups within which marriage is not allowed. There is some evidence of
totem descent. At Dhenkanal it is related of the Dumariya clan
that their ancestor was born from one of the figs after a man
had had sexual union with the fig tree; and the Toddy Palm
clan traces its origin to a woman who became pregnant when
her husband forced her to eat the fruit of the tree. In the list
from the borders of Pal Lahara and Keonjhar the following
explanations are given of some of the clans:

| | |
|---|---|
| Babijaribok.................... | Born from a bhilwan tree. |
| Barunbok...................... | Born from the sand of the Baiturni river. |
| Bhuitturiyabok................ | Born of a she-buffalo. |
| Kumakulibok.................. | Born of flying ants. |
| Nachingbok or Kariyabok | Born from a human father out of the belly of a hare. |
| Parsabok........................ | Born of a parsa tree. |
| Sarlabasuriyabok............. | Born from the bamboo. |

Of the Bhuitinar sept it is further related that its first member was born as a result of sexual union between a human
father (or Bhagwan himself) and a she-buffalo. The child was
Bas Deota, the bamboo god, from whom the Bhuitinar or Bhui-
turiya clan claims to be descended. The sept is associated with
a cult of the bamboo god.[99]

## The Savara (Saora)

The Savara live in Orissa, Madhya Pradesh, Madras and Bihar. Linguistically and culturally they are allied to the Munda-speaking tribes with whom they share many elements in common. Some writers believe that the Savara were formerly the dominant branch of the great Kolarian family pushed aside by other Kolarian tribes in the north and the east and by the Gond in the south, and that at one time they stretched right across middle and eastern India.[1]

The Savara described by Risley and Russell have exogamous clans or *bargas*, the names of which are 'usually totemistic'. Thus Frazer (using Risley as his source) mentions 8 clans with animal totems and related taboos; but Russell & Hiralal say that the north Savara have 52 or more bargas and the Uriya Savara 80, which are generally totemic. Risley adds that some of their exogamous septs are shared by the Bagdi and other tribes of West Bengal, that one or two names are taken from the Brahminic system, that in Orissa there are no septs, and that the Bankura branch may have picked them up locally.[2]

More recently Verrier Elwin made a study of the Hill Saora of the Agency tracts of Ganjam and Koraput Districts of the modern State of Orissa. He finds that the Hill Saora are different from those described by Risley and Russell. While the Savara or Saora described by Risley and Russell have totemic septs, the Hill Saora have none. 'The most remarkable thing', says Elwin, 'about the organization of Saora society is its lack of organization. Its endogamous divisions are vague and often disregarded and, in sharp contrast to all the neighbouring tribes, it has no exogamous totemic clans, no phratries, no moieties. The one essential unit is the extended family descended from a common male ancestor, but there are also divisions into aristocracy and proletariat and by villages.' The Savara of Midnapore (West Bengal) also have no trace of a clan or gotra organization, as a recent observer points out. But they are more or less Hin-duized.[3]

## The Gadaba and the Bondo

The Gadaba live in Orissa, Madras and Madhya Pradesh. They are related linguistically and culturally to the Munda-speaking tribes in general and to their close neighbours, the Bondo, in particular. Russell & Hiralal state that their tribal organization is not very strict, and others like a Bhatra, a Porja or a Muria may become a Gadaba.[4]

Thurston states that the Gadaba of Vizagapatam have five sections divided into exogamous septs. The septs have totemic names. The Gadaba of the plains, however, have forgotten their sept names, but will not injure or kill certain animals.[5] Russell & Hiralal also affirm the existence of exogamous septs named after animals and of totem taboos.[6] According to Fürer-Haimendorf, the units of society among the Bodo Gadaba of Koraput are three in number: they are the village community, the phratry (*bonso*) and the clan (*kuda*). Of these three only the clan is strictly exogamous. Every village has two or more phratries and many clans. The phratries are named after animals like the tiger, the snake, the bear; and show ' indications of totemism '. The clans, however, have no connexion with animals or natural objects.[7]

The Bondo system of phratries (bonso) and clans (kuda), says Fürer-Haimendorf, is akin to that of the Gadaba; marriage, however, is permitted within the bonso and the kuda, the only strict exogamous unit being the village community.[8] In his more detailed study of the Bondo, Elwin confirms the existence of three exogamous units—the village community which is strictly exogamous, the bonsos in which the exogamous rules have broken down, and the kudas in which the exogamous rules are fairly well observed. Of these three units, only the bonsos are totemic. There are totem taboos and myths (probably of relatively modern origin) in which an old couple in one myth begets three sons, one of whom has the head and shoulders of a tiger and becomes the ancestor of the Tiger bonso or race, and in another a woman conceives a cobra child and a human boy. Members of the Cobra bonso say that they are not allowed to even look at a cobra, still less kill one, as cobras are their brothers. The clans are named after village functionaries. Elwin believes that both village and clan exogamy have been borrowed from other Orissa tribes and near-Hindu castes like the Dom and the Pano. The bonso system, however, is the oldest exogamous system of the Bondo, and in former times chiefly controlled them. It is moreover ' a relic of a genuine dual organization with patrilineal descent '. Vague references among the Bondo to other than the Tiger bonso (Killo or Kukusa) and the Cobra bonso (Ontal) probably relate to the bonsos of neighbouring tribes like the Gadaba, the Parenga and the Didaya, who have more than two totemic bonsos. The origin and affiliations of the Bondo, Elwin adds, are obscure, but most of their affinities are with the northeast.[9]

## Other Probably Related Tribes

(i) *The Bhuiya* are a widely distributed and populous tribe, found in Bengal, Bihar, Orissa, Assam, Uttar Pradesh, Madhya Pradesh and Madras. They have been considerably Hinduized. S. C. Roy states that they are rightly included among the Kol or Munda tribes on cultural grounds, although racially they do not much differ from the Dravidian-speaking tribes. The Pauri or Hill Bhuiya have village, but no clan exogamy and no totemism. Traces of totemism found among the Plains Bhuiya are not accompanied by exogamous restrictions, and would appear to be due to borrowing rather than to survival. Some of their gotras—Naga (Snake), Gaja (Elephant), Kachhap (Tortoise), Kabutar (Pigeon)—show a tendency towards endogamy. Other totemic gotras are Komasta (a small bird), Mayur (Peacock), and Boraha (Boar). Russell regards the Baiga as a branch of the Bhuiya.[10] (ii) *The Majhwar* (Manjhi, Majhia): This is, as Russell & Hiralal point out, a mixed tribe originating from Gond, Munda and Kawar. In Mirzapur they have Gond septs; in Sarguja and Raigarh septs of Santal and Munda origin. There are totem taboos and other traces of reverence towards their totems.[11] (iii) *The Mahili* (Mahli). Located in Chota Nagpur and West Bengal, the Mahili have totemic septs like those of the Santal and the Munda. Risley lists 34 septs of which 15 are totemic. He surmises that they are a branch of the Santal and the Munda.[12] (iv) *The Chero* live in Bihar and Chota Nagpur and have totems similar to those of the Kharia. Dalton maintains that they resemble the 'Mongolians'; but Risley denies that the Kolarians are of a Mongolian origin, and asserts that the distinction between the Kolarians and the Dravidians is a linguistic one.[13] (v) *The Turi*: On physical grounds Risley says that the Turi are a Hinduized offshoot of the Munda. They still speak a dialect derived from Mundari, and have a large number of exogamous, totemic septs, some of which are identical with those of the Munda.[14] (vi) *The Kora* (Koda): According to Risley, they are probably an offshoot of the Munda tribe. Found in Chota Nagpur and west and central Bengal, they have in some areas well-marked totemic septs of the same type as those of the Munda. Totem taboos also exist. In other areas the totemic names have been dropped and the caste has been divided into four sub-castes. They affect to be orthodox Hindus.[15] (vii) *The Pahira*: In physical features the Pahira resemble the Kharia and the Santal. Their daily life is devoted to food-gathering and hunting. They have totemic 'divisions' but no bar against marrying within them, provided that the two 'families' concerned have separate graveyards. The numerical smallness of the tribe is a possible cause of the tendency towards clan endogamy. The totem taboos have also been relaxed. S. C. Roy is nevertheless of the opinion that their social and kinship organization was based originally on exogamous totemic clans.[16] (viii) *The Lodha:* According to a recent monograph, the Lodha are largely located in the jungle tracts of Midnapur (West Bengal) and seem to have at one time belonged to the Mundari group, but have today become very much Hinduized. They prefer to call themselves Savara, and speak a mixture of Bengali, Oriya and Mundari. In the jungle villages hunting and gathering are the main occupation; in the plains agriculture. They have patrilineal, exogamous, totemic clans. Of nine clans enumerated, eight have animal totems, one has a kind of yam and one has the moon as well as the grasshopper. Taboos of avoidance relating to the totems are mentioned for eight clans. In several cases the clan names are not identical with the totem names. There are two instances of mourning for the dead totem by the throwing away of earthen pots and bathing; and two instances of clans with two sub-clans regarded as superior and inferior respectively. Thus the Bhakta or Bugta clan (yam as totem) is divided into two sub-clans: Bara Bhaktas with the bigger variety of yams as their totem and the Chhota Bhaktas with the smaller. Some members of the Mallik clan, which has the makar or shark as its totem, say that the sal fish is also their totem.[17]

\*      \*      \*

In the immediately preceding section of this chapter we have brought together the relevant facts concerning totemism among the Munda-speaking tribes, quoting for that purpose both old and new sources. By new sources we mean studies, both ethnographic and other, made in the main after the publication of Niggemeyer's survey. These studies in alphabetical order are chiefly those of P. Bhowmick (1963), P. Biswas (1935, 1956), W. Culshaw (1949), T. C. Das (1931), N. Datta-Majumdar (1956), S. Dube (1951), V. Elwin (1942, 1948, 1950, 1955), C. Fürer-Haimendorf (1943b), J. Gausdal (1960), G. S. Ghurye (1950), W. Griffiths (1946), J. Hoffmann (1930-1941), W. Koppers (1943), K. Leuva (1963), D. N. Majumdar (1937, 1944, 1950, 1961), N. Parry (1932), S. Roy (1935) and W. Ruben (1939). We have thus before us an ample empirical base from which to draw certain broad conclusions.

The conclusions legitimized by the evidence before us are as follows:

(1) So far as the sources are concerned, the newer reports—speaking generally—expose various inadequacies in the older ones (Dalton, Risley, Russell), and indicate that totemism is still relatively strong among most of the tribes concerned, but that a decline is also manifest in all of them. This decline is evidently the result of a long process of Hinduization (or Sanskritization), coupled in more recent times with what may be called, for want of a better term, Westernization. A possible example of the transmission of totemism in its phase of decline to a probably non-totemic section of a larger group is the section of the Bhuiya tribe called the Plains Bhuiya. If it is true that the Baiga of Central India are an offshoot of the Bhuiya tribe, this would be confirmatory evidence, since the Baiga too exhibit very weak traces of totemism. That the strength of totemism among these tribes is not the result of a recent efflorescence, but a continuance from a somewhat remote past, unveiled by relatively more thorough field-investigations, is evidenced by the fact that these investigations have been conducted at a time when the forces adverse to totemism have accelerated.

(2) There are tribes in our list like the Kharia, the Pahira and the Bhuiya which have sections that eke out their existence by food-gathering and hunting or early forms of cultivation, and show no totemism or very weak traces of it. This implies the existence at one time all over India of tribes of hunters and food-gatherers without totemism. There is no evidence of a proto-totemic complex, but loose and floating forms of beliefs and practices of a more or less proto-totemic nature may be presumed to have existed at one time among tribes with various degrees of accentuation on hunting.[18]

(3) There is one tribe in the above list which is basically a food-gathering and hunting one, but possesses a strongly formed totemism. If clan-and-totem identification is a mark of group totemism at its maturest, the Birhor reveal this element to a conspicuous degree. Internal evidence seems to indicate that Birhor totemism was not borrowed from existing tribes in the neighbourhood. The Birhor would therefore seem to belong to that nucleus of tribes in which group totemism first grew and matured.

(4) Among the other tribes of the above list clan totemism exhibits the following elements in varying degrees: (i) Animal and plant names and to a less extent the names of inanimate objects: animal names predominate over plant names, and animal and plant names over those of inanimate objects. One tribe, the Korku, has in the main plant totems; this may be due to its western location allowing western influences to strike roots in

its social organization. In another tribe, the Juang, plant names appear to predominate, but an exhaustive list of totemic names is still wanting. (ii) Totem taboos (rules forbidding the killing, eating or touching of the totem object): Such taboos exist among most of the tribes (the Asur, the Birhor, the Munda, the Kharia, the Bhumij, the Bondo, the Gadaba, the Juang) on which adequate reports are available; their absence in other cases (when recent reports are available) may be ascribed to a decline of totemism, particularly when other traits point to the former existence of a stronger totemism among them. (iii) Totem exogamy: In India, as the observations of several earlier interpreters indicate (see Chapter III), totemism and exogamy have been closely associated all over, suggesting an early convergence and blending of the two phenomena. Among the Munda-speaking tribes, too, totemism and exogamy are closely combined, but a few instances of a dislocation of the two also appear. As the evidence indicates, however, this is mainly the result of Hinduization. (iv) Feelings of kinship towards the totem as among the Asur, the Birhor and the Bhumij are not so widespread among the Munda-speaking tribes. (v) Forms of respect and reverence (obeisance, mourning, burying) occur occasionally. Some tribes which manifest them are the Asur, the Birhor and the Kharia. (vi) Myths narrating encounters with the totem of the parallel-relationship variety are more frequent (the Birhor, the Ho, the Munda, the Kharia, the Santal, the Juang) than those narrating totem descent (the Juang, the Santal, the Kharia, the Agaria but not the Asur). From the above one can, therefore, conclude that totemism, now in various phases of decline, was relatively strong at one time among the Munda-speaking tribes.

(5) There are some groups within larger tribes which have no clan exogamy and no totemism or very weak traces of it. In these groups the family takes the place of the clan, and blood-relationship exogamy and territorial or village exogamy take the place of clan exogamy. These groups are the Hill Kharia of Mayurbhanj (Roy), the Pauri Bhuiya (Roy), the Hill Saora (Elwin), and the Kol of Central India (Griffiths). The Hill Kharia probably belong to the very old group of food-gathering and hunting tribes originally without clans and totemism. The Kol of Central India have obviously lost their clan organization and totemism in recent times through the impact of the surrounding Hindus. The Pauri Bhuiya and the Hill Saora stand in some measure in an intermediate position. If the Pauri Bhuiya are classed among the food-gathering and hunting tribes which have been 'Mundaized' to some extent, the Hill Saora appear to belong racially and culturally more to the core of the

Munda-speaking tribes than to those which have been superficially Mundaized; but Schmidt classes the Savara (Saora) and the Gadaba linguistically among the mixed groups.[19] It is likely that among the original Munda-speaking population in India a village consciousness had begun to displace the sense of clan solidarity. (6) Among the other Munda-speaking tribes a clan organization with patrilineal descent is the general rule. In some instances, as among the Kharia, clan consciousness is the result of a hankering after social solidarity. In other instances this type of consciousness has begun to pale under more modern influences. Among the Birhor, clan-and-totem identification has been ritualized. The totemism of the Munda-speaking tribes is overwhelmingly group totemism of the clan variety, the individual totemism of the Birjia Asur constituting a solitary exception. Both the Birhor and the Kharia, not to speak of other tribes in this area, thus illustrate the existence of the psychological factor which we have termed ' craving for complementarity and dependence ' and its projection into the clan-and-totem organization. (7) A detailed interpretation of the similarities and differences in the totemic phenomenon among these tribes demands the application of the historical as well as the structural and functional approach. Except for very broad interpretations and some inspired guesses, the history of the Munda-speaking tribes in all its particulars (mother-tribe, offshoots, assimilations, migrations, diffusion, acculturation and so on) has still to be written. Structural and functional studies are also scarce. In a broad study of this nature an interpretation of the totemic evidence can only give rise to broad lines of interpretation, as will be made manifest in due course.

We shall end this chapter by examining the ethnic components of the Munda-speaking tribes in an effort at locating the original bearers of totemism in the area. According to Heine-Geldern, the Munda-speaking tribes do not constitute either a racial or ethnographic unity. Racially three main components seem to have blended in their physical make-up. These are a complex primitive component with protomorphic features, a Mongoloid component and an ' Indid ' component.

The people with the Indid component (Dravidians and Aryans) have been mainly responsible for the transformation of the tribal cultures, since the time of their entry into India. The totemism of the Munda-speaking tribes could scarcely have stemmed from this quarter; for both, Dravidians and Aryans, were relatively advanced peoples and late arrivals in India, and had nothing to do directly with totemism, as we shall see.

On the extent of the Mongoloid infusion in these tribes opinions differ very much. Some deny its existence altogether; others make allowances for insignificant intermixtures; and still others see a fairly large admixture of the Mongoloid in them. The Mongoloid component has been traced to and identified with the bearers of the Mon-Khmer or so-called Austroasiatic languages. This view in turn has been called into question, as we have seen, by Gordon T. Bowles and a few others; but until such time as more intensive studies result in distinctly contrary certainties, the views of Schmidt and Heine-Geldern appear on merits to be the most valid of existing hypotheses. As alleged bearers of a neolithic culture, then, the ' Austroasiatic Mongoloids ' were doubtless looked upon as culture-bringers. It would therefore suffice if one presumes that the immigrants were not too numerous nor too few, and to ascribe the spread of the Austroasiatic languages and related cultural elements more to a process of linguistic and cultural ' Mundaization ' than to intermixture of an ethnic kind. The Mundaization in this sense would thus constitute a kind of enthusiastic absorption into a base of differing racial and cultural character. Totemism could scarcely have been brought by the Austroasiatic Mongoloids because in India it displays all the marks of a greater antiquity, and because the Austroasiatics elsewhere either do not possess totemism or show very weak traces of it. The techniques of cultivation, however, which came into this area with the Austroasiatics (involving, as they did, a greater measure of stability) must have served to strengthen clan totemism on the one hand, and to disturb and transform its ideological base on the other. In this connexion it must be pointed out that the parallel-relationship myths which occur so frequently among the Munda-speaking tribes might possibly represent a later form than descent myths, specially as they occur in great part among more differentiated cultures with a combination of gathering and hunting and early forms of cultivation.

This leaves the complex primitive component as the only possible bearer of totemism in this area. In an early article [20] Fürer-Haimendorf identified the bearers of totemism in India with the Melanid, an ethnic concept which Eickstedt introduced in his racial classification. Eickstedt classifies the races of India into three broad groups as follows: the Weddid or racially primitive people of the jungles, consisting of the Gondid and a still more primitive type, the Malid; the Melanid or racially mixed and dislodged groups of very dark-skinned people, consisting of the South Melanid and the Kolid (the Kolarian- or Munda-speaking tribes); and the Indid or racially progressive people of the open regions, comprising the Gracile-Indid and the North Indid.[21] Eickstedt's classification has been criticized in various ways but mainly on grounds of over-schematization.[22] This applies particularly to the term Melanid, thus invalidating it in a consideration of the bearers of totemism.[23]

## NOTES AND REFERENCES

[1] Grierson, 1927, 14.
[2] Schmidt, 1906; Mullan, 1932, 171.
[3] Grierson, 1906, 10; 1927, 34.
[4] Hutton, 1933, 358.
[5] Heine-Geldern, 1928b, 822.
[6] Risley & Gait, 1903, 279; Grierson, 1927, 34. Russell & Hiralal (1916, I, 66) mention in addition the Nahal, the Male, the Khairwar, the Baiga, the Bhunjia, the Bhaina, the Binjhwar, the Bhar, the Koli, the Bhil and the Chero as tribes of the Munda or Kolarian family; and Hutton would also prefer to include the Dom of Northern India and the Korava and the Kurumba of South India (1933, 364).
[7] Heine-Geldern, 1920, 1928a, 1928b, 1929, 1932, 1936, etc.
[8] 1932, 1934, 1935.
[9] 1938, 16; 1961, 64.
[10] 1943. See also T. A. Sebeok, ' An Examination of the Austroasiatic Language Family ' (*Language*, 1942, XVIII, 206-17).
[11] 1960, 103.
[12] 1935, 738.
[13] In *Anthropos*, 1946-9, XLI-XLIV, 924-9.
[14] 1945, 138.
[15] Roy, 1917, 568.
[16] 1930, I, 238.
[17] 1939, 45.
[18] Ruben, 1939, 4; Elwin, 1942, 64.
[19] 1891, I, 25; 1892, II, App. I, 2. For the Binjhia, whom he also calls Birjia and Binjhwar, he mentions 22 totems (Vol. II, App. I, 13).
[20] 1917, 567-71.
[21] 1939, 41, 44, 45.
[22] 1963, 2, 64.
[23] 1917, 567.
[24] 1930, I, 239-40.
[25] 1933, 443-4.
[26] 1939, 40, 140.
[27] 1942, 1, 3, 68-9; Roy, 1926.
[28] 1930, III, 729.
[29] 1925b, 93.
[30] Parry, 1932, 350.
[31] Majumdar in *Essays in Anthropology presented to Rai Bahadur Sarat Chandra Roy* (Lucknow, undated), 69.
[32] ibid., 61.
[33] In the foreword to Dube, 1951, i-ii.
[34] 1928b, 822.
[35] 1958, 19.

[36] Roy, 1925b, 1, 44-5, 59, 62, 67, 90-4, 98-109, 121-4, etc. See also Asutosh Bhattacharyya, 1953.

[37] 1933, 452.

[38] Hoffmann & Emelen, 1932, vi, 1763.

[39] 1872, 189.

[40] 1891, i, 320; 1892, ii, App. I, 60.

[41] 1927, 41, 44-7.

[42] 1937, 1, 55-6, 205-8; 1950, 28, 89, 90-4.

[43] Risley, 1892, ii, 101. But it also means an upright carved post with figures of the sun, the moon and various animals erected in honour of the dead (Driver, 1893, 131); and B. C. Mazumdar (1927, 49) adds: ' The term Munda signifies properly a well-to-do man of agricultural occupation and in this very sense the term is in use among the Ho people of Singhbhum who are sharply distinguished from the Mundas.'

[44] Tamaria, 1922, 176.

[45] 1872, 189.

[46] 1892, ii, 102; App. I, 102-9.

[47] Roy, 1912, 400, 404-11; Hoffmann & Emelen, 1933, viii, 2417.

[48] Hoffman & Emelen, viii, 2406-31.

[49] 1933, 612.

[50] 1937, i, iii, 1-2, 17, 21-2, 55, 122-47, 306.

[51] 1916, iii, 445.

[52] 1872, 158-61.

[53] 1891, i, 446.

[54] 1910, ii, 295.

[55] 1916, iii, 443.

[56] 1937, i, 22, 60-1.

[57] 1931b, 5.

[58] 1933, viii, 2333.

[59] Risley, 1891, i, 512.

[60] 1872, 221-30.

[61] 1891, i, 512; 1892, ii, App. I, 83.

[62] 1896, iii, 322-4.

[63] 1944, 2, 4, 33.

[64] Quoted by Biswas, 1956, 4.

[65] 1910, ii, 300.

[66] 1949, 2.

[67] Quoted by Biswas, 1956, 212.

[68] 1949, 2.

[69] 1916, i, 405.

[70] Bompas, 1909, 5; Majumdar, 1961, 122.

[71] Biswas, 1935, 9; 1956, 19.

[72] Tribal Map of India, Dept. of Anthropology, Govt. of India.

[73] 1872, 207-18.

[74] 1892, ii, 224-34.

[75] 1910, ii, 300-2. In addition to Dalton and Risley, Frazer depends on W. W. Hunter (*Annals of Rural Bengal*) for his information.

[76] 1935, 5, 6, 51-4, 55-8; 1956, 62-7, 68-73.

[77] 1949, 11, 65-71, 77.

[78] Datta-Majumdar, 1956, 41.

[79] 1949, 71, 73, 76.

[80] Gausdal's book (1960) is a detailed study of the Santal sub-clans.

[81] 1959, 240.

[82] 1961, 346.

[83] 1891, i, xviii, 117, 122; 1892, ii, App. I, 12.

[84] 1929, 95-115.

[85] 1931a, 23-7.

[86] 1916, iii, 500.

[87] 1957, 6-7.

[88] 1943, 14, 17.

[89] 1916, iii, 504, 512-13.

[90] 1946, 4.

[91] According to Russell & Hiralal, 1916, iii, 511.

[92] ibid.

[93] 1946, 32-5, 44, 52-4, 141-2, 178, 198-201.

[94] 1893, 128-32.

[95] 1916, iii, 550-69.

[96] 1891, i, 350-2; 1892, ii, App. I, 61.

[97] 1929, 47-53.

[98] See also Elwin, 1942, 84-5, and Lord Raglan's comments on Elwin's hypothesis in *Man*, 1945, xlv, 136.

[99] 1948, 12, 24-30, 120.

[1] Elwin, 1955, 1-2, 33. See also B. A. Saletore, *The Wild Tribes in Indian History* (Lahore, 1935).

[2] Risley, 1892, ii, 242-4; Frazer, 1910, ii, 229; Russell & Hiralal, 1916, ii, 500-8.

[3] Elwin, 1955, 6, 33, 50; Bhowmick, 1955.

[4] 1916, iii, 9-13.

[5] 1909, ii, 242-52.

[6] 1916, iii, 9-13.

[7] 1943b, 151. Somasundaram, 1949, says that there are very strong reasons to believe that the tribe was once formed after the totemic fashion. He adds that they have five ' clans ' divided into several ' families ' named after animals and trees, and that while the totems have lost much of their socio-religious significance today, they are still occasionally mourned or worshipped (36-45).

[8] 1943b, 163.

[9] 1950, 3, 24-5, 29-37.

[10] Roy, 1935, 1, 23, 26, 81, 146, 312; Risley, 1891, i, 108-15; Russell & Hiralal, 1916, ii, 305-18.

[11] 1916, iii, 149-53.

[12] Risley, 1892, ii, 40-2, 96-7; Russell & Hiralal, 1916, iii, 146-7.

[13] Risley, 1891, i, 199-202; Crooke, 1896, ii, 214-20.

[14] Russell & Hiralal, 1916, iv, 588-91.

[15] 1891, i, 506-9.

[16] Roy, 1920, 1921.

[17] Bhowmick, 1963, vii, 1, 7, 29, 34, 52-8.

[18] For evidence of remnants of food-gathering and hunting tribes in India and their distribution, see Heine-Geldern (Ed.) *Bulletin of the International Committee on Urgent Anthropological and Ethnological Research* (1958, i, 14-22; 1959, ii, 77-84; 1960, iii, 40-4, 45-51, 52-60).

[19] ' The Munda languages ', says Schmidt (1906, 19), ' break up into two groups, a more eastern, the Kherwari group with the languages or dialects, Santali, Mundari, Bhumij, Birhor, Koda, Ho, Turi, Asuri, Korwa, and a western which comprises the languages Kurku, Kharia, Juang, next to the two mixed languages Savara and Gadaba.'

[20] 1932a, 336.

[21] 1934, 144-85; 1944, 395-451; L. K. Ananthakrishna Iyer, 1935, i, 9-75.

[22] Elwin, 1934, 4; Guha, 1935, lxxi; 1938, 321-2; 1944, 19; Koppers, 1949, 232.

[23] In addition, Niggemeyer (1933, 590) points out that the so-called Melanid of the extreme south and of Ceylon, that is to say, the Tamil-speaking populations of these areas, have no totemism.

# V

## THE 'GONDID' TRIBES

IN HIS ATTEMPT at determining the ethnic character of the earliest totemists in India, Niggemeyer, operating with Eickstedt's racial classification, arrived by a process of elimination at the conclusion that the Gondid (or more specifically the Bhil, the Baiga, the Korku, the Gond, the Oraon, the Maria, the Kui and others) were its original bearers. Eickstedt, who seemed to have arrived at the same conclusion independently, also ascribed the earliest blade culture to the Gondid.[1] But Guha (and other British and Indian anthropologists) traced totemism to the Proto-Australoid, a term which is more widely conceived than its nearest equivalents (Gondid or Weddid) in Eickstedt's classification, and which embraces all the primitives in India except the submerged Negrito and the Palae-Mongoloid.[2] Schmidt, however, agreed with Niggemeyer but limited his choice of Gondid tribes in the main to the Gond, the Muria, the Khond and the Oraon, and confidently attributed a totemic culture circle of higher hunting to them.

In order to strengthen the above conclusion Niggemeyer quotes three additional proofs: (i) The habitat of the Gondid coincides with the area (Central India) in which totemism is in its most typical and most intensive form. (ii) The important Gondid tribes (as listed above) still retain a 'living' totemism which is the basis of their social life. (iii) In the southeast of the Central Provinces the Maria and the Muria, who are practically uninfluenced by the advanced cultures of the Indians and Europeans, are also totemic.

According to Eickstedt, the Weddid with the two sub-types, the Gondid and the Malid, are an old and special form of the Europid or Northern race, but occupy today the outlying and backward areas of the southern region. The Malid who occupy the hills and jungles of South India are physically somewhat more primitive than the Gondid who are largely found in Central India.

From the so-called Gondid tribes which Niggemeyer specifically

[1] For notes to this chapter see pp. 154-6.

mentions as being strongly totemic, the Korku can be eliminated without much ado. As the evidence presented in the preceding chapter demonstrates, the Korku, who are linguistically and culturally related to the Munda-speaking tribes further eastwards, do not have any totemic usages other than a few gotra names derived largely from plants and trees.

The Hill and Bison-Horn Maria and the Muria are culturally mixed and have strong affinities with the more eastern tribes; but they have been traditionally classed as Gond groups and will, therefore, be examined under that head. As the Khond (Kurukh, Kandh, Kui) and the Oraon speak Dravidian languages like the Gond, they will be taken in hand next. The Baiga and more so the Bhil, as modern research reveals, differentiate themselves from the Gond on various counts. The Bhil, therefore, merit a chapter to themselves.

## The Gond

Considering the spread (Madhya Pradesh, Orissa, Bihar, Andhra Pradesh and Maharashtra) and the numerical strength (3,264,332 in 1941) of the various groups called Gond or Koitur,[3] it is not astonishing that there is a Gond problem which in many of its aspects has so far resisted a satisfactory solution. The term Gond or Koitur refracts a spectrum ranging at the one extreme from a race of rulers who held sway at one time in Gondwana to groups of primitive forest-dwellers at the other. It is therefore no wonder that the Gond are not uniform in language, race or culture.

Linguistically they display a certain measure of diversity. A substantial number of them speak Gondi, a Dravidian language of the intermediate group, said by Grierson to be more closely related to Tamil and Kanarese than to Telugu. But others speak Hindi; and still others, the Koya, Telugu.[4]

On the question of their racial components views differ in some directions. R. C. Roy, who measured a hundred Hill Maria and fifty Bison-Horn Maria males, says that the basic element is Pre-Dravidian or Proto-Australoid modified by a considerable Dravidian infusion and tinged by ' Pareoean ' or Alpine traits. Roy is sceptical of assertions which ascribe a Mongoloid element to them.[5] On the other hand, Hutton is inclined to see a slight but definite Mongoloid element in the Maria.[6] Guha, who measured 103 adult Muria males, says: ' Taking all the characters together, I am inclined to the view that the Muria are not different from the Bhil of the Vindhyan ranges measured by me and belong essentially to what we have termed the Proto-

Australoid group. While this is really the basic type, it is possible that they have absorbed a little of the blood of a finer racial type (as a result probably of their contact with higher caste Hindus across the Godavari) as shown in the occasional occurrence of a longish face, thin lips, prominent chin, and well-developed prominent nose. In addition there is unmistakably a Mongoloid element, though very small, and it appears to be more marked in the Hill Maria and the Muria of the foothills than the Muria of the plains. How exactly this has to be accounted for, remains to be seen but I am inclined to agree with Hutton that the intrusion probably came from the eastern coastal regions.' [7] Regarding the Gond of Adilabad Fürer-Haimendorf says that there is no one racial type to which the majority conform, but nearly all have an indefinable common element in their bearing. He explains this diversity by ascribing it to a fusion of populations of different racial stocks in the distant past.[8] Weninger, studying anthropometric data supplied by Koppers on the Bhil, the Nahal, the Korku, the Baiga and the Gond, concludes that the metrical and morphological characteristics of the head, the face and the body yield a fairly uniform picture, that in every respect there is a marked relation to the Vedda of Ceylon, but that certain traits show a crossing of several racial strains primitive and non-primitive and perhaps even Mongoloid, and that environmental influences also cannot be ruled out.[9] Finally, Fuchs believes that the anthropometric evidence available is too scanty to indicate clearly to which racial group the Gond belong.[10]

Furthermore, recent ethnographers who have dealt with the Gond bear witness to the diversity of their culture.[11] On the one hand, Hutton, Aiyappan and Fuchs enumerate cultural parallels between the Gond and the tribes and castes of the south,[12] and on the other, Hutton and Fürer-Haimendorf see affinities between some sections of the Gond and the non-Dravidian-speaking tribes further eastwards. As Fürer-Haimendorf says, the Muria, the Hill Maria and the Bison-Horn Maria of Bastar differ considerably from the Gond of the Central Provinces, and show obvious affinities with the Munda cultures of Orissa and Chota Nagpur.[13] In addition to these elements from the south and east, others both primitive and non-primitive lend a variegated appearance to the cultural situation in the Gond habitat.

Who, then, are the Gond [14] and from where did they come to their present habitat? Russell opines that they came from the south between the ninth and thirteenth centuries after Christ.[15] But this is highly speculative. A more reasonable view is that of Fürer-Haimendorf, who believes that the tribes now known as

Gond are not the dispersed offshoots of a once homogeneous people, but that they acquired a certain very limited measure of cultural uniformity only when they came under the sway of the same dominant linguistic influence, that Dravidian is the language of the high civilizations of South India, and that a large-scale Dravidianization of the aboriginal tribes took place partly previous and partly parallel to the Aryanization which is still going on. Further, Fürer-Haimendorf visualizes the process of Dravidianization as an invasion of people (no longer exactly identifiable) who were limited in number but superior in organization and material equipment, and from whom the aborigines derived their language and some elements of their culture. He therefore holds that a tribe like the Muria were subject to a change of language rather than that they migrated from distant parts of South India.[16] Fuchs agrees with both Grierson and Fürer-Haimendorf, and thus lends additional support to the latter's view.[17]

With the Gond problem thus in focus, we can turn next to the various reports on totemism among the Gond.

Risley reports that the Gond of Bengal have four sub-tribes, and that the ' sections ' are totemic. One of them Besra (hawk) is also found among the Santal. In Appendix I, however, he mentions five sub-tribes and thirty-two septs of which fifteen are named after animals, and one after a tree. The meanings of eleven names are unknown; two are named after objects (iron, bead); one after a river; another after a city; and the third ' Ganga ' is translated as sea.[18] P. B. Bose, presumably referring to the Gond of Chhattisgarh, says that their language appears to belong more to the Tamil than the Telugu section of the Dravidian languages, and adds that they are divided into five gots which worship 3, 4, 5, 6, and 7 gods respectively. For the first got he mentions three subdivisions, for the second five, for the third five, for the fourth eleven, and for the fifth three. He gives the meanings of five of the subdivision names (Tekam: teak, Neitam: dog, Kariam: charcoal or cock, Singram: a variety of fish, and Marai: a tree). He states further that the three deities of the first got are the bull, the tiger and the crocodile and that they are not eaten.[19] Crooke, quoting Hislop on the Gond of the Central Provinces, says that they are divided into twelve and a half castes or classes in imitation of the Hindus and that of these twelve and a half, four (Raj Gond, Rajhuwal, Dodave and Katulya) are Gond *par excellence*. Six gotras or ' sections ' are named for the Raj Gond of the North-Western Provinces and Oudh, but the meanings of the names are not given.[20] C. Hayavadana Rao, dealing with the ' Wild Gonds ' of the

Madras Presidency, states that they have three exogamous subdivisions (Raj Gond, Bhuri Gond and Murya Gond) which are in
turn broken up into numerous totemic septs. As commonest
totems he mentions Suribons (sun), Bhagar or Bhagbons (tiger),
Nagbons (cobra), and Kachchimbons (tortoise). There are also
various customs which signify respect and veneration towards the
totems.[21] Russell & Hiralal, casting their net more widely but
not discriminating sufficiently between individual Gond tribes,
report that in one part of Bastar there are two great exogamous,
patrilineal classes, one with 90 and the other with 65 septs.
All the septs in each class are *dadabhai* or *bhaiband* to each
other, that is to say, in the relation of brothers, and so marriage
within the class is forbidden. But the septs in one class stand
in the relation of *mamabhai* or *akomama* to those of the other.
Mamabhai means 'maternal uncle's sons' and akomama apparently signifies 'having the same maternal grandfather'. Marriage
between the two classes is the general rule. Hence Russell &
Hiralal add: 'It will thus be seen that the smaller septs seem
to serve no purpose for regulating marriage, and are no more
than family names.' In another part of Bastar there are five
exogamous classes, each with a small number of septs. Among
the Muria of Bastar there are a few large exogamous septs named
in Hindi, each with sub-septs named in Gondi. Some examples
are Bakravans (goat race) with 4 septs (or sub-septs?), Kachhimvans (tortoise race) with 4 septs, Nagvans (cobra race) with more
than 5 septs. Other exogamous groups are Sodi (tiger), Behainsa
(buffalo), Netam (dog in Gondi), Chamchidai (bat) and one or
two more. Russell & Hiralal believe that in this case the exogamous clans with Hindi names are probably a late development
adopted either because the old Gond names had been forgotten
or because the septs were too numerous to be remembered. In
Chanda they report the existence of a classification according to
the number of gods worshipped. There are four main groups
worshipping 7, 6, 5 and 4 gods respectively, and each group has
10 to 15 septs. The number of gods worshipped also determines
the choice of marriage partners. Each group has a sacred animal
which it reveres, the seven-god group having the porcupine, the
six-god the tiger, the five-god the saras crane, and the four-god
the tortoise. In practice, however, the classification according to
the number of gods is being forgotten, the three lowest groups
having disappeared. In Mandla this classification has grown
weak, and in Betul it is entirely in abeyance. Many of the septs
are named after animals and plants, of which the commonest in
all the districts are the Markam (or mango tree), the Tekam
(or teak tree), the Netam (or dog), the Irpachi (or mahua tree),

the Tumrachi (or tendu tree), and the Warkara (or wild cat).
There are totem taboos which are, however, not always observed,
and traces of other practices indicating respect and veneration
towards the totem. In some cases some other object than the one
represented by their sept name is venerated, either because the
meaning of the sept name has been forgotten or because the
object concerned is no longer regarded as sacred. The members
of some septs (Marabi, Dhurwa, Uika) do not know the meanings
of their sept names. Most of the explanations which the Gond
offer for the totemic names of their septs describe incidents which
occurred at the Deo-Khulla (or god's place) or at the threshing-
floor relating to the animal, plant or other object concerned and
the ancestor or priest of the sept. Russell & Hiralal are of the
opinion that these stories were devised after the totems had
ceased to be revered as ancestors or kinsmen, and were therefore
associated with the gods as explanations of the sept names or
because of the sanctity still attaching to them.[22] Syed Siraj ul
Hassan reports the existence of four septs in the Adilabad district. The Chardeva or four-god sept has three totems (tortoise,
crocodile, and iguana) and nine sub-septs; the Pachdeo or five-
god sept has two totems (porcupine and saras) and eleven sub-
septs; the Sahadeo or six-god sept has the tiger as totem and
nineteen sub-septs, and the Satdeo or seven-god sept has two
totems (serpent and porcupine) and six sub-septs. There are
totem taboos. The preservation of the totems and the founders'
names and the replacement of the totemic names of the septs
by fanciful titles indicate, says Hassan, that the Hinduized Gond
are attempting to replace their totemic names by eponymous
ones in order to lend colour to their pretensions of a mythical
origin of the orthodox kind.[23] Finally, Niggemeyer, basing himself on C. Hayavadana Rao, Russell & Hiralal, and Hassan, summarizes the information from these sources as follows: *Sociology
of totemism*: The Gond have a series of endogamous sub-tribes
and exogamous totem groups (with two or three totems each in
Hyderabad); *the religious side of totemism*: rule of avoidance,
veneration at marriages, mourning for the totem, and in part
another totem than that indicated by the name is venerated.[24]

The new era in Gond studies can be said to have begun with
Grigson's monograph on the Maria Gond of Bastar (1938). The
Maria Gond of Bastar State in the extreme southeast corner of
the Central Provinces fall mainly into two divisions—the Hill
Maria of the Abujhmar Hills and the Bison-Horn Maria. The
distinction is based largely on differences in the cultural life of
the two divisions. Of the fifty Hill Maria clans enumerated in
Appendix II of Grigson's book, six have animals listed under

the column 'totem', one has a tree, one a type of grass, one
sunset, three or four various other objects, twenty-eight have
none, and ten were presumably not definitely ascertained.[25] For
the Bison-Horn Maria the position is as follows: the phratry
Marvi has the goat as a totem in some places, and the cobra in
others, and comprises nine clans of which one has the tortoise
as a totem; the phratry Kuhrami or Kadiari has the cuckoo as
a totem, and ten clans of which two have the hornbill, one the
screech-owl, and one the buffalo as totems; the phratry Sodi or
Odi had the tiger as a totem but has replaced it by the buffalo,
and of its three clans two have the buffalo as a totem; the phratry
Markami has the tortoise as a totem, and twenty-one clans of
which three have totems (a kind of flower, the goat and the
buffalo); and lastly, the phratry Kawasi or Wanjami has the
tortoise as a totem, and eight clans with no totems mentioned.
Six clans could not be traced to phratries.[26] Furthermore, Grigson denies the existence of a 'two moieties' system among the
Hill Maria, which Russell & Hiralal had maintained, but concedes the existence of 'something approaching phratries' of
which the Hill Maria 'perhaps are not conscious'. But these
phratries or 'suppositious groups' are not associated with the
totems like the phratries of the Bison-Horn Maria of Bastar
or the Muria; nor are there necessarily five of them like the
three-god, four-god, five-god, six-god and seven-god phratries of
the Chanda, Nagpur and Chhindwara districts. Traces of related
taboos are few, weak and confused among the Hill Maria. Hence
Grigson concludes: 'It is thus clear that traces of totemism
among the Hill Marias are very slight, and affect individual
clans, not groups. There is no connexion at all between totemism
and the taboos, nor does it figure in the cult of the clan god.'
Among the Bison-Horn Maria, of 57 clans enumerated by Grigson, only 10 have totems; and it is the clan totem, not the
phratry totem, that matters, as several examples of clans with
and without totems of their own not observing any taboos towards the phratry totems demonstrate. Therefore Grigson educes
two conclusions: (i) that certain clans in the phratry with
different totems did not split off from the parent clan, but were
added later because of contiguity; (ii) and that, as the association
of totems with clans and phratries is not universal and plays an
insignificant part in the life of the whole tribe, 'it is either
something, borrowed from another culture, but not really assimilated, or else a relic of something that has decayed with antiquity'. The only legend among the Bastar Maria deals with the
origin of the tortoise totem, and relates how, during a great
flood long ago, a tortoise carried the brothers Markam and

10

Kawasi across to safety.²⁷ Two further reasons suggesting that
the totems are not of real significance and that the phratries
grew out of the desire to extend the marriage field are (iii) that
a man in the Markam Tortoise phratry can take a wife from
the Kawasi Tortoise phratry or the Hemla Tortoise clan in the
Goat phratry, and the same holds good for the Goat and Buffalo
phratries and the Goat and Buffalo clans in other phratries;
(iv) and that each village is regarded as the *bhum* (earth or soil)
of the individual Bison-Horn clan that first settled there, and
not of the phratry. Finally Grigson lists the traditional origins
of certain Hill and Bison-Horn Maria clans (actually ten in
number) and rightly says that nothing totemic seems to enter
into them.²⁸

Totemism among the Gond was next examined by Buradkar,
who followed Frazer largely in his interpretative approach.
Buradkar's study suffers from the fact that his totemic material
is neither exhaustive nor always systematically arranged in terms
of areas or tribal distinctions, that he does not clearly indicate
to what extent the information offered is derived from his own
field-researches or to what extent his own field-researches confirm
the evidence derived from older sources like Russell & Hiralal,
Grigson and so on, and that his interpretations are often intem-
perately speculative. Attempting a brief general statement on
Gond totemism he says: Most of the totemic clans do not have
totem taboos, and those which have them do not observe them
with scrupulous care. Many do not know the significance of
their totems, and some clans have adopted eponymous, territorial
or titular names. Thus the totems are now mainly nothing but
clan names, and totemism is of the exogamous or social variety.

Most of the Gond totems are derived from the flora and fauna
of their habitat. Others were added with the advance of civilization and the knowledge of agriculture, metals and so on. In
a list which is not exhaustive the following totems (apparently
from the entire Gond area) are enumerated: (i) *Beast totems*:
Three clans with the tiger as totem, three with the horse (of
which one is a colt), two with the buffalo, two with the wild
cat, two with the goat, and one each with the dog, the porcupine, the ass, the heifer, the cow and the she-rat—that is, 18
beast totems in all. (ii) *Bird totems*: Seven in all (three species
of hawk, the goose, the crow, the peacock and a kind of crane).
(iii) *Fish and other aquatic totems*: Three clans with the tortoise as totem, two with the crocodile and four with various
kinds of fish—9 in all. (iv) *Reptile totems*: Two clans with a
large lizard, two with the cobra and one with the iguana—5 in
all. (v) *Vegetable totems*: Seventeen in all. (vi) *Other totems*:

Natural objects: Six in all (iron, pearl, stone, salt, fire, sea); and artificial objects: five in all (axe, basket, earthen pot, arrow, whip). (vii) *Cross totems* (inclusive of more than one species, otherwise called multiple totems): Eight in all. (viii) *Split totems and Cross split totems*: Five in all (female organ of generation, paw of an animal, bowels, head of a kid and blade of corn).

Some of their legends indicate totem descent. In the Betul district it is narrated that the ancestress of the Gond, Sukama-devi-Velar, and her brother, Adi-Rawan-Parial, were born from two eggs laid by the Singmali birds;[29] and in Chhattisgarh and Chota Nagpur a legend relates the birth of the totem animal, the tiger, from the human ancestress, the wife of the eldest of five brothers, Kusru, Suri, Markam, Netia and Sarsum. Deified and worshipped as Bageshwar, the tiger-spirit is supposed to appear at weddings in the person of a possessed man. This is considered a favourable omen among the Gond, who claim descent from the aforesaid brothers. Among other Gond who also worship Bageshwar or Bagh-Deo, he is merely one of the many spirits to whom propitiatory offerings are made, and his origin is ascribed to other causes.[30] The Tumrecha (Tendu) Uika clan has a legend in which the ancestor and his wife who was with child were walking in the forest. The wife saw some tendu fruit and longed for it, and the husband gave it to her to eat. In the Raipur district of the Chhattisgarh country the Gond till recently believed in their descent from their totems.

Among some Gond clans there is evidence of mourning for the dead totem in a like manner as for a dead clansman. In Jashpur State this is so for the tiger, and in Mandla district for the crocodile, which is also revered and offered sacrifices at marriages.

The totem taboos observed are on the whole few, and differ to some extent from clan to clan and place to place as a result of the different levels of culture attained. There are traces of totem taboos in the Jashpur State, the Mandla and Betul districts, the Nagpur plains and other adjoining areas.

Buradkar believes that there are traces of the consumption of the totem in certain rituals connected with Nag Deo or the cobra god—a former totem which evolved into a 'totem god'. In this ritual the Gond cook and eat the body of a cobra in the month of Asharh (July) under the belief that by doing so they will protect themselves from the effects of poisonous substances that they might happen to eat.

Fusion of totemic clans among the Gond is evidenced by the disconnected totem taboos (to the Por-tai or Basket clan tigers and crocodiles are tabooed); by the crest of the Gond royal family at Chanda, which is composed of the winged tiger and the elephant; by the phratry totems which were once the clan totems of the leading clans in the phratries; and by clans with cross or multiple totems. Fission of clans and their totems is perhaps indicated, as Frazer believed, by the split totems of which some instances exist among the Gond.

Buradkar claims that exogamous phratries exist among almost all the Gond sub-tribes, but that phratry totems are found mainly in the Chanda district. The phratries are identified by the number of gods each of them worships. In the Betul district, however, they have in addition other names—thus, the seven-god clan and the six-god clan are called Dhurwa and Uika respectively. Among the Hill Maria the phratries do not have names; and among the Bison-Horn Maria and the Muria they have totemic names. In the Chanda district the exogamous phratries have the following totems: the Satdeve or seven-god phratry has the porcupine (*sui*) as its totem; the Sahadeve or six-god phratry, the tiger (*bagh*); the Panchdeve or five-god phratry, a kind of crane (*saras*); and the Chardeve or four-god phratry, the tortoise (*marpachi*). The members of the clans comprising the phratries reverence their phratry totems and hold them in superstitious awe. Both the Muria Gond of Bastar (as Russell & Hiralal report) and the Bison-Horn Maria (as Grigson shows) have exogamous, totemic phratries. The phratry totems are of later origin, and evolved out of the clan totems. Among all the Gond tribes the inheritance of the totem is patrilineal.[31]

Elwin's elaborate study of the Muria Gond of Khondagaon and Narayanpur Tahsils in Bastar is the next milestone in Gond studies.[32] Although the clan system among these Muria Gond has fallen into considerable disorder, the clans can be classified roughly into five phratries as follows: (i) The Nag or Cobra phratry with 12 clans, 3 of which have the cobra as totem, 4 the goat (one being a she-goat), one both the goat and the horse, and one each the bullock, the wild buffalo, the dog and the Kassi tree. (ii) The Kachhim or Tortoise phratry with 7 clans all of which have the tortoise as totem, and one the dog as an additional totem. (iii) The Bakra or Goat phratry with 7 clans, of which 5 have the goat as a totem, one the Kassi tree, and one the goat and the Kassi tree. (iv) The Bagh or Tiger phratry with two clans, one of which has the tiger, the buffalo and the bod-fish as totems, and the other the buffalo. (v) The Bodmink or Fish phratry with 6 clans, of which 2 have the bod-fish as totems, 2 the Kassi tree, one the Kumot bird and one the Usi bird. There are four clans which Elwin could not fit into the phratry scheme; further, the clans were sometimes arbitrarily

divided into these phratries. The rules governing clan behaviour
are: (i) *Clan and phratry exogamy*: The members of a clan are
*dadabhai* or brothers to one another, and so are the clans within
a phratry; (ii) *Totem taboos*: Members of a clan and phratry
must in many instances avoid injuring or eating their totem
animals or plants and must usually give them special honour
and worship. Mourning for the dead totem as for a human being
occurs in many clans; (iii) *Special rules*: There are a number
of these, as for example, the rule forbidding members of the
Naitami clan from wearing bangles. Most of the clans trace their
origin and their totems to a journey involving the crossing of
a river. This legend is known throughout Central India, and
among the Muria there are several versions of it. Most versions
concern Lingo Pen and other Gond ancestors and the tortoise
in its role as a rescuer. Other clans give local and special reasons
for their origin such as dreams, divisions of families and migrations. A belief in the clan bhum or earth still exists. The clan
system retains its vitality in that it regulates marriage relations,
organizes its members round the clan-god, celebrates particular
festivals and governs funerary rites and memorial customs.
'Totemism', says Elwin, 'is less important, but is still far from
moribund. The whole complex of ideas and customs is greatly
confused, but the very confusion is perhaps a sign of its
vitality.'[33]

In 1948 Fürer-Haimendorf published the first volume of his
ethnographic investigation of the Raj Gond of Hyderabad and
the Central Provinces. The Raj Gond are important because they
occupy a central position among the Gond, because they consider themselves the true exponents of Gond culture and language
and the traditional Gond religion, and because being less exposed
to the more intolerant propagators of Hinduism they have preserved more of their old culture than most of the Gond in the
Central Provinces. They have a system of four nameless phratries
described as seven-wen kin-group, six-wen kin-group, five-wen
kin-group and four-wen kin-group.[34] The origin of the phratries
is attributed to the mythical culture-hero, Pahandi Kupar Lingal.
Each phratry has one or more totem animals which may not be
killed or eaten by its members. Each phratry is strictly exogamous
and consists of a number of pari or clans. The clans are
numerous, and even the Gond are unable to enumerate all the
clans of their respective phratries. Consequently, Fürer-Haimendorf's list consists only of those clans that occur in some strength
in the Adilabad district. Thus, the seven-brother phratry or
Yerwen Saga consists of seven clans; the six-brother phratry or
Sarwen Saga has two sub-phratries, the Pandwen Saga with

eighteen clans and the Sarpe Saga with eight; the five-brother phratry or Siwen Saga also has two sub-phratries with seven and fourteen clans respectively; and the four-brother phratry or Nalwen Saga has fourteen clans. Each pari or clan worships a clan-god called Persa Pen or great god, and in many instances the shrine of the Persa Pen still lies within the ancestral clan land. We are not told if the clans like the phratries are associated with totems, presumably because a more detailed account of the social organization of the Raj Gond of Adilabad was to have been given later in Volume II of the work. It is, therefore, regrettable that Volume II has not yet for one reason or another been published.[35]

The Gond in Eastern Mandla (Central India) have been recently studied by Stephen Fuchs. The Gond call their endogamous division *biladeri* (brotherhood) or *jat* (breed). It is subdivided into three types of exogamous units: the *garh* which is territorial, the gotra or clan, and the phratry. The Hindi word *garh* means literally 'fortress', 'citadel' or 'hill'; but it also signified a territorial unit. It would therefore appear that the Gond were originally organized into exogamous, territorial groups, and that the later exogamous groups, the gotras or clans, were originally localized. Garh exogamy, however, is not strictly enforced nowadays. Most of the Gond clan names in Eastern Mandla and elsewhere are in Gondi. It is therefore a safe assumption that the system is as old as their use of the Dravidian language. The clan system and its accompanying totemism may be older than the adoption of the Dravidian language; but the territorial exogamy of the Gond which seems to be older renders that view unlikely. Of the thirty clan names for which Fuchs could find meanings, eight are those of animals, seven are those of trees, and most of the rest bear little resemblance to totemic names. The Gond clans of Eastern Mandla are grouped into phratries of eighteen clans each. Each phratry has its own totem and taboos. In some villages there is even a moiety system. The grouping of phratries in terms of the number of gods worshipped is found in Western Mandla and other areas but not in Eastern Mandla; and with the exception of the Kusro clan, which worships the tiger, no Gond clan of Eastern Mandla worships any special clan gods.

As the totemism of the Gond is of a very dilute kind, Fuchs disagrees with Niggemeyer that the Gond together with the Bhil, the Baiga, the Korku, the Oraon, the Maria, the Kui and others are the true representatives of totemism in India. This dilute form of totemism is also found among many castes of Central India who could not have been strongly influenced by the Gond.

Further, the Panka, a semi-aboriginal weaving caste in Gond-wana, have clan names which indicate a more pronounced totem-ism, all the clan names, moreover, being of an Aryan origin. Again, there is no evidence that the totem is regarded by the Gond as the ancestor of the tribe or clan; nor is clan exogamy strictly enforced. Hence this dilute form of totemism could either have been introduced into the country by the Rajputs, or could even be of an older date. For instance, the Rajputs have a clan named after the tortoise, Kachhwaha. It is possible that the Gond clans (Markam, Kusro, Tekam, Tilgam, Pusam and others) which venerate the tortoise may have derived this totemic in-fluence from the Rajputs. On the other hand, some of their legends which narrate the experience of their ancestors in cross-ing a river show the tortoise in the role of either a rescuer or an evilly disposed creature.[36]

There are some tribal groups and castes which, it has been alleged, are offshoots of the Gond or have been influenced by them in varying degrees. Some of these are: (i) *The Ahir*: These are also known as Gaoli, Rawat, Mahakul, etc., and are cow-herds, milkmen and cattle-breeders by occupation. Russell & Hiralal (Central Provinces) identify them with the Abhira who, it is claimed, entered India from central Asia at about the be-ginning of the Christian era. Today they are a purely occupa-tional caste largely recruited from the indigenous tribes. They have exogamous units of the titular or totemic kind. Hassan (Hyderabad) reports six endogamous divisions with a large number of exogamous units, some of which are totemic. Enthoven (Bombay) states that there are no exogamous units except fami-lies bearing the same surname. In Khandesh and Poona there are some totemic traces.[37] (ii) *The Agaria*: Risley states that they are a sub-tribe of the Asura of Chota Nagpur and that they are divided into four sub-tribes with some totemic septs. In Mirza-pur Crooke reports the existence of seven exogamous, totemic septs with totem taboos. Russell & Hiralal regard them as an offshoot of the Gond tribe who, having taken to the occupation of iron-smelting, now form a separate caste. They have two endogamous divisions, and most of their exogamous units have generally the same names as those of the Gond. They do not know the meanings of their sept names and hence have no totemic observances. Elwin, however, who devoted an entire monograph to the Agaria, says that the totemic customs of the tribe are highly developed and of great significance. They have a number of endogamous divisions subdivided into exogamous, patrilineal and totemic septs. The names of the septs vary from place to place owing to the influence of their neighbours, the main influence stemming from the Gond and the Munda-speaking tribes. Some of their legends point to descent totemism. Thus, the Kusro sept claim descent from the offspring of a bird and a girl, and the Kerketa, Baghel, Somvani and Aindhar septs trace their origin to jungle dogs, tigers, kerketa birds and an eel, from which their ancestors were born or emerged. Other legends trace the origin of the septs to various incidents which occurred during the flight from the stricken city of Lohripur or to other experiences and occurrences. There are totem taboos and other indications of totem veneration. The Agaria do not form a homogeneous tribe, for everywhere they take on the colouring of their neighbours—Gond, Baiga, Korwa, Munda as the case may be. They are, however, distinct from the Lohar and other Hindu blacksmiths in the Central Provinces and elsewhere. They are a primitive tribe with a distinctive and striking mythology and a uniform iron-smelting technique, which makes possible the tracing of an Agaria belt across the centre of India in spite of cultural differences from place to place. Both Agaria and Asur are probably descendants of a tribe which was known to the early Aryans as the Asura and was defeated and reduced to the level of demons by them. Their totemism which ' is still a powerful social and religious factor ' probably was ' a highly developed system in antiquity '.[38] (iii) *The Bhattra*: Found in Bastar State and south of Raipur, the Bhattra are akin to the Gond, say Russell & Hiralal. They have the usual set of exogamous septs named after animals and plants. It is said that they formerly tattooed representations of their totems on their person and that the Tiger and Snake septs ate the flesh of these animals at a sacrificial meal. They still display attitudes of respect and veneration towards their totems, apologizing to them when they accidentally kill them, burying or burning their bodies, and when rich distributing alms in their name. Elwin reports that they are rapidly becoming a Hindu caste.[39] (iv) *The Kamar*: Regarded as an offshoot of the Gond by Russell & Hiralal, the Kamar, according to them, have two subdivisions and a few gots, all of which have the same names as those of the Gond septs. The meanings of the names, however, have been forgotten. In his more detailed study of the Kamar (1951), Dube shows that the tribe located in Chhattisgarh (Central Provinces) is divided into a number of gots or clans which are totemic, exogamous and patrilineal. Many of their clan names and their legends of clan origins resemble those of the Gond. Some traces of totem descent also lie in their legends. Thus, a Sori woman gave birth to a tiger and a snake, hence there are Wagh and Nag Sori; and the Kunjam got traces its origin to the children of a girl

and a black he-goat. The Kamar are not very interested in their
clans; nor are they keen on asserting their relative superiority
or antiquity. There are no clan councils or ritual clan meetings.
Their folk-lore is poor in myths of clan origins. Nevertheless,
the clans as exogamous units still occupy a significant place in
their social organization. The totemic significance of some of
their clans has been lost, and in some cases the totem taboos
and allied practices have begun to decline. Dube opines that the
clan organization of the Kamar was probably borrowed from
some more advanced neighbours like the Gond. With this
opinion Fürer-Haimendorf concurs, pointing out that the Kamar
together with the Baiga, the Reddi and other similar tribes
belong to a stratum midway between food-gatherers and primitive agriculturists. The tribes of this layer practise both shifting
cultivation and food-gathering and hunting. They have no complex social organization, the family and the local group being
more important than the clan. The totemic clan system seems
to have been superimposed on an older system of territorial
units.[40] (v) *The Kolam*: Russell & Hiralal maintain that they
are hardly distinguishable from the Kunbis or Hindu cultivators, but point out also that they are considered to be akin to
the Gond. They speak Kolami, a Dravidian language of the intermediate group. Many of their family names resemble those of
the Marathi-speaking castes. Fürer-Haimendorf states that the
most primitive racial types in Adilabad are found among the
Kolam (also known as Kolavar or Mannevarlu). Gond influence
on them is considerable. They have exogamous clans with names
like those of the Gond. The clans are grouped into phratries
after the manner of the Gond into 7-brother, 6-brother, 5-brother
and 4-brother clans. But the Kolam phratries have no mythological sanctions. It is, therefore, ' almost certain that they have
been formed by the coordination of existing exogamous units
with the Gond clan system '. In Berar the Kolam have Marathi
sept names and in the Telugu areas house-names or *intiperulu*
like their Telugu neighbours.[41] (vi) *The Parja*: In Bastar, Russell & Hiralal think, the Parja appear to be the oldest Gond
settlers subdued by later immigrants of their race. They have
exogamous, totemic septs. There are totem taboos and other
forms of totem veneration such as mourning and praying for
forgiveness when the totem is accidentally killed. But the Parja
beyond the Jeypore border comprise, as Grigson points out,
seven different tribes, some speaking Munda, others Dravidian,
and still others Aryan dialects, and varying very much in customs
and cultural progress. The Bastar Parja now call themselves
Dhurwa. They differ most in their style of dancing which

resembles that of the Gadaba in neighbouring villages.[42] (vii)
*The Pardhan*: Russell & Hiralal regard the Pardhan as an
inferior branch of the Gond tribe, who act as priests or minstrels
to the Gond. The name is of Sanskrit origin, and means a
minister or agent. They have many endogamous divisions; and
their exogamous divisions are the same as those of the Gond.
They tattoo on their left arm a dotted figure which represents
their totem. Shamrao Hivale, who published in 1946 the results
of several years of personal study of the Pardhan in the Dindori
Tahsil (Mandla district, upper Narbada valley), also regards
them as a branch of the Gond tribe. Both the Gond and the
Pardhan have the same clans, the same mythology, the same
religious practices, the same festivals; and they mix together very
naturally. In Dindori they have two sections, and in other areas
still others. As Hivale puts it, ' Since the Pardhan economic and
religious system depends on the community of clans between
the Gonds and Pardhans, the clan organization of the latter
closely resembles that of the Gonds and in its main outlines
is based upon it. In detail, however, and especially in the development of local sub-clans, there is considerable divergence.'
There is no clear-cut phratry system or classification of the clans
according to the number of the gods worshipped; but groups
of clans do regard themselves as related, and the Dhurwa and
Parteti clans worship five gods, suggesting the former existence
of a classification based on the number of gods worshipped.
There are also indications which suggest that the clans were
formerly territorial units. Today, however, the clan system is in
a state of decline and confusion. Hivale lists five groups of clans
among the Pardhan of Patangarh. Members of each of the first
four groups must marry outside their clans and groups of clans.
There is some vagueness among the Pardhan about their matri-
monial relations towards members of the other groups, but in
the main they can marry members of the other groups. The
relations of the fifth group to the others could not be determined. The first group contains 17 clans, of which seven have
totems (the hawk, the tiger, the palm tree, the horse, the cockroach, and two clans with the tortoise); the second has 10 clans
with no totems identified; the third has 13 clans, of which the
Marabi clan has the cobra and the bones of cattle as totems; the
fourth has 7 clans with no totems; and the fifth 15 clans, of
which seven have the following names—buffalo, thief, crow, betel-
cutter, oilseed, tiger and wild cat. The Kumra clan, not mentioned in the above list, has the goat as its totem and related
taboos. Its myth of origin (as also that of the Khusro clan) is
the same as that of the Gond. The sub-clans of the Marabi clan,

which has a vague reverence for the goat and does not sacrifice
it to the gods, have arisen as a result of offerings made to Bara
Pen at the time of worship or as a result of other acts and
experiences. The Markam clan, which is a very old and widespread clan or clan-name, has the mango tree as its totem and
related taboos. (In Hivale's list, however, the Markam clan
appears in the first group and has the tortoise as a totem.) The
Parteti clan has a myth of origin similar to that of the Potta
clan among the Agaria. The Syam clan has probably the porcupine as totem, the Tekam the teak tree, and the Urweti the
cockroach. In his reference to the Pardhan (1948) Fürer-Haimendorf regards them as culturally aboriginal, but racially far more
advanced than the Gond. The Pardhan in Adilabad and the
adjoining areas of the Central Provinces are hereditary bards of
the Gond and do not exercise priestly functions among them.
They have the Gond system of phratries and clans, and they
follow the Gond pattern in social observances, marriage customs
and funeral rites. They are nevertheless regarded by the Gond
as inferiors in rank and social standing. Differing from Russell
and Hivale, P. S. Rao affirms that the Pardhan were professional
bards of the Rajput chiefs, who, with the decline of those chiefs,
associated themselves for economic reasons with the Gond rather
late in the day, lost caste on that account and therefore assimilated large segments of Gond culture. Fürer-Haimendorf agrees
with Rao.[43] (viii) *Other related tribes and castes*: There are
other tribes and castes in adjoining areas which bear similarities
in customs, clan-names and totemic traditions with the Gond.
They have been regarded either as offshoots or close connexions
or recipients of Gond influence. Some of them, according to
Russell & Hiralal, are the Arakh, the Bhunjia, the Dhimar, the
Gauria, the Ghasi, the Manjhwar and the Sonjhara. Others add
a few other names. In suggesting the measure of racial and cultural ramifications, these identifications serve to underline the
complexity of the Gond problem.

## The Oraon

With a population of 1,122,926 in 1941, the Oraon are distributed
in Bihar, West Bengal, Orissa and Madhya Pradesh.[44] They have
a tradition, which crops up in most references to the tribe
(Dalton, Risley, Gait, Baines, Russell and Roy), that they lived
originally in the west, probably in the Karnatak, and that they
came up the Narbada and then settled in their present habitat.
Grierson claims that their language is more closely allied to
Kanarese than to any other Dravidian language. They are

cultivators and claim to have brought plough cultivation to the neighbouring tribes.

They are a distinctly totemic people, as all observers agree. Dalton mentions 10 exogamous totemic clans with related totem taboos. Of the totems eight are to all intents animal totems and two vegetable.[45] Risley lists five sub-tribes and 71 exogamous, patrilineal septs, of which 65 are probably totemic. Of these 65 totems, 41 are animals.[46] Hahn enumerates 27 septs, and adds that each sept has its own totem which is held sacred in some way or other. Of these totems eighteen are animal (the Kispota clan, as Dalton also states, does not eat the stomach of a pig), seven are vegetable (mostly trees and plants) and two are mineral (salt and iron).[47] Dehon gives 22 exogamous, patrilineal, totemic septs. Of the totems 14 are animal, 6 are vegetable and 2 mineral. Dehon claims that they do not know the origin of their totems and do not seem to attach very great importance to observances connected with them.[48]

It is, however, to S. C. Roy that we are indebted for more detailed information on the Oraon of Chota Nagpur (1915, 1928). Roy enumerates 68 clans, of which 43 have animal totems, 19 vegetable totems (mostly plants and trees), 2 mineral totems, 2 place totems (an embanked reservoir of water and a marsh or surface spring), and 2 split totems (rice soup and pig entrails). Most of the totems are derived from the flora and fauna of their habitat. A few have been more recently added after they had acquired a knowledge of agriculture and metals. They have no individual totems or sex totems. They have very few legends of totem origins, and no traces of descent totemism. Some legends indicate that the totem was of help to the human ancestor of the clan, others on the contrary that the human ancestor was of help to the totem, and still others to other experiences and incidents. Totem taboos of the usual variety (abstention from hurting, killing, eating or using the totem) prevail generally. But modifications of the taboo to enable use of indispensable articles of diet or household use have in some instances occurred. Thus the members of the Khes or Paddy clan abstain only from eating the scum that forms on rice-soup when it stands in a cool place. Similar modifications have been made by the Salt clan, the Iron clan, the Pig clan and the Bara clan. Hence split totems, Roy opines, might have arisen from such considerations as also from the segmentation of a single original clan, as Frazer suggested. In other cases the taboos have been extended on the basis of similarity to other objects. Men of the Tiger clan, for instance, also abstain from eating the flesh of the squirrel as its striped skin resembles that of the tiger. In some cases two totems seem to have arisen out of the desire to adopt a more respectable name than that implied by the original totem. In some villages, to quote an example, members of the Kispotta (Pig Entrails) clan gave as their gotra name the kassi tree, but observed taboos towards both pigs and the kassi tree. Fusion of clans may be another possible explanation of this phenomenon.

A few Oraon clans offer divine honours and sacrifices to their totem emblems. In one village where the Bhuinars, or descendants of the original Oraon founders of the village, belong to the Ekka or Tortoise clan, a wooden image of a pig and two wooden images of the tortoise (which, it was claimed, are the offspring of the pig) are kept in the village priest's house. On the day before the *jatra* or dancing-tryst held periodically in the neighbourhood, the images are brought out, ceremonially bathed, painted in appropriate colours, anointed with vermilion, and offered a libation of rice-beer and the sacrifice of a chicken. In another village two wooden images of tigers, and in still another wooden images of a fish and of crocodiles receive similar honours. Offerings to these images are also made by other Oraon during the transportation to the jatra grounds. There are likewise a few variations in the form of the custom in points of detail from place to place. But in the majority of the cases the wooden or metal images carried nowadays to the jatras are recently and arbitrarily adopted emblems, and do not represent the totems of the Bhuinars or other Oraon. In the few cases in which these emblems represent the totems of the Bhuinars, they reflect the arrested evolution of totems into totem deities. At any rate they are believed to be connected with the luck of the village or federation of villages (*parha*) concerned, and in many instances have been replaced by flags.

Although the social system of the Oraon is still based on totemism, clan exogamy, and patriliny, totemism and the sense of clan solidarity have begun to decline. Thus the violation of the totem taboos does not entail any serious consequences, although the older people still say that it is unsafe. The parha or federation of villages has begun to replace the clan as a social unit, and blood-relationship exogamy extending to three generations also serves as a regulator of marriages.

The Oraon, as Haddon emphasized, have been considerably influenced by the Munda; and Hutton goes so far as to believe that they actually gave up a Munda language in favour of their present Dravidian one. Roy's description of their physical traits demonstrates that they are not much different from the other tribal groups classed broadly together as Proto-Australoid, or somewhat more narrowly as Gondid. As compared with the

Munda, however, Basu says that while they have many characters which closely agree, there are basic differences by which they can usually be distinguished from one another. So far as their totem cult is concerned, Niggemeyer believes that, as compared with their exogamous totemism and related taboos, it is a relatively recent development which has deviated into a side-track and has grown rigid there.[49] As for the Maler, who are supposedly related to the Oraon, they have no totemism at all.

A recent study (1963) of the Oraon of the Sunderban area (West Bengal), a population which had begun to migrate from Chota Nagpur about a hundred years ago, offers an excellent opportunity for a comparison of the totemic organizations in the two areas. The Oraon of the Sunderban area still continue to have a number of exogamous, totemic clans known as gotors or gotros, but the village forms the most important social unit. There are no sub-clans or single-clan villages. The clan today serves merely in the regulation of marriage, the decline of clan consciousness being ascribed to the impact of Hinduism. There is little or no knowledge of the origins of the totems; though sometimes it is explained that their ancestors were helped in some way by the totems. A few instances of the violation of clan exogamy have also occurred; but in such cases the parents of both parties have to pay a fine to the village panchayat, after which the culprits are allowed to lead a normal social life. If the fine is not paid, they are regarded as outcastes and cannot participate in the communal activities of the village. As among the Oraon of Chota Nagpur, so also among those of the Sunderban area: when the totem is an object of daily necessity or indispensable household use the totem taboo is modified to suit the convenience of the people concerned. Thus the members of the Dhanwar or Paddy gotro only abstain from eating a particular variety which is not common in the area. Totem taboos have in general been much relaxed. Split totems, which are found in Chota Nagpur, occur also in the Sunderban area. An example is the Kisputta clan whose totem is pig's entrails. Multiple totems are few among the migrant Oraon, and not as clear as among those in Chota Nagpur. Curiously, although surrounded by Hindu castes and otherwise much influenced by Hinduism, the Oraon of the Sunderban area do not offer instances of the desire to change their totem names to more respectable ones, a few examples of which had been registered by Roy for the Oraon of Chota Nagpur. But some members of the Kinduar clan often say that they also belong to the Shol clan because the meaning of both the clan names in the Sunderban area is the same, a kind of fish. The same holds true of some

members of the Kiss, the Suar and the Kalaharin clans, which
have the meaning ' pig '. There is no totem worship among the
Oraon of West Bengal of the kind noted by Roy in Chota Nagpur, in which brass or earthen figures of animals played a role.
A number of clans mentioned by Dalton, Risley and Roy are
totally absent among the Oraon of the Sunderban area, and new
ones have sprung up among them. Of 39 clans listed for the
Sunderban area, 27 have animal names, 6 those of trees, plants
or their products, 3 of inanimate objects, and 3 were unidentified.[50]

## The Khond (Kandh, Kui, etc.)

Apart from brief references to animal descent by Campbell [51]
and to their animal and plant names by Macpherson [52] and one
or two others, we have to depend for information on Khond
totemism mainly on J. E. Friend-Pereira's article in the *Journal
of the Asiatic Society of Bengal* (1904). Located in Orissa, Andhra
Pradesh, Bihar and Madhya Pradesh, the Khond speak a language, Kui, which bears considerable resemblance to Telugu,
Tamil and Kanarese in grammar and vocabulary.[53] Dalton regards them as a mixed race of Kol, Gond and Aryans and reports
the practice of human sacrifice (*meriah*) and female infanticide
on a large scale. They are patrilineal and strictly agricultural
with a religion related to the fertility of the earth, and have
bachelors' and girls' dormitories.[54] Risley states that they live by
hunting and rude cultivation, that in spite of ' stringent inquiries ' no exogamous divisions could be traced, and that marriage is regulated by prohibited degrees. Later, however, he learnt
of fifty *gochis* or exogamous septs of a territorial nature in
Orissa. Each gochi has sub-septs or *klambus*.[55] Thurston & Rangachari tell us that in the bridal procession they carry brass figures
which include those of peacocks, chameleons, cobras, crabs, horses,
deer, tigers, cocks and elephants.[56] Russell & Hiralal say that they
have two main divisions—Kuttia or Hill Khond and Plains
Khond. The Plains Khond have endogamous divisions of which
the Raj Khond are the highest. Traditionally they claim 32 exogamous septs, but the number has now increased. The septs are
localized and take their names from villages, titles or nicknames.
The septs are divided into sub-septs such as Bachhas (calf),
Chhattra (umbrella), Hikoka (horse), Kelka (kingfisher), Konjaka
(monkey), Mandinga (earthen pot) and Kadam (a kind of tree).
The names of the septs appear to belong to the Khond language,
but those of the sub-septs are all Uriya words, indicating their
recent origin. The totems are considered sacred, and there are

indications of totem taboos. Septs and sub-septs are exogamous, the same sub-sept being sometimes found in several different septs.[57]

Friend-Pereira deals with the Malua or Mal Khond of the northern section, who are more primitive than the Plains or Uriya Khond. The Malua or Mal Khond are divided into communes or confederacies and septs or sub-septs. The Chhota Paju or Chhota Padki commune consists of six territorial areas called *mutha*, which form three pairs of sub-communes. In each of the six exogamous muthas there are families of various stocks with different totems, the six muthas together forming an exogamous unit also. Eleven stocks are mentioned, of which seven have ' totems '. These are the elephant, the cudgel, the clarinet, the cane, the chameleon, the potter's hammer and the kettledrum. The Tin Pari or Borgocha commune comprises three dominant septs or communes—Dela Pari with a twig as a totem and traces of an allied taboo; Kalea Pari, the totem of which could not be ascertained; and Sidu Pari, the members of which will not enter caves or dig wells or tanks. The Bengrika commune has two muthas—Bhetimendi and Tuniamendi, the Bheti being the dominant stock in the former and the Bengri in the latter. The totem of the Bheti stock is a torch made of twisted rope. The Ath Kombo communes are a loose confederacy of eight divisions, consisting of two communes with four sub-communes each. Each sub-commune has numerous totem stocks. A numerically important totem sept is the Hansari (wild duck), which traces its origin to the egg of the wild duck. A totem sept of the Tol Charo Kombo has the *siali* or giant creeper as its totem. The creeper is taboo to the sept. The Tin Kombo communes have the following totems: the tender shoot of the bamboo, the fruit of the sal tree, the horn of an animal, the trunk of a certain tree, the branch of the same tree, the she bear, the cloth worn round the loins by women, the lac insect, and the palas tree. Some totems of the wilder Khond of the west and Gumsar are the frog, the snake, the button quail, the lesser florican, the crow pheasant, the mohul tree and grass. The Khond have a series of exogamous circles extending from the smallest unit to one of truly stupendous magnitude. But the actual exogamous circle is the commune within which marriage is strictly forbidden although it consists of different totem stocks. Thus the exogamy of the Khond is based on real or fictitious blood-relationship between the members of the various stocks constituting the commune, but is also always subject to the wider totemic circle of prohibition that lies outside the limits of the commune. Hence Friend-Pereira concludes that totemism is ' merely a guide for the observance

of the rules of exogamy', and not its cause, that the origin of
totemism lies in the sphere of religion, and that the totem is
the protecting spirit or tutelary deity of the stock which bears
its name. For instance, when a Khond of the Chita Krandi stock
sees the totem animal, the chameleon, he immediately turns his
back and says in an awed whisper to his relations, ' I have seen
our god '. A propitiatory sacrifice is then performed to discover
why the god manifested himself.

More recently F. G. Bailey noted the existence among the
Badri Khond of two types of clan—the dispersed clan which is
significant only in the kinship system and the localized clan
which is a political unit. The dispersed clan has no single name,
but is identified in terms of pairs of ancestors. The modern
mutha is a territorial group and not a clan. As regards their
totems Bailey says: ' Most of those I questioned did not seem
surprised that they might have a totem but few could say, or
would say, what their totem was ': and as regards some of the
totem taboos described by Friend-Pereira in 1904, he adds: ' I
saw no sign of this behaviour sixty years later. . . .'[58]

Shortly after these paragraphs on the Khond had been com-
pleted I learnt from H. Niggemeyer that his book on the Kuttia
Kond, based on personal investigations in the field, had just been
published in Germany. From page proofs of the relevant material
which he very kindly sent me comes a somewhat dramatic confirmation that the Khond were not originally totemic, or at any
rate not at all strongly so. Niggemeyer investigated the clan
organization of the Kuttia Khond in the central Kuttia area, but
believes that things are the same in the other Kuttia areas. The
Kuttia Khond of the central area have about fourteen patrilineal,
exogamous clans or *godsi* in which membership depends on a
belief in descent from a common ancestor. The meanings of
most of the clan-names have been forgotten, but some signify
geographical locations and others—six in all—as the meanings
available or the myths indicate, refer to animals—the pig, the
goat, the dog, the owl and the wood-worm, and to a tree. The
Sukubitsa clan has the following story to tell: One day
Ururengan-Renarengan went on a hunt. In the hole of a withered
tree he found a rat and ate it. As Nirantali-Kapantali heard of
this, she said, ' What you have done is not good. You shall, therefore, be called Sukubitsa ' (*suku* is a kind of wood-worm). Therefore, the Sukubitsa are not allowed till today to eat rats which are
found in a hole made by wood-worms. The story related by the
Gundsika clan is somewhat similar. But in this case it was a kind
of owl that was eaten. No taboo is however reported in connexion
with the owl. The Urlaka clan has a tradition that its ancestor

11

came out of the earth at a certain place beneath the urlaka tree. The Garanga relate how various persons came out of the earth in a certain order and that as the Garanga had a dog with them, they were called Nakuri-Garanga (*nakuri*: dog). Evidence indicates that the clans were once localized, but are seldom so today. Nowadays the village has acquired greater significance than the clan, which is important only so far as exogamy is concerned. Judging from the remnants of their traditions and their clan names, Niggemeyer therefore concludes that the clans are evidently of different origin. Some clans show traces of totemic notions, but only in one instance is there a related taboo. Hence there is no occasion to suppose that all the clans of the Kuttia were once totemic. In a personal communication Niggemeyer adds: I believe that totemism has scarcely if ever played a great role among these people. If other Khond tribes are more strongly totemic, that signifies nothing much in my opinion; for I believe that the Khond or Kui-speaking tribe was originally made up of different tribes, all of which need not have been totemic.[59]

## *The Baiga*

According to Russell & Hiralal, the Baiga are divided into seven sub-tribes, each of which has exogamous septs. Many of the septs have names like those of the Gond such as Markam, Maravi, Netam, Tekam and so on. The meanings of the sept names have been forgotten and no instances of totemism are known. The Binjhal or Binjhwar of Chhattisgarh and the Bhaina of Bilaspur are probably offshoots of the Baiga tribe which, as is very likely, is in turn a branch of the Bhuiya tribe of Chota Nagpur. The Binjhwar, however, have some totemic septs (Bagh: tiger, Pod: buffalo, Kamalia: lotus, Panknali: water crow, Tor: date-palm, Jal: net, and others) and the Bhaina a number of them (Nag: cobra, Bagh: tiger, Chitwa: leopard, Gidha: vulture, Besra: hawk, Bendra: monkey, Kok or Lodha: wild dog, Bataria: quail, Durgachhia: black ant, and so on). Totem taboos and other signs of respect and veneration towards the totems, such as worship of the totem at marriages and mourning for the dead totem, also exist among the Bhaina.[60]

Verrier Elwin, however, was the first to undertake a systematic study of the Baiga. From his monograph (1939) we learn that the Baiga tribe is divided into a number of endogamous units called jat which are in turn subdivided into exogamous garh and goti. The garh are the more important of the two and are territorial and not totemic. The goti, as Baiga traditions indicate, are borrowed from the Gond. There are faint traces of totem taboos among some Baiga, but speaking generally no real totemism, the one exception being a village in Amtera in which totemism was alive and ' obviously not borrowed '. In this village there were seven exogamous goti, each with a different tree as a totem and related rites. The Belgaria Durwa believe that the bel tree is their Bara Deo, and once a year they take a branch of the tree, bury it, and sacrifice a coconut over the place. The Karraiya Durwa believe that the karra tree is their Bara Deo. They take a cooking-pot or karaiha to the karra tree, cook bread there and sacrifice it to the tree. The Tiljaria Durwa have the tilwan tree as their totem. They grind some of it, make it into bread and then offer it. The Bartaria Durwa have the bar tree as their totem, to which they offer a *barhai* or she-goat. The Sachera Markam have the sachera or saj tree as their totem. They cook its leaves in fresh rice and offer it to the tree. The Thaurgaria Markam have the thaur tree as their totem. They also make fresh rice mixed with its leaves and offer it. Lastly, the Jhinjhigaria Markam have the bamboo clump as their totem, to which they offer bamboo shoots.[61]

Fuchs, who next investigated the Bhumia, a sub-group of the Baiga in Eastern Mandla, also found a system of territorial or *kher* exogamy [62] and gotra exogamy, both of which are contained in the endogamous tribal division called *biladeri* (brotherhood) or *jat* (breed). Fuchs confirms further that the Baiga have no real totemism, and that their gotra system together with some animal and plant names and traces of totem taboos were evidently borrowed from the Gond. The Bhumia appear to be the oldest settlers in their present habitat, but in all tracts where there are Baiga the population is ' overwhelmingly Gondish '. It is therefore not surprising that the Baiga reveal a high degree of economic and cultural dependence on the Gond. Fuchs regards the Nahal as in all likelihood the westernmost branch of the Baiga, and thinks that the Bhaina, a section of the Baiga, borrowed their totemism from the Kawar of eastern Madhya Pradesh.[63]

Russell's view that the Baiga (who are located in Madhya Pradesh, Bihar and Orissa) are a branch of the great Bhuiya tribe which numbers more than half a million in Bihar, Orissa and Bengal, is shared with varying degrees of conviction and reservation by Roy, Elwin and Fuchs. This identification would thus relate the Baiga to the Kolarian or Munda-speaking tribes. Further, both Hutton and Elwin are inclined to accept Russell's hypothesis that there were two separate settlements of Munda-speaking tribes into the region: the first comprising the Bhar, the Bhuiya, the Baiga and other related tribes which lost their own language, and the second comprising the tribes which still speak Munda languages and retain to a fair measure the elements of their own culture. On the other hand, Fürer-Haimendorf classifies the Kamar, the Baiga and the Reddi together for reasons referred to earlier, and thus relates them to a cultural stratum which even antedates the ' neolithic Austroasiatics '. The Reddi of the Bison Hills in the Godavari area have clan exogamy, but no totemism. They are racially mixed but are basically much more primitive than the Bastar Gond, the Koya and the Khond.[64] Quite in contrast to these views, however, is that of Walter Ruben. Ruben believes that the Baiga, the Bhaina, the Birhor, the Bhuiyar, the Birjia and similar groups were the original bearers of totemism in India, and that the Baiga lost their totemism through Gond influence.[65]

As has been pointed out earlier, the Bhil merit a chapter to themselves. We shall therefore confine our critical remarks on the totemism of the ' Gondid ' tribes to the end of the next chapter.

## NOTES AND REFERENCES

[1] Heine-Geldern, 1936, 252.

[2] Guha, 1944, 7-29.

[3] The Hinduized or detribalized sections call themselves Gond, the Gondi-speaking sections Koitur (Fürer-Haimendorf, 1948, 1).

[4] Grierson classifies the Dravidian language groups as follows: Dravida, Intermediate, Andhra (Telugu), North-West (Brahui), and semi-Dravidian hybrids. The Dravida group consists of Tamil, Malayalam, Kanarese, Kodagu, Tulu, Toda and Kota (1927, 83-4). Other languages of the intermediate group are Kolami, Kandhi, Kurukh, Malhar and Malto (1927, 88).

[5] Grigson, 1938, 318.

[6] His introduction to Grigson, 1938, xiii-xiv.

[7] Quoted by Elwin, 1947, 19-20.

[8] 1948, 39-41.

[9] 1952, 145-8.

[10] 1960a, 11-12.

[11] Grigson, 1938, xii; Fürer-Haimendorf, 1948, 1; Fuchs, 1960a, 14.

[12] Grigson, 1938, xv-xvi; Aiyappan, 1955, 43; Fuchs, 1960a, 12.

[13] 1948, 3-4. See also his article on the Megalithic Cultures in Middle India (1945a).

[14] In spite of various attempts at an explanation, the origin of the term Gond remains obscure. Crooke (1896, II, 430-5) states that it probably means inhabitant of Gauda or Western Kosala, but Hislop derives it from the Telugu *konda*, a hill, and Oppert traces it to the Dravidian root *ko, konda*, that is, a mountain.

[15] 1916, III, 506.

[16] 1948, 1-3.

[17] 1960a, 12-13.

[18] 1891, I, 292-4; 1892, II, App. I, 54. Ghurye (1959, 243), however, thinks that Risley's septs are really sub-septs.

[19] 1891, 276-87.

[20] 1896, II, 430-5.

[21] 1910, 791-7.

[22] 1916, III, 41-94. For a criticism of Russell & Hiralal, see Grigson, 1938, 235-9. Grigson locates Russell's five classes in the Bison-Horn country and its cultural extension, the Dorla country. The moieties mentioned by Russell, says Grigson, could only have reference to the Hill Maria country. But Grigson himself found no system of moieties among the Hill Maria and explains Russell's 159 clans as against his own 50 for the Hill Maria as probably implying the inclusion of many areas that are not occupied by the Hill Maria.

[23] 1920, I, 216-21.

[24] 1933, 609.

[25] That is to say, these ten have a question-mark under the column ' totem '.

[26] Russell & Hiralal mention 19 septs, manifestly for the Bison-Horn Maria, Grigson 57. Grigson adds: ' Like the Muria phratries mentioned by Russell and Hiralal, these phratries are often described as the *bans*, a Hindu word for race, of their totems: the Marvi phratry in most of the Bison-horn country is the *Bakrabans* or Goat race, and in Sukma and the south the *Nagvans* or Cobra race; the Kuhrami phratry is the *Kadiarbans* or Cuckoo race; the Sodi phratry is the *Baghbans* or Tiger race; and both the Markami and the Kawari phratries are *Kachhimvans* or Tortoise race ' (1938, 240).

[27] This legend, says Grigson, is the only trace among the Bastar Maria of the Ramcharsa legend of the origin of the Gond. As Trench has it in his *Grammar of Gondi* (Vol. II), the ancestors of the Gond were blocked on their way to worship the Great God by a great flood. So they plunged hastily into the river, and one caught hold of a tendu log, another a sirras, another a palm tree, another a teak, another an iguana, another a tiger and so on, and thus crossed the river. Later they asked one another what they had caught hold of; and Addi-rawan-pariol added, ' Then your *pari* will be the palm tree, yours the teak, and yours the tiger '. And so paris were found for all of them (Grigson, 1938, 241).

[28] 1938, 3, 204, 207, 236-43.

[29] The rest of the legend is the same as described in footnote 27. The source is likewise Trench. The Gond of Jashpur State have a similar story.

[30] Buradkar (1940, 122) thinks that the legend of Bageshwar has a true totemic ring and points clearly to the former identification of the clansmen with their totem.

[31] Buradkar, 1940; 1947.

[32] An earlier study is that of Indrajit Singh, 1944. Singh concentrates attention on the Gond in the hills and jungles of the Central Provinces and Bastar, and is concerned more with the economic than with the social side of Gond life. His treatment of totemism is cursory and sweeping, and does not contribute much new material or lend new insights to the problem. Elwin's *Maria Murder and Suicide* (Bombay, 1943) and other works on the Gond are much more narrowly conceived than the present one.

[33] 1947, 5, 59-69.

[34] Fürer-Haimendorf (44) prefers to speak of the 7-brother phratry, 6-brother phratry and so on rather than of 7-god phratry, 6-god phratry, etc., because the word ' wen ' is better translated as ' divine ancestor ' than as ' god ', and the members of each phratry trace their origin to 7, 6, 5,

and 4 mythical brothers respectively, who are now revered as ancestors.

35 1948, 5-6, 44-5.

36 1960a, 19, 71, 133, 141-9, 152-8; 1960b, 43-51.

37 Russell & Hiralal, 1916, ii, 18-34; Hassan, 1920, i, 3; Enthoven, 1920, i, 17-26.

38 Risley, 1891, i, 3-14; 1892, ii, App. I, 1; Crooke, 1896, i, 1-12; Russell & Hiralal, 1916, ii, 3-6; Elwin, 1942, xxvii, 2-23, 68-92.

39 Russell & Hiralal, 1916, ii, 271-6; Elwin, 1947, 11.

40 Russell & Hiralal, 1916, iii, 323-30; Dube, 1951, i-vii, 1-5, 68-73, 174.

41 Russell & Hiralal, 1916, iii, 520-4; Fürer-Haimendorf, 1948, 32-7.

42 Russell & Hiralal, 1916, iii, 62; iv, 371-8; Grigson, 1938, 36, 40-1.

43 Russell & Hiralal, 1916, iv, 352-6; Hivale, 1946, 1, 3, 10-12, 20-7, 29-42; Fürer-Haimendorf, 1948, 47-9; 1951; P. S. Rao, 1949, 56-7.

44 Tribal Map of India, Dept. of Anthropology, Govt. of India.

45 1872, 245-63.

46 1892, ii, 138-49, App. I, 113-14. Roy (1915, 327) points out that in Risley's list some of the totem names are given twice, once in Oraon and again in Hindi.

47 1904, 12-19.

48 1906, 160.

49 Roy, 1915a; 1915b, x, xiii-xiv, 1, 10-11, 81, 309-44; 1928, 82-4; Hutton, 1933, 358; Basu, 1933-4; Niggemeyer, 1933, 451; Sarkar, 1938; Vidyarthi, 1963.

50 Das & Raha, 1963, 87-102.

51 Quoted by Frazer, 1910, ii, 304.

52 1865, 78.

53 Winfield, 1928, xiii.

54 1872, 285-301.

55 1891, i, 397-409.

56 1909, iii, 391.

57 1916, iii, 464-73.

58 1960, 43, 47, 59, 88.

59 1964, 45-8.

60 1916, ii, 77-85, 225-33, 329-34.

61 172-5.

62 Elwin speaks of it as garh exogamy, which Fuchs avers is a term used by the Gond for their territorial, exogamous units.

63 1960a, 3-11, 15-18, 133-7, 139-41.

64 1945b, vii, 15, 26, 161-6.

65 1939, 177.

# VI

# THE BHIL

WITH A POPULATION strength of 2,246,570 in 1941, the Bhil are the third largest tribal group in India. They are found in Rajasthan, Gujarat, Madhya Pradesh, Maharashtra and Andhra Pradesh, but are concentrated mainly in the northwest or the Vindhya, Aravalli and Satpura Hills. Early officials, missionaries and travellers had of course not failed to register their observations on the Bhil, but the turning-point in Bhil research came with Koppers' systematic work *Die Bhil in Zentralindien* (1948). Since then interest in Bhil studies has gathered pace, and works on this important tribal population by qualified persons have steadily grown in number.

An early reference to totems and taboos is that of E. Barnes in his article 'The Bhils of Western India' (1906-7). Speaking of the Naik who are reckoned among the southern Bhil, Barnes says that many of their clans are totemic, and asserts the existence of totem descent, totem taboos, totem tattooing and a high degree of reverence towards the totem. The question is, however, whether Barnes' report can be fully trusted;[1] and Shah, who recently made a brief study of the tribe, found no totemism among them, but reports the custom of wooden or clay images of the tiger, the elephant, the horse and the camel being presented to the gods, who are invoked at a small wooden post near their houses.[2]

By far the best of the earlier reports is that of Luard (1909). Referring to the Bhil of Malwa, Luard points out that the septs are differently given from place to place, mentioning several corroborative lists in his appendices, that considerable difficulty was experienced in tracing totems, that the usual reverence is paid to the totem object, that its representation is never tattooed on the body, and that the Bhil do little cultivation. In his main list Luard enumerates 122 septs, of which 23 are connected in some way or other with trees, 19 with animals and 15 with other objects.[3] Taboos are mentioned for approximately 24 of these animals, trees and other objects, worship at marriages for 26;

---

[1] For notes to this chapter see p. 167.

and for five (the lizard, the crab, the wild boar, the peacock, the spider) effigies are made and worshipped at marriages. The other groups mentioned by Luard—the Bhilala, the Patlia, the Rathia, the Mankar and the Tarvi Bhil of Barwani—appear to be of mixed descent or strongly influenced by the Bhil, and show fewer traces of totemism.[4] Russell & Hiralal report that the Bhil of the Central Provinces have two subdivisions—the Muhammadan Bhil and the remainder. Both divisions have exogamous clans named after plants and animals which they revere. In a list which is not exhaustive the authors mention 4 septs with trees as totems, 4 with animals (the peacock, the horse, the cat and a fish), one named after the grinding mill and another, which has 4 sub-septs, after the sun; two worship particular goddesses and several have names of Rajput clans. There are traces of totem taboos and other forms of veneration.[5] Enthoven, referring mainly to the Bhil of Gujarat and Khandesh, says that they have numerous clans named after other tribes, after animals and trees and miscellaneously. He lists 17 totem clans, of which 12 have animal, and the others vegetable totems (trees, flowers, etc.). All have related taboos. Furthermore, the tiger is worshipped, and grief is expressed at its death. The pumpkin is also worshipped, red lead being smeared on it and slices offered to the gods.[6] Sarat Chandra Roy, who studied the Black Bhil of Jaisamand Lake in Rajputana and embodied his findings in a small article, notes that the Black or Kalia Bhil are wilder in expression and darker in skin colour than the Ujla or Mina Bhil. Unlike the Palia Bhil (a name given to the other Bhil by the Kalia Bhil) who depend mainly on agriculture, the Kalia Bhil eke out their existence through fishing, food-collecting and rudimentary agriculture. The Kalia Bhil have totemic clans, of which more than one are found in a village. But totemism among the Kalia Bhil is only a mechanism for regulating marriage, and has nothing to do with their religion. On the other hand, the totemic groups of the Palia Bhil are localized, and totemism has 'retained or acquired' a religious aspect among them. The members of the Suan got or Black Nag Serpent clan, for instance, light a lamp and burn incense every evening in the name of the totem, maintain the usual taboos towards it, and are in duty bound to cremate the dead body of the totem if they come across one. The Palia Bhil forbid marriages not only within the clan but also between persons of different clans who sacrifice to the same clan gods. The Kalia Bhil appear to have no traditions of totem descent or legends narrating the origins of clans.[7] Paul Konrad's *Zur Ethnographie der Bhil*,[8] which is both incomplete and in some directions inaccurate,[9] merely adds a fact or two to the list of 122 septs contained in the *Census of India* 1931. Most of the other reports which preceded Koppers' study either make no reference to totemism at all or very general allusions to it.[10]

Koppers carried out his personal investigations chiefly in Jhabua State, which to all intents and purposes is the heart of the Bhil territory. He reports the existence of numerous exogamous, patrilineal clans, but very few traces of totemism. In Rambhapur approximately 36 clans were discovered, of which one, the Parmar clan, has two sub-clans and three other clans associated with it in an exogamous bond. Two other clans, the Pargi and the Mero, are also associated together in a similar way. Of the 36 clans 3 are connected with animals (the porcupine, the crab), 4 with trees and 3 with other objects (dagger, stick, axe). Of the rest no meanings could be traced. In the Nandurbar area (West Khandesh) several sub-tribes and clans were found which differed entirely from those in the Jhabua area. Traces of totemism in the Nandurbar area are exceedingly scanty. Three groups—the Mauchi, the Pawrya and the Ambura —do not fell teak trees or use their leaves during the period from the Diwali feast to Dashahra. It is believed that if this taboo is infringed, tigers or snakes will revenge themselves on the culprits. In Ambapara, apart from a limited number of new clans (eight in all), essentially the same situation prevails as in Rambhapur. One of these eight clans has the pig as a totem and the usual taboo. Violation of the taboo brings a kind of nettle-rash all over the body as a punishment. In the Udaipur-Kherwara area the clan names are again the same as those in the Rambhapur and Ambapara areas. Six new clans were discovered, but the existence of totems remained doubtful.[11]

Towards Luard's findings Koppers takes the following stand. Considering the difficulties experienced in procuring information on clan relations (as Luard himself states), the results are accordingly not in every respect satisfactory. Again, it appears that in the investigations more goodwill than expert experience was involved, and so a number of clan names which do not occur in the area were noted down. Therefore, if one leaves out all the clans which are locally not present and also other doubtful cases, 43 clan names remain over, which agree in the main with Koppers' list. Of these 43, 19 are connected in some way or other with plants, 17 with animals and 7 with other objects. As Koppers himself encountered far fewer examples of such relations he suspects that in this respect, too, the informants were overwhelmed with leading questions. Further, there is no evidence of totem descent, and the relation to the animal, plant or other object is general and vague. In most instances the names of the clans are identical with those of the animals, plants or objects concerned; but that is not always the case. In these relations plants (or trees) are frequent. In almost half the number of cases, the plant or parts of it are used in the marriage celebrations. There is talk of a general respect towards the plants concerned, and in some instances the rule to avoid felling the tree or eating its fruits is also mentioned. Towards the animals or parts and products of animals there is a kind of reverence which is accompanied by the rule to avoid killing or eating them. In seven instances the animals appear in the marriage ceremonies. Three of the seven other objects also appear in the marriage ritual. Koppers' critical evaluation of Luard's findings is of fundamental importance, since Luard's report is the best of the earlier ones.[12]

Koppers points out further that the clan names of the Bhil and those of the Rajputs and the Gujars agree only in a few cases. Hence he concludes that the Bhil were in possession of their 'totemic' clans before they came into close contact with the Gujars and the Rajputs. This does not signify that totemic clans were necessarily and originally characteristic of the Bhil. In the strict sense of the word there is no localization of clans today; but there is some evidence to show that at one time a strong localization of clans prevailed among the Bhil.[13]

Naik's work (1956) deals with the Bhil of Rajpipla and West Khandesh in Gujarat. He enumerates 36 clans which differ from those listed by Koppers. Some of these clans are named after villages and other places of origin, and some after other tribes. The others seem to have a totemic origin, says Naik; but apart from three—Henglya (bidi-leaf tree), Dogrya (mountain), and Wanariwala (monkey)—he gives us no other instances of totemic clans or of meanings which could be regarded as totemic. There are no traces of respect or veneration towards the totems, and apart from the use of the names as means of identifying clan members, the significance of the totems has evaporated. In the Panch Mahals and Sabarkantha there are a number of large, patrilineal descent groups or *atak*, consisting of a number of lineages, bearing the same name and claiming descent from the same mythical ancestor, and hence regarding one another as kin. There is no mention of totemism with regard to these groups.[14]

Nath, too, finds but few traces of totemism among the Bhil of Ratanmal and Kathiawar. There are, he says, a large number of patrilineal, exogamous clans or atak bearing names which seem in the main to be eponymous. He finds no totemic practices of the type described in the *Census of India* (1931) in Ratanmal and Kathiawar; and apart from matters of descent, identification and exogamy the clans have little significance to the Bhil. To the Bhil of the Aravalli-Malwa region Nath assigns 60 clans without mentioning the existence of any totems. The Bhil clans break up into lineages which vary in depth from six to seven generations. Nath finds further that Venkatachar's totemic data in the *Census of India* (1931) are too meagre and inconclusive, and suggests that the worship of the dagger may relate more to the martial traditions of the people than to some past totemic belief. Finally, actuated by his functional and structural interests, he records some instances of the emergence of new sub-clans through the process of fission. The new sub-clans (or clans) adopt eponymous names or more often names which refer to some historical incident.[15]

From among the mixed groups two—the Bhilala and the Grasia—may be singled out for brief mention as illustrative instances. The Bhilala have been regarded as descendants of Rajputs and Bhil by Forsyth, Luard, Russell and others.[16] Luard states that there is a lack of unanimity in Malwa about the names and number of their septs, that practically no septs are now traceable to totemic origins although many names possibly once had totemic meanings, that many names are of local and others of Rajput origin, and that they constitute a large endogamous group divided into 42 septs.[17] Russell & Hiralal, alluding to the Bhilala of Nimar and Hoshangabad in the Central Provinces, say that they have exogamous groups called *kul* or *kuri*, some of which have Rajput clan names and others totemic ones. The totems mentioned are the jamun tree, the san hemp tree, the sona tree and the pipal tree. There are also traces of totem taboos.[18] More recently Haekel, who undertook a field study of some groups of the Bhilala, found next to no traces of totemism among them.[19] The Grasia, inhabiting the states of Gujarat and Rajasthan, are likewise in all probability of mixed Rajput and Bhil descent. A recent work on this group mentions the existence of exogamous divisions or gotras, but no totemism.[20]

Considered in their entirety the Bhil are linguistically, racially and culturally heterogeneous. Their language, Bhilli, is clearly related to Gujarati, but also shows varying admixtures of other Aryan languages such as Rajasthani and Marathi. Some have sought to relate Bhilli in its origin to the Munda languages; others to the Dravidian; but Koppers, going still further backward, holds out the possibility that it was once a pre-Munda and pre-Dravidian language. Racially Eickstedt regards the Bhil as predominantly but not purely North Gondid; referring to the Bhil of West Vindhya Guha sees a similarity between them and the Chenchu and (to a less extent) the Kadar; D. N. Majumdar regards the Bhil of Gujarat as a hybrid group with a recognizable tribal substratum and a high degree of admixture with the Rajputs and other more advanced castes; and others connect them variously with the Oraon, the Gond, the Santal and the Koli. Many observers speak of their dark or very dark skin colour, thus pointing perhaps to tribes more primitive than the Gond, the Oraon and the like. Others derive their name from the Dravidian word for ' bow ', which, if correct, may be interpreted as a Dravidian designation for the primitive food-gatherers and hunters of the subcontinent. Russell & Hiralal say that they have been recognized as the oldest inhabitants of South Rajputana and parts of Gujarat, and in confirmation add the custom whereby some Rajput chiefs have to be marked on the forehead with Bhil blood on their accession to power. On the other hand, Robert Shafer (1954) affirms the belief that they occupied a vast area from the Ganges to the western coast, and from the Himalayas to the northern edge of the present Dravidian territory, and that Nahali which represents the remains of the Bhilli language identifies them with the pre-Dravidian type which once occupied much of India.

As Koppers points out, however, the Bhil are in part related to the Chenchu, the Reddi and other old tribes which are both pre-Munda and pre-Dravidian. Originally hunters, fishers and food-collectors, they later acquired primitive cultivation and absorbed at different times both different influences and different strains. From the Gujars they got their present language and stock-breeding; and some elements from the Mundas and the Dravidians. The paucity of totemic elements among them seems to indicate that they had no totemic clan organization to start with; and that they adopted it in a weakened form from some tribal neighbours.

The later history of the Bhil may be described in terms of two possible hypotheses: (i) the loss of their common cultural heritage through a process of adaptation to other regional cultures, and the retention of a consciousness of kind rooted in the belief of a common origin and basic unity; or (ii) the classification of a number of different tribes under the generic term Bhil by more advanced populations who established their rule over the aborigines, and as a result the gradual growth of a common tribal consciousness. Majumdar, Fürer-Haimendorf and Nath incline to the second of these two hypotheses. But whatever the origin of the term Bhil and however widely it has been extended, the fact remains that the core of this 2,246,570-strong population shows a series of traits which connect it with an old cultural stratum that was both, as Koppers suggests, pre-Munda and pre-

Dravidian with food-gathering, hunting and fishing as its economic basis, local rather than clan exogamy as one of its sociological traits, and little or no totemism.[21]

\*    \*    \*

With the totemic evidence culled from both old and new
sources before us, we are thus in a position to test the accuracy
of Niggemeyer's conclusion that the important Gondid tribes—
the Bhil, the Baiga, the Korku, the Gond, the Oraon, the Maria,
the Kui and others—still retain a living totemism which is the
basis of their social life. From this evidence it follows clearly
that the Bhil, the Baiga and the Korku do not have a strong
or very old type of totemism, and must therefore be excluded
from Niggemeyer's list. The Bhil must be excluded because the
new and more accurate sources (Koppers, Naik, Nath) present
but few traces of totemism among them, because the evidence
offered by the principal old source (Luard), when critically
examined, undergoes a considerable shrinkage, and because the
nature of the remaining evidence (predominance of plant totems,
worship at marriages) points towards external influences. The
Baiga must also be excluded because, as both old and new
sources (Russell, Elwin, Fuchs) show, totemism is negligible
among them. As the Baiga are everywhere in close contact with
the Gond, the few traces of totemism among the former may
be ascribed to Gond influence, the one exception, according to
Elwin, being the tree totems prevailing in a village at Amtera.
But here again the fact that the totems are trees and are worshipped as divinities seems to point towards external influences
from a population other than the Gond, the influences being
' islanded ' so to say as a result of various other local factors.
It is furthermore indubitable that territorial exogamy and not
clan exogamy was and is the prevalent form among the Baiga.
The Korku, too, must be excluded from Niggemeyer's list not
only because they belong linguistically and culturally to the
Munda-speaking tribes, but also because the totemic evidence
available is too meagre and of a kind which points towards a
westward orientation.

This leaves us with the Gond (including the Maria and the
Muria), the Oraon and the Khond. This shortened list coincides
in the main with that of Schmidt who believed that the four
Gondid tribes—the Gond, the Muria, the Khond and the Oraon
—possess the oldest form of totemism in India.

If we, then, first turn our attention to the Gond, and assume
with Fürer-Haimendorf that a number of tribes localized in Central India and immediately adjoining areas were ' Dravidianized '

by a small, advanced but no longer identifiable group arriving from the south, we may classify the Gond tribes into two broad groups—the Hill Maria, the Bison-Horn Maria and the Muria of Bastar would thus form one group, and the rest of the tribal Gond in the former Central Provinces and elsewhere the other. The Hill Maria, the Bison-Horn Maria and the Muria show several cultural similarities with the Munda-speaking tribes of Orissa and Chota Nagpur, and therefore stand somewhat apart from the rest of the Dravidianized tribes bearing the common name Gond or Koitur. From Grigson's data on the Hill Maria (and Grigson's monograph is about the most reliable source on the Maria that we have at our disposal) it is clear that traces of totemism are very slight among them. It may therefore be inferred that the Hill Maria secured their weak totemism from some external quarter. The Bison-Horn Maria have both phratries and clans. All the phratries have totems, but only ten of the fifty-seven clans have them. Further, from the fact that the phratry totems are of less importance than the clan totems, and from certain additional evidence pointing towards the weak and confused character of their totemism, Grigson concludes that the totemism of the Bison-Horn Maria was either borrowed from another culture or is now in a phase of considerable decline. Not far removed from the Maria, however, are the Muria of Narayanpur and Khondagaon, among whom, as Elwin shows, totemism exists in relative strength—a fact which casts a measure of doubt on the ascription of the present state of Bison-Horn totemism to factors of decline and decadence only. It would, therefore, seem preferable to explain the totemism of the Bison-Horn Maria as borrowed but not really assimilated rather than as a decadent phase of an inherent and once flourishing totemism. From this it follows that the Hill Maria and the Bison-Horn Maria probably acquired their elements of Munda culture before, and the Muria after, they had acquired their totemism.

The totemism of the rest of the Gond tribes can be well described in general terms as dilute (Fuchs) or decadent (Buradkar). As with the Munda-speaking tribes, so with the Gond and their immediate neighbours: in the main the decline of totemism must be ascribed to the pervasive and corrosive effects of the Hindu culture, and is to that extent a relatively recent phenomenon.

Other conclusions arising from the evidence summarized above may be listed as follows: (i) There are a few faint traces of totem descent among the Gond (Buradkar), and among a few related or influenced tribes like the Khond (Campbell, Friend-Pereira), the Kamar (Dube), and the Agaria (Elwin). Apart from these few instances, the other myths of origin are of the parallel-relationship variety—that is to say, they recount experiences and encounters with the totem animals or plants of a kind with other than descent connotations. Schmidt, therefore, concludes that parallel-relationship totemism can be of an equal age as descent totemism. As most of these myths in India, however, seem to be secondary justifications of totemic phenomena which had already lost much of their ideological roots, this is an issue which can only be resolved by considering the total situation in each case. (ii) Animal totems predominate over totems of the other two kinds. In this respect the Gond resemble the Khond, the Oraon and the Munda-speaking tribes. Their totemism is therefore older than that of the Bhil or of the West coast, but is not, as we shall see, the absolutely oldest form in India. (iii) Totem taboos, not always faithfully observed and no longer everywhere in existence, establish the extent of the decline in recent times, and suggest the existence at one time either among the Gond or among some other neighbours of theirs of a more consistent totemic organization. Other forms of respect and veneration and other beliefs and attitudes pointing to a stronger ideological basis in a forgotten past also show up here and there. (iv) Totemism in this area as also in that of the Munda-speaking tribes is by and large of the clan variety, and is associated with the notion of clan exogamy. Some evidence of a doubtful nature may be interpreted as referring to other forms of totemism. Individual and sex totemism do not exist among the Gond, or for the matter of that, among the Gondid. (v) Gond totemism may be said to differentiate itself broadly from that of other tribes and areas in India in terms of the following features: (*a*) the existence of phratries often classified according to the number of gods worshipped (who are probably the deified founding fathers of the original clans) and associated with one or more totems; (*b*) the fairly frequent occurrence with variations of the flood-and-tortoise myth narrating the origin of the clans and their totems. Variations of this myth occur elsewhere, but not so frequently or elaborately as among the Gond; (*c*) a series of clan names which differ linguistically from those of the Munda-speaking tribes and the tribes further south and west.

When we turn to the Khond we are confronted by the striking fact that both early and recent observers, with the exception of Friend-Pereira, do not proffer any ample evidence of the existence of totemism among them. Furthermore, Friend-Pereira's article is characterized by the use of a confused and confusing terminology and by the incompleteness of his observations. It is of course evident from Friend-Pereira's article that the more

primitive Khond of the northern areas have totems of all three
varieties—animal, vegetable and inanimate, and that perhaps
somewhat more than half the number of the units mentioned
(communes, sub-communes, septs, sub-septs, stocks and families)
have totems. Although his report is incomplete, one can perhaps
presume that animal totems exceed vegetable totems by a small
margin, and that inanimate totems are comparatively numerous,
although fewer in number than the other two kinds. Traces of
totem taboos of the usual kind seem to be few. If one next recalls
to mind Russell & Hiralal's statement, referring no doubt to the
less primitive Khond of the Central Provinces, that the septs
have Khond names and are non-totemic, whereas the sub-septs
have Uriya names and are totemic, one can scarcely conclude
with conviction that totemism was originally inherent among
the Khond or that it is of the kind which can be legitimately
described as living and fundamental in their social organization.
To this conclusion Niggemeyer's recent work on the Kuttia
Khond lends added strength.

With the Oraon, however, we are better informed, and can,
therefore, draw more definite conclusions. Most of the reports,
even that of Dalton, mention a series of totems of all three kinds.
The animal totems predominate over the plant totems, and the
plant totems over the inanimate ones. But there is no totem
descent, no individual or sex totemism, and but few myths of
origin which are of the parallel-relationship variety. Totem
taboos of the usual kind are frequent. There are some instances
of divine honours being paid to the totem emblems; and modifications and unpunished violations of the totem taboos and also
other evidence indicate that a decline of their totemism has been
going on for some time. If, following Niggemeyer, we conclude
that the offering of divine honours to the totem emblems is a
relatively recent development (and the evidence appears to
justify Niggemeyer) we may—going further—infer from the predominance of animal totems and the frequency of the totem
taboos that totemism among the Oraon is a comparatively old
phenomenon, but the absence of a definite identification between
clan and totem in inner and outer relations and other similar
pointers suggest that it is not the oldest form in India.

It thus follows that in identifying the Gondid as the original
bearers of totemism in India, Eickstedt and Niggemeyer, and,
following them, Schmidt, were casting their net much too widely
and not discriminatingly enough. The view that the totemism
of the Gond, the Muria, the Oraon and the Khond is not the
oldest in India will be examined further and vindicated in due
course.

# NOTES AND REFERENCES

[1] Koppers, 1948, 122.

[2] 1959.

[3] Venkatachar (1933), who reproduces Luard's facts in the *Census of India*, 1931, gives the following classification: of 122 Bhil septs, 52 seem totemic, 23 are tree or plant totems, 17 animals, 14 objects, 6 Rajput, 2 local, 25 no explanation and others miscellaneous. Totems worshipped 33, taboos mentioned 22; and four or five effigies are made. Koppers (1948, 118) gives 19 plants, 17 animals and 7 objects.

[4] 1909a.

[5] 1916, ii, 278-92. But Russell's survey, says Koppers (1948, 17) is only of moderate importance.

[6] 1920, i, 152-7.

[7] 1924, 97-113. Koppers (1948, 18) adds that the inquiries he made in Udaipur did not confirm Roy's view that the Kalia Bhil are an old and special form.

[8] 1939, 23-117.

[9] Koppers, 1948, 21.

[10] See Koppers' excellent examination of the earlier literature (1948, 3-41, 116-22).

[11] 1948, 109-16.

[12] ibid., 116-19.

[13] ibid., 122-3.

[14] 1956, 56-8.

[15] 1960, 72-82. In his book *Die Bhagoria Bhil* (Wiesbaden, 1964), which has just come to hand, M. Hermanns gives a list of clan names collected by the Capuchin missionaries in the Thandla district and surrounding areas. Of 57 clan names listed, 14 are those of animals, 13 of plants and 7 of inanimate objects. Eighteen instances of worship at marriages occur. Totem taboos are mentioned in nineteen cases. Twenty of these clan names agree with those in Koppers's list. Although their myths contain accounts of peculiar relations between spirits and magicians on the one side and animals and plants on the other, of which birth from a tree or fruit and transformation into animals are examples, there is no trace of descent totemism among these Bhil. According to one of Hermanns's informants, the totem animal is regarded as the father's sister. Hermanns has not made a critical evaluation of the Capuchin list, as Koppers did in regard to Luard's. Hence the question of its total validity remains open.

[16] Forsyth, 1872, 135; Luard, 1909a, 1; Russell & Hiralal, 1916, ii, 293.

[17] 1909a, 1-2.

[18] 1916, ii, 293-7.

[19] Haekel was among the Bhilala in 1960-1 and 1964.

[20] Dave, 1960.

[21] Crooke, 1896, ii, 48; Russell & Hiralal, 1916, ii, 279; Majumdar, 1950b, 24; 1961, 56-8; Shafer, 1954, 8-9, 12; Naik, 1956, Fürer-Haimendorf's foreword, x-xiv; Nath, 1960, Fürer-Haimendorf's foreword, v. For other references see Koppers, 1948, 3-41, 114. Koppers (1948, 179) is inclined to include among the Pre-Dravidian and Pre-Munda (or Pre-Austroasiatic) groups related to the Bhil also the Nahal, the Baiga, the Koli and perhaps the Balahi.

# VII

## SOUTH INDIA AND MAHARASHTRA

THE AREA to which we now turn our attention covers in the
main the following political units according to the latest delimitation of their boundaries—Andhra Pradesh, Madras, Mysore,
Kerala and Maharashtra. In the hills and jungles of this vast
area there are a number of very primitive tribes with little or
no totemism and elsewhere a very large number of castes, some
of which still retain certain tribal traits and many of which display totemic features in varying degrees. We shall here examine
a representative sample of these tribes and castes in the following order: primitive tribes, Telugu-speaking castes, matrilineal
castes, patrilineal Tamil-speaking castes, patrilineal Kanarese-
speaking castes and Marathi-speaking tribes and castes.

### Primitive Tribes

*The Kadar*: Among the primitive tribes in the more or less
inaccessible areas of South India, which, it has been claimed from
time to time, still retain some traces of Negrito ancestry, the
following are frequently mentioned: the Kadar, the Pulayan,
the Urali and the Kanikar. Adequate information on most of
these tribes is lacking. On the Kadar, however, there is Ehrenfels's full-length, ethnographic work (1952). The Kadar of Cochin,
says Ehrenfels, together with the Malapantaram of Travancore,
the Paliyar of the adjoining parts of the Madurai district, the
Paniyar of North Malabar, the Irular of Tamilnad and the
Chenchu of Telengana are among the few tribes in India which
still retain a predominantly hunting and food-gathering way of
life. In his foreword to Ehrenfels's book, however, Schmidt points
out that the Kadar are no longer at the pristine food-gathering
level, but already show advancements in material culture and
religion. There are some cultural similarities between the Kadar
and the Negrito of Malaya. Racially both Guha and Hutton
regard the Kadar as being predominantly Proto-Australoid with
some Negrito elements. The Kadar have no clan organization
or totemism. But they have a belief in male and female spirits
who live in trees, and it is said that if a person cuts the branches

of a particular tree and falls sick thereafter, he has offended the
tree spirit who has caused the sickness. There is a taboo on
buffalo flesh because the animal is considered unclean, and on
the flesh of the tiger, the bear and the elephant out of respect
towards them. A few statements refer to rebirth in animal form,
but the belief appears to have stemmed from Hinduism. The
white monkey is not eaten because it is said to resemble the
Kadar; but the flesh of the black monkey is prized as a delicacy.
In the avoidance of white monkey flesh, Ehrenfels sees a resemblance to certain Negrito beliefs (as reported by H. N. Evans
and P. Schebesta) in which some types of monkeys appear as
friends of their ancestors—‘ a sort of totemism in the making,’
says Ehrenfels.[1]

*The Kanikar*: About the Kanikar L. A. Krishna Iyer reports
the following facts: They are a hill tribe in South Travancore,
have a bachelors’ hall which is taboo to females, a type of pile
dwelling, and an exogamous dual organization in which the
moieties are named Muttillom and Menillom. The origin of the
moieties is traced to the finding of an elephant. The man who
saw the haunches and hind limbs of the elephant became the
founder of the Muttillom (*mutt*, haunches, *illom*, clan) moiety;
and the man who saw the trunk, the founder of the Menillom.
The Kanikar of Mankutty relate the following story to explain
the origin of their clan system. A sambhur (*Cervus unicolor*), it
is said, did great damage to their crops. Therefore the man who
shot and killed it with an arrow belonged to (or became the
founder of) the Kurumillom; the man who sat on a fence and
observed the event became the founder of the Vellillom; the
man who watched the fun at a distance, the founder of the Vela-
natillom; the man who cut off the head of the sambhur, the
founder of the Muttillom; the man who carried away the fore-
limbs, the founder of the Kayyillom; the man who bundled up a
small quantity of the flesh in leaves which swelled its appearance,
the founder of the Perimanillom; the man who removed the
udder of the carcase, the founder of the Mangotillom; and the
man who left a python in the water, the founder of the Perin-
chillom. The Kanikar of another area have a similar story, but
substitute an elephant for the sambhur. The other illoms are
named after localities. The Kanikar are matrilineal. They practise
both shifting and permanent cultivation, but also propitiate the
spirits of the hunt before undertaking a hunting expedition, and
make offerings of parts of the animal afterwards. The sun and

[1] For notes to this chapter see pp. 206-9.

the moon are both worshipped, the former being female and the latter male.[2]

*The Vedda*: According to Eickstedt the Vedda of Ceylon belong racially to the type called Malid, found mainly in the remote recesses of South India.[3] They practise hunting and food-gathering and also shifting cultivation. In broad terms their social organization may be described as consisting of exogamous clans with female descent. There is considerable evidence that a territorial grouping of clans once prevailed. Their religion is essentially a cult of the dead. Some of the nicknames applied to the men are those of animals, others represent personal peculiarities or habits. The flesh of the following animals is tabooed but no reasons are assigned: buffaloes, elephants, leopards, bears, jackals, wild and domestic fowl, lizards, bats, snakes and porcupines. The Seligmanns believe that these food restrictions are not connected with totemism or derived from Hinduism. The Vedda have no ceremonies for the control of game, but believe in a vague and indefinite way that the *yaku* or spirits can give success in hunting, yam-digging and honey-gathering. The ancestral spirits, Konde yaka and Bilindi yaka, are invoked for success in hunting, and offerings of the killed animal are made to them. It is believed that if these offerings are neglected bad luck will attend the hunters in the future, and they might be attacked by bears and bitten by snakes. Other spirits of the dead are also invoked for success in hunting. One of the Vedda clans, Morane, seems to have derived its name from the mora tree growing on a hill; the other clan names are probably names of localities. There is an almost total absence of myths among the Vedda, and so they have no legends about the origin of their clans. On the other hand, the Sinhalese have legends of origin for four or five of the Vedda clans. These are of the type common in India and describe incidents in the lives of the ancestors. In one of these legends the children of the ancestress fled into the jungle and lived on the fruits of the mora tree. In another a chief's daughter on the way to her bridegroom's cave drank water from a bamboo; hence her descendants were called Unapane (*una*, bamboo, *pane*, water). In the third a Morane girl became pregnant and refused to give the name of her lover; she was therefore beaten and driven away from the group and gave birth to her child in a hole dug by a wild boar, *uru*—hence Uru waruge or Uru clan. In the fourth an Unapane girl left her child under a tree while she went to dig for yams; on her return she found that red ants (*aembaleo*) had blinded her child; hence the child was called Aembali and her descendants formed the Aembala clan. In the fifth an Aembala woman gave birth to her child under a namada tree; the girl was, therefore, named Namadi, and from her descendants arose the Namadewa clan.[4]

*The Chenchu*: Located in the Eastern Ghats (Andhra Pradesh), the Chenchu resemble the Vedda of Ceylon in several ways. They are semi-nomadic food-collectors with some primitive cultivation. Thurston & Rangachari report that they have exogamous septs or inteperu, some of which are Gurram (horse), Arati (plantain tree), Mavla (trees), Tota (garden), Makala (goats), Indla (houses), Savaram (sovereign or gold coin), and Gundam (pit). Khan reports in the *Census of India*, 1931, that they have five septs, the origins of which are doubtful. Thus, Thakalu means tail in Telugu, but another version has it that it is derived from squirrel; Nimalu are Chenchu who lived in a lime grove; Erravalu refers to a man who relishes certain red roots; Siggilu is regarded as a corruption of Sigiri, the tender, edible leaves of the tamarind tree; and the origin of Maindlu is obscure. Khan thinks that ' some form of totemism exists among them '. The Chenchu have a belief in the temporary incarnation of the *jiv* or soul in an animal. Fürer-Haimendorf points out that as the idea of the dead appearing in an animal shape is also found among Indian tribes hardly touched by Hinduism, the Chenchu belief need not be ascribed to Hindu influence. In the Chenchu pantheon two deities are outstanding. These are Bhagavanturu and Garelamaisama; the former lives in the sky and no offerings are made to him; the latter lives in the jungle, has a female character perhaps derived from contact with a matrilineal, cultivating culture, and, as a powerful sylvan deity indigenous to Chenchu culture, receives offerings of parts of the animals killed and of first fruits. Garelamaisama occupies a more prominent place in the beliefs and practices of the Chenchu than Bhagavanturu. Since hunting is the most ancient of Chenchu activities, the belief in Garelamaisama as the deity who controls the activities of the wild animals of the forest and brings luck in the chase must be given a great antiquity. When the Chenchu goes hunting, when he brings down an animal, and when he returns home with his kill he prays to Garelamaisama in whose hands lie the success or failure of the hunt. The goddess also causes flowers to blossom and fruits to ripen. She is sometimes viewed as if she were male. Some Chenchu clans worship particular minor deities; further, deities connected with particular localities are believed to follow the worshippers when they migrate to other places. The Chenchu do not have many myths or legends; in one of their legends, however, a girl marries a bear and gives birth to several bear-children. The principal units of Chenchu society are the family, the patrilineal, exogamous clan

and the local group. There is hardly any tribal feeling. Of these
units the family is the most outstanding, the clan having scarcely
any functions other than that of exogamy. The clans were
probably at one time regional units, and clan exogamy was local
exogamy. But this system was disturbed through the opening
of the forest and the intrusion of outsiders. The original significance of the clan names is unknown, and there is no descent
from a common ancestor. Although some of the clan names refer
to animals or plants, the stories explaining them do not suggest
a totemic origin. Nor do the Chenchu have totemic food taboos.
Indeed, they are not very interested in their clans. The absence
of clan cohesion, the existence of optional residence, and the
lack of full correlation between the kinship terms and the clan
system, therefore, leads Fürer-Haimendorf to the conclusion that
the Chenchu borrowed their clan system from some patrilineal
tribal neighbours, after they had already absorbed some matrilineal influence from another source. Most of the Malid jungle
tribes in southwest India like the Kanikar, the Mudavan, the
Manne and the Urali have matrilineal, exogamous clans, thus
contrasting with the Chenchu who are strictly patrilineal in
clan descent and personal property. The Hill Pantaram of
Travancore are an exception; they are patrilineal, but do not
have a proper clan system.[5]

*The Iruliga (Iraliga)*: Probably an offshoot of the Kurumba,
they are a jungle tribe in Mysore, speaking a mixture of Tamil
and Kanarese. They are the darkest of the hill tribes, their very
name Iruliga, meaning night, indicating this fact. Their features
are also very coarse. They have no endogamous groups, and some
even question the existence of exogamous clans. However that
may be, Nanjundayya & Iyer state that some of their clans are
named after family gods and others after inanimate objects and
trees. They are patrilineal and practise primogeniture. Their
myth of origin and several other beliefs and practices are
Hinduistic, thus indicating considerable acculturation.[6]

*The Sholiga*: A forest tribe of Mysore, they have four endogamous groups and five exogamous clans showing traces of
totemism. We are, however, not informed what these traces are.
They live by hunting and food-gathering and use the digging-
stick. They are dark and short-statured, lie outside the caste
gradation and dwell outside the village.[7]

*The Kasuba*: The Kasuba are a forest tribe of the Nilgiri
Hills and some adjoining areas. Their language is a mixture of
Tamil and Kanarese. They seem to be related to the Irula, but
unlike them they have totemic clans with totem taboos and
other forms of veneration. Members of the Cobra clan do not

kill the cobra, and when they see one they bow to it and burn incense before it; those of the Silver clan do not wear silver ornaments on their toes; and those of the Earth clan burn incense in honour of the earth on festival days. Four other clans have been mentioned by C. Hayavadana Rao, but their totems have not been ascertained. Frazer assumes that the clans are exogamous, although Rao does not say so expressly.[8]

*The Toda*: The Toda inhabit the Nilgiri Hills, are a purely pastoral tribe with a complicated ritual centring in the care of buffaloes, differ remarkably in general appearance from the other inhabitants of Southern India, and are divided into two distinct endogamous groups, Tartharol and Teivaliol, each with several exogamous clans. Each clan owns a group of villages and derives its name from the chief of those villages. Further, each clan has a clan god believed to have been the ruler of the clan when the gods and men lived together. As the Toda may eat the flesh of the sambhur, but of no other animal except ceremonially, W. H. R. Rivers suggests the possible existence of totemism among them at one time in their earlier home, the cult of the buffalo swamping the probably earlier cult of animals and with it totemism. In actuality, however, the clan system is territorial, and 'no trace of its having been totemic' could be discovered. Descent is always patrilineal.[9]

## *Telugu-speaking Castes*

*The Golla*: Thurston & Rangachari state that the Golla are a pastoral caste of the Telugu people, that their social status is fairly high and that they have many subdivisions. Like the other Telugu castes they have both exogamous septs or *inteperu* and gotras. The following 'examples' of 'totems' are offered: cow, horse, sheep, jackal—tamarind, henna, onion, brinjal—fire, ears, stone, woman's cloth, dagger, dumb, cold rice or food and service. Some of the septs occur among the other castes; and some of the gotras have certain forms of veneration towards certain trees and objects. For instance, members of the Raghindala (*Ficus religiosa*) gotra do not use the leaves of the sacred fig or pipal tree as platters for their food; and those of the Palavili gotra never construct small booths or *palavils* inside the house for the purpose of worship. Hassan reports that they are not a homogeneous 'race', that they are patrilineal, have a number of sub-castes of which 18 are mentioned, and exogamous, totemic 'sections' with taboos. Nanjundayya & Iyer point out that they claim to have 101 exogamous septs. Of 51 septs of the Uru Golla listed, 29 are connected with trees and the like, 11 with

animals, and 8 with inanimate objects. One is a descriptive term
(hunch-backed), and another a European game (golf). They have
a number of endogamous groups of which two, Uru and Kadu,
appear to be superior to the others. The Kadu Golla have a
tradition which points to Delhi as their original home. They
have three primary exogamous divisions—the Bear, the Moon
and Rama Gauda's descendants. The members of the Bear division believe that their ancestors were nourished by a bear; and
those of the Moon division have a vague story of a princess
having conceived by association with the moon. There is also a
belief that the Golla owe their origin to two children of a princess and a bull, who later married and begot the two tribes of
Golla. The Bear division has two exogamous clans (Bear, Pot);
the Moon division six, of which three are connected with the
milk-hedge, the he-buffalo and the moon respectively; and the
third division has ten, of which one is the name of a place, one
the name of a person, two the names of a deity, and the others
those of a plant, the flail, the hoe, the pestle and gram, and the
meaning of one is unknown.[10]

*The Bestha*: Thurston & Rangachari report that the Bestha
have inteperu or exogamous septs and gotras, and that some
of the gotras maintain taboos of a totemic type. Thus, the members of the Malle gotra must not touch the jasmine plant (*malle*),
and those of the Ippala gotra must not touch and use the ippa
tree. Nunjundayya speaks of the existence of exogamous clans
or *kulas*, some of which are named after gold, silver, the sun,
the moon, cloud, the marriage chaplet, musk, coral bead, jasmine
and the word for goddess. Members of the Silver clan do not
wear silver ornaments except at marriages. Their hereditary occupation, it is said, was hunting and fishing, but they have now
taken largely to cultivation. They profess the Hindu religion,
have myths of origin which are Hinduistic, have adopted the
names of some of the Brahmanic gotras in order to raise their
caste status, are patrilineal according to Hindu usage, and have
rules regulating interdining and intermarriage. However, they
allow a girl to remain unmarried, dedicate girls as *basavis* or
temple prostitutes, permit widow marriage, and usually bury
the dead.[11]

*The Kapu (Reddi)*: The Kapu form a very large caste of cultivators in Andhra Pradesh and have several subdivisions and
exogamous septs. Of the septs enumerated, 7 are named after
animals, 5 after trees, plants or their products, and 6 after inanimate objects. At Conjeeveram where totem taboos are in
existence, the Panta Reddi septs are named after the following:
*Bassia longifolia*, cot, *Paspalum scrobiculatum*, tamarind seeds

and water melon. A probable offshoot of the Kapu Reddi caste is the Balija caste. By occupation traders and cultivators, the Balija are considerably mixed, admitting outsiders into their caste without scruple. They have both exogamous septs or inteperu and gotras. Five of their sept-names are animal in origin, four vegetable, and eight are those of inanimate objects. Although the sept-names listed for the Kapu and the Balija coincide in only one or two instances, most of them occur among other caste groups in the surrounding areas.[12]

*The Komati*: The Komati are traders or vaisyas, and are found in Andhra Pradesh, Mysore, Madras, Maharashtra and elsewhere. Thurston & Rangachari state that they speak Telugu everywhere, have two endogamous sections, Gavara and Kalinga, and several exogamous septs of a totemic nature. They claim to have collected 120 sept names; and of those they list a large number are names of trees, plants or their products, six are those of animals, and two are named after the sun and the moon respectively. The totem groups are termed variously *gotram* in imitation of the Brahmin gotras; *vamsam*, a term commonly used in Ganjam, Vizagapatam and the Godavari districts, and derived from the word *bams* or bamboo denoting a family whose branches are as numerous as those of a bamboo; and *kulam* as an equivalent of group or family. There are totem taboos and other forms of respect. It is believed that those who violate the taboos relating to the plant totems will be born as insects for seven generations. It is, however, possible to avoid this calamity by performing the funeral ceremonies of the totem ancestor every year at Gaya where the Hindus generally perform the obsequial ceremonies for their ancestors. In an effort to raise their status the Komati have in recent times sought to arrange their totems under various Brahminic gotras and have accordingly appropriated their *pravaras* (names of quasi-deified ancestors). In the northern parts of the Madras Presidency the septs are further divided into exogamous inteperu (house names), named after a distinguished ancestor or the original home of the family. The Komati claim to be related to the Madiga. Nanjundayya & Iyer report the existence of three endogamous groups, and add that they also speak Kanarese, that they are patrilineal after the Hindu fashion and have many other Hindu beliefs and practices. Their gotras have both *rishis* (quasi-deified ancestors of the upper castes) and totems. Of the 101 gotras mentioned, 89 have vegetable totems. There are no animal totems. A few are inanimate objects—curds, sandal, red earth, alum, camphor and white silk.[13]

*The Madiga*: Thurston & Rangachari state that the Madiga constitute the leather-working caste of the Telugu country corresponding to the Chakkiliyan of the Tamil area. They have endogamous divisions with several exogamous septs. Seven of the septs are named after animals, three after trees and their products, and thirteen after inanimate objects, abstract nouns and the like. Nanjundayya & Iyer add that they are lower than the Holeya, that both Madiga and Holeya are known as the black people, and that they stand outside the four castes of the *sastras* (ancient books of Hindu law). They speak Kanarese and Telugu, have two endogamous divisions based on language, which in turn have three endogamous divisions. The latter are further divided into a number of exogamous groups known as *kulas* or *bedagus*, most of which are named after various material objects, trees and animals. Some still retain the usual taboos, but most have forgotten the implications of their names and taboos. Of the 55 clan names listed, 10 are those of animals, 11 are those of trees, plants and their products, 13 are those of inanimate objects, and one is a person—chief man. They are patrilineal in accordance with Hindu usage, but retain many customs which seem to point to a remote racial and cultural past.[14]

*The Togata*: The Togata are Telugu weavers, and have exogamous septs like other Telugu castes. Some of these sept names, according to Thurston & Rangachari, are: old, pillar, indigo, plough, pot, cummin seed, food, goat, alms, *Chrysanthemum indica*, horse, a god and treasurer. The members of the Gurram sept are not allowed to ride on horseback. Nanjundayya & Iyer state that their myth of origin is Hinduistic, that inheritance is in the male line, that they have a fairly high position in the caste system, and that they are divided into four endogamous groups with, it is claimed, 360 exogamous clans. Most of the clans are totemic, that is to say, they are named after animals, trees or other objects, to which the usual respect is shown. Some of the names are those of places and many represent family names. Of the 34 exogamous septs listed, 5 are named after animals, 7 after trees and plants, 8 after inanimate objects, 7 after places and the like, and one is the word for God.[15]

*The Devanga*: The Devanga are a caste of weavers who speak Telugu or Kanarese, and are found all over the Madras Presidency. Their myth of origin and rule of inheritance are Hinduistic. They have many endogamous sections, but practically speaking only two of these, the Kanarese and the Telugu, are of importance. The Kanarese section has adopted Brahminic rituals to a greater extent than the Telugu. Of the 52 sept-names of the Telugu section, about 40 are derived from other than the animal or vegetable kingdom. The majority of them are Saivites, and in some parts of Ganjam they keep a large number of

Brahminy bulls, and when one dies they hold elaborate funeral rites in its honour. The exogamous septs of the Kanarese Devanga also bear names derived mainly from other than the animal or vegetable kingdom.[16]

*The Nayindia*: Located in Mysore, the Nayindia are a caste of barbers whose occupation is not looked on as very auspicious. There are two main endogamous sections based on language—the Kanarese and the Telugu. The Kanarese section has a few gotras with rishis; and the Telugu section has a number of exogamous septs named after animals, plants, flowers and other objects with the usual prohibition of killing, cutting or using them. Some of their sept names are those of a tree, horse, a kind of seed, the tree *Pongamia glabra*, the karu tree, jasmine, chrysanthemum, peacock, turmeric, and the plant *Achryanthes aspera*. They are also patrilineal after the Hindu manner.[17]

*Other Telugu-speaking Castes*: There are, of course, several other Telugu-speaking castes with exogamous, totemic clans, and sometimes with other divisions, both endogamous and exogamous. All of them are strongly Hinduistic, although the caste status varies from group to group. All are also patrilineal in descent and inheritance. Most of them have a large number of clan names, often a very large number, derived from inanimate objects and other non-animal and non-vegetable sources, many of which are obviously of a relatively modern origin. Niggemeyer calls these clan names non-genuine totems. Some examples of such castes are the Gamalla (toddy-tappers), the Janappan (manufacturers of hemp gunny bags, probably an off-shoot of the Balija), the Jogi (mendicants), the Kamma (originally soldiers, now agriculturists and traders), the Karna Sale (weavers), the Mala (pariahs), the Mutracha (hunters, fishers and palanquin-bearers), the Odde or Vodda (navvies), the Padma Sale (weavers belonging to the right-hand faction), the Tottiyan (cultivators), the Helava (beggars), and the Rajawar or Rachewar who claim Kshatriya descent. A few of the Telugu groups lie outside the fourfold division of castes, many are Sudras or Vaisyas, and a few claim Kshatriya ancestry. Some like the Devanga and the Rajawar have two endogamous sections based on language—the Kanarese and the Telugu sections; the Ganiga (oil-pressers) have three main sections—the Kanarese, the Telugu, and the Tamil; and the Meda (workers in bamboo) are found in the Telugu, Kanarese, Oriya and Tamil areas. The Konda Dora are a caste of hill cultivators found chiefly in Vizagapatam; they have two well-defined divisions—Pedda (big) and Chinna (little) Kondalu. The Pedda Kondalu have retained the totemic divisions (Naga, cobra; Bhag, tiger; Kochchimo, tortoise) occurring among the other hill castes; whereas the Chinna Kondalu have adopted the Telugu system of inteperu as exogamous septs. The twofold division of a more or less similar nature is also shared by the Mutracha, the Kurni, some Oriya castes like the Pentiya and the Omanaito, and a few other groups elsewhere. The Yanadi, regarded by Eickstedt as belonging in the main to the Melanid stock, are a Telugu-speaking, dark-skinned, platyrrhine tribe. They are treated here to exemplify influence from the Telugu castes. Of their exogamous septs listed by the old sources, four have names derived from animals, and the rest (fifteen in all) from inanimate objects. A more recent investigator, Raghaviah, however, reports the existence of two main subdivisions: Manchi (superior) and Challa (inferior). There are several clans which correspond to house names (inteperu). Some clan names mentioned are knife, shirt, gun, slivers, fighters, tiger-killers, bowmen, lime tree or peacock, quantity of grain, tending goats, fly, thoughts or having a door frame, parrot catchers, star, bear, and the name of a sect. Twenty-three clan names refer to hills and other localities. Raghaviah maintains that there is not much support for the view that the Yanadi surnames have a totemic basis, that totem descent, totem taboos or any special veneration for the animals which appear as house names are non-existent, that several house names probably crept in from other castes as a result of admixture on the male side, that several house names are traceable to the Balija, the Reddi, the Kamma and even the Brahmins, and that certain surnames indicate an occupational origin. Some taboos relating to a few animals or plants have other than a totemic origin.[18]

## Matrilineal Castes

Niggemeyer lists fifteen groups in the South which trace their totems in the female line. In terms of the pre-independence political units, five of them reside mainly in South Kanara (the Bant, the Devadiga, the Kelasi, the Madivala and the Nalke), five in both South Kanara and Mysore (the Bili Magga, the Billava, the Halepaik, the Holeya and the Patvegara), one in North Kanara and Mysore (the Kotte Vakkal), one in South and North Kanara, that is to say, it has matrilineal clans in both areas (the Moger), one in North Kanara (the Nador), one in Mysore (the Hasalar), and one in the Tamil area (the Maravar).[19] As the establishment of matrilineal totemism in this area is relatively significant, we shall examine the castes concerned in all their relevant particulars.

The Bant are land-owners and cultivators, Hindus by religion and Sudras by caste. They have four main subdivisions, and a number of *balis* or exogamous septs. Of the balis mentioned, four are named after animals, four after trees, plants or their products, one after the word for weaver, and another after the term for one who removes the evil eye. In South Kanara the language spoken is Tulu, and both clan membership and property are matrilineally inherited with the exception of a few sectarians. In North Kanara the language is Kanarese and property is patrilineally inherited.[20]

*The Kelasi* belong to the barber caste and have the following balis: gold, weaver, salt, cap made of the areca-palm leaf, and sugarcane. They have a tradition that matriliny and some other customs were imposed upon certain castes by a king. They speak Tulu in South Kanara and are matrilineal in clan membership and property inheritance there. But in North Kanara they speak Kanarese and are patrilineal in property inheritance.[21]

*The Nalke*: Thurston & Rangachari state that the Nalke are a caste of mat, basket and umbrella makers, that they have numerous exogamous divisions or balis evidently borrowed from the Bant and Billava, that they are held to be Holeya or pariahs, and that they follow the male line, although living in the midst of 'female line' castes. Saldanha, however, places them among the castes in South Kanara which trace their balis through females; and Niggemeyer sets them down as matrilineal in clan membership, but patrilineal in property inheritance. They speak Tulu in South Kanara, and Kanarese in North Kanara.[22]

*The Bili Magga*: Weavers by occupation, the Bili Magga speak Tulu in South Kanara and Kanarese in Mysore. They are said to have 66 exogamous clans or gotras in Mysore, which are divided into two groups known as the Siva and the Parvati or the male and the female groups. Each group has 33 gotras, most of which are named after animals, plants, implements and so forth. Members of the clan seem to think it sinful to injure the things whose names they bear. Of the clan names listed, 7 are those of animals, 13 are those of trees, plants and their products, and 15 of inanimate objects and the like. In South Kanara the clan names are matrilineally, and property patrilineally, inherited.[23]

*The Billava* are a caste of toddy-tappers mostly found in South Kanara. Their name is regarded as a contraction of Billinavaru, or bowmen. In South Kanara they speak Tulu, and in Mysore Kanarese. Like the Bant they have a number of exogamous septs or balis, and are matrilineal in clan membership and property inheritance.[24]

*The Halepaik*: Also a caste of toddy-tappers, the Halepaik

are found in the northern taluks of the South Kanara district, in Mysore and in North Kanara. Their name signifies 'old soldiers'. Thurston & Rangachari report that the Halepaik of South Kanara have exogamous septs or balis which run in the female line. Of the examples given, two are named after trees, one after an animal (the wolf), one is known as Devana (god), and another as Ganga. In the Kanara district of the Bombay Presidency the balis are named after animals or trees which are held sacred by their members, and seemed to have once been considered the common ancestors of the members of the respective balis. They are worshipped and tabooed. Thus the members of the Nagbali, apparently named after the nagchampa flower, will not wear it in their hair as this would involve injury to the plant; those of the Kadavebali will not kill a deer, after which they are named. The Halepaik of South Kanara, however, do not seem to attach such importance to their sept names; but they avoid eating a fish called *srinivasa* as they think that the streaks on its body bear a resemblance to the Vaishnavite sectarian mark. Nanjundayya & Iyer state that they have numerous family groups or balis (ways, lines of descent), which are named after plantains, gold, diamond, turmeric, the pepper plant, the deer, the wolf and so on. Twenty-two of them seem to suggest totemism, but not in South Kanara. In a list of the most important balis—23 in all—14 are named after trees, plants or their products, 7 after animals, one after gold, and another after a river. The balis are traced in the female line and are exogamous. In Mysore property inheritance is patrilineal, but on the west coast it is either matrilineal or Hinduistic. Saldanha points out that the Halepaik and the Moger of North Kanara also trace the balis in the female line, but that they might have migrated north; and Niggemeyer sums up the facts as follows: in South Kanara clan membership and property inheritance are matrilineal; but in North Kanara property inheritance is patrilineal, and there is both the rule of avoidance and totem veneration.[25]

*The Holeya* are found mainly in South Kanara and Mysore, are field labourers and agrestic serfs, and in South Kanara are considered a polluting caste. Thurston & Rangachari, referring to the Holeya of South Kanara, state that they have a large number of exogamous septs or balis. Of the examples given two are named after animals, three after plants or flowers, and seven after inanimate objects. Their three divisions differ widely from one another: among the Bakuda descent is matrilineal, among the Mera patrilineal, and among the Mari the headman follows in the female line of succession. Frazer, quoting Nanjundayya's earlier findings for Mysore, lists 5 kulas or septs named after animals, 10 after trees, plants and their products, and 20 after inanimate objects—that is, 35 in all. Some instances of totem taboos are likewise indicated. Nanjundayya & Iyer, however, enumerate 3 kulas named after animals, 23 after trees, plants and their products, 26 after inanimate objects, and 2 after the terms for shepherd and headman—54 in all. Clan descent is traced in the male line only, and in property inheritance they follow the Hindu law. They are also divided into many endogamous groups. Their myths of origin and several other beliefs and practices are Hinduistic. Enthoven describes them as an aboriginal and impure tribe of South India, and adds that their language in the south of the Bombay Presidency is Kanarese and in the Deccan Marathi. In the Deccan they have several endogamous divisions, and exogamous septs known as *bhavkis* in Sholapur and kuls elsewhere. Every kul has a separate *devak*, and similarity of devaks is a bar to marriage. Some of their devaks are the axe, the whirler of the spinning-wheel, the sunflower and the *panchpalvi*. Niggemeyer, basing himself on Sturrock, Saldanha and others, condenses the facts as follows: in South Kanara they speak Tulu and acquire clan membership matrilineally and property patrilineally. In Mysore they have the rule of avoidance.[26]

*The Patvegara*: Thurston & Rangachari describe the Patvegara as a Kanarese caste of silk-weavers located in South Kanara. They are divided into exogamous balis, are patrilineal in the Hindu fashion, worship Siva and Vishnu, wear the sacred thread and employ Brahmins. Nanjundayya & Iyer, following Enthoven, suggest that they were probably immigrants from Bombay and that they speak a mixture of Gujarati, Marathi and Hindustani. They have some endogamous-territorial groups and exogamous clans, all named after flowers symbolizing the rishis. Sturrock and Saldanha aver that the Tulu-speaking section in South Kanara inherit clan membership matrilineally.[27]

*The Kotte Okkalu (Kotte Vakkal)* are gardeners and field labourers and have exogamous balis closely resembling those of the Halvakki Vakkal. But unlike the latter they inherit the balis matrilineally. Some of their totems are the moon, the wolf, the plantain and a river.[28]

*The Moger* are a caste of fishermen inhabiting both South and North Kanara. In the south they speak Tulu and inherit clan membership and property matrilineally; in the north they speak Kanarese and inherit property patrilineally. Thurston & Rangachari mention the following exogamous balis for the Tuluspeaking section: the elephant, a fish, the tortoise, *Pterocarpus marsupium,* another fish and the wolf. For the Kanarese-speaking section Enthoven lists five balis named after animals, five after trees, and one after a god. The meanings of two are unknown. They reverence the balis or totems and abstain from injuring them. While the balis are inherited matrilineally, the main body of the caste follow the Makkalasantana law or succession through males; the rest (only a small minority) following the Aliyasantana law or succession through females.[29]

*The Hasalar* are a forest tribe in western Malnad (Mysore) and carry bows and arrows in hunting. They speak both Tulu and Kanarese and claim relationship with the Medar. They have five endogamous groups which are subdivided into exogamous balis tracing descent through females. Nanjundayya & Iyer mention ten balis without giving their equivalents, and add that they are said to be totemic. They are also found in North Kanara, where they have two endogamous groups, and totemic, exogamous clans. The totems here are the elephant, the toddy tree, a fish, cane, virgin, and a tree (*Gynandropsis pentaphylla*). Property is inherited patrilineally.[30]

*The Maravar* are found in Madura and Tinnevelly and are mainly herders, cultivators and traders. Fawcett, writing on the Kondayam Kottai Maravar, adds that they are very dark in skin colour and are the purest of tribes, being least influenced by modern civilization. This is an odd statement to make, considering the facts that their myth of origin is Hinduistic, and that the names of some of their *khilais* are those of Brahminic rishis. They have six trees or *kothus,* each of which is subdivided into three khilais or branches. Fawcett calls the kothus sub-tribes and the khilais septs; whereas Niggemeyer regards the former as clans and the latter as sub-clans. Members of khilais belonging to the same kothu have to seek marriage partners outside the kothu. There are also certain marriage restrictions among the kothus. The six kothus are named as follows: Pepper-vine, Betel-vine, Coconut, Areca-nut, Dates and Palmyra. Of the eighteen khilais, two are named after Brahmin rishis, one seems to mean ' a king's crown-bearer ', another ' one of the old Pandiyan kings of Madura ', and three others probably mean ' the wife of Gautama ', ' the one being of the world ', and ' a monkey king with a bear's face who lived long, long ago '. The meanings of the others are not known. On marriage a girl joins her husband's sept, but retains the name of her own sept, and the children belong to the mother's and not the father's sept. Property is inherited patrilineally, but the prohibited degrees are reckoned through the women. Another group in the Tamil area, which has exogamous septs called khilais or branches that run in the female line, are the Nattar Kallan of Sivaganga, one of the ten endogamous divisions of the Kallan. Some of the other endogamous divisions of the Kallan name their exogamous septs after streets, gods or other fanciful designations. The Kottai Vellala, the Nangudi Vellala and the Pallan, also in the Tamil area, have exogamous khilais which run in the female line, but are very likely non-totemic.[31]

*The Devadiga, the Madivala and the Nador*: The first two of these three castes inhabit South Kanara and speak Tulu; both are matrilineal in clan membership and property inheritance. The third inhabits North Kanara, speaks Kanarese, and is matrilineal in clan membership but patrilineal in property inheritance.[32]

*The Bakkaru, the Gudikara and the Nadu Gauda*: Niggemeyer does not allude to these three. The first, also known as Baggaru or Bagga Holeya, speak Kanarese and are probably immigrants from South Kanara. They have no endogamous groups, but many exogamous balis traced through females. They appear totemic, although they do not admit being so. The second are a caste of sandalwood carvers who follow Hindu customs and the rites of the Brahmins except in matters of food. They were originally Kshatriyas. They have exogamous clans or gotras, each with a family god or goddess. The six gotras mentioned are named after rishis, but some of their taboos appear totemic. Thus, members of the Bharadvaja gotra do not ride a horse; those of the Gautama, Kasyapa and Kamshya gotras do not kill a scorpion; and those of the Kaulanda do not kill a cobra. Inheritance occurs in both lines, in Mysore in the male, and in North Kanara in the female line. The third are an agricultural caste with two endogamous divisions. They are an endogamous group of the Bant, are found mostly in South Kanara, and follow inheritance in both lines. They have twenty gotras or balis corresponding to the Brahminic gotras, but traced in the female line. Thus they are not totemic, but must have once been so.[33]

## Patrilineal Tamil-speaking Castes

*The Konga Vellala* are a caste of cultivators who live in the neighbourhood of Trichinopoly. They have two endogamous divisions called Konga Vellala proper and Tondan, the latter comprising the offspring of girls and widows of the caste and outsiders. Both divisions have a large number of exogamous septs named after animals, trees and the like, which are tabooed.

Three examples of their totems are the quail, a pot herb, and *Celosia argentea*.[34]

*The Saliyan* are a Tamil-speaking 'class' of weavers in the Tanjore district, and contrary to the usual custom of the Tamil castes they have exogamous septs or *vidu* (house). Of those listed as examples, three are named after animals, two after trees, eleven after various inanimate objects and six after persons. Two are descriptive terms. They have also acquired gotras named after the rishis.[35]

*The Vallamban* are a small Tamil cultivating caste in the Tanjore, Trichinopoly and Madura districts, and have five sub-divisions, of which one has exogamous septs like Chola, Pandyan, Jackal and Tiger.[36]

## Patrilineal Kanarese-speaking Castes

*The Kappilyan* are Kanarese-speaking farmers in Madura and Tinnevelly and have a large number of exogamous septs and sub-septs, some of which, at any rate, are named after animate and inanimate objects such as the elephant, the tiger, the lizard and a hamlet. Certain septs have particular deities.[37]

*The Toreya*: Originally fishermen and palanquin-bearers, the Toreya are a Kanarese 'class' now living in the Tamil districts of Coimbatore and Salem. They have endogamous divisions and many exogamous septs with traces of totem taboos. Thus members of the Silver sept may not wear silver toe-rings; those of the Snake sept worship anthills which are the homes of snakes; those of the Onne (*Pterocarpus marsupium*) sept do not mark their foreheads with the juice from the trunk of this tree; those of the Kazhal or Flute sept throw away what remains of their food if they hear the sound of a flute during a meal; and those of the Rakshasa or Giant sept do not celebrate the Diwali feast to rejoice over the death of a *rakshasa*. Other septs are named after gold, diamond, clouds, small bronze bells, a kind of knife, the buffalo, and a Hindu saint.[38]

*The Kuruba*: Thurston & Rangachari hold that the Kuruba speak a dialect of Kanarese and are subdivided into clans or *gumpus* which derive their names from the clan headmen. The clans are divided into gotras or septs, mostly of a totemic origin. Of the 67 gotras, 10 are connected with animals, 15 with trees, plants and derivatives, 37 with various inanimate objects, one is an adjective (noble), one an abstract noun (darkness), and three are of a personal nature (devil, headman, Muhammadan). Among the 37 inanimate objects the following metals appear—silver, gold, and bell metal; the following natural phenomena—the moon, the sun and the ocean; and of the rest several are clearly of a more or less modern origin. One gotra is named after saffron, which was originally tabooed; but as this was inconvenient, the korra grain instead has become an object of taboo. Their rule of inheritance is patrilineal in accordance with Hindu usage. Nanjundayya & Iyer say that they are a Sudra caste of shepherds, that their myths of origin are Hinduistic, and that they have three endogamous groups and several exogamous clans. Agriculture is gradually replacing sheep-tending and weaving as their occupations. Of 111 clans enumerated, 13 have animal and 35 vegetable totems; the totems of 10 could not be ascertained; and of the rest, that is to say 53, most are inanimate objects of ancient or modern derivation. In several instances the usual totem taboos exist. The Kuruba are found in Coorg, Mysore, Andhra Pradesh and Madras.[39]

*Two Brahmin Castes*: (a) The Stanika are temple servants in South Kanara and claim to be Brahmins, but other Brahmins do not accept their claim. They have two sections—Subramanya and Kumbla. Members of the Subramanya section state that they have Brahminic gotras named after the rishis Visvamitra, Angirasa and Bharadvaja, and also twelve exogamous clans. Of the eight septs or clans enumerated, three are named after trees, two after inanimate objects (cart, tassel for the hair-knot), and the meanings of three are not given. (b) According to Sturrock, the Shivalli Brahmins have 252 gotras, of which 10 appear to be totemic. Of these ten, two are named after animals, six after trees, plants or their products, and two after inanimate objects. Saldanha states that the Shivalli Brahmins, who are Deshasth Brahmins of South Kanara, have a tradition that they came to this locality without women of their own, took local women as wives, and thus acquired their balis. They speak Tulu in South Kanara and Kanarese in Mysore.[40]

*The Ager* are salt-makers by occupation and are located mainly in North Kanara. Enthoven reports the existence of six exogamous balis, of which three are named after animals, two after trees, and one after a fruit. There are also taboos which forbid the killing or cutting of the totem concerned. The inheritance of the totem and of property are in the male line.[41]

*The Halvakki Vakkal* are a caste of cultivators who live in North Kanara, and were the earliest settlers on the coast. They have a number of exogamous balis named after animals, trees, inanimate objects or in other ways. Enthoven lists 20 balis, of which 7 are named after animals, 10 after trees, plants or their products, and one after an inanimate object. One is the word for goddess and the meaning of another is unknown. There are traces (actually three instances are described) of the usual totem taboos. ' Descent in reference to *balis* ', says Enthoven, ' is traced through males, the caste in this point differing from the majority, who either trace their *bali* through females or through both sexes, the latter presumably being the intermediate stage between the older fashion and the modern system.' The related cultivating castes—the Gam Vakkal in North Kanara and the Kare Vakkal in North Kanara and Mysore—also have patrilineal, exogamous balis. For the former Enthoven lists 14 balis, of which 3 are named after animals and 9 after trees and their products. The meanings of two are unknown. There are totem taboos. The Gam Vakkal, adds Enthoven, will not readily disclose their balis, probably because they are ashamed of them. In property matters they follow the Hindu law of inheritance. Like the Gam Vakkal, the Kare Vakkal also have balis which are traced in the male line.[42]

*The Mukri* are inhabitants of North Kanara, speak Kanarese, and had some former connexion with the Halvakki Vakkal. They have exogamous balis, of which five are named after animals and four after trees. One is the word for virgin. There are also traces of the usual totem taboos. Both clan membership and property are inherited in the male line.[43]

*The Bedar (Beda, Boya)*: Located in Mysore and Andhra Pradesh, the Bedar are, according to Thurston & Rangachari, cultivators and herdsmen. Both the Kanarese-speaking Bedar and the Telugu-speaking Boya have two endogamous divisions: the Uru or Village men and the Myasa or Grassland men. These are again divided into exogamous, non-totemic *bedagas*, of which the following are the best known: Yemmalavaru or Buffalo Men, Mandalavaru or Men of the Herd, Pulavaru or Flower Men and Minalavaru or Fish Men. Each bedaga has its own god, to which its members pay special reverence. Since the names of the bedagas are the same among the Bedar and the Boya, it is concluded that they belonged in the past to one homogeneous caste. Of the 62 exogamous septs of the Boya, 17 are connected with animals, 12 with trees, plants and their products, and 33 mostly with inanimate objects. Many of the sept names are also found among other castes or tribal castes of the area. Nanjundayya & Iyer claim that they pursue hunting and agriculture in Mysore, that they have flat noses, frizzled hair and a dark skin, and that they belong to the same stock as the Vedda of Ceylon. They spoke Telugu originally, but those in the Kanarese districts now speak Kanarese. They are divided into six endogamous groups and several exogamous, totemic clans. Of the 42 clans ascertained, 8 have animal and 6 vegetable totems. Of the rest, one is named after

a place, another after seven hills, and six after inanimate objects.
There are totem taboos. They are considerably Hinduized.[44]

## The Marathas and Marathi-speaking
## Castes and Tribes

The Maratha: We shall first examine the nature of the exogamous units and devaks of this large and influential population
and leave the question of their origin for somewhat later consideration. An early observer, James Campbell, noted that the
Marathas of the Bombay Presidency were divided into families,
each with its devak or sacred symbol. The devaks were patrilineally inherited, and worshipped at marriages and other
important occasions. Persons with the same devak were not permitted to marry. Of the devaks listed, eighteen are trees and
their products, and nine are inanimate objects. One evidently
refers to a Brahminic rishi or ancestral sage but is equated with
the ' feather of a crow pheasant ' in the source, and the meaning
of another is unknown. One of the devaks is the *panch pallav*
or the leaves of five trees—the *Ficus indica*, the *Ficus religiosa*,
the *Cynodon dactylon*, the *Bauhinia racemosa* and the *Eugenia
jambolana*. Campbell classed the Maratha devaks and the Kanarese balis together, and regarded them as guardian spirits and
ancestors and heads of houses.[45] So far as the Marathas in the
Central Provinces are concerned, Russell & Hiralal report that
they have several exogamous clans with Rajput names (Chauhan,
Panwar, Solanki, Suryavansi), others named after animals or
natural objects (iguana, date-palm), and still others of a titular
nature.[46]

The most detailed accounts of the Maratha devaks, however,
have been given to us by Enthoven. Referring to the Marathas
proper, to the Maratha Kunbis, and to the Maratha occupational
castes (the Bhandari, the Chitrakathi, the Gavandi, the Kumbhar,
the Lohar, the Mali, the Nhavi, the Parit, the Sutar, the Takar,
the Taru, the Teli and so on), he says that their exogamous
groups have devaks or marriage guardians which in their origin
seem to have been the exact equivalents of the Kanarese balis.
The devaks of the Marathas and related castes are not as highly
revered as the balis; but similarity of devaks is a bar to marriage,
and some of the Maratha kuls are named after devaks (More
after *mor*, Salunke after *salunki*). The devak is usually some
common tree like the bel (*Aegle marmelos*), the pipal (*Ficus
religiosa*), the vad (*Ficus indica, Ficus bengalensis*), or the shami
(*Prosopis spicegera*). In its commonest form it is the leaves of five
trees, of which one is held specially sacred and was the original

devak of the section. The devak is worshipped at marriages,
at the time of entering a new house, when the threshing-floor
is prepared at harvest time, and during the thread ceremony. In
Maratha marriages the installation of the devak is an important
part of the marriage ceremony. The nature of the ritual, however, varies in details among the various castes that practise it.
In general it takes the following form: The persons concerned
go to the woods, worship the tree involved and cut a twig from
it. A visit is then made with the twig to the temple of Maruti
where the devak is formally worshipped. In some instances a
potter's house is visited also. The twig is then brought to the
marriage booth and tied to one of its posts or placed among the
household gods. Lights are waved before it, and a lamp is kept
burning in front of it for the entire period of the ceremony.
No mourning is observed during this period. After the marriage
ceremony the devak is once again worshipped. Two or four days
later it is requested to depart; and then together with the marriage coronet is taken to a distant place and left there. Often
the devak is also installed at the bride's house with a similar
ceremony; and sometimes an image of it takes its place. Of the
80 devaks listed 60 are trees, plants, fruits and flowers, 11 are
animals and the rest of other kinds, many being instruments
of industry. (In a later article the number is put down at 120,
of which 80 are trees and the like, 24 animals and the rest other
objects.) There is also evidence of totem taboos. The predominance of trees among the devaks may be due to the belief
that the ancestral spirits live in trees, and thus the trees become
guardians or devaks. The Kanarese castes do not have the composite totem or *panchpalvi*, a combination of separate devaks.
In their attempts to rise in the social scale the tribes and castes
manifest a common process of evolution by discarding their
totemic divisions for *kuls* or family stocks, which in turn are
replaced by Brahminic gotras. The devaks which possess or once
possessed all the attributes of real totems are therefore survivals,
and are hence a valuable indication of racial origin. In addition
to their kuls or surnames, the Marathas also claim gotras named
in the Brahminic fashion. But the majority of the caste do not
know to which gotra they belong, and there is a great confusion
in the assignment of kuls to gotras. Furthermore, the sameness
of gotras is not necessarily a bar to marriage, whereas the sameness of kuls and devaks is. Therefore Enthoven concludes that
the kuls and gotras were adopted after the tribe rose in social
status.[47]

To turn lastly to an Indian investigator of kinship organizations in India, in her book on that subject, Irawati Karve points

out that some clan names of the Marathas are of Rajput origin, others are names of animals, qualities or artefacts (the tiger, the peacock, black, white, the pick, the axe and so on), and still others of other types. A totemic connexion between the clan and the animal name it bears does not always seem to be present, although sometimes the flesh of the animal is not eaten by the clan concerned. The rule of exogamy, however, depends not on the clan name, but on the symbol or *devaka* connected with the clan. A devaka may be a living thing or an inanimate object like a kind of grass, a javelin or the leaves of five particular trees. Worshipped at the time of marriage, the devaks have an exogamous force, but are borne as family names only by a few. Nor do many people know what their devaka is, the elders in the main being repositories of this knowledge. The Maratha system of exogamous, totemic clans is analogous with that of the South and might have been derived from there. On the other hand, like the Rajputs and the Khatris of northern India, the Marathas also have a hypergamous arrangement of clans. While the family in Maharashtra is patrilocal and inheritance is in the male line, there are many customs in the area which are unknown in the north of India, but are found universally in the south.[48]

There are a number of occupational castes in the Marathi-speaking area, which are related to or influenced by the Marathas. The devak phenomenon occurs among many of them.

*The Bhandari* are found everywhere in the Bombay Presidency, have eight endogamous divisions and several exogamous kulas. Some kula names are shared with the Marathas. Members of the kulas show reverence towards the devaks—the banyan tree (*Ficus indica, Ficus bengalensis*), the pipal tree, the kadamba tree (*Anthocephalus cadamba*), the umbar tree (*Ficus glomerata*), and the mango tree. The kulas are referred to by the names of such trees. The devaks are reverenced by not being cut, burnt, or injured, and by being worshipped at marriages. In some places, however, persons with the same devak nevertheless marry. Some Bhandari have now begun to claim Brahminic gotras. They are toddy-tappers by occupation, drink alcohol and eat flesh, are Shaivites and are patrilineal in the Hindu fashion.[49]

*The Maratha Chambar* of the Deccan, Konkan and Karnatak have no exogamous divisions other than families. But marriages are also prohibited among those who worship the same devaks, which are mainly trees and the panchpalvi. They profess Hinduism.[50]

The fishermen caste of *Gabit* in Kanara and Ratnagiri have recently adopted gotras, but traces of kuls and devaks suggest that they are of Maratha origin. Among the 8 devaks listed, 7 are trees and one the panchpalvi. Although similarity of devaks is not necessarily a bar to marriage, they still retain traces of totem taboos; for instance, by not dining on the leaves of their devak trees, or by not cutting them or burning their wood. Like the other Marathi-speaking occupational castes they are patri-lineal and profess Hinduism.[51]

*The Gavada,* a caste of salt-makers in Kanara and Ratnagiri are, says Enthoven, in the course of passing from ' a primitive totemistic organization by *devaks* into the Brahmanical one of *gotras* through the Maratha system of Kuls '. Some families still show reverence towards the trees representing their devaks by not cutting them or touching them or dining on their leaves. But devak exogamy is fast dying out, its place being taken by kul exogamy. The kuls are identical with the surnames. Most reports state that Kashyap is the gotra of the entire caste; but another gives in addition the gotras Vatsa and Bharadvaja, and adds that marriages are prohibited between members of the same kul and also of the same gotra. Members of the Kashyap gotra, however, are allowed to intermarry. One account states that the entire caste has the same devak—the Kalamb (*Antho-cephalus cadamba*) tree; others, on the other hand, assert that every kul has a separate devak. In Vengurla the devaks are the sword, seven kinds of earth, seven kinds of flowers, rice grains, coconuts, betel-nuts, a piece of cloth, and a twig of the kalamb tree; in Shiroda it is the kalamb tree. They follow the Hindu religion and are patrilineal according to Hindu usage.[52]

*The Kumbhar* or potters have 23 endogamous divisions. The chief of these are the Maratha, the Konkani, the Gujarati and the Pardeshi. The Maratha Kumbhar resemble the Maratha Kunbi in dress and appearance. They have exogamous units based on surnames. In Poona the devaks or marriage guardians are a wristlet of a creeping plant, the maryadvel (*Ipomea biloba*) tree, the potter's wooden platter and the hoe; in Satara the mango tree, the jambul tree (*Eugenia jambolana*) and the vad tree; in Sholapur the potter's platter and the panchpalvi; and in other places only the panchpalvi. In Nasik, when the leaves of the five trees or panchpalvi are not available, mango leaves are substi-tuted. Enthoven therefore maintains that this fact supports the hypothesis of one object as the original devak, the composite devak being adopted later as the caste advanced socially and took up the custom of prohibiting marriages between persons bearing the same surname. He adds that the totemic origin of the devak is further strengthened by the fact that the Ahir Kumbhar, who have borrowed several customs from the Marathas, have separate devaks for each family even today. Similarity of surnames is a bar to marriage among the Maratha Kumbhar, but similarity of devak is no longer so. The Konkani Kumbhar claim to be Marathas in origin and have many devaks, most of which are leaves or trees, but in Ratnagiri also earth or anthill and peacock feathers. The Konkani Kumbhar hold their devaks in great reverence and some affirm that a similarity of devaks is a bar to marriage. Their exogamous divisions are local in origin. The Gujarati Kumbhar have several exogamous divisions named after Rajput clans; and the Pardeshi Kumbhar have exogamous kuls with surnames. Each kul among the Pardeshi Kumbhar has a separate deity, called *dhiradi*, which represents its devak. The custom, as they themselves admit, is borrowed from the Marathas. The dhiradis are worshipped at marriages. Among them are a clay figure of a cobra besmeared with red lead; the fruit of the bel tree; two coconuts, two betel-nuts and an idol of silver; coconut and turmeric; and so on. The Pardeshi Kumbhar are said to have come from northern India.[53]

The term *Kunbi* (Marathi for husbandman) corresponds to Kanbi in Gujarat and Kurmi in the United Provinces. The Kunbi are found all over the Bombay Presidency and have five territorial groups—the Maratha, the Konkani, the Khandeshi, the Talheri of Thana and the Kale of Kanara. Together with the Marathas, the Maratha Kunbi belonged originally, says Enthoven, to the same caste; and both their exogamous kuls and exogamous devaks are identical with those of the Marathas. Enthoven opines that the totemic nature of their devak system suggests that they are largely of a non-Aryan origin. The Konkani Kunbi in north Ratnagiri and south Kolaba do not claim to be Marathas or Kshatriyas, but are content to be known as Sudras. Smaller and darker than the Marathas, they have no kuls but surname exogamy. The Kale Kunbi in Belgaum and Kanara speak Konkani and resemble the Halvakki Vakkal in dress and ornaments. They have a number of exogamous kuls or clans, each with special gods and goddesses. The Talher Kunbi or lowlanders comprise two sections: the local who are but little different from the Son Koli, and the foreign who are principally Marathas with surnames and devaks.[54]

The *Mali* or gardeners (Sanskrit: *mala*, garland) are found all over the Deccan and north Gujarat and to a less extent in the Konkan, the Karnatak and the Kanara areas. In all probability they were originally Kunbi who turned their attention to gardening. There are three territorial groups—the Maratha, the Gujarati and the Kanarese. The Maratha Mali have thirteen endogamous divisions, and exogamous kuls represented by surnames. But sometimes a group of surnames appear together under one kul on the ground that their bearers are descendants from a common ancestor. In addition some of the Maratha Mali have gotras adopted in imitation of the Brahmins. In the beginning every kul or group of kuls had a separate devak, but today the devaks have ceased to be exogamous among all but the Jire Mali of the Nasik district; and the panchpalvi has become the common devak of the entire caste. Of the devaks listed for the Maratha Mali (not including the Jire Mali), three kuls have the maryadvel tree, two have the red mace, one the sun-flower, one the feather of the salunki or blue jay, one a kind of grass, and six the panchpalvi. Of the six devaks of the Jire Mali listed, four are trees, one is the feathers of the blue jay, and another the feathers of the peacock.[55]

The *Nhavi* or barber caste of the Bombay Presidency are mostly Hindus of the Lingayat sect, a small number being Muslims. Like many other functional castes of the Deccan, they are identical with the Marathas in names, surnames and religio-social practices. Enthoven therefore believes that the Marathas, the Maratha Nhavi and other functional castes of the Deccan belonged originally to one tribe. The Maratha Nhavi have two territorial, endogamous divisions—the Maratha in the Deccan and the Konkani in the Konkan. The Maratha Nhavi have kuls and devaks like the Marathas. The Konkani Nhavi have two divisions: the Konkani Nhavi proper and the Shinde or bastards. The Konkani Nhavi have surnames like those of the Maratha Nhavi, and their exogamous divisions are based on exogamous devaks. The kuls and their respective devaks listed are as follows: Bagkar—pankanis (red mace); Bhagwat—panch-palvi; Bide—mango and axe; Chavan—gulvel (*Tinospora cordi-folia*); Gaikwad—leaves of the sag (teak), the umbar, the mango, the jambul, and the pipal; Jadhav—pankanis (red mace); Kadam—the kalamb tree; Korde—panchpalvi; Lad—the umbar; Pavar—sword-blade; Raut—horse and the umbar; Shinde—velu (bamboo); Vagh—sunflower; and Vaghchavare—panchpalvi. In the Savantwadi area the most frequent devaks are trees—the kalamb, the umbar, the vad, the mango, the phanas (jackfruit), and the pipal. The devaks may not be touched, cut or otherwise used, and they are worshipped at marriages. Placed on a new winnowing-fan or on a piece of cloth strewn with rice, the devak is installed near the house gods, where a lamp is kept burning till the end of the marriage ceremony. The Konkani Nhavi are like the Bhandari in religion and social practices.[56]

The *Taru,* found chiefly in Ahmednagar, Nasik district and Savantwadi, say that they were originally Marathas. They have no endogamous divisions, and no exogamous ones other than family surnames. Similarity of devaks is a bar to marriage. Every 'section' has a separate devak. The principal devaks are the feathers of the peacock, the panchpalvi, the sunflower and the maryadvel tree.[57]

*The Jingar and the Shimpi*: The Jingar are an impure caste of leather-workers in the Deccan, the Konkan, the South Maratha country, Khandesh and Kanara. They claim to be of Kshatriya origin and have ten gotras. But their gotra system has been recently adopted to confirm their assumed Kshatriya origin. For in deciding marriage alliances attention is paid mainly to the surnames, which are exogamous. Every section has a separate devak, and their chief devak is the panchpalvi. Thus their origin, says Enthoven, seems to be the same as that of most of the lower castes in the Deccan. The Shimpi or tailors also claim to be of Kshatriya origin. They are found all over the Deccan, the Konkan and Karnatak. They have many endogamous divisions, and are an occupational caste formed from numerous castes and tribes. They have many exogamous surnames, and some claim to belong to gotras. But the latter are not guides to marriage. Their devaks in the Deccan and Karnatak are: (i) a pair of scissors, needles and a measuring rod; and (ii) the panchpalvi (leaves from the mango, the umbar, the jambul, the palas [*Butea frondosa*] and the sag); and in the Konkan (i) mango leaves and umbar twigs, and (ii) pipal leaves. In the Deccan the devak is taken to the temple of Maruti and then tied to a post of the marriage booth; but in the Konkan it is kept in a winnowing-fan near the house gods. Both the Jingar and the Shimpi belong to the Hindu religion and follow the Hindu law of inheritance.[58]

The *Tambat* or coppersmiths are found in the Deccan, Konkan and Bombay city, and are supposed to have come from the Karnatak and Telengana a thousand years ago. They may be described as a Brahmin caste in the making; for they call themselves Brahmins, have Brahmin gotras, wear the sacred thread, and have even made efforts to train their own caste-men as priests, but to little avail as the occupation of a coppersmith is more profitable than that of the priest. On the other hand, Enthoven adds that they have still traces of a totemic organization, exemplified by the survival of the devaks or gods of their exogamous sections. Like the Marathas they have also kuls or family stocks. The exogamous kuls have different devaks, and marriage is forbidden between persons who worship the same devaks. In the Deccan, however, this practice has become obsolete and its place has been taken by gotra exogamy. In their marriage ceremonies betel-nuts, palas twigs and mango leaves are placed in a winnowing-fan and worshipped. There are special days for the worship of the banyan, the pipal, the umbar, the avali and the tulsi (*Ocymum sanctum*). The devaks of the Konkan Tambat are the leaves of the mango, the pipal, the banyan, the payari (*Ficus rumphii*) and the jambul. Further, on certain occasions they worship the implements of work. The banyan, the avali, the pipal and the tulsi are special objects of worship among the Tambat women. Hence Enthoven concludes that the common Maratha devaks may have once been of equal importance to them in regulating marriage restrictions and that the gotras are a modern innovation which have displaced an earlier totemic organization. It is noteworthy that they eat flesh and drink liquor.[59]

The primitive tribes of the region display the phenomenon of the devak in varying strength or not all. We shall examine them in the following order—the Katkari, the Warli, the Thakur, the Mahar, the Koli and the Dubla.

*The Katkari*: Niggemeyer, basing himself on Risley (*The People of India*, Calcutta, 1908, 98), concludes that totemism among the Katkari is doubtful. Enthoven's information is also not very conclusive. He states that they are probably of Bhil origin and are believed to have come from the north. They have five endogamous divisions and thirty-two exogamous ones represented by surnames. 'It is commonly alleged', he adds 'that many of the above names such as More, Vaghmare, etc., are totemistic in origin, though reverence for the totem is no longer observable.' There are also some traces of the devak ceremony during marriages, such as the tying of umbar and jambul leaves to the marriage post. In 1934, however, Weling published a somewhat fuller account of the Katkari from which we learn that they have numerous clan names or surnames[60] which are exogamous. Some of the surnames refer to animals, trees or other objects (Bokya, a male cat; Bhople, a pumpkin; Dukre, a hog; Diva, a lamp; Gaikar, a cow; More, a peacock; Savra, *Salmalia malabarica*; and Phopli, betel-nut tree), others are names of various tribes and castes (Ahir, Bhoya, Jangam, Gosavi, Koli), and still others suggest territorial origins (Ghogarkar, Mandavkar, Patkar) and occupations (Katkar, Khopkar, Waghmare). Jadhav, Nikam, Dalvi, Chavan, Jagtap and Pawar are surnames of highly placed Maratha families; and Dhulia, Shetga, Nirguda and Gaikar are found among the Kunbi. Mukna, Misal and Murkute are surnames of the Mahar, and Kambdi that of the Kumbhar or potters' caste. None of the above surnames belong exclusively to the Katkari. Some Katkari have devaks. Among

the Marathas of the Bombay Presidency, adds Weling, the devak
is a sacred symbol which might have originally been a totem;
among the Katkari, however, there is a good deal of confusion
between totems and devaks, suggesting the mixture of two systems of somewhat differing beliefs and practices. For instance,
a Katkari with the surname Wagh (tiger) says that he does not
kill a tiger, but at the same time claims the kumbha tree (*Careya
arborea*) as a devak. The Jadhav and the Mukna have the same
devak, the mango tree, but they intermarry. A Valvi does not
eat the flesh of the animal called *valvi*, but a Phopli (betel-nut
tree) chews betel-nut without hesitation. Furthermore, the Katkari are not clear about the restrictions and ritual connected
with the devaks. A Jadhav who has the mango tree as a devak
eats mangoes, but a Bhoplya (pumpkin) says that he must avoid
eating pumpkins. Nor are the Katkari particular about hanging
a branch or the fruit of the devak on the marriage booth or
worshipping it during the marriage ceremony. Weling therefore
concludes that the Katkari are not a distinct tribe, but judging
from their surnames, their practice of admitting members of the
surrounding tribes and lower Hindu castes into their fold, and
some other evidence, are a considerably mixed group. The traces
of totemism among them might thus have been acquired in this
fashion; although the contrary view that the Katkari were a
totemic tribe which has today lost much of its totemism is held
by Abbott. The habitat of the Katkari is the hilly parts of the
Deccan or the Western Ghats, their territory ranging from Thana
in the north to Ratnagiri in the south. They are a people of
the jungle, and depend by preference and inclination on hunting, fishing and food-gathering and rude forms of cultivation
for their existence. Their plough-cultivation and other economic
activities are a recent acquisition. They live in local groups of
10 to 150 members. The entire community is divided into two
endogamous sections—Son and Dhor—which are again divided
into exogamous septs. The Dhor Katkari are also known as
Marathas, and might have thus separated themselves recently.
Descent is patrilineal, and the language Marathi.[61]

Another aboriginal tribe in the Bombay Presidency is the
*Warli* tribe. The Warli live in the northeastern part of the
Thana district and are therefore in contact with the Katkari.
Enthoven opines that they are a subdivision of the Bhil. They
have four endogamous divisions and 200 exogamous clans or
kuls. Among the clan names some refer to animals (tiger, deer,
jackal, bear, crocodile, peacock and cock), others to trees and
their products (six are listed), and still others to titles (five
mentioned), occupations (five), localities (three), and so on. Some

are of Rajput origin. There are no totem taboos or any other indications of respect or reverence towards the animals, trees and other objects after which some kuls are named. There are also no devaks as among the Marathas. Therefore Save questions the existence of totemism among them. They are patrilineal. In the north their dialect is largely influenced by Gujarati and in the south by Marathi.[62]

The *Thakur*, an ' early tribe ' living in or near forests, are also neighbours of the Katkari. Their language is Marathi. They have two endogamous divisions, and had originally three exogamous surnames, each with a separate devak—Jadhav, gold; Nargude, sunflower; and Pavar, the blade of a sword. In course of time, however, they adopted other surnames, all of which have the common devak comprising the twigs of the mango, the umbar, the jambul and the teak (*Tectona grandis*). They have, says Enthoven, a number of exogamous divisions or kuls, each consisting of a group of families bearing different surnames. A more recent investigator, L. N. Chapekar, does not mention totemism, but says that they have certain *kulis* or families which cannot marry into certain others, and in their marriage cere- monies they establish the devak, which is ' a collective term for the deities worshipped on an auspicious occasion ', in both the bride's and the bridegroom's homes. They have certain taboos relating to animals, and trees. They are patrilineal and patri- potestal, and have today thoroughly assimilated the plough culture.[63]

The *Mahar* are an impure or untouchable caste of menials, labourers and village watchmen in the Maratha country. Russell & Hiralal state that their name was probably derived from Maharashtra, that they are an aboriginal, pre-Aryan tribe, and that they were the oldest residents of the plains of Berar and Nagpur. They have a number of territorial subdivisions and numerous exogamous, totemic ' groups ', of which fifty-seven were recorded in the Central Provinces. Most of the common animals (tiger, cobra, peacock, jackal, lizard, elephant, lark, scor- pion, calf and so on) have septs named after them. Other objects which lend their names to the septs are mirror, sword and shield, sour milk, and coconut kernel. Still other sept names are rat- killer, incendiary, blind man, dog-killer, and vegetable-eater. Enthoven regards the Mahar as ' an assembly of tribal units ' comprising ' the broken residue of many former aboriginal tribes '. The Koli, the Bhoi, the Katkari, the Ramoshi and the Bedar have much in common with them. They are found throughout the Marathi-speaking areas of the Presidency, have several endogamous divisions and numerous exogamous surnames. The evidence, adds Enthoven, points to the fact that each of their exogamous units at one time owned and worshipped a devak or totem closely corresponding to the bali of the Kanarese 'tribes'. 'The object represented by the devak is worshipped, protected from injury by the section owning the devak and brought into prominence at the time of the marriage ceremony.' Families possessing a common devak are exogamous. Of the devaks listed, seven are animals, sixteen trees and their products, and two inanimate objects. In many instances the devak has become obsolete and has been replaced by a 'composite totem' or panchpalvi—the leaves of five trees which are similarly worshipped in the marriage ceremony. In Poona and Nasik the trees concerned are the mango, the pipal, the rui (*Calotropis gigantea*), the shami and the umbar; in Khandesh the arkathi, the borkathi, the jambul, the mango and the ruchkin; and in Satara the babul (*Acacia arabica*), the banyan or vad, the jambul, the mango and the rui. The Mahar profess Hinduism and are patrilineal after the Hindu usage. Robertson reports that they have many endogamous sub-castes and numerous exogamous kuls or clans marked by surnames often identical with those of the Marathas, and devaks or clan totems. 'So it usually happens', says Robertson, 'that parties of the same surname cannot marry; but the final basis of judgment as to who may marry is the *kula-devaka* or the clan totem. That is to say, no two persons who have the same devaka may marry. Some families bearing different surnames have the same devaka.' The devaka or godling is represented by a small metal *taka* or plate bearing the likeness of the clan totem. The devakas are as a rule animals (the buffalo, the tortoise, the mouse-deer, the crab, the cobra, the peacock) and trees (the umbar, the palm, the nandruk [*Ficus benjamina*], the mango, the champa). The taka are becoming obsolete and are being replaced by the panchpalvi or bunch of five leaves. Many Mahar surnames belong to the Kunbis and Marathas, some to Brahmin families, and others are shared by the Katkari. Kula descent is patrilineal. Robertson concludes that the Mahar are 'the remnant of an ancient people widely spread and divided into clans or tribes on whose social structure there supervened the organization of Brahminical society and culture'.[64]

The term *Koli*, Enthoven maintains, is a vague one and covers a number of tribes of low status which have little in common beyond a position inferior to the Kunbi or cultivating caste. Thus the Gujarati Koli differ very much from the Deccan or Konkan Koli. In the Deccan and Konkan there are many endogamous divisions. The Mahadev Koli had 24 clans or kuls originally, but these were later subdivided into 218 according to

Mackintosh. Similarity in devaks is also a bar to intermarriage. Hassan tells us that their sept names show a very curious mixture of different elements, but reports no totemism. Ghurye points out in his recent monograph on the Mahadev Koli that the only traces of totemism among them are that the women of the Bote family, whose family deity is Kolaba, are forbidden to wear black clothes and that the families which have Ghorapad (iguana) as their deity do not eat the iguana. The sept names mentioned by Mackintosh are no longer in existence, but their ‘spirit and content’—the exogamous restrictions—are still in force. A group of exogamous families is known as *gotribans* (gotra brothers), and according to tradition but not in actuality, each gotriban consists of twelve families. Ghurye points out further that no marriage takes place between individuals having the same family name. The District Gazetteer of Ahmednagar, however, affirms that the exogamy of the Mahadev Koli is based on devaks rather than on family names, the devaks being certain totemic objects towards which a number of Marathi-speaking castes maintain certain observances and on which they base their exogamous restrictions. Persons having the same devak or the same number cannot marry one another. The Maruti or monkey-god cult connects the Mahadev Koli with the Kunbis, the Marathas and other high castes of Maharashtra; and the Vagh-deva or tiger-god cult connects them with the Thakur, the Warli and other tribes of Maharashtra, and also with the Gond. In Maharashtra the Son Koli are fishermen, but the Mahadev Koli are agriculturists and cattle-breeders. According to Vijaya B. Punekar, the Son Koli are the highest of the Koli groups and have no devaks, no clans or totems. All the Koli groups are of course patrilineal.[65]

The *Dubla* of the Thana district and the talukas of Surat and Broach (South Gujarat) are today a group of serfs and landless labourers. Enthoven says that they have about 20 clans, but a recent monograph shows that they have nowadays no ‘definite idea of clans’. Nor is there any reliable evidence of totems and devaks. Although largely oriented towards Gujarat, the Dubla have been considered here to illustrate the proposition that the further northwards that one moves, the rarer becomes the devak phenomenon.[66]

*        *        *

It is regrettable that the external and lower castes of India have so far constituted a comparatively neglected field from the standpoint of detailed ethnographic investigations. Accordingly, for information on this important intermediate sector of the

population in South India we have had by and large to fall back
on the 'Tribes and Castes' series, or more precisely, on the
tantalizingly brief accounts in the compilations of Thurston &
Rangachari, Enthoven, Hassan, and Nanjundayya & Iyer. When
we add to this information whatever additional evidence on
totemism is available on the tribes and tribal castes of the area
in more recent monographs, the following picture emerges:

The extreme south—that is, the Tamil and Malayalam areas—
and Ceylon are generally speaking non-totemic areas. In Ceylon
the Vedda have exogamous clans with matrilineal descent, but
no totemism. There are some myths of the parallel-relationship
variety, but they stem from the Singhalese side, and are not an
integral part of the Vedda culture which is characterized by an
almost total absence of myths. The Tamil population of Ceylon
and the Singhalese are also non-totemic. The tribes and castes
of Travancore and Cochin (Kerala), as the evidence presented
by the Iyers in their ethnographic compilations indicates, are
almost entirely non-totemic. The Kanikar have matrilineal clans,
and an instance or two of legends which seek to explain the
origin of their clan names in a manner which is reminiscent of
legends in other totemic areas of India. But apart from these
legends no other traces of totemism are evident. Both the Kadar,
a primitive tribe of food-gatherers and hunters, and the Nayadi,
an untouchable caste, on which we have full-length monographs,
are likewise non-totemic.[67] There are a few castes in the Tamil
area which have exogamous septs with traces of totemism. But
this, as Thurston in reference to the Saliyan phrases it, is contrary to the usual custom of the Tamil castes. Therefore, these
castes may be considered migrants from the Telugu area or from
the Kanara area or recipients of diffused elements from these
areas.

The castes and tribal castes of the Telugu area have exogamous
clans named after animals, plants and inanimate objects with
occasional traces of relevant taboos. An outstanding characteristic
of this area is the predominance in most instances of inanimate
objects, adjectival terms and the like as clan names—non-genuine
totems, as Niggemeyer labels the latter category. Several of
these objects are evidently of recent origin. The inheritance of
the clan name is patrilineal; the myths of caste origin are
Hinduistic; and there is ample evidence to demonstrate considerable Hinduization of the Telugu-speaking castes.

In the Kanara area two facts stand out. The first, so far as
the incomplete reports permit an inference, is a trend towards
an increase in totems of a vegetable type—trees, plants, fruits,
flowers and the like; and the second is the matrilineal inheritance

of the totem. The base area in which the totems are matrilineally inherited is South Kanara, where the language is Tulu. From here matrilineal totemism has spread or has been carried southwards—the Kondayam Kottai Maravar; westwards—the Bili Magga, the Hasalar and others; and northwards—the Moger and the Nador. As one moves from South Kanara northwards into North Kanara and westwards into Mysore, patrilineal influences begin to assert themselves. This is exemplified by the facts that some castes which inherit the totems matrilineally in North Kanara and Mysore inherit property patrilineally; and that castes like the Bant, the Moger, the Halepaik and the Kelasi which are found in both South and North Kanara are matrilineal in totem and property inheritance in the south, but patrilineal in property inheritance in the north. There are a few castes in South Kanara also which inherit the totems matrilineally but property patrilineally—these are the Nalke, the Patvegara, the Holeya and the Bili Magga. South Kanara, however, is the only area in the south in which both the totems and property are inherited matrilineally—in Niggemeyer's list the number of such castes is seven. The nature of the totemic evidence suggests that totemism has considerably declined in the area; and that the initial form of totemism here must have been of a superficial, more or less external, variety.

Our principal informant on the devaks of the Marathi-speaking area is Enthoven who is also the most zealous advocate of the conception that the devaks among the Marathas and the surrounding castes and tribes are in essentials totemic in nature, and were once much more so. Devaks are found among the Marathas, among a number of occupational castes in the Marathi-speaking area, and to a less extent among the primitive tribes like the Katkari and the Thakur. From Surat northwards into Gujarat and Kathiawar the devak phenomenon declines considerably in frequency of occurrence, and occasional manifestations of it in these areas may be ascribed to migrations or influences from the area of Maratha domination. Towards the south, in Kanara, balis take the place of devaks, and Enthoven sees affinities between the two. He notes that there is a remarkable resemblance between the guardians or devaks of the Maratha castes in the Deccan and the balis of North Kanara. The following trees, animals and inanimate objects, for instance, occur as both devaks and balis: the nagchampa (*Mesua ferrea*), the jambul, the banyan, the screw-pine (*Pandanus odoratissimus*), the mouse-deer, the tortoise, the axe, gold and turmeric. Furthermore, in North Kanara it is a common practice to keep and worship in the village temples carved tablets depicting the *vansh* or five ancestors of the village community. Enthoven identifies these five ancestors with the panchpalvi or leaves of five trees, the most frequent of the devaks in the Marathi-speaking area, which, however, does not occur as such among the Kanarese castes. Enthoven therefore concludes that these facts point to a similarity of origin between certain tribes and castes in the Marathi-speaking area and those further south in the Kanarese area.

Saldanha gives the following derivations of the term bali: (i) from *balli*, *tadbhava* of Sanskrit, a creeper, a line; hence that which traces descent; (ii) from *bale*, a bracelet of glass worn by females; the female inheritance of the bali in many cases in the Kanarese area is adduced in support of this derivation; (iii) *bali*, a Dravidian word, means a way, a road, and hence that which traces one's lineage, sept or clan. Enthoven gives the following meanings of the term: (*a*) way, road, (*b*) place, spot, (*c*) vicinity, nearness, company, (*d*) way, order, (*e*) race or lineage, (*f*) navel. Enthoven adds that it is further the term for the exogamous sections and also for the totems among the castes of the Kanarese tracts, and that it corresponds to the term *bari* in Tamil and *bedagu* [68] in Telugu. The balis or exogamous sections may be named after some well-known animal, fish, bird, tree, fruit or flower; and the members of the sections not only worship the animal or object after which they are named but also follow strict rules framed to protect them from injury. Either the bali or an image of it in stone or wood is usually installed in a rude shrine near the village, and coconuts and other offerings are made to secure its favour and protection. At certain seasons members of the section gather together with the caste priest and make special offerings. The inheritance of the bali through the mother was probably the earliest practice, and this was later displaced by descent through the father.

Further north, in the Marathi-speaking area, says Enthoven, a similar organization is also to be found. Of the 120 devaks discovered the most common are the mango, the kadam (*Anthocephalus cadamba*), the peacock, the pipal (*Ficus religiosa*), the rui (*Calotropis gigantea*), the shami (*Prosopis spicegera*), the umbar (*Ficus glomerata*) and the vad (*Ficus indica*). A large number of the devaks are trees. Among many groups the possession of identical devaks is a bar to marriage; among some the exogamous kuls are named after the devaks; in Sholapur persons bearing the names of animals or trees (wolf, tiger, pig, buffalo, parrot, cormorant, and snake-gourd) hold that they are descended from them; and a significant point of the devak worship is that it must not be injured by those who acknowledge it. It is, however, at marriages and other special occasions that the devaks receive special worship.

Enthoven analyses the course of social development as follows: At first each exogamous unit had its own devak. With the progress of the primitive tribes towards greater social unity, the panchpalvi came into existence, and became a frequent composite totem, leading to the decline of totem exogamy. This is evidenced by the fact that of the five trees from which leaves are taken to form the panchpalvi, one is regarded with special reverence by the family stock concerned, who do not injure it or make use of it in any way. After the panchpalvi come the kuls or family stocks named after human progenitors, the Marathas claiming 96 of these kuls. In other words, social evolution in the Bombay Presidency shows progress from ancestor worship in the guise of trees and animals to a system of family stocks in which a human progenitor displaces the totems of an earlier stage. Later, the human progenitor is in turn displaced by the eponymous rishi of a gotra in imitation of the Brahmins.

Enthoven thus maintains that the Marathas contain a much stronger pre-Aryan racial element than was hitherto believed. The fact that the Marathas have a totemic organization, that they and the Maratha Kunbis share some of their devaks with primitive tribes and low castes like the Bhoi, the Bhil, the Mahar, the Chambhar, the Burud and the Koli, and that neither the Vedas nor the subsequent orthodox Hindu texts contain any mention of the worship of trees, animals and other objects regarded as ancestors of groups which are exogamous are pointers to a pre-Aryan origin of the Marathas; and this despite their Aryan language, their quasi-Rajput stocks and claims of a Kshatriya origin. Many of the occupational castes like the Parit, the Nhavi and the Kumbhar were originally Marathas who lost status as a result of their occupation. The Kunbi cultivators are also Marathas but of a somewhat inferior social standing. The Maratha claim to belong to the ancient 96 Kshatriya families has no foundation in fact and may have been adopted after the Marathas became with Shivaji a power to be reckoned with.

The origin of the word Maratha (Enthoven tells us) has been traced variously as follows: (i) to Maharashtra which, according to Sanskrit writers of the north, comprised the great Deccan plain; (ii) to a combination of *maha* (great) and *rashtrika* (a Sanskrit term for petty chiefs in the Deccan); (iii) to a combination of *maha* (great) and *ratha* (a chariot-rider or warrior). The earliest reference to the Marathas occurs in an inscription of about 100 B.C. The term Maratha embraces three classes: (i) the Marathas proper or chiefs, land-owners and warriors of the

Deccan and Konkan who claim to be Kshatriyas and avoid widow marriage. They are socially superior to the cultivating castes of Kunbis, with whom, however, they maintain in places a hypergamous relation; (ii) the Maratha Kunbis or cultivators; there is little or no difference between the Marathas and the Kunbis; (iii) the occupational castes. Judging from the devaks all these three classes appear to have had a common origin.[69]

The views of some other writers on the origin of the Marathas may be added here for purposes of contrast and comparison. Colonel James Tod regarded them as the offspring of Rajputs and the local population. Risley believed that they originated in groups of Scythians who were driven from the pasture-lands in Western Punjab towards the south where they intermixed with the Dravidians. Crooke, however, affirms that there is no historical or traditional evidence of a Scythian migration into the Deccan and that the Marathas are closely connected with a mixed race of cultivators who are found in a vast area from the Deccan to the valley of the Ganges and are known as Kunbis or Kurmis. In course of time they asserted their superiority over the humbler Kunbis, but took brides from them while at the same time refusing to give their own daughters in marriage to them. In some places they have secured the right of marriage with certain Rajput clans. Their totemism points to a pre-Aryan origin. Russell & Hiralal say that they are a military caste of south India, mainly derived from the peasant population of Kunbis. They claim Rajput origin and several of their clans have Rajput names. They are a caste of purely military origin recruited from the various castes of Maharashtra. Some of their families may have had Rajput ancestors. Syed Siraj ul Hassan states that they are the chief fighting, land-owning and cultivating caste of the Deccan, Berar and the Central Provinces. The term Maratha comprises all the classes of society in Maharashtra —the Brahmins, the low castes like the Nhavi and the Parit, and the unclean classes like the Mahar and the Mang. More specifically, however, it refers to the fighting and land-owning groups on the one hand, and the agricultural Kunbis on the other. Some of the higher groups appear to be of Rajput descent.[70]

Enthoven's view that the devaks are totemic survivals has been called into question by Abbott. As Niggemeyer, basing himself on Enthoven, characterizes the phenomenon as Maratha totemism and offers a series of interpretations emanating from this conception, Abbott's denial of the totemic character of the phenomenon is worthy of careful attention. Abbott's criticism runs as follows: (i) On the basis of the evidence derived from the Katkari it is impossible to ascribe a totemic origin to the devak.

There are a few examples of the survival of genuine totemism in the Bombay Presidency, as among the Katkari for instance. But the totemic organization of the Katkari is for practical purposes a thing of the past. The totem plays no part in the invocation of the dead, in the marriage ceremony or in other rituals practised by the Katkari. The Katkari also have devaks which are more or less identical with those of the Marathas, but tradition indicates that groups with different devaks constitute one and the same original family. Further, unlike the totem, the devak plays an important part in the marriage ceremony. Thus, the Katkari have both totems and devaks. (ii) The existing definitions of the term devak are many and do not have the same connotation. Frazer calls the devaks sacred symbols which appear to have been originally totems. Enthoven, too, accepts the connexion between the devak and totemism, but has differing views on its inner nature. In 1909 he called it a marriage guardian; in 1922 he spoke of it as a ' god of the exogamous section ' and identified the devaks of the Pardeshi Kumbhar with their family deities, and of the Bari with their ' house goddess '; and in 1926 he phrased his view of the matter as follows: the devak is ' the totemistic spirit contained in some tree, animal or material object which in addition to being the subject of special worship, regulates the marriage laws of many primitive sections of the population. In origin it appears to have been an ancestral spirit '. To Campbell the devak was a marriage guardian. But the kula devata or family gods of the Hindus are not ancestral spirits; nor do the Marathas identify their devaks with ancestral spirits. The offerings that are made to the *pitri* or ancestors are not made to the devaks. There is also a ceremony in which an ancestral spirit is invoked at a marriage. It is called *Mulapurusa* and is practised among castes which have devaks; but it has no connexion with the installation of the devak and may even be performed together with the devak ceremony at marriages. Finally, the only explanation which the Marathas offer of their devaks is that they were originally objects by which the families took an oath. (iii) There is some identity of names between Maratha families and their devaks; on the other hand, it is easy to find families which have devaks other than the animals or trees which the family names signify. In fact, the number of families with names similar to their devaks is smaller than that of families with no such similarity. Again, there is reliable evidence to suggest that punning or play on words and names may lead to the choice of a devak, the extension of its meaning, the erection of taboos and forms of charms on the ground that there is *sakti* or power in a name.

(iv) The source from which the devak is taken is not invariably revered, and when it is, the reverence is not necessarily totemic. Enthoven's assertion that the devaks are totemic, as the objects they represent are not touched, cut or otherwise used, contains several inaccurate surmises. Some of the objects reverenced acquire their sanctity as the result of a general Hindu belief and practice; and there are many instances of trees from which devaks are cut which are not reverenced except when the devak is taken from them. (v) Other considerations which discredit the hypothesis that the devak is or was a totem are the facts that the family sometimes extends the meanings of its devak when it divides (the Powars have a sword or knife as devak, the Dhar Powars stick a lemon at its point, the Har Powars put a garland of onions or umbar around it and so on); that many families have more than one devak which they use alternatively, one of them being an easily obtainable object; that families which claim no interrelationship at all have the same devak and vice versa; that the substitution of one devak for another is a frequent occurrence when there is a similarity of names; that there are villages in which a number of racially different groups and different sects have a common devak; that when a family migrates from one village to another it often adopts the devak which is common in the area; and that the similarity of devaks is not a universal bar to intermarriage. (vi) The panchpalvi and craft tools can be called devaks only in a loose sense, and the reasons quoted to justify the view that they are totems are irrelevant. The number of trees used in the panchpalvi is limited in relation to the number of devaks known. Nor does the panchpalvi act as a bar to consanguineous marriages. Again, there is no evidence to suggest that one leaf in the panchpalvi receives special reverence. Further, the panchpalvi occurs frequently in Hindu ritual, but its use as a devak is precisely restricted. So far as the craft tools are concerned, many craftsmen tie their tools to the marriage booth, but do not call them devaks; and when they do, it very likely signifies that the tools are imbued with sakti or divine power. (vii) The devak is, therefore, not a totem or a family god, but a symbol into which the sakti of a deity is temporarily invoked, according to the Hindu practice of *avahana*. Among the Marathas and related castes the sakti of the often identical village or family god is invoked into the devak to ensure the presence of the deity in the marriage booth during the marriage ceremony. The ritual followed in the installation of the devak is in accordance with the ordinary canons which guide the practice of avahana. There are also parallel customs in the Karnatak (the halgamba), among the Jains in Gujarat (the manekstambha or ruby pillar), among the Tamil Christians (the arasani kallu), among the Rajputs (the vedikhamb), and among the Ahir Gauli immigrants from Mysore (the manda), which have no connexion at all with totemism, but with the invocation of sakti. Thus both internal and external evidence indicates that the devaks are not totems but temporary repositories of divine sakti. The devak institution is found mainly in the Deccan and Konkan, and probably had its origin in the latter area.

Hence Abbott sums up the matter as follows: ' To go from the *manda*, the *manekstambha*, and the *vedikhamb* through the *halgamba* to the Maratha *devak* is merely to proceed in orderly stages from the use of a single symbol by a whole caste to a differentiation of symbols among families which reaches its most perfect form in the *devak*. To assume *a priori* that the *devak* is a totem is to neglect altogether these other customs which are so alike in ritual detail and meaning and to which no totemistic origin can be attributed. The whole theory of totemism in fine as applied to the *devak* institution is a loose construction based on deduction from a few premises, moulded by assumed analogy and framed without consideration for one of the principal and fundamental axioms of Indian thought.' [71]

## NOTES AND REFERENCES

[1] 1952, 3-5, 130-1, 156-7, 180-1, 274, 295.
[2] 1937, i, 1-74. Mukherjee (1953, 38), however, denies the existence of the Muttillom and Menillom moieties as reported by Iyer.
[3] 1934, 183.
[4] 1911, 30-2, 36, 41, 73-5, 78-9, 102, 104, 150-3, 178, 180, 191-2, 195, 197, 203, 416, 422.
[5] Thurston & Rangachari, 1909, ii, 26-45; Khan, 1935, 209-12; Fürer-Haimendorf, 1943a, 4, 75, 87-96, 107, 157-8, 180-2, 184-6, 189, 190, 195-6, 224-8, 279, 281, 284, 292.
[6] 1930, iii, 378-92.
[7] Nanjundayya & Iyer, 1931, iv, 592-9.
[8] C. H. Rao, 1909; Frazer, 1910, ii, 232-3. Frazer uses Rao's data.
[9] 1906, 6, 18, 34-6, 183, 432, 455-6, 540.
[10] Thurston & Rangachari, 1909, ii, 284-92; Hassan, 1920, i, 204-9; Nanjundayya & Iyer, 1930, iii, 201-40.
[11] Thurston & Rangachari, 1909, i, 218-22; Nanjundayya & Iyer, 1928, ii, 239-57.
[12] Thurston & Rangachari, 1909, i, 134-41; iii, 222-43.
[13] Thurston & Rangachari, 1909, iii, 306-43; Hassan, 1920, i, 340-5; Nanjundayya & Iyer, 1930, iii, 536-82.
[14] Thurston & Rangachari, 1909, iv, 292-322; Nanjundayya & Iyer, 1931, iv, 125-69.

15 Thurston & Rangachari, 1909, vi, 170-2; Nanjundayya & Iyer, 1931, iv, 625-36.
16 Thurston & Rangachari, 1909, ii, 154-66; Nanjundayya & Iyer, 1931, iii, 118-38.
17 Nanjundayya & Iyer, 1931, iv, 429-51; Frazer, 1910, ii, 275.
18 Thurston & Rangachari, 1909; Nanjundayya & Iyer, 1928; 1935; Raghaviah, 1962, 117-24.
19 1933, 440-2, 601-19.
20 Thurston & Rangachari, 1909, i, 147-72; Sturrock, 1894, i, 158, 160, speaks of 20 balis; Saldhana, 1909, 386-7.
21 Sturrock, 1894, i, 171; Thurston & Rangachari, 1909, iii, 268-77.
22 Sturrock, 1894, i, 179; Thurston & Rangachari, 1909, v, 141-6; Saldanha, 1909, 387; Niggemeyer, 1933, 441.
23 Sturrock, 1894, i, 167; Thurston & Rangachari, 1909, i, 240-2; Saldanha, 1909, 387; Frazer, 1910, ii, 274; Nanjundayya & Iyer, 1928, ii, 277-87.
24 Sturrock, 1894, i, 172; Saldanha, 1909, 387; Thurston & Rangachari, 1909, i, 243-8; Nanjundayya & Iyer, 1928, ii, 290-5.
25 Sturrock, 1894, i, 173; Saldanha, 1909, 387; 1912, 262; Thurston & Rangachari, 1909, ii, 320-1; Enthoven, 1922, ii, 34-6; Nanjundayya & Iyer, 1930, iii, 278-94; Niggemeyer, 1933, 442, 610.
26 Sturrock, 1894, i, 174; Thurston & Rangachari, 1909, ii, 329-51; Frazer, 1910, ii, 271-2; Nanjundayya & Iyer, 1930, iii, 320-49; Saldanha, 1909, 387; Enthoven, 1922, ii, 75-6; Niggemeyer, 1933, 441, 610.
27 Thurston & Rangachari, 1909, vi, 187-8; Nanjundayya & Iyer, 1931, iv, 476-81; Sturrock, 1894, i, 167; Saldanha, 1909, 387.
28 Nanjundayya & Iyer, 1931, iv, 1-3; Enthoven, 1922, ii, 47-55, 271.
29 Thurston & Rangachari, 1909, v, 65-70; Enthoven, 1922, iii, 59-61; Saldanha, 1912, 273; Sturrock, 1894, i, 168.
30 Nanjundayya & Iyer, 1930, iii, 296-307; Enthoven, 1922, ii, 67-8.
31 Fawcett, 1903; 1915, 186-7; Thurston & Rangachari, 1909, iii, 71-5; iv, 35; v, 22-46, 246, 472-7. More recently L. Dumont made some study of the Maravar groups in the field. See his *Une Sous-Caste de l'Inde du Sud* (Paris, 1957), ' Hierarchy and Marriage Alliance in South Indian Kinship ' (Occasional Papers of the Royal Anthropological Institute of Great Britain and Ireland, No. 12, 1957) and his notes on the Maravar subcastes in Bala Ratnam (Ed.), *Anthropology on the March* (Madras, 1963). Dumont questions Fawcett's information that the Kodayam Kottai Maravar are divided into 18 units grouped by threes into 6 larger groups. He could himself only discover eleven. Nor does Dumont mention plant totems.
32 Sturrock, 1894, i, 170; Thurston & Rangachari, 1909, ii, 154; Saldhana, 1909, 387; 1912, 260-5, 273; Enthoven, 1922, iii, 117-19, 353-5; Niggemeyer, 1933, 441-2, 607, 614, 616.
33 Nanjundayya & Iyer, 1928, ii, 94-8; 1930, iii, 260-8; 1931, iv, 397-401.
34 Thurston & Rangachari, 1909, iii, 417-18.
35 Thurston & Rangachari, 1909, vi, 277-8.
36 Thurston, & Rangachari, 1909, vii, 299-300.
37 Thurston & Rangachari, 1909, iii, 215-18.
38 Thurston & Rangachari, 1909, vii, 299-300.
39 Thurston & Rangachari, 1909, iv, 138-55; Nanjundayya & Iyer, 1931, iv, 27-73.
40 Thurston & Rangachari, 1909, i, 382; vi, 402-4; Sturrock, 1894, i, 150-1, 154-5; Saldanha, 1909, 382; 1912, 263; Nanjundayya & Iyer, 1918, ii, 542-4.
41 Saldanha, 1912, 264, 273; Enthoven, 1920, i, 5-7.

[42] Saldanha, 1912, 265, 273, 276; Enthoven, 1920, I, 353-4; 1922, II, 47-55, 162.

[43] Saldanha, 1912, 264, 273; Enthoven, 1922, III, 65-9.

[44] Thurston & Rangachari, 1909, I, 180-209. See also Frazer, 1910, II, 231. Frazer, basing himself on W. Francis in the *Census of India*, 1901, xv, Madras, Part 1 and on Thurston & Rangachari, 1909, I, speaks of 101 totemic clans of the Boya with the usual taboos. Of the examples given, 15 are animal, 4 vegetable and 13 various other totems. Nanjundayya & Iyer, 1928, II, 197-237.

[45] Quoted by Frazer, 1910, II, 276-8; Enthoven, 1911, 65.

[46] 1916, IV, 198-204.

[47] 1909; 1911; 1922, III, 3-40; 1924a; 1924b; 1924c, 18-20, 208-21. For a variation in the form of devak worship, see Enthoven, 1924b, 210-11.

[48] 1953, 156-63.

[49] Enthoven, 1920, I, 96-103.

[50] ibid., 263-8.

[51] ibid., 347-50.

[52] ibid., 359-63.

[53] Enthoven, 1922, II, 276-82.

[54] ibid., 284-314.

[55] ibid., 422-5.

[56] Enthoven, 1922, III, 127-34.

[57] ibid., 370.

[58] Enthoven, 1922, II, 99-100; III, 327-31.

[59] Enthoven, 1922, III, 361-4.

[60] Weling mentions 80, and adds that the list is not exhaustive and that they had these clan names from an early period. Mackintosh mentions 4, Hearn 3 and the *Bombay Gazetteer* 8.

[61] Niggemeyer, 1933, 611; Enthoven, 1922, II, 170-81; Weling, 1934, 1, 49-51, 52-7, 85-6, 121. Abbott says, ' The Katkari illustrates a totemistic organization which for practical purposes is now a thing of the past. He calls his totem brother, and has vague ideas that he may be re-born as his totem; he also pays a certain respect to the totem, but this figures in none of his ritual. It plays no part in his celebration of *Sarvapitri Amavasya*, when through the medium of symbols, usually *tak* or engraved pieces of copper, he invokes the spirits of his dead, and its absence from his marriage ceremonies is still more marked ' (1932, 448). See also Manndorff, 1960, 41.

[62] Enthoven, 1922, III, 445-7; Save, 1945, 1, 5, 12-17, 189.

[63] Enthoven, 1922, III, 376-81; L. N. Chapekar, 1960, 2, 15-16, 53, 56-7, 96, 104, 215.

[64] Russell & Hiralal, 1916, IV, 129-44; Enthoven, 1922, II, 401-15; Robertson, 1938, 9, 17, 52-5, 57; Karve, 1953, 16-17.

[65] Enthoven, 1922, II, 245-55; Hassan, 1920, I, 332-6; Ghurye, 1957, 2-3, 6-7, 26, 40-8, 96-7, 105, 123, 215; Russell & Hiralal, 1916, III, 534-6; Koppers, 1943; Punekar, 1959.

[66] Enthoven, 1920, I, 341-2; Shah, 1958, 11, 26, 30, 33, 171.

[67] Ehrenfels, 1952; Aiyappan, 1937.

[68] But the more usual Sanskritic meaning equates *balli* with *pinda* from *pind*, to press together; hence balls of rice offered to the *pancha bhuta* (living beings). See Raja Radha Kanta Deva's *Shabda-Kalpadruma*, Part III, 400ff. At every meal orthodox Hindus (*smartas*) must set apart before commencing their meal five little heaps of rice (*pinda, bali*) for the pancha

bhuta. Among the bhuta are ancestors, devas and different categories of animals. These offerings are made because it is the householder's obligation to sustain the entire world.

69 1909, 1911, 1920-2, 1921, 1924a, 1924b, 1924c.

70 Risley, 1915, Crooke's Introduction, xx-xxi; Russell & Hiralal, 1916, IV, 198-204; Hassan, 1920, I, 473-91.

71 Abbott, 1932, 448-60, 461-4, 526-7. Of the devaks listed in App. I in Abbott's book (461-3) approximately 119 are trees and creepers, 19 are animals, 32 various other objects, and of 44 the meanings are not known.

# VIII

## THE NEGRITO OF THE ANDAMAN ISLANDS

THERE ARE TWO REASONS why the Negrito of the Andaman Islands are examined here. The first is that Radcliffe-
Brown, as we have seen, traces the phenomenon of totemism to
certain ritual relations towards animals and plants among tribes
with or without totemism such as the Eskimo and the Andaman
Islanders, and that Baumann has demonstrated the existence of
a complex of beliefs and practices among specialized hunting
tribes, which he calls 'proto-totemism' and which he and some
other ethnologists regard as the background of group totemism.
The second is that some anthropologists like Guha and Hutton
affirm the existence of a Negrito substratum in India, traces of
which are found particularly among the primitive tribes in the
hills and jungles of south India and to a less extent among some
of the Naga tribes in the extreme northeast.

Frazer, basing himself on E. H. Man, says: 'The Andamanese
appear to have individual totems, for every man and woman
is prohibited all through life from eating some one (or more)
fish or animal; generally the forbidden food is one which the
mother thought disagreed with the child; but if no food disagreed with him, the person is free to choose what animal he
will avoid.' Radcliffe-Brown, however, was not able to confirm
Man's observation that it was necessary for every person to have
some forbidden food; nevertheless, in his essay on totemism he
refers to the ritual attitude towards the turtle and other animals
and plants among the Andaman Islanders, which expresses itself
in mythology or in which the animal species are personified and
regarded as ancestors or culture heroes, and suggests that totemism arises from or is a special development of this general ritual
relation between man and natural species.[1]

Racially and culturally the Andaman Islanders are a branch
of the Asiatic Negrito exemplified further by the Semang of the
Malay Peninsula and the Negrito of the Philippine Islands. The
distribution of the Asiatic Negrito indicates that they must

[1] For notes to this chapter see p. 214.

have wandered over a wide area in southeastern Asia hundreds or thousands of years ago. Almost entirely isolated in their island home, the Andaman Islanders may be thus considered the direct descendants in physical character, in language and in culture, of the original Negrito race. The Andaman Islanders, says Radcliffe-Brown, are pure hunters and food-gatherers, and have nuclear families, local groups and tribes, but no clans.[2] Lidio Cipriani asserted in his report on a survey of the Little Andaman during 1951-3 that in each communal hut of the Onge there was an exogamous clan tracing its origin from a common ancestor; but changed his mind thereafter.[3]

The relevant beliefs and practices of the Andaman Islanders in their ceremonial life and mythology are as follows: (i) In North Andaman there is a kind of association between the un-born souls of babies, the green pigeon and the *Ficus laccifera* tree. It is sometimes stated that the souls of unborn children live in Ficus trees, and that if the baby dies before it is weaned its soul goes back to the tree. Another statement has it that the soul of the baby goes into the mother when the green pigeon is calling. The green pigeon is fond of the fruit of the Ficus tree, and both green pigeon and Ficus tree are denoted by the same term—*renko*. Although the Ficus tree is to some extent tabooed, that is, it must not be cut or damaged, the Andamanese do cut it and use the bark of its aerial roots for personal ornaments. The green pigeon is not tabooed. (ii) Among some tribes there are several myths in which the monitor lizard appears as the first ancestor of the Andaman race with a dove or a civet cat as its wife, and a woodpecker as their son. These ancestors are sup-posed to have taught the arts and crafts to the Andamanese. (iii) Other myths speak of the transformation of human beings into animals such as crabs, lizards, turtles, fishes, birds and jungle beasts. In many versions of a great catastrophe which befell the ancestors, the legend relates how the ancestors were transformed into fishes and birds. In North Andaman one of the ancestors, Kolo by name, made wings for himself out of palm leaves, was thus able to fly, lived a solitary life on the top of a tree, and in the end became a sea-eagle. This species of bird still bears his name, and the Andamanese regard the entire species as if it were human. (iv) Many trees and animals or substances from them are endowed with magical properties. Examples are the *Ficus laccifera*, the *Hibiscus tiliaceus*, the *Anadendron paniculatum*, the tree lizard, the rat, the civet cat, the flying fox, beeswax and so on. (v) The personification of animals is a common feature of the myths. Thus, a species of ant makes a turtle-net and goes fishing. In South Andaman the monitor lizard is said to have invented scarification; the prawn discovers yam, cooks it on a fire and eats it; the fly hunts pigs and so also does the dove. (vi) Many personal names are names of trees, fishes and other animals, or objects like rope and mat. During the menstrual ceremonies, the girl is referred to as *alebe* or *toto*, toto being the name of a species of pandanus from which women's belts are made, and the leaves of which are used in the menstrual cere-monies. At this time the girl receives a new or flower name by which she is addressed from then on. The new name is that of a plant or tree which happens to flower at that time. (vii) The Andamanese believe in forest spirits which are, however, assumed to be spirits of dead men or women and dangerous to the living. Further, Radcliffe-Brown connects the spirit Biliku with the wind and reports that the spider (*biliku*), a certain species of insect like the cicada, a species of beetle, two species of fish, a mollusc, and a certain bird must not be killed, or Biliku will be angry and send violent storms. Again, a species of bird, *col*, is supposed to possess supernatural powers. Radcliffe-Brown states further that there is no fixity or unanimity of beliefs among the Andamanese. The beliefs are floating and lacking in precision, and the various versions of the myths are often contradictory.[4]

In explaining the beliefs and practices of the Andamanese in their ceremonial life and mythology, Radcliffe-Brown indicates the inadequacy of both the intellectualist hypothesis which views the beliefs of aborigines as an attempt at explaining the pheno-mena of life and nature and the hypothesis which attributes primitive beliefs to the emotions of surprise and terror, or awe and wonder. Following in the footsteps of Durkheim, Hubert and Mauss, he notes that every custom and belief plays a part in the social life of the community, and that therefore the study of customs necessitates a kind of social psychology. The existence of a society depends on a certain system of sentiments in the minds of its members. This system regulates the conduct of the individual in conformity with the requirements of the society. Every event or object which affects the well-being or cohesion of the society becomes a part of the system of sentiments, and thus has social value. These sentiments are not innate, but are developed by the action of the society on the individual. The ceremonial customs which give collective expression to the senti-ments on appropriate occasions maintain and transmit the senti-ments from generation to generation. The social value of a thing may be positive or negative in so far as it promotes or detracts from the well-being of the society. In the affective atti-tude of the individual towards the social order there are two chief moments—the sense of the individual's dependence on society, and his need of conforming to its requirements. The Andamanese believe like the Melanesians in a power or force inherent in all objects which in any way affect the social life; and it is by means of this power that these things can aid or harm society, that is, this power is able to produce either good or evil. Contact with this power is dangerous, but the danger can be avoided by ritual precautions. The degree of power in things is directly proportional to the importance of their effect on the social life; and the power in one thing may be used to counteract the power in other things. This power, then, is inherent in plants and animals and other phenomena of nature, in the world of the spirits, in certain individuals, and also in society. The society is the chief source of protection for the individual, and the well-being of the society depends on these powers. Although these powers are fundamentally the same, in a sense each kind of thing has its own peculiar power. In the final analysis, this power is the moral force of the society acting directly or indirectly on the individual. The personification of natural phenomena in the myths is one of the methods by which the moral forces experienced in society are projected outwards. To the primitives the natural laws are moral laws.[5]

In the above interpretation Radcliffe-Brown perpetrates what David Bidney calls the sociologistic fallacy; in other words, he assumes with Durkheim that society is the ultimate ontological entity *sui generis*. But the fact is that there is a determinative, substantive and ontological human nature which is logically and genetically prior to human society and culture. If there were no such determinative human nature, there could be no characteristically human society and no culture. There is, of course, a relationship of polarity and complementarity between human nature on the one side and society and culture on the other. This relationship implies that while there is some degree of independence or autonomy of the factors involved in it, there is also some degree of interdependence.[6] Among other things human nature is characterized by a basic finitude or inadequacy, from which arises a sense of dependence on the world of spirits and nature and on society, and a craving for complementarity. Thus the Andamanese believe that a man who comes into contact with the spirits and is not intimidated by them will acquire magical powers, that their medicine-men possess supernatural powers, and that their ancestors were bigger and more powerful than themselves and had magical powers. Their belief in a pervasive power or force like the mana of the Polynesians follows genetically from the actual fact of human finitude, and is then projected into the world of spirits, of nature, and of society.

Turning to the question of a Negrito substratum in India, it may be pointed out that it has from the inception divided students who have dealt with it into two groups: those who deny the existence of Negritos in India and those who affirm it. Two prominent scholars who in comparatively recent times have denied the existence of Negritos in India are Eickstedt and Majumdar; two equally outstanding scholars who have on the other hand recently affirmed their existence at one time on the subcontinent are Guha and Hutton. Both Guha and Hutton accept certain anthropological features of certain backward tribes in south India and in the extreme northeast as surviving traces of the former existence of Negritos in India. Hutton regards the Negritos as the earliest human inhabitants of the Indian Peninsula, and holds that the sacredness of the pipal tree in India can possibly be traced to their influence.[7] The Andaman Islanders are the nearest surviving group of Negritos to India.

## NOTES AND REFERENCES

[1] Frazer, 1910, I, 52; Radcliffe-Brown, 1933, 115; 1952, 126.
[2] 1933, 6, 23.
[3] 1953, 61-82; 1963. What Cipriani's investigations clearly show, however, is that the isolation of these islands was not total.
[4] 1933, 89, 91, 93-6, 118, 136, 140, 156, 161, 163, 170, 181-4, 193-6, 206-10, 217-23, 387-8.
[5] 1933, 229-30, 232-4, 264, 306-7, 310, 313, 323, 326, 381, 384.
[6] Bidney, 1953, 120, 126, 140-1, 154, etc.
[7] 1961, 2, 3, 7, 8, 223, 231.

# IX

## THE TRIBES OF ASSAM

In the extreme northeast of India, that is to say, in Assam, there are traces of totemism among the Naga and other tribes, which have been interpreted in various ways. One of the early interpreters, Hodson, regarded these traces as proving ' the existence in this area not so much of totemism as of a mental attitude, a *Weltanschauung*, which in other parts of the world have permitted totemism to flourish and prosper '.[1] Later, Hutton surveyed some of the evidence anew and came to the conclusion that Hodson's view was not far off the mark.[2] Thereafter, Fürer-Haimendorf in an early article maintained that at one time there existed in ' Further India ', and particularly in Assam, a totemic culture or a mixed, matrilineal-totemic culture basically similar to that of the South Seas.[3] Lastly, Niggemeyer, whose study of totemism in India we have summarized in an earlier chapter, held out the possibility that the totemic substratum of Assam and Further India could have once been connected with the totemism of India or even have been identical with it.[4]

The totemic evidence as found in this area is as follows:

*The Konyak Naga*: In his field investigation of the Konyak Naga, the results of which were published in 1941, Fürer-Haimendorf could find no myths of clan origin among the tribe of the kind reported for the Ao. The Konyak, however, believe that their ancestors, as also all mankind, issued from a mythical bird. One clan has some connexion with the frog, which is believed to devour the sun and thus cause eclipses. Hutton asserts that in some Konyak villages an entire clan has dark brown skin and fuzzy hair suggesting the Negrito type. The Konyak have a tradition of having driven out an earlier race of monkey people.[5]

*The Ao Naga*: Both J. P. Mills, author of a monograph on the Ao Naga, and Fürer-Haimendorf point out that among the tribes of this area totemism is strongest among the Ao. The Ao have patrilineal, exogamous clans and phratries. The Wozukamr clan claims descent from a woman who, it is believed, was impregnated by the feather of a hornbill. The bird is taboo to the members of this clan. The great hornbill is regarded with respect and veneration by all Naga, who see in it an emblem of bravery, its tail-feathers being the insignia of the successful warrior. Another clan claims to have originated from a gibbon caught in a trap, which later turned into a man. Still another clan claims descent from a dog, which also turned into a man when the great hero Chongli went out on a hunt with it. But the members of this clan do not avoid eating dogs. Still another clan claims descent from a plantain tree. Other clans are possibly connected with the sparrow, the worm and the gourd. The members of the sun clan are supposed to be descendants of a woman who fainted in the sun and was thus impregnated by it. An earlier investigator, W. C. Smith, speaks of a lime fruit clan and partial totems.[6]

*The Sema Naga*: The clan organization is weak as compared with the village. Some clans have certain food restrictions which seem to hint at totemism. The Wotzami clan abstain from killing and eating the hoolock ape, and acknowledge a vague blood-relationship with it, but do not always like to be reminded of this fact. They also believe that some members of the clan turned into hoolock apes after their death. All Sema abstain from eating and touching the hornbill. Another clan seems to be descended from the red plantain, and some abstain from eating it. But there are also other explanations of the origin of this clan. Still another clan does not eat a species of edible fungus because it grows in large numbers at the place where the ancestors of the clan emerged from the earth. There is a somewhat similar taboo concerning the winged ant. Hutton, however, maintains that, apart from the Wotzami clan, not a single clan genuinely traces descent from an animal or plant and that there are no definite totems. He also reports the belief that a woman of the tribe had three children, of which one was a spirit, another a human being and the third a tiger. But the tiger is not a totem. The hornbill, the tiger and the python may be classed together because the Sema surround them with the same attitude of awe and respect. The Sema have a vast number of food taboos. They are confirmed lycanthropists, and believe that the soul conceived as a shadow may occupy the body of a leopard or a tiger during life. After death the soul may sometimes take the form of a particular species of hawk. A possible hint at sex totemism also occurs here. In the more southern villages of Zumoni and Asimi, it is believed that the sand-lizard informs the spirits of the birth of male children. This enables the spirits to come together and to destroy the new-born child. Hence, men kill the sand-lizard if they happen to see it; but women always let it go unharmed, because it does not leave its hole when a female child is born. It is reported that, if men try to kill the sand-lizard, the women sometimes make a fuss and endeavour to protect it.[7]

*The Angami Naga* have patrilineal, exogamous clans, but no traces of totemism. Fürer-Haimendorf at one time explained the absence of totemic traces among them and the Naga of Manipur by maintaining that the elements of the ancient culture preserved by the Konyak and the Ao are proportionately weak among the Angami and the Naga of Manipur. Hutton reports that he personally came into contact with an Angami who refused to kill snakes, the reason being that snakes were taboo to him and his household. It appeared that a snake was found in his house, and later when he removed to a new house, the snake was present there too, and persisted in remaining in the vicinity. His kindred, therefore, said that such a snake should not be killed by the household concerned. Hutton sees in this case a possible basis of group totemism.[8]

*The Lhota Naga* have three phratries divided into clans which in some cases are further divided into kindreds. Two clans are said to be descended from jungle men. The Worore clan has more or less the same myth of origin as the Wozukamr clan of the Ao, and is probably of Ao origin. The hornbill is taboo to this clan, but not strictly or universally. The Lhota have stories of a union between a girl and a tiger and between a woman and a hairy caterpillar, and of children turning into catfish and monkeys and women into gibbons. They have also numerous food taboos.[9]

*The Rengma Naga* have six exogamous groups with exogamous clans. One clan is named after the sideshoot of a tree. In another case the first male ancestor of a sub-clan was supposed to be the offspring of a union between a woman and a hairy caterpillar. The belief prevails that if anyone gets stung by touching the poisonous hairs of this insect, all he has to do is to get a member of the Tselauyu clan to spit on the affected spot and scratch it, and the irritation will instantly cease.[10]

*The Naga Tribes of Manipur* have patrilineal, exogamous clans named after common ancestors. Luang is the name of one of the Meithei clans and also of a river fish. A folk tale portrays the ancestress of the Marram Naga as semi-animal in form. Traces of totemism among these tribes are extremely scarce. They have, however, a number of food taboos. Frazer was of the opinion that the objects which are taboo to Meithei clans could be provisionally called totems. But Hodson does not concur. He does not accept the Manipuri *yek* as a totemic division, as Colonel

Shakespear was once inclined to do. Instead, he concedes the possible existence of a mental attitude conducive to totemism in the area.[11]

*The Lakher*: Parry's detailed monograph on the Lakher illustrates the likelihood that less detailed investigations often ignore shreds and patches of beliefs and practices which are sometimes of the greatest significance ethnologically. The Lakher are a Kuki tribe with Naga affinities. Like the Chang and the Angami they claim kinship with the tiger and regard the python as an object of awe and more or less taboo. They believe in *saw*, a power which causes sickness or ill-luck and attaches to certain animals like tigers and leopards and also to men in certain circumstances. Every person has a tutelary deity or guardian angel called *zang*. All animals have souls, and in Lakher folklore they predominate and are personified. In the past the Lakher probably also had a belief in tiger men. When a hunter has killed any of the larger animals he performs on his return a sacrifice called *Salupakia*, the object of which is to give him power in the next world over the spirit of the animal he has killed, to please the dead animals, and also to help him to kill many more animals in the future. If a man is very lucky at hunting and manages to shoot many wild animals, he is known as *lasisapa*. His good luck is attributed to the fact that he is a favourite of the *Lasi*, the spirit that looks after wild animals. But unlike the Lushei, the Lakher perform no sacrifice to the Lasi. It is believed that shortly before a lasisapa dies he sees his own Lasi, generally riding on a huge animal. The Lakher practise shifting cultivation. They have six groups divided into clans. But the tribal unit is the village rather than the clan, and clan exogamy has considerably weakened. Only four clans seem to have a totemic origin. Two claim descent from the python which, it is believed, assumed human form and had connexion with a girl. The members of these clans are forbidden to touch or kill a python, and one who violates the taboo will die. The python is a good spirit and special protector of all the members of the two clans. The Tiger clan has a special reverence for tigers, which are taboo; and the members of the Hornbill clan state that to eat a hornbill is like eating one's father and mother. Like the above-mentioned tribes the Lakher are patrilineal; but some matrilineal traces also exist.[12]

*The Kachari* belong, like the Garo, the Mech and the Chutiya, to the Bodo family. They have a myth in which the tribe is forced to cross a river. Some saved themselves by catching hold of rushes (*khangris*) growing on the bank, and are called Khangrabaria; others caught hold of reeds (*nals*), and are called Nalbaria. Endle

believes that their social organization rested originally on a
totemic base, although today a real regard for the totems is to
be found only here and there. Endle also affirms that the
totemic divisions are strictly endogamous, but Gurdon has grave
doubts if that is really so, and points out that among the related
Garo and Mech the divisions are exogamous. Among the
Kachari the Tiger folk claim kinship with the tiger
and go into mourning on hearing of the death of a tiger.
The Sesamum folk hold that plant in special honour. The
Leech folk are not allowed to kill leeches under ordinary circumstances. The Jute folk hold the jute in special honour. The Leech
folk and the Jute folk have the odd obligation of chewing the
leech and the jute respectively on certain religious and ceremonial occasions. Other divisions are named as follows: Heaven
folk, Earth folk, Jungle Grass folk, Areca folk, Fern folk, Squirrel
folk, Bamboo Grove folk, Bamboo Water-vessel folk, and so on.
Some of these names do not seem to have a totemic significance.
The Kachari are an agricultural people, and some maintain that
their original home was Tibet or China. The related Dumara
appear to be divided into forty men's clans and forty women's
clans. The Mech have sixteen exogamous clans of which four
appear to be totemic.[13]

*The Galong and Abor*: One clan among the Galong seems to be
totemic and to be descended from the frog spirit. The frog is
not eaten. The tradition runs that a frog married a woman and
from this union the Tig people are descended. The related
Abor have sacrificial rites to the frog spirit.[14]

*The Garo*: Although related to the Kachari, the Garo are matrilineal. Hence, Bampfylde Fuller surmises that they got their
matrilineal features from the neighbouring Khasi with whom
some Garo tribes have freely intermarried. Their agriculture is
of the *jhuming* variety. They have three phratries subdivided
into many clans or sibs (*machongs* or motherhoods). Both
phratries and clans are exogamous and matrilineal. Playfair
denies that the larger groups or phratries are totemic, but adds
that the clans in many cases show totemic traces. Descent from
the totem is claimed, but no respect or reverence towards it
exists. One machong has the bear for its totem, and the myth
connected with it traces the ancestry of the clan members to a
woman who had sexual relations with a bear. Another machong
has the dove as its totem, the relevant myth relating how the
ancestress as a girl turned into a dove. A third machong has
the hen for its totem because the ancestress had an ornament
which could cluck like a hen. A fourth machong is named after
a basket because their rich, old ancestress was carried in one.

Other machongs are named after streams or hills in the vicinity. The related Lalung have only one distinct totemic clan, the Pumpkin clan, to which the pumpkin is taboo.[15]

*The Khasi*: Surrounded by tribes which speak Tibeto-Burman languages, the Khasi stand out by reason of their Austroasiatic language and their strongly formed matrilineal organization. Linguistically and to varying extent culturally and racially, they are related to the Mon-Khmer tribes in the east and the Munda-speaking tribes in the west. They practise agriculture of the jhuming variety, erect megalithic monuments with greater zeal than most other tribes in the area, and have a considerable number of matrilineal-exogamous clans tracing descent from ancestresses. Some of these clans—a proportionately very small number—have a quasi-totemic character. Reports mention a Pumpkin clan, a Crab clan, a Monkey clan, and some named after trees. Myths of origin tracing descent from these objects also apparently exist. If the *Census of India* (1891) is to be believed, these objects were also tabooed in earlier times. Gurdon, however, is emphatic that the clan members do not abstain from killing, eating or using the objects after which they are named, and that there is no evidence to show that the clansfolk ever regarded the above animals or objects as their totems. Fürer-Haimendorf, on the other hand, seeks to explain the contradiction between the statements contained in the *Census of India* (1891) and Gurdon's emphatic denial of the existence of totemic taboos by pointing to the rapid breakdown of the old Khasi customs and the consequent dissolution of the taboo rule. But the full trustworthiness of the information supplied by the Census cannot be taken entirely for granted, especially as the time-lapse between 1891 and Gurdon's observations was not very great.[16]

\*          \*          \*

There are three obvious possibilities by means of which the origin of the totemic traces in Assam might be explained.

The first possibility would consist in attempting to connect these traces with some centre of totemism located somewhere in the vast region to the east of their present occurrence. This is what Fürer-Haimendorf at one time attempted to do by presuming the existence in this area of a fuller totemic stratum at an earlier period and by associating this stratum with the totemism of the South Seas.[17] But in his field investigation of the Konyak Naga, undertaken later, Fürer-Haimendorf could find among them no myths of clan origin as among the Ao, or any other phenomena which could be distinctly pronounced totemic in character. In his article on the community-life of the Konyak Naga published in 1941, he therefore made the following pronouncement: 'My supposition expressed at that time that perhaps totemic traces would be found among them to a greater extent than among the Ao has not been confirmed thereafter, and I have in general grown extremely sceptical in regard to a connexion of particular elements of the Naga culture with the so-called "totemic" complex of the South Seas.'[18] Fürer-Haimendorf's pronouncement is thus in keeping with the prevailing ethnological standpoint which frowns on attempts at affirming distant connexions between cultural elements or groups of them, when clear-cut proofs are lacking.

The second possibility would consist in affirming a connexion between the totemic traces in Assam and some centre of totemism located elsewhere on the subcontinent. It is this possibility which Niggemeyer holds out. But, as Fürer-Haimendorf has demonstrated, the totemic elements are strongest among the Ao, and decline considerably as one moves westward. If the spread of totemism had taken place recently from some centre in the west, the contrary would have occurred.

Nevertheless, while the possibility of totemic stimuli issuing from a totemic centre in India cannot altogether be shut out, let us consider the third alternative. This would consist in maintaining with Hodson that a mental attitude conducive towards totemism exists in the area, and has given rise more or less independently to phenomena which Hutton rightly characterizes as quasi-totemism because of their weak and sporadic nature. A certain number of animalistic beliefs and practices not amounting to a full-fledged proto-totemic complex, but justifying the assertion that a mental attitude conducive towards totemism exists in the area, appear in the evidence presented above. This is so particularly in relation to the Lakher; but is also manifest less strongly among the other tribes of the area, as the peculiar attitude towards the hornbill, the python and the hoolock ape and other evidence such as the veneration of a snake by an Angami household as reported by Hutton, or the belief in lycanthropy which is so widespread here, bear witness. This mental attitude is likewise illustrated by the Lynngam myth (found also with variations among the other tribes of Assam) which traces the origin of the Nongsobhar clan to an ancestress who was impregnated by the falling of a flower of a sobhar tree on her, while she was sleeping in the jungle. It is possible that Negrito influences have added somewhat to this attitude of mind, but the evidence of such influences is not conclusive. When one, however, weighs all the facts and considerations bearing on the

problem of totemism in Assam, the scales can be said to be
tilted in favour of the view that the totemic traces in this area
represent what we have called primary quasi-totemism or group
totemism in its early stages, which has arisen independently of
outside influences. The arrest of the phenomenon at this level
may be ascribed to the fact that the region has been the target
of many cross-cultural influences.

So far as the totemic traces of the matrilineal Khasi and Garo
are concerned, these may be attributed to influences absorbed
from the surrounding countryside through contagion.

## NOTES AND REFERENCES

[1] 1911, 199c.

[2] 1921a, 397.

[3] 1932a.

[4] 1933, 426.

[5] Fürer-Haimendorf, 1932a, 32-3; 1941, 77, 83; Mills, 1922, xxiii.

[6] Mills, 1926, 13, 27; Fürer-Haimendorf, 1932a, 329; W. C. Smith, 1925, xi-xv, 50.

[7] Hutton, 1921b, 121, 122-7, 129, 201, 208, 236-7, 393; 1921a, 392-3.

[8] Fürer-Haimendorf, 1932a, 332; Hutton, 1921a, 109, 117, 397.

[9] Mills, 1922, 87-9; 1928, 277, 283, 305-8.

[10] Mills, 1937, 11.

[11] Hodson, 1911, 71, 199a-c.

[12] Shakespear, 1912, 213-24, reported no totemism among the Lakher. Parry, 1932, x-xii, 75, 143, 232-6, 130-40, 145, 477, 559-60, 542.

[13] 1911, 9-12, 24-8, 82.

[14] Duff-Sutherland-Dunbar, 1915, 1-91.

[15] Risley, 1915, 101; Playfair, 1909, xvi, 16-17, 22-3, 33, 64-7.

[16] Gurdon, 1907, xxi-xxiii, 65-6, 195; *Census of India*, 1891, 258; Fürer-Haimendorf, 1932a, 334.

[17] 1929, 1932a.

[18] 1941, 83. Fürer-Haimendorf, however, does not deny historical connexions with areas further east so far as certain non-totemic elements are concerned.

# X

## *INTERPRETATIONS*

In the immediately preceding chapters of this work we first outlined a series of general interpretations of the totemic phenomenon in India by various students of the subject and briefly indicated some of their inadequacies. We next surveyed the evidence among the Munda-speaking tribes, the ' Gondid ' tribes in Central India, and the tribes and castes of South India together with the Marathi-speaking population. We then turned our attention to the Negrito of the Andaman Islands, and passed finally to the tribes in Assam. We have thus at our disposal a vast corpus of empirical material on which to base our own general interpretations.

A few words, however, are first necessary on the *modus operandi* followed by Niggemeyer. In an alphabetical list of 200 totemic tribes and castes appended to his study published in *Anthropos,* he supplies in abbreviated form information on their habitat, the sociological and religious sides of their totemism and the sources of his information. Among other things, the list is meant to indicate more concretely and more completely than was possible in the text of his study the extent in space of totemism in India by presenting briefly information in a condensed form on totemism or traces of it among all the tribes and castes on which evidence was then available. Niggemeyer's list outruns earlier lists of totemic tribes and castes in point of number. As he himself points out (p. 602), Frazer presents fairly ample information on 85 to 90 totemic groups (1910: ii: 218-335), and Karandikar's list (1928: 240-7) comprises 75 groups only.[1] Niggemeyer, however, does not seem to have entered very deeply into the problem of affiliations in compiling his list. However that may be, the text of his study falls neatly into two broad parts. The first and larger part is mainly descriptive, analytic and classificatory; and the second and smaller interpretative; the description and classification pave the way for the interpretation. Instead of following in Niggemeyer's footsteps however, and first describing and classifying the phenomenon

[1] For notes to this chapter see pp. 262-5.

and then interpreting it in general terms, we propose in this chapter to deal with the problems of its original bearers, its development, and other such general questions, describing and classifying where and when the interpretation requires it. The extent to which we differ from Niggemeyer will thus become clear as we proceed. The justification for this procedure lies in the two facts that we have already presented a substantial empirical base for it in the immediately preceding chapters, and that Niggemeyer's own study (a detailed summary of which has been presented earlier) obviates to a certain measure the necessity of following the course he did and of enduring the tedium of repetition.

*                 *                 *

If we now take up the question of the original bearers of totemism in India, we can unhesitatingly exclude the Indo-Aryans because, as Niggemeyer has clearly demonstrated and as our re-examination of the evidence also shows, the northern areas of India, which are the principal habitat of the Indo-Aryans, are almost entirely non-totemic. Moreover, the totemic elements among the castes which occupy a more or less low position in the Hindu social organization can be explained through the absorption of these elements from totemic tribes with which they came into contact or through the transformation of totemic tribes into Hindu castes. Again, the few instances of animal and plant names which occur in the old Vedic literature can be explained in other ways than the totemic.[2] We can likewise exclude the original bearers of the Dravidian languages as the original bearers of totemism in India. Although the Dravidian problem still remains largely unresolved,[3] we can ascribe a high degree of probability to the following propositions: that the Dravidians were the bearers of a relatively advanced culture and that they came originally from somewhere in the west. It is, therefore, unlikely that they were the bringers of totemism to India. The totemism of the Telugu-speaking, the Tulu-speaking and the Kanarese-speaking castes can be explained by the fact that they acquired their relatively weak, totemic elements from totemic sources within the frontiers of India itself. As for the Tamil-speaking population in Ceylon and South India, they are also largely non-totemic. This leaves us with two ethnic groups as possible original bearers of totemism in India—the Munda-speaking tribes and a still older racial group. In all probability the bearers of the Munda languages were originally a neolithic group with little or no totemism. It is true that the nature of their early culture, their exact original habitat and their racial

character have of late become controversial questions. Nevertheless, the view that the chief bearers of the Munda languages
were a Palae-Mongoloid group who came mainly from the east
can still be accepted as a working hypothesis until such time as
stronger positive proofs to the contrary are brought forward
than those offered by Hevesy, Bowles and Dani. For these
reasons the bearers of the Munda languages can be excluded
as bearers of totemism in India.

As we have seen, however, totemism among the Munda-
speaking tribes in the northeastern areas of Central India (Bihar
and Orissa) and among some other neighbouring tribes in eastern
Madhya Pradesh is comparatively strong. Hence the original
bearers of totemism in India can be described as an ethnic group
which was pre-Aryan, pre-Dravidian and pre-Munda. From an
early period, however, varying degrees of Mundaization, Aryanization and Dravidianization have made themselves felt in the
ranks of the primitive tribes in India. So far as the process of
Mundaization is concerned, we may put the matter as follows:
the original bearers of totemism exchanged their language for
Munda languages and together with them absorbed many features of the Munda culture and to a less extent Munda ethnic
elements also. However, they retained their original totemism
in a somewhat modified form. The most striking of these modifications was the loss of a strong clan-and-totem identification.
If, then, the original bearers of totemism in India were pre-
Aryan, pre-Dravidian and pre-Munda, totemism on the subcontinent can be said to be of great age.

\*       \*       \*

On the question of the place of origin of the totemic forms
found in India, two alternative possibilities lie before us: (i)
in the remote past India had received totemic elements from
outside either through diffusion or migration, and these elements
were then further developed within the country; or (ii) forms
of group totemism grew up within India itself from proto-
totemic elements in the country. Decisive proofs for the one or
the other of these two possibilities are lacking on account of the
great gaps in our ethnographic information on India and the
adjoining areas of the world, and on account of the other inadequacies of the available material and the contradictory interpretations of related disciplines like physical anthropology,
palaeontology and prehistory. The question must therefore remain open until more complete, all-round information is available. Nevertheless, there are indications which lend a somewhat

greater probability in the present state of research to the second of the two possibilities mentioned above.

The general indications of this fact may be described briefly as follows: (1) In discarding the culture-circle concept, the historical ethnologists of today have also discarded the older view that phenomena like group totemism, which occur in widely separated regions of the world, must necessarily go back to a single origin in some geographically delimited location. Substantial factual and methodological reasons have been quoted for this shift in viewpoint. (2) The development of the concept of animalism or proto-totemism as background from which group totemism took its rise has lent strength to the view that group totemism can arise more than once in various geographically delimited areas. (3) The psychological tendency towards complementarity and dependence, which arises directly from the fact of human finitude, and which expresses itself in various forms, among which proto-totemism stresses its individual expression and clan totemism its social expression, can to a certain extent be accepted as an adequate explanation of the similarities of the totemic phenomenon everywhere in the world. (4) The high variability of totemic complexes to which Goldenweiser drew attention in 1910, and which recently both Haekel and Henninger have acknowledged, coupled with the process of convergence (which includes diffusion, independent invention and development) through which these complexes arise, is further evidence in favour of the view that the totemic phenomenon has had more than one geographical origin. Thus each complex comes to have a form of its own.

Hence, on the basis of our empirical material and in the light of the above general considerations, the course of totemic development in India can be sketched as follows:

*The Proto-totemic Background*: There is no evidence of a proto-totemic complex anywhere in India. But beliefs and practices connected with animals and plants of a ritual nature are found at all cultural levels in the Indian population.[4] They range from the merest magical notions to actual worship of animals and plants in the form of spirits or deities, or as symbols of spirits and deities, or as objects closely associated with them in one way or another. Most of them lie scattered in shreds and patches at various cultural levels. Some of them have evidently had a late origin and are presumably connected with the development of Hinduism as such, others probably originated with the aborigines and then entered the folds of Hinduism at its lower reaches, and still others seem to have a hoary antiquity. Among the Andamanese and the Lakher, they are more frequent, although loose and floating; and among the rest of the tribal population in India they appear sporadically.

There is no conclusive proof that the Negrito contributed to any kind of proto-totemic beliefs and practices in India. But the anthropometric traces (if acknowledged as such) of a Negrito substratum in the hills and jungles of South India and in Assam hold out the possibility of some such contribution. This, however, can no longer be clearly isolated, and therefore ascribed to that ethnic source.

The earliest primitive population in India consisted no doubt of hunters and food-gatherers, as is evidenced by the small groups of such tribes who still survive in the hills and jungles of South India and, to a less extent, elsewhere on the subcontinent. If we divide the concept of proto-totemism, as we have done in an earlier chapter, into beliefs and practices of a ritual nature relating to animals and plants of a loose and floating character and the proto-totemic complex proper which is an organized form of such beliefs and practices found mainly in the ranks of specialized hunters, there is no adequate reason to deny the existence of beliefs and practices of the first type among the early food-gathering and hunting tribes in India. The scarcity of the evidence relating to such notions can partly be attributed to losses resulting from other cultural influences which have played on these early cultures from early times, and partly to the inadequacy of ethnographic investigations.

There are no tribes of higher hunters in India, and Schmidt's attempt at reconstructing such a complex is highly problematic. If, however, we turn to the economically more advanced groups of the tribal population, which are characterized by the pursuit of elementary forms of cultivation, and which constitute the overwhelmingly greater part of the tribes in India, we find a series of notions relating to animals and plants which resemble proto-totemic ones, but which exist sporadically and in a seemingly attenuated form. Some examples of such notions are the belief in lycanthropy and the transformation of certain individuals into various other animals, the belief in the incarnation of the soul in animals, worship of spirits of the hunt, veneration of the tiger and so on. The widely spread but scattered distribution of these elements perhaps hints at an extreme age, which could possibly have reached back into a fuller proto-totemic past, because the proto-totemic complex, according to Baumann, was widely distributed in the earlier ages. In this sense these elements can be regarded as surviving remnants; and a more thorough investigation into their occurrence in India would no doubt be very enlightening. But that is a task which cannot be undertaken in this general study of totemism in India.

Perhaps another example of the proto-totemic mentality, which however is the only example of its kind in India, is the individual totemism of the Birjia Asur. For reasons which we have already stated, we are inclined to the view that it is a survival from a somewhat fuller proto-totemic phase—'an early form', as Roy says, and not a new development, as Hoffmann and Niggemeyer maintained. Roy's report is unfortunately neither detailed nor complete; and, as Niggemeyer says, it seems that every person has two totems: his own which is acquired at birth from a relative or neighbour, and the clan totem. If this conclusion from Roy's incomplete information is correct, the Birjia Asur would illustrate a state of incomplete convergence. That is to say, in this case individual totemism is associated not with the spirits of the parents, but with those of relatives and neighbours, and is seemingly unrelated to their clan totemism in which the totems are changed, sometimes regularly and sometimes every third or fourth generation.      '

Still another example of the preservation of the proto-totemic mentality is contained in the myths which focus attention on individual ancestors and their individual totems, later inherited by their progeny and then claimed as clan totems. In most cases the myths are of the parallel-relationship variety, that is, they narrate various encounters of the clan ancestor with the totem; in some cases, however, they talk of actual descent. In the parallel-relationship myths there are some instances in which the totem plays the role of helper or friend; but in others the connexion expresses not so much help received as an accidental contact of a not very meaningful nature. In the first type of parallel relations one might perhaps see the reflection of a proto-totemic mentality, and in the second the displacement of that mentality and of descent totemism by some cultural occurrence antithetical to them.

A possible example of a tribe which occupies an intermediate position between the phase of proto-totemism and the next phase of quasi-totemism is that of the Chenchu. They are a nomadic food-collecting tribe, but also practise some primitive cultivation; and still retain elements which resemble proto-totemic ones such as the temporary incarnation of the soul in an animal, which Fürer-Haimendorf is convinced does not necessarily stem from Hindu sources, a myth in which a girl marries a bear and gives birth to several bear-children, and a goddess of the forest, who controls the activities of the wild animals. The latter conception bears resemblances to the proto-totemic ' Lord of the Animals '

to which Baumann and other ethnologists have drawn attention
and which Schmidt regarded as a deviant from the concept of
the Supreme Being.[5] Thurston & Rangachari say that they have
exogamous clans (inteperu) and that some appear to have totems.
Fürer-Haimendorf, on the other hand, while conceding that
some of their clans have animal and plant names, was not able
to find totemic myths and totemic taboos among them. Furthermore, they have no strong clan consciousness, and it is possible
that their clan organization and the clan names which are
derived from those of animals and plants were borrowed, as
Fürer-Haimendorf believes, from some patrilineal neighbours.
Raghaviah connects them with the Yanadi, but the Yanadi, too,
have very weak traces of totemism. Thus the Chenchu illustrate
the complexity of cultural interactions and the intricacy of cultural development even at low levels of economic pursuits.

*Quasi-Totemism*: The next phase in the growth of totemism in
India can be appropriately termed quasi-totemism. As we have
pointed out earlier, quasi-totemism or clan totemism in its early
period of growth has two forms: primary quasi-totemism in
which no outside influence is distinguishable, and secondary
quasi-totemism which is caused by such influences. The term
quasi-totemism, however, is confronted by two difficulties. The
first is the difficulty of tracing the gradual cumulation of individual events converging into a form or complex; and the second
is the difficulty of distinguishing an early stage of growth from a
stage of decline. It is only when individual events tend to acquire
a repetitive character or, in other words, to become institutionalized and to coalesce into a complex that the study of
cultural origins and of cultural growth becomes possible. This
fact, therefore, offers a criterion by which one might distinguish
quasi-totemism, as we have defined it here, from totemism in
decline. The former is positive, convergent, developing; the
latter negative, disjointed, disintegrating. The former exhibits
a tendency towards the cumulation of related elements; the latter
towards their scattering. Two other criteria are the probable
predominance of proto-totemic elements and the contrasting concept of apical or full-blown group or clan totemism. As Baumann
and Haekel point out, with the advance of group totemism the
social aspect tends to displace the ideological or proto-totemic
aspect, or, in other words, the older the group totemism, the
stronger the proto-totemic elements. The continuance in existence
of quasi-totemism as such is an instance of the socio-cultural
inertia of arrested growth. The arrest in growth may be due to
one or more of several factors such as weakness in clan consciousness, the prevalence of localized clans with territorial

names, substitutes other than totems (clan gods, for example) as focal points of the urge towards complementarity and the relationship of dependence, the impact of matrilineal elements before the process of totemic development has reached its apical point and various other circumstances, which a detailed and localized historical interpretation can alone unravel.

The area in which quasi-totemism predominates is the extreme northeast, or Assam. In terms of descent and inheritance the tribes of this area fall into two groups, the larger being patrilineally organized and the smaller matrilineally. In the rest of India the early quasi-totemic phase has largely given way to apical group totemism, to formal social totemism and in more recent times to the phase of totemism in decline. Survivals of primary quasi-totemism are, therefore, few and scattered in the central and southern parts of the subcontinent.

The totemic traces in the extreme northeast have been characterized as primary quasi-totemism or clan totemism in its early phase, which is largely independent of outside influences, because the attempts at connecting them with centres of totemism either to the east or west of them have failed to bring forward conclusive evidence in their favour, and because of the somewhat more frequent occurrence of proto-totemic elements in this area or the existence of a mental attitude conducive towards totemism. From this proto-totemic mentality there must have issued the first impulses towards a totemic organization of clans in the area, as several myths of the Assamese tribes, which narrate how individual ancestors acquired their animal or plant totems, which were then inherited by their descendants, bear witness. The arrest of clan totemism at the quasi-totemic level in Assam may be attributed to many factors, of which perhaps the following are the more outstanding: the gradual displacement of clan consciousness by village consciousness, the canalization of the urge towards complementarity and dependence into fertility cults, ancestor cults and megalithic rites, and in general to the fact of several cross-cultural influences to which this area has been long subject.

The matrilineal quasi-totemism of the Khasi might very likely have been acquired from the primary quasi-totemism of their neighbours, the Naga tribes, through the occasional occurrence of intermarriages, even as the matrilineal elements of the Garo have been so acquired from the Khasi. An alternative possibility is that the quasi-totemic elements among the Khasi grew up as independent events nourished by the diffusion of a proto-totemic mentality in the area. The arrest of the phenomenon at this level among the Khasi might have been due to the fact

of matriliny, which is less favourable than its counterpart, patriliny, to the growth of totemism. The totemic traces among the
Garo, the Lynngam and the Lalung, who possibly acquired their
matrilineal elements from the Khasi, can be interpreted along
similar lines.

When we turn our attention to the quasi-totemic phenomena
in the rest of India, that is, in all areas other than Assam, the
concept of apical group totemism, as it occurs among the Birhor,
serves as an important dividing-line between the two varieties—
primary and secondary quasi-totemism. Traces of primary quasi-
totemism must evidently be sought among the more primitive
tribes such as the Kadar, the Kanikar, the Vedda and the Chenchu. As our empirical evidence indicates, however, these traces
are neither relatively plentiful nor clearly primary. Therefore it
can be concluded with some measure of justification that primary
quasi-totemism has not left many traces of its occurrence among
the tribes in the rest of India, principally because totemism has
developed all over India into more advanced forms. Secondary
quasi-totemism can be accepted as existing among tribes like the
Kamar, the Baiga and others, which had no strong totemism of
their own, but which borrowed some totemic elements from their
neighbours like the Gond, and also among some lower castes like
the Balahi in Central India[6] and others elsewhere in India.

In the south the sheer primitivity of most of the very simple
tribes must have acted as a retarding force towards the growth
of primary quasi-totemism, and in later times the acquisition
of other cultural elements from external sources must have
stifled whatever tendencies in that direction that were ever present among them. In the northeastern areas of Central India
(Orissa, Bihar and eastern Madhya Pradesh), it may be assumed
that a convergence of favourable circumstances accelerated the
pace of development, and primary quasi-totemism blossomed
into apical clan totemism, leaving behind, as is to be expected,
very few traces of its former existence.

*Apical Group or Clan Totemism*: The third phase in the development of totemism in India is apical group or clan totemism.
Its best preserved form is found among the Birhor of Chota
Nagpur. It is in the northeastern areas of Central India that
totemism is at its strongest and that relatively older forms prevail. Therefore it is no wonder that the best preserved form of
apical clan totemism is also found in the same region, but confined to a smaller location and limited almost to a single tribe.

In identifying the northeastern areas of Central India as the
region in which totemism is at its strongest and in which relatively older forms of it are found, we exclude by implication

16

other areas like Andhra Pradesh, Madras, Mysore and Maharashtra from that claim and ascribe their totemism to a later period of secondary or tertiary development. In doing so, we confirm Niggemeyer's conclusion that the northeastern areas of Central India possess relatively strong and old forms of totemism, but reject his affirmation that the totemism of the ' Gondid ' tribes is the strongest and oldest of its kind.

In this connexion Walter Ruben's attempt at locating the ancient bearers of totemism in India is interesting because he excludes the Gond from that category and limits the original bearers to a smaller number of tribal groups. Ruben does not agree with Niggemeyer that the Gond belong to the original bearers of totemism in India because they have come from the south in relatively recent times. On the other hand, the Birhor with their monkey hunt and ignorance of bows and arrows are, according to Ruben, mesolithic hunters, and it was with their culture that patrilineal totemism and the sun cult first came to Chota Nagpur. The Birhor stand closer to the Baiga, the Korwa, the Birjia and the Bhuiya than to the Oraon and the Munda. But how have the Baiga such weak traces of totemism today? Like the Bhaina, the Birhor, the Birjia and the Bhuiya, who are still totemic today and to whom they are related, the Baiga were also once totemic; but the superior, largely matrilineal and agricultural Gond superimposed themselves on the ethnologically more primitive Baiga who, as a consequence, took Gond names for their exogamous clans and largely lost their totemism into the bargain.[7]

As we shall see, Ruben runs in the right track when he focusses attention on the Birhor as the earliest, full-fledged totemists in India. But his association in this respect of the Baiga with the Birhor scarcely holds water; for, as we have seen, both Elwin and Fuchs, who have made detailed ethnographic studies of this tribe, show that their weak totemism has been borrowed from their Gond neighbours. Furthermore the Bhaina, who are pronounced totemists and have been generally regarded as a sub-group of the Baiga, may not in reality belong to that tribe. If, however, they do, they could have acquired their totemism from the Kawar of eastern Madhya Pradesh with whom they are closely connected and with whom they frequently intermarry.[8] Again, the Korwa and the Bhuiya show certain affinities of a general nature with the Birhor, but they can scarcely be bracketed with them on totemic grounds.

Totemically speaking, Haekel has likewise drawn particular attention to the Birhor. He believes that the totemism of this tribe occupies a special position up to a certain measure. Thus it appears that the Birhor were already totemic when they took over the Munda language and that they represent the remnants of an old pre-Munda, pre-Dravidian tribal group which was possibly the bearer of an old form of totemism. The reasons for this view are that the Birhor have patrilineal, exogamous clans with predominantly animal totems and strict totem taboos, that there is a strong feeling of kinship between the human members of the clan and their totems, and that, although the clans are today scattered among several local groups or tandas, their traditions point to specific hills and other places where they were originally localized. The totem cult of the Birhor also suggests this localization, and at the same time emphasizes the close identification between clan and totem. So, too, the Birhor believe that the clan increases to the same extent as the totem species, which is an additional indication of the close relationship between the human group and the animal species. Finally, although their legends of origin narrate mere encounters with the totem and not descent, the Birhor are the only known case of a hunting tribe with a strongly formed totemism in India. It is true that one section of the tribe has already taken to cultivation, but their original hunting life is still recognizable among them.[9]

Let us now turn our attention to Petri's study of Australian totemism in order to find out if useful suggestions can be derived from it by means of which we might be able to locate the position of Birhor totemism on the curve of totemic development in India. According to Petri, territorial-clan and cult totemism appear to be the historically oldest basic form on that continent. There are three reasons which justify this view: (i) The continental distribution of the phenomenon. (ii) The spiritual centres as mid-points of the spiritual, historical, social and economic life of the tribes concerned. (iii) The existence of proto-totemic elements. Petri, however, adds that the proto-totemic complex as such, which Baumann worked out for Africa, does not exist any more in Australia, though it might have existed in Tasmania at the time of its discovery. Therefore, the Australian territorial-clan and cult totemism can perhaps be regarded as one step further towards group totemism and away from the preceding, proto-totemic phase. The widely spread social clan totemism can be considered as having issued from the archaic cult totemism. But an exact proof of this in terms of inner and outer factors leading towards it is still wanting. The totemism of the dual system and of the sections is a relatively more recent development in Australia and was brought to the South Seas and Australia in the early neolithic period.

Birhor cult totemism does not have a subcontinental spread, but is in fact confined to a single tribe. It therefore does not fulfil Petri's first criterion of age. There is, however, other evidence to indicate its extreme antiquity, which may be enumerated as follows: (i) In a country in which totemism is widespread the Birhor are the only hunting group with a strongly formed totemism in both its internal and external aspects. (ii) There is no proto-totemic complex of the type described for Africa by Baumann; but some proto-totemic traces are present: the identification of the daemon of a guest with animals or things seen in a dream, the acquisition of an individual guardian spirit by the Birhor spirit doctor in a vision or dream, but not in the shape of an animal, the belief that the *orabongas* or hill and forest spirits have each a particular species of animal for their vehicle and are sometimes dreamed of as coming from the direction of their native hills riding their favourite animals, and the belief in animal spirits like Baghbir (tiger god), Hundarbir (wolf god) and Bandarbir (monkey god) who have to be propitiated with sacrifices. The latter, it is believed, interfere in hunting expeditions if not propitiated, thus suggesting their origin in an early period of cultural growth.[10] The paucity of proto-totemic elements is an indication of the ascendancy of the social or clan principle (Baumann, Haekel), and therefore a pointer to the age of the phenomenon. (iii) The ascendancy of the social or clan principle among the Birhor—at one time much more so than today—is suggested by their cult totemism. Their cult totemism stresses two features—the original localization of the clans, today scattered among various local groups, and the close identification of the clans and their totems. Both these features, again, suggest that the phenomenon of totemism among the Birhor reaches back into a remote past. The localization of the clans, as Schmidt rightly points out, precedes their scattering; and there is a good deal of evidence to substantiate the proposition that in India the clans were likewise originally localized. The close identification of the clan and its totem exemplified in both its internal and external aspects is totemism at its apex. This apical group totemism contrasts with the succeeding phase in which the internal elements of clan-and-totem identification grow weak and scattered or disappear entirely from existence, leaving behind the external trappings of a formal brand of totemism. Thus, the existence of both the internal and external manifestations of clan-and-totem identification is evidence of the relative antiquity of the phenomenon in question. Birhor totemism, then, is apical group totemism because clan-and-totem identification is found among them as ritual belief and practice, and also in the outward trappings of totemism. The ritual side of this relationship takes vivid form in their cult which of course does not dominate the entire range of their cultural life, as the totemic cult does in Australian tribes.[11] That it does not do so may be ascribed to the peculiar circumstances of Birhor cultural history. The clan-and-totem identification is also manifest in the Birhor belief of kinship with the totem, in their strict totem taboos, in their fancied resemblance to their totems and in other aspects of their totemic organization. The absence of descent myths among the Birhor but their sporadic occurrence among a few other tribes like the Juang, the Garo, the Kawar, the Agaria and some clans of the Gond would seem to militate against the view that Birhor totemism is a relatively old form. But two explanations are possible: that all else apart the legends of parallel-relationship encounters are a secondary acquisition wherever they are found (Roy, Hoffmann, Niggemeyer) or that they are as old as the myths of totem descent (Schmidt).

The special position of the Birhor in relation to the internal and external manifestations of clan-and-totem identification is further emphasized when one considers the nature of the totemic evidence among remnants of the hunting tribes in the northeastern areas of Central India. These are the Pahira of Chota Nagpur and the Hill or Wild Kharia of Orissa. The totemism of the Pahira is today in a state of considerable decline as is evidenced by the fact that there appears to be no bar against marrying within the totem division provided that the two families have separate graveyards and live in different settlements, that the social unit is now the settlement and not the clan, and that the totem taboos have become very lax. Roy opines that the decline of Pahira totemism is due to the 'numerical smallness' of the tribe, and adds that their original social and kinship organization appears to have been based on exogamous, totemic clans. From the evidence available, however, there is no valid reason to deny the possibility of Pahira totemism having been acquired rather late from some neighbours with formal social totemism, that is, totemism without the internal signs of clan-and-totem identification. The Hill Kharia are, as the Roys inform us, food-gatherers and hunters with occasional shifting cultivation. The Hill Kharia of Mayurbhanj have practically no clan organization or totemism, and those of Manbhum and Singhbhum show some traces of both. The original clan names found among the two more advanced sections, the Dudh and Delki Kharia, do not occur among the Hill Kharia. Nevertheless, it is possible that the totemic traces among the Hill Kharia

were acquired from other neighbouring tribes and not fully
assimilated because of their primitivity.

All the other tribes and tribal castes of the northeastern areas
of Central India are economically more advanced than the
Birhor, the Pahira and the Hill Kharia, and are either rude
cultivators or have even taken to cultivation with the plough.
With the exception of the Oraon who are plough cultivators,
none of these groups show any evidence of a developed totemic
cult. The Oraon cult in which divine honours and sacrifices are
offered by a few Oraon clans to their totem emblems may be
said with Roy to exemplify the arrested development of totems
into totem deities, and with Niggemeyer to represent a relatively
recent and deviant growth which has ceased to rise beyond its
present level. Many of the emblems are recently and arbitrarily
adopted ones and do not represent the totems of the Bhuinars
or original settlers. They are believed to be connected with the
luck of the village or federation of villages concerned, and in
many instances have been replaced by flags. They therefore
illustrate a process analogous to that in which clan or group
totemism arises—the ascendancy of a social unit and of a sense
of unit solidarity and the association with it of a suitable symbol.
In group totemism the symbols are primarily animal or plant
species and the units mainly clans; among the Oraon the symbols
are mainly flags and other objects and the units villages or
groups of villages.

Thus, in terms of the cultic aspect of clan-and-totem identification, the Birhor are separated from their economically more
advanced neighbours by a measure of ' totemic distance '. They
may therefore be regarded as a remnant of a larger tribal population in which localization of clans was once a common feature,
in which hunting had begun to acquire a somewhat greater
measure of attention, and in some groups of which, localized in
the northeastern areas of Central India and represented today
by the Birhor alone, apical group totemism took its rise as a
result of specially favourable circumstances. From these groups
totemic stimuli and elements radiated outwards, giving rise to
formal social totemism. A less plausible alternative is to regard
apical group totemism as having been as widespread in the past
as formal social totemism today, and to consider formal social
totemism as the consequence of the population now possessing
it having outgrown apical group totemism for one reason or
another. The implausibility of the second explanation arises from
the fact that the evidence of apical group totemism is so meagre,
confined, as it is, to one small tribe.

*Formal Social Totemism*: The next or fourth phase of totemic development in India may be described as formal social totemism. By formal social totemism we mean the existence of the outward forms of totemism with perhaps diffused, disjointed and sporadically appearing elements of the internal aspect of clan-and-totem identification.

The emergence of this phase may be visualized as follows: From the totemic complex of the Birhor and perhaps other groups related to them but no longer identifiable as such, totemic stimuli and elements diffused themselves into the adjoining areas of the northeastern region in Central India. The tribes receiving these stimuli and elements could absorb them readily to a certain degree because of the following favourable conditions: (i) The existence of a hunting mystique. (ii) A greater stabilization of life-conditions through the adoption of early forms of cultivation. (iii) The dispersal of clans requiring some means of identifying clan-members other than the outmoded territorial names. Thus through the process of convergence emerged the patrilineal, formal, social totemism of the area. Local circumstances engendered local variations, and here and there fortuitous factors and individual experiences no doubt added their mite to the totemic organization (Hutton, Elwin). With the advance of modes of cultivation, village sentiment began to displace clan consciousness and totemism commenced to lose its inner cohesion still more.

The tribes which best represent formal social totemism are the Santal, the Juang, the Oraon, the Khond and the Muria Gond. Hoffmann's analysis of Munda totemism demonstrates its considerable weakness, which is obviously due in part to recent forces of acculturation. Many of the other Munda-speaking tribes and the rest of the Gond (excluding the Hill and Bison-Horn Maria) can be considered as having acquired their patrilineal, formal, social totemism by a process of secondary diffusion; and the Hill and Bison-Horn Maria, the Bhuiya, the Baiga, the Kamar, the Kharia, the Bhil, and perhaps the Pardhan by a process of tertiary diffusion, and so on. In some of these instances, the alternative term—secondary quasi-totemism—would also apply.

The totemism of the northeastern areas in Central India can be again divided into that of the Munda-speaking tribes and that of the Gond. The first is characterized by totem names which are largely different from those of the Gond, and were caused by the Mundaization of the tribes concerned. The characteristic totemic names of the Gond clans were the result of Dravidianization. A phratry organization, often defined by the number of gods worshipped, is likewise typical of the Gond, but as this characteristic does not directly arise from totemism as such, Gond totemism with which it has come to be closely connected might well be described as a totemic system, that is to say, as a combination of totemically characteristic and other elements more or less integrated with one another.

The tribes with formal social totemism in the northeastern areas of Central India have the following features: (i) Patriliny (which they share with totemic tribes all over India excepting the Khasi and the Garo in the extreme northeast and certain Kanarese castes in the southwest). (ii) Early and advanced forms of cultivation. Plough cultivation is evidently a recent acquisition and disrupts rather than consolidates totemism. (iii) Predominantly animal totems (with some local exceptions which can be ascribed to inadequacies in the reports or local and western influences). (iv) Totem names derived from the fauna and flora of the country and to a less extent from inanimate objects or natural phenomena and the like. In a few cases the totem units have names other than those of their totems; this is a symptom of totemic disintegration. (v) Totem taboos forbidding the killing, eating, felling, touching or using of the totems. This element is co-extensive with totemism in India, but is also in varying stages of decline, more so in other areas than in the northeastern region. (vi) Exogamy (co-extensive with totemism in India, also in varying stages of decline, perhaps somewhat more in other areas than here). (vii) Parallel-relationship myths. (viii) Elements found scattered unevenly in this area: totem descent and mourning for the dead totem.

*Totemism in the South of India*: The totemism of this large area owes its origin to all intents and purposes to stimuli and elements emanating from the northeastern region, the primary centre of totemism in India; and can therefore be considered a later ramification, fifth for convenience of classification in the line of emergence. Totemism in this area can be classified into three sequences: (i) The patrilineal totemic complex of the Telugu-speaking castes. (ii) The totemic complex or system of the castes in Kanara. (iii) The half-formed totemic system of the Marathi-speaking castes.

Considered in the light of the total evidence, it is improbable that totemism in the south could have had an independent origin. The primitive tribes of the hills and forests in the south must be excluded as its bearers because, as we have seen, they have either no totemism or sparse traces of it. Whenever traces of totemism are found among them, they can be explained as a borrowing from the more advanced totemic castes in their neighbourhood. In their ethnic make-up the totemic castes of the south are more non-primitive than otherwise; they belong, to use Eickstedt's term, mainly to the Indid race, and both divisions of the Indid race are basically non-totemic. So far as the Dravidians are concerned, the Malayalam-speaking and the Tamil-speaking groups are non-totemic; and totemic traces among certain castes in northern India, the main centre of the Aryans, can be ascribed to influences arising from the primitive population not far removed from them.

Whence, then, arose the totemism of the lower castes in South India? A clear pointer to its source is the fact that the Telugu-speaking castes of the southeast occupy an area not far removed from the primary centre of totemism in India, and must have therefore been subject to stimuli emanating from that quarter, and particularly from tribal castes on its fringes. Absorption of totemic elements through some ethnic intermixture can also be taken for granted. For most of the Telugu-speaking castes with totemic units occupy a comparatively low position in the caste system, and are generally Sudras and Vaisyas. While some claim to belong to the Kshatriya caste, a few lie outside the pale of the caste system by reason of their lowly occupations. The relatively low status in the caste hierarchy of the totemic Telugu-speaking castes would, therefore, not preclude their absorption of outsiders even from the ranks of primitive tribes surrounding them. Of the Balija it is, for instance, reported that they admit outsiders without scruple; and of the Shivalli Brahmins in Kanara that they migrated to that area without women of their own, hence married local women and thus acquired the totemic bali-organization of the Kanarese castes. Some Telugu-speaking castes like the Kapu and the Kadu Golla, both of which have totemic features, have traditions of having come from northern India. Thus ethnically the Telugu-speaking castes can be regarded as a fusion of Aryan and Dravidian stocks, with a varying infusion of tribal blood among the lower castes. The existence of totemism among the lower castes is to a certain extent a proof of the tribal element in the racial constitution of these castes.

In their turn the Telugu-speaking castes extended their influence and the sphere of their operations across the southern belt of the subcontinent into Mysore and right up to the coastal strip in the southwest. Therefore the totemism of the Tulu-speaking and Kanarese-speaking castes can be attributed to influences springing from the Telugu-speaking castes. From the Kanarese-speaking castes in turn influences radiated upwards, where the devak system of the Marathas and related castes absorbed but did not fully assimilate them.

A conspicuous feature of Telugu totemism is the predominance of inanimate objects, natural phenomena, adjectival terms and so on as totems—non-genuine totems, as Niggemeyer calls them. Among the Golla, the Bestha, the Balija, the Madiga, the Devanga, the Boya and other Telugu-speaking castes such terms and objects outrun animals and plants as totems. There are also some instances of objects of a clearly modern origin functioning by association and absorption as totems. The significance of this fact is that it enables us to locate Telugu totemism on a rough time-scale. Just as the predominance of animal totems is a pointer to the antiquity of the totemic complex in which it occurs, so the predominance of inanimate objects as totems can be accepted as a pointer to the dilution of the original totemic conception, and is therefore a recent phenomenon. Another factor which suggests that Telugu totemism is a relatively recent development is its dilute character as a whole in comparison with the totemism of the northeast. Thus totem taboos are weak and sporadic, totem kinship and the internal aspect of clan-and-totem identification occur less frequently and strongly, if they do occur at all; and the over-all picture is one of considerable attenuation and formalism. A third factor pointing to the recent emergence of Telugu totemism is the predominance of the Indid element in their ethnic make-up.

Like the Marathas in the west and the other Indid groups elsewhere (with the exception of the matrilineal castes of the lower southwest) the basic unit of the Telugu-speaking castes was no doubt originally the patri-family of which the term *inteperu*, translated as house-names, bears some evidence. The extension of the term to cover the concept of sept or clan and the adoption of a clan organization can with a high degree of probability be viewed as an absorption and borrowing at the time and in the manner in which totemic elements were -absorbed by these castes.

This view is further strengthened by the opinion expounded by Karandikar and adopted by Niggemeyer that the gotra exogamy of the Brahminic and other Hindu castes owes its ultimate inspiration to the clan organization of the overwhelmingly clan-organized tribal population of the country. John Brough, however, maintains that Karandikar's suggestion to the effect that ' the Brahmans transformed their ritual colleges into exogamous societies with which they came into contact would seem to go beyond all bounds of probability ', and that his handling of his material on gotra and pravara is so inept that his theories are hardly worthy of a refutation.[12] Yet Brough himself points out that it is not till the Sutra period that the prohibition of marriage within the gotra is evidenced in Indian sources, that the two regulations (sapinda or prohibited degrees and gotra exogamy) were originally independent, and that 'the historical situation represents a fusion of two distinct cultural traditions '.[13] Furthermore, as Irawati Karve says: 'The Brahmins also occasionally married outside their caste. There are records of famous sages getting Kshatriya princesses as wives. Sometimes they also married women belonging to non-Aryan aboriginal tribes and lived among the tribal people. There are instances of such unions in the Mahabharata. They had early contact with the non-Aryans and may have known their system of exogamous clans.'[14] Finally, in a recent work on the family and kin in Indo-European culture, Ghurye states it as his considered opinion that the primitive Indo-European people had not developed a unilateral kin-organization of the gens, clan or sept variety. This follows from his analysis of the available evidence and from the fact that the early Indo-Aryan records which are much older than the earliest records of Greek culture make no mention of such an organization at that early period.[15] Thus the development of the extended family into the exogamous gotra among the Brahmins must have no doubt been stimulated into existence by contact with the primitive population in this country and by some experience of their clan-organization.

That the Telugu-speaking castes were responsible for carrying the concept of totemism westward is evidenced by the following facts: the Madiga, a leather-working caste, the Nayindia, a caste of barbers in Mysore, and the Devanga, a caste of weavers, have two endogamous sections based on language—the Telugu and the Kanarese. According to Nanjundayya & Iyer, the Bedar or Boya spoke only Telugu in the beginning, but now one section has adopted Kanarese. The Ganiga or oil-pressers have three sections—the Telugu, the Tamil and the Kanarese. The Meda or bamboo-workers are found in the Oriya, Telugu, Tamil and Kanarese areas. The Komati are likewise widely spread, and are found in Andhra Pradesh, Madras, Mysore, Maharashtra and elsewhere. One of their sections speaks Kanarese. In Mysore the Golla, who are Telugu pastoralists, have more trees as totems than animals or inanimate objects. This is true of the Komati also, and is an indication of an influence from the west. The Kapu, a Telugu-speaking caste, show some matrilineal influences derived from the southwest; on the other hand, the Kuruba who are Kanarese-speaking, but are found in Mysore, Andhra Pradesh and Madras, have more inanimate objects than animals or plants as totems. Again, the Kelasi, a caste in Kanara, have, judging from the information available, more inanimate objects

and the like than trees and their products, and more trees and
their products than animals as balis.

Totemism among the castes in Kanara, concluding from the
inadequate reports at our disposal, is characterized by a slight
trend towards an increase of trees, plants, flowers and the like
over animals and inanimate objects as totems, by a convergence
of matriliny and totemism, and by a generally weak, over-all,
totemic organization. Since the affinity between matriliny and
totemism is much less than between patriliny and totemism, it
would seem preferable to regard matriliny as an external element, and therefore to dub the matrilineal totemism of the
castes in Kanara a totemic system rather than a totemic complex.

As Niggemeyer's analysis clearly demonstrates, the centre in
which matriliny and totemism in the south combine, blend, and
maintain a more or less proportionate balance is South Kanara,
where the language is Tulu. It is in this area that a number
of castes are matrilineal in both bali and property inheritance.

The Tulu area in turn owes its matriliny in all likelihood to
the Malayalam area further south, where the Nayars constitute
its principal centre of radiation. The Nayars, says Hutton, form
' a more or less military society in which the men tend to go
off on fighting or marauding expeditions leaving their wives to
live in their own maternal homes, a state of society familiar also
in Malaysia '.[16] According to Kathleen Gough, when and whence
the Nayars came is uncertain; however, the most plausible view
is that they were a matrilineal hill tribe in the Ghats under the
control of chiefs who owed a tenuous allegiance to the Chera
kings, and might have come down into the Kerala plains about
the fourth century when the Chera kingdom collapsed.[17] Ranking immediately after the Nambudiri Brahmins in the caste
hierarchy of the south, the Nayars once possessed a fuller system
of inheritance through females than today.[18] The other castes
and tribes of the area with matrilineal elements show similarities
with the Nayar system, and can be said to have largely acquired
them from that source. Ehrenfels's view that motherright in India
is older than totemism [19] is based on an over-schematization of
the data (the facts can be explained by percolation and elaboration) and by a preconceived ascription of single traits to a
motherright complex or culture-circle (whereas some of these
traits at any rate might have had other functional roles and
relations and might have thus arisen independently, or at least
independently of matrilineal conglomerates). The hypothesis
that we suggest is therefore that the Nayars, a Dravidian people,
brought with them from abroad certain proto-matrilineal elements which later grew into a somewhat fuller system under the

spur of the fact that the men were away from home on military
or predatory expeditions frequently and for long periods of
time. Other castes and tribes acquired features of this system
by percolation and by imitation of their social and military
superiors, and adapted them in varying degrees to their own
ways of life.

The advance of the patrilineal totemism of the Telugu-
speaking castes westwards shows itself further in the super-
imposition of patrilineal elements over matrilineal ones among
some Kanarese castes in Mysore such as the Halepaik and the
Holeya, which retain a matrilineal inheritance of the totem, but
are patrilineal in property inheritance. The Halepaik, moreover, show other regional differences in terms of matriliny and
patriliny. The matrilineal totemism of South Kanara advanced
northwards into North Kanara where matriliny tended to give
place to patriliny (thus the Bant, the Moger, the Halepaik, and
the Kelasi are matrilineal in bali and property inheritance in
South Kanara, but matrilineal in bali and patrilineal in property inheritance in North Kanara); and further upwards into
the heart of Maharashtra where patriliny displaces matriliny in
both the inheritance of the devak and of property.

That the Marathas and the occupational castes related or
influenced by them very likely acquired their totemic stimuli or
elements largely from the south is attested by the facts that the
Marathi-speaking population represents a cultural compromise
between the northern and the southern patterns of kinship
organization,[20] that a large number of the devaks are trees, that
a number of trees, animals and inanimate objects, as Enthoven
points out, occur as both balis and devaks (the nagchampa, the
jambul, the banyan, the screw-pine, the mouse-deer, the tortoise,
the axe, gold and turmeric), and that the totemic elements in
the devak system are much weaker than among the Kanarese
castes, indicating their acquisition at the third or even fourth
remove from the original source of totemic stimuli in India.
This of course does not exclude the possibility of some influences
derived directly from the Telugu-speaking castes or other tribes.
All in all, however, we can well agree with Karve that the clan
system and its totemic elements among the Marathi-speaking
population have analogies with the system of the south and
might have been derived from there.[21]

However, for reasons stated so ably by Abbott and recorded
earlier in this work, we believe that the devak was originally
and essentially not a totem but a symbol into which the sakti or
power of a deity was temporarily invoked, according to the
Hindu practice of avahana. With the encroachment of totemic

influences into the area, the devak concept and the patri-family (kul) of the Maratha castes tended to converge with the clan and totem system of the south, producing the half-formed totemic system of the Maratha castes. The process was probably interrupted, among other factors, by the unquenchable urge of the lower castes, egged on by the example of the Marathas, to imitate their superiors and thus raise their status in the caste hierarchy.

Devaks are found most frequently among the Marathas and the occupational castes related to or influenced by them in the Maratha country, and less frequently among the primitive tribes of the area like the Katkari, the Thakur and the Mahadev Koli. The Warli and the Son Koli, as recent ethnographic studies indicate, have no devaks. The tribes and castes in Gujarat do not display the phenomenon generally. Therefore it follows that the primitive tribes of the area picked up the devak system from the Marathas and the related castes, and that whatever isolated traces of it occur beyond Surat spread or were carried there from the Maratha country.

The devak system of the Marathas is characterized by two features: the worship of the devak or its image at marriages and the predominance of trees and plants among the devaks. Now, as Niggemeyer points out, the worship of the totem or an image of it at marriages is found among a few castes, tribal castes and tribes in Central India. One or two instances of it occur in the south also. The groups in Central India which have this practice are the Burud, the Chadar, the Basor, the Dahait, the Khadal, the Khangar, the Chauhan, the Kawar, the Bhaina, and even some clans among the Gond. In the south the Toreya and perhaps the Bestha show traces of it.[22] The Bhil in northwestern India, as Luard's evidence indicates, also have several instances of the worship of the totem or its image at marriages. Some of the groups worship a painted image of the totem (the Chadar, the Basor and the Dahait). The Khadal make an offering of flowers, sandalwood, vermilion and rice, and throw clothes and ornaments meant for the bride to the totem at marriages. When the actual totem is not available, the Chauhan make an image out of flour and worship it. Among the Kawar the bride and bridegroom in one sub-caste make images of their totems out of flour, bake them in oil and show them to the families of their marriage-partners as proof of their descent and totem membership. Among the Bhaina the father of the bride makes an image of the bridegroom's totem out of clay and sets it up next to the marriage-post. The bridegroom worships the totem-image, lights a sacrificial fire before it, and sacrifices vermilion, which he afterwards applies to the brow of the bride. Further, an image of the bride's totem is made in the house of the bridegroom and the bride worships it after she returns from the marriage ceremony. In Coimbatore and Salem the snake clan of the Toreya worships ant-hills at marriages because they are regarded as the dwelling-place of snakes; and among the Bestha in Mysore the members of the Silver clan, who are normally forbidden to wear silver rings, are allowed to use silver ornaments at marriages. Niggemeyer, therefore, concludes that the worship of the totem at marriages has spread from the area where it is at its most intense, that is, in the Maratha country, far into Central India among some of the tribes and castes there. Some of these tribes and castes also have a predominance of plant totems. With this view we are in agreement, and note further in its support that the spread of the Marathi-speaking population into Central India, spurred by the spirit of expansionism and adventurism of the Marathas, could have thus served as a channel of diffusion. The making and worship of totem images can be ascribed in general to the Hindu practice of idol-worship, of which the devak image is a specific example. Thus the totemic character of the devak and the worship of the totem or its image at marriages is a relatively recent development; and the cross-currents of cultural influences—totemic influences from the south converging on the devak system of the Marathas, and the worship of the devak at marriages converging on the totemic organization of certain Central Indian tribes and castes—underlines the complexity of cultural history in India.

This complexity is particularly accentuated in the more accessible parts of Central India where an interplay of advanced and primitive cultures, languages and races has been going on down the ages. Fission and fusion of ethnic and cultural elements are perhaps exemplified by the Basdewa, the Bhaina, the Bharia, the Chadar, the Halba, the Manjhwar and a series of other tribal groups and tribal castes, and it is often difficult to determine group identities because of the complex web of affinities and affiliations. Thus the Basdewa have exogamous septs with various names. Some are those of Brahminic gotras and Rajput clans; others are nicknames or names of villages; and still others are derived from animals and plants. The Basdewa are a caste of wandering beggars of mixed origin, according to Russell & Hiralal.[23] The Bhaina, as we have seen, are regarded as a sub-group of the Baiga. But Fuchs is not inclined to agree because the Bhaina are pronounced totemists, whereas totemism is not very strong among the other Baiga subsections. According to Russell & Hiralal, the Bhaina are of mixed descent and are mainly derived from the Baiga and the Kawar. Their exogamous divisions show that they have failed to preserve the purity of their blood. Some of their got or sept names are names of other castes or tribes: Dhobia (washerman), Ahera (cowherd), Mallin (gardener), Panika (from Panka), Gond and others. The members of these septs respect any man belonging to the caste after which their septs are named, and also worship the family gods of the caste concerned. Other septs are named after animals and plants. Some of these are Nag (cobra), Bagh (tiger), Chitwa (leopard), Gidha (vulture), Besra (hawk), Bendra (monkey), Bataria (quail), and Durgachhia (black ant). They have totem taboos, and also worship the totem-image at marriages, a custom which, as we have already seen, has been probably acquired from the west. If they see the dead body of the totem animal or hear of its death, they throw away an earthen pot and bathe and shave themselves as for a member of the family, a practice with its principal location in Central India. It is also reported that women are often tattooed with representations of their totem animals and men swear by them as their most sacred oath. Inanimate objects after which some septs are named are likewise respected. Members of the Gawad sept will not burn cowdung cakes for fuel; those of the Mircha sept do not use chillies; and those of the Sun sept perform formal rites of mourning as for a totem animal on an eclipse of the sun. Some of the groups have two divisions—male and female—which are almost separate septs. Examples are Nagbans Andura and Nagbans Mai (or male and female cobra septs), Karsayal Singhara and Karsayal Mundi (or stag and doe septs), and Baghchhal Andura and Baghchhal Mai (or tiger and tigress septs).[24] Closely allied to the Kol and the Chero, the Bharia originally belonged to the Munda group, but in the Central Provinces (Madhya Pradesh) are regarded as Gond. They have a number of exogamous divisions, the names of which suggest the heterogeneous elements of which the tribe today consists. Of 51 such divisions, 15 or 16 are names of other clans or castes, indicating intermarriages or the admission of a family of outsiders. Other divisions are named after animals, plants and inanimate objects.[25] The Halba, according to Russell & Hiralal, are a caste of cultivators and farm servants in Kanker and Bastar, and are everywhere divided into two groups of pure and mixed Halba, which are endogamous. Many of their exogamous septs are named after other castes; others have territorial and titular names; and still others are totemic. This also indicates their mixed origin. In Bastar they revere the totem animal or plant, and will not injure or kill it. There are also traces of mourning rites for the totem, but the breaking of earthen pots is not general. In Bastar the totemic groups are called *barags,* but many men belong also to a *thok* which has a titular name and is used as a surname; and marriages are nowadays avoided among persons with the same thok or surname and the same barag.[26] These examples, then, suffice to show the intricate affiliations of many tribal groups and tribal castes in Central India and adjoining areas. Other small tribal groups and tribal castes show more uniform and distinct affinities, and these are either with the Gond or the Munda-speaking tribes or with both. Some of these latter groups have been examined in an earlier chapter.

The depressed or exterior castes occupy a social position of their own—although a despised one—in the caste system. According to an earlier standpoint, both untouchables and Sudras were descendants of the indigenous inhabitants of India, who were subdued by the later invaders and reduced to the status of serfs and menials. But this is a sweeping hypothesis, and is untenable as such on both socio-cultural and ethnic grounds.[27] There are a large number of such castes, particularly in northern and central India, which are anthropometrically, serologically, and to a predominant measure socio-culturally closer to the Kshatriyas and allied upper castes than to the primitive population. On the other hand, as Hutton points out, when tribal groups come into the Hindu system, they tend to be regarded automatically as depressed because of the Hindu prejudice against certain occupations and certain kinds of food.[28] Even those lower castes however, which are otherwise little related to the primitive population, have some elements which relate them to the primitive peoples. This can be explained in terms of their low status in the Hindu caste hierarchy—a fact which must have to a certain measure at least permitted the absorption of some socio-cultural elements and even made possible some ethnic intermixture.

One of these castes is the menial caste of the Dom found in Bengal, Bihar and Uttar Pradesh. Risley calls them a Dravidian menial caste, and is inclined to the view that they were originally at least one of the aboriginal tribes. They have an intricate internal organization which is due to the large area over which the caste is distributed. They have numerous exogamous sections and subcastes. In Bihar their exogamous sections are territorial and titular; in Bankura they are totemic; in central Bengal there is a tendency to replace them by Brahminic gotras; and in the eastern districts the exogamous sections have disappeared altogether and marriages are regulated by prohibited degrees down to the fifth generation in descent from a common ancestor. Their religion is a chaotic mixture of survivals from the animistic cults of the aboriginal races and observances borrowed haphazardly from whatever Hindu sect happened to be dominant in the particular locality. Crooke seems also of the opinion that they are one of the aboriginal tribes of India, and adds that in the North-Western Provinces and Oudh (Uttar Pradesh) they have exogamous gotras which have names of occupations, of animals and plants, and of other tribes. The Doms have not been systematically studied to this day; but it may be noted that Majumdar relates them anthropometrically to the Kshatriyas on the one hand and to the Chamars on the other.[29]

The Chamars are a caste of tanners and menial labourers in Northern India. Risley and Crooke report no totemism, but exogamous divisions of a territorial or local nature exist. Russell & Hiralal, however, point out that they have numerous endogamous subcastes and exogamous divisions. The latter reveal great diversity. Thus, some of the exogamous divisions are named after Rajput clans and others after other castes; some have nicknames and others territorial ones. Many are of a totemic variety; for instance: peg, sandalwood, sword, plum, chillies, whisk, wasp, skin, silk and the lotus plant. Totemic observances occur only in one or two instances. G. W. Briggs, who studied the Chamars somewhat more intensively, affirms that they are essentially non-Aryan, but are today heterogeneous. They are Hindus, and their subcastes are endogamous. The subcastes are broken up into smaller exogamous or 'family' groups (got, kul) which have the names of some mythical saint, hero or other person, or of a village or other locality, or refer to a totem. Of the gots listed, 15 are named after trees, plants and their products, 12 after animals, and the rest after saints, gods, places, diseases, and so on. Dust, leper, Krishna, Kali, milk and strength are some examples of the odder type of names. Traces of totem taboos are also reported—members of gots named after the gular, the pipal, the jhand and the neem trees do not use the wood of these trees as fuel for cooking purposes, and the members of the Sheep got do not eat the flesh of the sheep, or drink its milk, or use woollen blankets. They have likewise a number of Rajput clan names.[30]

The Balahis, too, are reckoned among the 60 million depressed classes. Fuchs, who devoted an entire monograph to the Balahis of the Nimar district in the Central Provinces (Madhya Pradesh), found a clan organization among them but no distinct elements of totemism. Some of the clans, however, have beliefs and practices which suggest traces of totemism. Thus the members of the Hirwa clan, founded by a Rajput, worship the owl and are not allowed to kill it. It is said that an owl protected the child of a Rajput farmer. The members of the Khandgar clan, a genuine Balahi one, have a clan goddess and are prohibited from cutting an astra tree or burning its wood. They are also not allowed to kill a snake or use a broom. The members of the Nirguya clan, which is of Rajput origin, are not allowed to touch the nirguya plant; and those of the Varmandal clan, whose ancestors were Ahirs, are not allowed to sit in the shade of a banyan tree or to cut it and burn its wood, or use its leaves as plates.[31] Of these four cases, the two clans of Rajput origin show relatively more distinct traces of totemism than the other two. Their totemic elements may therefore be interpreted as examples of secondary quasi-totemism, ' secondary ' because they are evidently the result of the surrounding totemic atmosphere, and ' quasi ' because they have not grown into full-fledged totemism. The taboos of the other two clans bear similarities to some of the totemic taboos among many totemic groups, but could also have origins other than totemic. The banyan, for instance, is widely revered in India, and taboos generally regarded have a complex etiology.[32] On the other hand, they may also represent the last remnants of a somewhat fuller totemism that perhaps once prevailed among some groups of the Balahis.

The three instances of depressed castes dealt with here thus show varying degrees of mild totemism. The possibility that the lower Hindu castes and untouchables represent the remnants of the former population of the Indus Valley Civilization, dispersed, subdued and reduced to the status of menials and untouchables by the later Aryan invaders, cannot altogether be ignored.[33] The totemic traces among them, however, can scarcely be ascribed to the Indus Valley Civilization itself; for of totemism or totemic traces there is scarcely any evidence from that quarter. Hence the sources of these totemic traces must be sought among the tribes and castes in the area in which these lower castes eke out their existence.

Like the Kunbis in Maharashtra, the Kurmis of Upper India are a cultivating caste, and occupy a higher and more respectable status in the caste system than the depressed castes. Dalton thought that they were degraded Aryans, and Risley that the Kurmis of Bihar were probably Aryans and those of Chota Nagpur ' Dravidian ' tribes. They have several endogamous subcastes; and Risley adds that in Chota Nagpur and Orissa their exogamous sections are totemic, whereas in Bihar they are titular and tend to be replaced by prohibited degrees. In Chota Nagpur and Orissa the tribal beliefs have only a thin veneer of Hinduism. The Kurmis of the North-Western Provinces and Oudh

(Uttar Pradesh) have totemic usages, but no elaborate totemic
system as in Chota Nagpur. In religion, says Crooke, they are
like the other Hindu castes of a similar standing. The word
'Kurmi' has been traced to the Sanskrit *kutumba* (family), to
the Sanskrit *krishi* (cultivation), and to *kurma* (tortoise), an
incarnation of Vishnu, either because it supports the earth, or
because it is worshipped by the Kurmis and other agricultural
castes or tribes, or because it was the 'tribal totem'. Russell &
Hiralal, referring to the Kurmis of the United Provinces, Bihar
and the Central Provinces, state that each subcaste has a number
of exogamous septs of all types. Some have Brahminic names;
others those of Rajput clans; and still others are titular or the
names of villages. The Chandnahu subcaste has 6 clans named
after animals, 5 named after trees and their products, 9 after
inanimate objects, 5 after rishis, 3 after villages, 4 after various
qualities, 5 after persons with various occupations, and 5 as
follows: famine, God, Saturday, air and Ganges. The Gabel
subcaste has 3 named after animals, 2 after inanimate objects,
3 after villages, 3 after persons, 1 after a quality, 1 after a Rajput
clan, and 3 as follows: Ganges water, ocean, and small sea. The
Santara subcaste has two named after towns, four after villages,
and two as follows: embankment and wooden pestle. The Tirole
subcaste has one named after an animal, 3 after trees and their
products, 4 after Rajput clans, 2 after qualities and one after
an inanimate object. The Gaur subcaste has 4 named after
villages, 2 after towns, 4 after persons with various occupations,
2 after trees and their products, and 2 after inanimate objects;
and the Usrete subcaste has 3 named after animals, 10 after
villages, one after a town, and 4 as follows: hunter, fort, stump
of a tree, and to roll. Many Kurmis claim to belong to the
Kashyap gotra.[34] All in all, therefore, we may conclude that the
Kurmis are not strongly totemic; though differences in totemic
intensity which are regionally significant manifest themselves.

The Rajputs, generally classed as Kshatriyas, have exercised
considerable influence on the surrounding tribes and lower castes
in Central India and elsewhere. In the west the Marathas and
related castes have Rajput clan names, and in the east their
sphere of influence extends right up to the coastal areas roughly
from the Godavari upwards. The heart of the Rajput country,
Rajputana (Rajasthan), is the northwest, but the martial traditions and adventures of the Rajputs have extended the range
of their influence far and wide; and so a claim to Rajput descent
and imitation of Rajput customs has become a means to social
advancement, an alternative to the imitation of Brahminic gotras
and ceremonies. There are, for instance, a number of tribes and

castes in Central India, as Russell & Hiralal bear witness, which have Rajput clan names. Some of the Rajput clan names themselves refer to animals and plants; and, as we have seen, one or two Balahi clans of Rajput origin have quasi-totemic features. This therefore raises the question whether in fact the Rajputs are quasi-totemists, and, if so, whether the quasi-totemism of some tribes and castes in the upper areas of India can perhaps be attributed to this source.

The origin of the Rajputs is still shrouded to some extent in obscurity. Crooke (in his Introduction to Tod's *Annals and Antiquities of Rajasthan*) affirms that a great gulf lies between the Vedic Kshatriyas and the Rajputs of medieval times, that many of the Rajput clans date from the Saka or Kushan invasion which occurred about the middle of the second century before Christ or from the time of the Gupta empire about the year 480 after Christ, that the Gurjara tribe connected with the White Huns adopted Hinduism, and that most of the Rajput families sprang from them. When these families in turn adopted Brahminism, they concocted myths of descent from the sun and the moon to maintain their status. Therefore, adds Crooke, it may be accepted that the nobler Rajput septs are descended from the Gurjaras and other foreigners, while the others are closely connected with the autochthonous races. Risley states that most of the original septs of the Rajputs are of the territorial type, but that they also recognize Brahminic gotras, which one recent writer maintains (not without challenge) are an ancient possession, thus lending support to the view that the Rajputs are an old class of fighters and rulers in India.[35]

Traditionally the Rajputs have 36 clans. Some of these clans have names which refer to animals. Thus, as Russell & Hiralal inform us, Meshbansi signifies descendants of the sheep, the Baghel clan derives its name from the tiger, the Kachhwaha clan from the tortoise, the Haihaivansi clan from the horse, the Nagvansi clan from the cobra and the Tomara clan from a club. Furthermore, some clans show a special reverence for particular trees. For example, the Bundelas revere the kadamb tree, the Panwars the neem tree, and the Rathors the pipal tree. Russell & Hiralal see in this veneration a relic of totemism. It appears also that in former times each clan had a clan god. Enthoven calls the Rajputs hereditary soldiers and landowners, and adds that the bulk of the tribe has lost the purity of its blood by marriages with the Bhil, the Koli and other primitive tribes. Their chief peculiarity is their exogamous clan organization. The smaller clans appear to have split off from the larger ones when the latter grew in size and spread widely, and thereafter took the name of a distinguished ancestor or the place of residence. In other instances the clan names were derived from occupations or even from trivial changes of customs. Apart from their clan and local characteristics, however, the Rajputs do not differ from other Hindus in their religious beliefs and practices. The Jats, who are probably related to the Rajputs, have two territorial divisions, one of which has ' sections ' which, according to H. A. Rose, might be totemic, but reverence is seldom paid to the ' totem '. Examples of their so-called totems are a tree, hatchet, young heifer, monkey, jackal, sword, axe, the pipal tree, the jand tree, louse and blue cow.[36]

From the evidence available it is therefore clear that the ' totemic ' traces among the Rajputs are exceedingly sparse and weak, and could scarcely have been the source of the ' diluted form of totemism ' found among the Gond and other castes in Central India, which cannot be said to have been strongly influenced by the Gond. On the contrary it would seem more likely that the Rajputs acquired their totemic traits, or at any rate the stimulus leading up to them, from below, or in other words, from the primitive tribes of Central India among which totemism has been relatively strong. Other evidence which favours this view is that the Rajputs have intermarried with the tribes and castes with which they came into contact, that the Gujarat areas are largely non-totemic, and that there is no positive proof that the foreign component in the Rajput community was originally totemic even in quasi-totemic terms. Hence, of the two possibilities held out by Fuchs that this dilute form of totemism could well have been introduced into the country by the Rajputs or that it could be of an even older origin,[37] the 'facts would seem to favour the second. That is to say, the dilute form of totemism found in these parts is the end-product of tribal history and development in India itself. The same process of reasoning would perhaps apply also to some extent to the clan system of the Rajputs, the stimuli for which could have emanated from the primitive population, or even from the higher Hindu castes, and local peculiarities could be ascribed to local factors. However, the possibility that the foreign component (White Huns or Scythians) originally contained non-totemic clans cannot altogether be excluded.[38]

That totemic stimuli and elements have tended to creep upwards from a primitive base is also exemplified by the Oriya Brahmins who have gotras named after the Vedic rishis, but who at the same time identify their gotra names with the local names of certain birds, beasts and other objects, and observe restrictions towards them which resemble totemic taboos.

Examples are Bharadvaja (blue jay), Parasara (pigeon), Gargiyasa (a bird), Saimilya (a bird), Kasyapa (tortoise), Bachhasa (calf), Gautama (cow), Krishnatreya (black buck), Lahityana (fire), Mudgala (ring), Dallabhya (monkey), Kausika (owl), Bhargava (a tree), Kaudinya (a deer), Agastya (pot), Maitreya (frog), and Sandilya (bull). The Oriya Brahmins, however, have a Hinduistic myth to explain these animal names.[39]

As totemism crept upwards from its primitive base, it no doubt gave rise all along its trail to examples of secondary quasi-totemism—a form of dilute totemism which is not due to forces of disintegration, but which traces its source of inspiration, its origin, its centre of diffusion elsewhere than in the group in which it is found. Obviously the phenomena which the term ' secondary quasi-totemism ' seeks to conceptualize are not subject to clear delimitation, but the term itself is nevertheless useful in that it condenses the two factors of diffusion and dilution at the beginnings of clan-totemic growth into a short phrase.

The view that totemism has probably had a multiple origin in India (Roy) is based upon a loose use of the phrase ' multiple origin ', and is in any case difficult to prove.[40] It is for instance difficult to prove that individual tribes with totemic elements in India have not received totemic stimuli from the general totemic atmosphere prevailing among the many totemic tribes and castes in the country, or that they have not acquired more concrete elements from those tribes and castes. This is of course not to deny the rise of certain totemic clans from individual and accidental experiences (Elwin) or the accretions of other elements which later secured a more or less totemic colour (Hutton).

\*　　　　\*　　　　\*

There is no evidence of sex totemism in India. The hints of something of the kind among the Bhaina, as reported by Russell & Hiralal, are too vague to be interpreted as such. Nor can the report be entirely trusted in relation to the statements bearing on them. The evidence from the Sema Naga which Hutton reports is also not conclusive.

There is likewise no definite evidence of the ritual eating of the totem in India. The instances quoted by Russell & Hiralal refer either to vague claims of its former existence or are subject to explanations extraneous to totemism. Thus it is said that the Tiger and Snake clans of the Bhatra tribe formerly ate their totems at a sacrificial meal, that the Gond, who worship the cobra as a household god, eat its flesh once a year because they believe that by so doing they will be immune from snake-bite throughout the year, that on the festival of Nag-Panchmi the

Mahar make an image of a snake out of flour and sugar and eat it, and that the Singrore Dhimar must eat the flesh of a crocodile at their weddings.[41] The Gond custom, however, might have arisen as a result of a belief in the efficacy of snake-flesh as a preventive against snake-bite in an atmosphere of magic and religious emotion; and the Mahar practice may also have its roots in part in the festival with which it is associated. The authenticity of the other instances is doubtful. Hence Buradkar's attempt at deducing from the above-mentioned Gond custom and from vague reports of cannibalism among a community of Gond the earlier existence of a ' stage of totemic development in which the Gond savage killed and ate his totem to identify himself physically with it '[42] is strained and unwarranted.

The problem of a dual organization in India has been variously tackled. The first to assert its former existence in India was W. H. R. Rivers, who was of the opinion that the prevalence of cross-cousin marriage in South India was a proof of that fact. But Westermarck denied its existence in India, and F. J. Richards explained cross-cousin marriages in other terms. Next, Hodson pointed out that a dual organization was still existent in the extreme northeast; and Ghurye, supporting Rivers, endeavoured to prove its former existence in Dravidian India in conjunction with matrilineal descent from an analysis of kinship terms.[43]

Adopting Graebner's standpoint, Niggemeyer accepted exogamy and the matrilineal inheritance of membership in the two classes as the chief criteria of the dual organization, and took up the question of its existence in India because the fact of its association with the presumed older, matrilineal complex would be of immense help in tracing the cultural stratification of India and a proof of the existence of a totemic-matrilineal mixed culture on the subcontinent. The following tribes and castes were found in the main to be divided into two groups, most of which, again, break up into exogamous-totemic sub-groups: Omanaito (Oriyaland), Pentiya (Jeypur), Konda Dora (Vizagapatam), Bedar or Boya (Mysore and Hyderabad), Kurni (Bellary), Korku (Central Provinces), Gadaba (Vizagapatam), Bhulia (Sambalpur), Agaria (Sambalpur and Bilaspur), Konga Vellala (Trichinopoly), Andh (Berar and Hyderabad), and Halba (Raipur and Bastar). However, the two groups into which they are divided are mostly endogamous. Driver does not mention whether the two groups of the Korku are endogamous or otherwise; and the Gadaba have five endogamous groups of which two break up further into totemic sub-groups. None of these tribes and castes is matrilineal. Furthermore, in most instances the two groups are named big and little, and in other instances superior and inferior (Agaria), genuine and non-genuine (Andh), and pure and mixed (Halba). Hence, Niggemeyer concludes that the above-mentioned tribes and castes have no dual organization in Graebner's sense of the term, and that the division into two endo-gamous groups is a relatively recent development resulting from the fact that some members of these groups married outside their tribe or caste, their offspring being, therefore, regarded as mixed or inferior. An additional proof of this interpretation is the fact that among some of these groups (the Omanaito, the Pentiya and the Konda Dora) only the section called ' big ' breaks up into totemic groups, and that there are other castes also in which an endogamous sub-group regards the others as inferior (the Stanika in South Kanara, the Bavuri in Ganjam). There are, however, two or three dichotomous castes in South India which break up into two exogamous groups. These are: (i) The Janappan in North Arcot divided into two great exogamous groups consisting of 16 and 8 exogamous, totemic gotras respec-tively. Thurston & Rangachari unfortunately give no informa-tion on the way the two moieties are named or on the principle of descent, but patriliny seems to prevail. (ii) The Korava in Arcot have two exogamous sub-groups called masculine and feminine respectively, which in turn break up into a series of exogamous, totemic clans. (iii) The Bili Magga in Mysore like-wise have two groups named masculine or Siva group and femi-nine or Parvati group, which consist of 33 totemic clans each; but there is no information on whether the groups are endo-gamous or exogamous. Niggemeyer, however, is not inclined to accept Schmidt's view that these are traces of the two-class system for the following reasons: (a) that the castes concerned are patrilineal, (b) that there are castes in which the two groups are named after a god and goddess respectively, but are endogamous (for example, the Chadar in the northern parts of the Central Provinces, who are also patrilineal), and (c) that the two groups into which these castes are divided do not consist exclusively and respectively of men and women, but of both men and women. Therefore Niggemeyer leaves the question of the exis-tence of a dual system in India open.[44]

According to Ehrenfels, who next tackled the question of a dual organization in India, there are genuine traces of the system in the grouping of a number of castes in South India into two reciprocal parties, that is, the right-hand and the left-hand factions.[45]

But the most thorough and searching study of the problem for its time was that of W. Koppers.[46] Koppers, quoting Grigson, points out that there are no convincing traces of the

dual organization among the Gond and that their phratry system
is of comparatively recent origin, that there are no convincing
traces of the system among the Malayalis as revealed by more
careful research and hence evidence derived from the Tottiyan,
the Golla and the Korava (Ghurye) must be treated with caution,
that there is no dual organization among the Bhil and the
Bhilala or among the Bhuiya of Orissa, that the right-hand
and left-hand factions are not of great antiquity but are connected with the restoration of Brahminism in South India, that
as with the various castes listed by Niggemeyer so with the
Munda, the moieties are endogamous and have arisen through
contact with Hinduism, and that the Garo and other Tibeto-
Burman tribes of Assam have a genuine dual system, but not
the Khasi. Therefore Koppers concludes that an ethnological
dual organization or the division of a primitive tribe into two
exogamous moieties (which may also exist in a patrilineal system)
does not occur (apart from Assam) on the subcontinent.

Koppers' view has been recently challenged by Verrier Elwin
on the basis of evidence garnered from the Bondo Highlanders,
a small Munda-speaking tribe in Orissa. The Bondo have three
exogamous units—the village community, a number of patrilineal clans or kuda named after village functionaries, and two
great moieties (or bonsos), the Ontal and the Killo or Kukusa.
Elwin regards both territorial and clan exogamy among the
Bondo as a recent acquisition from their neighbours, and bonso
exogamy as the oldest of the tribal exogamous regulations. He
then attempts to show that the Bondo society is really bisected
into two divisions, that the bonsos were once much more strictly exogamous than today, that some of their kinship terms (following Ghurye's lead in his analysis of the Dravidian material),
although partly explicable on other grounds, certainly suggest
an original dual system, and that (taking a cue or two from
Ehrenfels), although there is no apparent rivalry or hostility
between the two moieties, they are closely associated with totemism. Hence Elwin draws the following conclusion: ' On the
whole, therefore, although the social picture is not quite in the
sharpest focus, I believe that we have in the Cobra and Tiger
bisection of Bondo society a relic of a genuine dual organization
with patrilineal descent.' [47]

Some points which appear to have a negative bearing on the
question of Bondo dual organization may, however, be noted
here. The Bondo and the Gadaba are culturally very similar
and the former may even represent an offshoot of the latter
(Fürer-Haimendorf). But the only evidence of a possible dual
organization among the Gadaba is that Thurston speaks of five

sections divided into exogamous clans and Fürer-Haimendorf adds that every village has two or more phratries named after animals such as the tiger, the snake, the bear, showing indications of totemism. The Dire (Didaya), who also speak a Munda language akin to that of the Bondo, have likewise a phratry or bonso system. The bonsos which run through the entire tribe are exogamous and are named after animals like the tiger, the cobra, the bear, the tortoise and the monkey. Fürer-Haimendorf, who reports on the Dire, considers them to be more primitive than the Bondo, from whom they got a good deal of their culture, but does not speak of a dual organization among them.[48] The Parenga, too, have more than two phratries; and the Bondo themselves have vague traditions of other bonso groups—the Sun, the Monkey, the Fish and the Bear. The bonso system of the area may, therefore, be regarded for all practical purposes as a cultural unit lending to the tribes concerned a sense of community. This bond is further strengthened by other ' Munda ' traits which these tribes have in common, of which a strong village sentiment is but one instance. It is therefore possible that the Bondo moieties are remnants of a larger system, the other units of which have withered away under adverse influences.[49]

Not far removed geographically from the Bondo and the Gadaba are the Gond. Fuchs, who examined the evidence afresh in 1952, concludes that the clan and village organization of the Gond does not by itself prove conclusively the existence of a dual organization in this tribe, but that other evidence like the formation of two groups of exogamous brother clans, certain kinship and affinity terms, the practice of giving daughters in marriage to a well-defined group of affines (*nat*), cross-cousin marriage, grandparents-grandchildren marriage, the classificatory system of relationship and the position of the nat relatives in the social life of the tribal unit, point, though again not conclusively, in that direction. So far as the ideological aspect is concerned, some signs of social antagonism exist in actuality as well as in the myths, but material suggesting cosmic antagonism, colour contrasts and the coupling of two animals is wanting. Fuchs therefore affirms that ' there is rather much in favour of the assumption that in former times the Gond had a dual social system or had been strongly influenced by a people with a dual organization '.[50]

If, now, as Haekel points out, the dual system is rooted in a certain ideological attitude, in a polar world-view and diverse

dualities in nature and the cosmos, and has nothing to do as
such with so-called motherright or fatherright,[51] one can safely
conclude that a full-fledged dual system does not exist in India.
The evidence presented by Elwin and Fuchs may be interpreted
to imply the former existence of such a system, but under the
present state of research on the problem the question is best
left open.

*                    *                    *

As the empirical evidence brought together in the preceding
chapters and our attempt at tracing the development of totemism in India in this one indicate, the phenomenon occurs in a
wide expanse of territory on the subcontinent. Radiating from
its primary centre in the northeast of Central India, it has spread
far into the south, largely avoiding the Malayalam area and
tapering off in the adjoining Tamil area. Niggemeyer's southern
frontier, shown by a line drawn from Mahe to Madras, is an
approximate indication of the southern limits of Indian totemism. Its northern frontier is best suggested, according to Niggemeyer, by a line drawn from the Gujarat peninsula in a curve
over Allahabad and along the Ganges up to its estuary. It must
be noted, however, that the area now known as Gujarat (that
is, including Kathiawar) is mainly non-totemic, that Rose
registers 'totemic traces' among certain castes even as far north
as the Punjab (the Chuhra who are sweepers and scavengers,
the Bania who are traders, the Ghirth, the Jat, the Khatri, and
the Arora, a leading caste in south-west Punjab),[52] and that L.
Adam would even prefer to interpret certain food taboos among
the Rai and other tribes in Nepal as totemic traces.[53] If these are
indeed totemic traces, they do not alter the situation to any
great extent. Assam or the extreme northeast stands apart with
its primary quasi-totemism. In this vast area over which totemism has spread there are of course some tribes and castes which
are non-totemic. The non-totemic tribes are a proof of the fact
that sweeping terms like 'Proto-Australoid' and 'Gondid' cannot be equated with the original bearers of totemism in India,
at any rate in their entirety. When Hutton and Niggemeyer
affirm these equations, they cast their nets too widely. So far as
the castes are concerned, the following generalization seems to fit
the facts to a large measure: The less totemic the caste, the
higher its status.

The features which characterize totemism everywhere in India
are totemic names, totem taboos and exogamy. The weakening
of these three features is roughly proportional to the distance

of their location from the primary centre of totemism and to the intensity of acculturative forces released by the higher cultures. All the other elements found in India are limited to specific areas or occur sporadically. Thus the worship of the totem or its image at marriages has its centre, as we have seen, in Maharashtra and has radiated from there to surrounding areas. Mourning for the dead totem, specially in the form of breaking or casting away of earthen pots (the Bhaina, the Bhatra, the Chadar, the Dhanwar, the Gond, the Halba, the Kawar, the Kharwar, the Kol, the Parja, the Rautia, the Savara, the Songhara, the Kachari and a few others) is confined mainly to the northeastern areas of Central India, though weak forms of it also occur occasionally in other places. Niggemeyer locates its centre in a small area of the eastern Central Provinces (Madhya Pradesh). It is possible that this practice is a local development of relatively recent origin like the practice of salaaming the totem when it is encountered, which is, judging from the instances of its occurrence (as among the Bhil), a northern custom. Myths of descent are much less frequent than parallel-relationship ones, as several students of the subject have noted. The distribution of totem-descent myths is sporadic, with perhaps some degree of concentration in the northeastern areas of Central India. In most instances (the Agaria, the Gond, the Garo, the Kadu Golla, the Kamar, the Kawar, the Kharwar, the Santal and others) they may not after all be very old and can possibly be explained as independent inventions resulting sporadically from a totemic mentality or the logic of totemic facts. If this is so, it is all the more likely that the parallel-relationship myths in part preceded the descent-totemism myths, and in part arose later. Among the Kamar, one or two instances of totem-descent myths exist and might have been invented after the acquisition of their totemism from the Gond. Totem-descent among the Kadu Golla is evidently a recent development. Totem tattooing occurs scarcely at all in India. Russell & Hiralal report its existence among the Bhaina, the Bhatra, the Kawar and the Pardhan; and Barnes claimed to have found it among the Bhil. But these reports could have arisen as a result of faulty observation and hasty interpretation—a view which secures some justification from the fact that none of the other sources, either old or new, confirms its occurrence among the Bhil;[54] and as Luard (*Tattooing in Central India*, Bombay, 1905, p. 1) puts it, ' One thing is certain and that is that the wearers of these devices only look upon them as ornamental and decorative devices with no deeper significance '.[55]

\* \* \*

Totemism in India goes back obviously to a remote past, when man was still a hunter, as the Birhor tribe bears witness. It could have emerged into existence perhaps in the Palaeolithic, and must have spread with the growth of population and a more stable form of existence in the Mesolithic and early Neolithic, adapting itself to the new conditions by suitable modifications. Its disintegration might be approximately dated with the advent of metals. As for Assam, some facts suggest that the primary quasi-totemism of the area emerged into existence in a setting of early cultivation. These are of course exceedingly broad statements, but the facts of prehistoric archaeology in India or for the matter of that elsewhere in the world do not permit of narrower and more precise correlations.

An attempt at the correlation of the course of totemic growth in India, as outlined in this chapter, with the racial and other cultural facts would run as follows: If we begin with the Negrito because, as we have seen, they possess loose and floating beliefs and practices of a proto-totemic nature, and assume that they once existed in India, we can take for granted from their distribution in Asia today that they entered India in small groups through the northeast at some early date. They were simple food-gatherers and hunters and had no clans or clan-totemism. The faintness of their traces in India can be ascribed to the fact that they were numerically weak, and were therefore pushed back into the remote recesses of the country and finally absorbed by a numerically stronger group coming from the northwest, who are known in anthropological literature as Proto-Australoids (Hutton, Guha and others) or Weddids (Eickstedt). So far as the Proto-Australoids or Weddids are concerned, two hypotheses relating to their social organization are possible: first, that when they entered India they were food-gatherers and hunters with loose notions of a more or less proto-totemic character but without clans or clan-totemism, and that they later developed localized clans in India with territorial and other designations. The Kadar in South India have no clans, and the other primitive tribes in that region which do may be presumed, on grounds of their primitivity and the nature of their clan system, to have acquired them from some outside source. Second, that the Proto-Australoids or Weddids entered India in two or more waves, the first consisting of simple food-gatherers and hunters without clans or clan-totemism, and the second with localized clans but without clan-totemism. With the growth of population and the resulting migrations in India, the clans became dispersed, making them receptive to a form of clan-totemism. In the meanwhile, in the northeastern areas of Central India, the tendency for the clans to disperse converged with the then existing proto-totemic elements and other favourable factors and resulted in the apical group totemism of a small population ancestral to the Birhor. (The possibility that certain hunting tribes brought a kind of clan-totemism from the east or west, or received it from somewhere outside India, cannot, as we have already pointed out, be altogether excluded, but has not been proved.) The apical group totemism of the Birhor no doubt developed in a culture in which hunting was important, but not necessarily accompanied by all the elements which Schmidt ascribed to the hypothetical culture circle of higher hunters. For one thing, there is no such complex in India today, and for another, the facts of cultural development in India indicate a much greater complexity, as the ethnographic and archaeological evidence bear witness or, to take a particular instance, as the nature, origin and distribution of youth-dormitories and community houses in India, investigated afresh by Fürer-Haimendorf (1950), indicate.

The later phases of totemic growth in India may be described as follows: The clan-totemism of the Birhor spread among the neighbouring tribes with dispersed clans, and in the process lost much of its cultic intensity and its core of clan-and-totem identification. As a result, totemism in India obtained its typical form as a largely social phenomenon with its emphasis on exogamy. The next group to enter India was in all probability that of the Palaemongoloid Austroasiatics who came from the northeast. Relatively small in numbers but culturally advanced, they were absorbed by the local tribal population, which has shown since then Mongoloid features in varying degrees. The Austroasiatics were in large measure non-totemic, but gave their language and other elements of their culture to the Munda-speaking tribes of the present day without weakening their relatively strong totemism very much, but perhaps adding to its formal social character. Approximately at this time the Indus Valley Civilization was in full bloom.[56] Next the entry of the Aryans and the end of the Harappa civilization can be put down with Heine-Geldern at 1200-1000 before Christ;[57] and in the middle of the first millennium before Christ the Dravidians, according to Wheeler, Gordon and Fürer-Haimendorf, entered India either by sea or along the coastal land-route,[58] but this view is controverted by other scholars, especially Indian.

## *NOTES AND REFERENCES*

[1] If one includes tribes and castes mentioned in less detail by Frazer in Volume II of his *Totemism and Exogamy* and adds to them some of the other groups in *Totemica* (1937, 365-402) which were not previously mentioned in his 1910 work, Frazer's list would reach the approximate figure of 120 totemic tribes and castes.

[2] MacDonell (1897, 153) writes: ' . . . there are possibly in the RV some survivals of totemism or belief in the descent of the human race or of individual tribes or families from animals or plants. " Tortoise ", the name of a seer (9, 114) and of a priestly family (AB 727), is also frequently found in the AV and the later Vedic literature as that of a cosmogonic power nearly related to or identified with the Creator Prajapati. In a passage of the SB (7, 5, I) Prajapati appears in the form of a tortoise (*Kurma*). Here it is remarked that as *Kurma* is identical with *Kasyapa*, " therefore men say: all beings are the children of the tortoise (*Kasyapa*)". The RV (7, 18, I) mentions as tribal names Matsyas (Fishes), Ajas (Goats), and the Sigrus (Horseradishes). As names of Vedic priestly families also occur the Gotamas (Oxen), the Vatsas (Calves), the Sumakas (Dogs), the Kausikas (Owls) and Mandukeyas (Frog-sons). The father of Samvarana, a name occurring in the RV (5, 53), from whom the kings of the Kurus claimed descent, is in the Epic called Riksa (Bear). Hopkins, however, expresses a doubt whether the names of animals ever point to totemism in the RV.' See also C. D. Chatterjee, ' Totemism in Ancient India ' (paper read at the 26th Annual Session of the Indian Science Congress, Lahore, 1939) and N. G. Chapekar, ' Traces of Totemism in the Rigveda ' (*Sociological Bulletin*, 1952, I, 95-8). But John Brough (1953, xvi) writes: ' It is natural in considering a society with exogamous clans to inquire whether the clans are also totemic; and Kosambi, reviving the argument from animal gotra-names, holds that totemism was in fact characteristic of the gotras, at least in their origin (D. D. Kosambi, *Studies in the Brahmanas,* Thesis for the Ph.D. degree in the University of London, p. 28; also *JBBRAS*, 1946, 22, 44). See also Oldenberg, *Religion des Veda,* pp. 82-3, who quotes names such as Vatsas, Sumaka, Kausika, Mandukeya, etc. For a detailed list of proper names taken from animals and plants, see J. A. van Velze, *Names of Persons in Early Sanscrit Literature* (Utrecht, 1938, pp. 95ff). It seems to me that the evidence is altogether too slender to support the hypothesis. A number of animal names admittedly occur in the gotra lists, for example Tittiri and Kapinjala . . . but these are names of small families within the clan, and it is prima facie unlikely that such small subdivisions should possess their own totems. By themselves these names are no better evidence for totemism than English surnames such as Fox or Heron. From the names of the larger clan-groupings, Kosambi gives four which he considers to be totemic, but these are likewise unconvincing. Thus *Gotama* is merely " the possessor of excellent cattle ", or " best provided with cattle ", and is no evidence for a bull-totem. *Bharadvaja* is " he who brings booty ", and if the word also means a skylark, this is clearly secondary, and presumably results from observation of the bird carrying food to its nest. *Kausika* admittedly means owl, but it would seem that *Kusika* does not; and hence at the best the bird may have been named after the clan or the eponymous *rishi,* and not the clan after the bird—if indeed

Kausika here does not mean " Indra's bird ". Even the well-known sense of " tortoise " for *Kasyapa* may be secondary, since we have also the Prakritic *Kacchapa* " tortoise ", presumably connected with Skt. Kaksa- ; and it is not improbable that *Kasyapa* " tortoise " results merely from a folk-etymology. The essential feature of totemism which we should look for is the definite identification of an individual with his totem; and there seems in fact no evidence of this among the Vedic Aryan clans. The tortoise built into the fire-altar which Kosambi cites from SB VII, 5, I seems to be no more totemic than the toads used in medieval witches' potions.'

The Hindu deluge story in which Manu is rescued by a fish, and the fish is interpreted as ' probably a totem ' is characterized by Washburn Hopkins as a typical case of ' invented totemism ' (1920, 573). In this connexion, see also Haekel on the concept of ' Pseudo-Totemism ' (1938). Haekel, however, no longer accepts the validity or utility of this concept (1956, 60).

3 The older view placed the Dravidian migration into India well before the Aryan. The advent of the Aryans, according to this view, resulted in the retreat of the Dravidians towards the south where Dravidian languages predominate today. Heras identified the Dravidians with the Indus Valley population, and sought to uphold a westward drift as far afield as the British Isles (1953). A more recent view is that of Fürer-Haimendorf (1954) who, basing himself on the excavations of Sir Mortimer Wheeler at Brahmagiri (*Ancient India*, 1948, No. 4), put forth the ' working hypothesis ' that the Dravidian immigrants came to India by sea round about 500 B.C.; and thereafter ' Dravidianized ' the surrounding tribal population. Gordon (1960, 185) also shares this view in its basic features. But others, D. Sircar (' The Dravidian Problem ', *Man in India*, xxxv, No. 1, 1955) and B. Subbarao (1958, 118-23) oppose it, the latter pointing out that ' it is premature to make any attempt to identify the Dravidians '. See also H. D. Sankalia, 1962, 103-4. In a personal communication (27 April 1964) Heine-Geldern says: ' I still think that Fürer-Haimendorf is right with regard to the late immigration of the Dravidians into southern India, but things are much more complicated than he thought. I have proposed several conceivable solutions which are compatible with both the archaeological and the linguistic evidence. Of one thing I am certain: the Dravidian languages came to India either from Iran or at least via Iran. Moreover, there must have been at least two Dravidian invasions into peninsular India.'

4 See, for instance, the relevant sections of Crooke, 1894; Abbott, 1932; Enthoven, 1924 and his *The Folklore of Gujarat* (undated); and also Ghurye, 1962b, 1-4.

5 Jensen, 1960, 159.

6 Fuchs, 1950, 245-52.

7 Ruben, 1939, 140, 176-7.

8 Fuchs, 1960a, 5.

9 1952, 40.

10 Roy, 1925, 93, 122, 290, 294; Bhattacharyya, 1953, 8.

11 Petri, 1950. See also W. Lloyd Warner (1958) for a vivid description of this fact.

12 Brough, 1953, 3, 12.

13 ibid., 2-3.

14 Karve, 1953, 53-64.

15 1962b, 217.

[16] 1961, 13-14.

[17] Schneider & Gough, 1961, 303.

[18] Fawcett, 1915, 186; Schneider & Gough, 1961, 631-52.

[19] As developed in his book on that subject.

[20] Karve, 1953, 162-3; Fürer-Haimendorf, 1954, 165.

[21] 1953, 157-62.

[22] Hassan, 1920, I, 136, 141; Russell & Hiralal, 1916, II, 400, 210, 446; I, 376; Risley, *Census of India*, 1901, Ethnographical Appendices, 166; Russell & Hiralal, 1916, II, 427; III, 392; II, 229; III, 68; Thurston & Rangachari, 1909, VII, 176-7; I, 221.

[23] 1916, II, 204-5.

[24] Russell & Hiralal, 1916, II, 225-33.

[25] ibid., 242-50.

[26] Russell & Hiralal, 1916, III, 182-96.

[27] See Fürer-Haimendorf's foreword to Fuchs, 1950. As Majumdar (cited by Fürer-Haimendorf) puts it : ' The " Dravidian " theory places the Dom alongside the tribal groups but on anthropometric and serological evidence this is difficult to uphold. On the one hand the Dom approach the Kshattriya in stature, sitting height and other characters, on the other they show close relations with the Chamar. . . . Whatever be the cultural status of the Dom, their dissociation from the tribal group . . . is definitely established.'

[28] 1961, 197.

[29] Risley, 1891, I, 240-5; Crooke, 1896, II, 312-17. See footnote 27.

[30] Risley, 1891, I, 175-7; Crooke, 1896, II, 169-94; Russell & Hiralal, 1916, II, 403-14; Briggs, 1920, 11, 17, 19, 35-6, 122, 126-7. See also the article on the Chamars in Rose, 1911-19.

[31] 1950, 245-52.

[32] Webster, 1942.

[33] Fürer-Haimendorf in his foreword to Fuchs, 1950 and Fuchs himself, 134.

[34] Risley, 1891, I, 528-35; Crooke, 1896, III, 346-54; Russell & Hiralal, 1916, IV, 55-73, 100-3.

[35] Tod, 1920, I, xxxi, xxxv. Tod's observations were made in 1804-22. Risley, 1892, II, 184-7; 1915, 102; Karve, 1953, 141. See also Luard, 1909b, 23-4.

[36] Russell & Hiralal, 1916, I, 90; IV, 411-22; Enthoven, 1922, III, 269-89; Rose, 1911, II, 376. See also Crooke, 1896, III, 25-38 and Luard, 1909b, 10.

[37] 1960, 153-4.

[38] For a discussion of the relevant evidence, see Karve, 1953, 140-3.

[39] Roy, 1933, 322-3.

[40] This is of course not to deny that under the present state of research totemism appears to have had an independent origin in the extreme northeast, as we have already indicated.

[41] 1916, I, 16-17.

[42] 1940, 134-40.

[43] See Koppers, 1944, 72-3; Hodson, 1922, 85; Ghurye, 1923.

[44] 1933, 419-23.

[45] 1940-1.

[46] 1944.

[47] 1950, 33-7.

[48] 1945b, 328-33.

[49] Elwin, 1950, 3, 24, 29.

[50] 1952, 204-17.

[51] 1956, 72-3.

[52] 1911, ii, 16-21, 60, 206-7, 287-95, 376, 518-19; Risley, 1891, i, lix, says that among the Tibetans and the Limbus of Darjeeling many septs are known by nicknames but some are totemic.

[53] I have not been able to see Adam's article in *Zeitschrift für Vergleichende Rechtswissenschaft*, 1935, L, 165-75, but am quoting from a short summary in *Anthropos*.

[54] Niggemeyer, 1933, 460-1, is inclined to accept the evidence available as pointing to the existence of totem tattooing in India, but leaves the question of its culture-historical age open.

[55] Quoted by Elwin, 1939, 18.

[56] Wheeler, 1953; Gordon Childe, 1954.

[57] 1956.

[58] Wheeler, 1947-8; Gordon, 1960, 171-5; Fürer-Haimendorf, 1954.

# XI

## TOTEMISM AND ACCULTURATION

A PENUMBRA of vagueness has clung to the term 'acculturation' from the time of its first systematic definition (by Redfield, Linton and Herskovits in 1936) to the present day; and in spite of much field-work aimed at registering its effects, the harvest of large generalizations capable of universal application has been exceedingly poor. This is due to a double complexity—the complexity of culture change of which acculturation is a special case[1] and the complexity of modern civilization and its impact on tribal cultures which is the primary focus of interest of anthropologists concerned with the problem of acculturation. Despite its complexity and the relative poverty of its general results, however, the concept has a pragmatic utility, and when applied to geographically limited areas can prove very fruitful. Acculturation has been defined as a process (either unilateral or bilateral) by which culture is transmitted through continuous first-hand contact of groups with different cultures, one often having a more highly developed form.[2] From this definition it follows that acculturation is a process of extreme antiquity, and not something new which has come into existence with the expansion of modern civilization and its infiltration in relatively recent times into areas of tribal habitation.

The purpose of this chapter, however, is to study the consequences following from contact between Hindu civilization and the tribal population of India and between the civilization of the West and the same aboriginal groups. The impact of western civilization on the aboriginal population is very much more recent than that of Hindu civilization, and has in the main taken two forms—administrative measures initiated by the British, and influences percolating through the filter of Hinduism. The impact of Hindu civilization has in comparison been much longer, much deeper, and has produced a series of complex consequences which are therefore often not open to clear analysis and classification. The main object of this chapter is

[1] For notes to this chapter see p. 279.

to trace the results of this impact on the totemic organization, and not on the entire expanse of tribal society and culture.

The effects of the contact between the advanced groups and the aborigines have evidently not been one-sided; and some competent scholars have tried to combat the once deeply entrenched view that Indian culture is entirely the product of the advanced population.[3]

So far as the totemic organization of the aborigines and its effects on Hindu civilization are concerned, there is first the view (represented by Karandikar and Niggemeyer, and more recently by Karve) that the gotra exogamy of the Brahmins owes its origin or inspiration to the clan exogamy found among almost all the tribes of the subcontinent. (The clanless tribes in existence today can be counted on the fingers of one hand.) The word ' gotra ' meant cow-stall in the Rig Veda, but was used with a diversity of meanings in the older literature. As the Brahmins had no fixed locality connected with the family (a mobility probably arising from the nature of their duties as priests and ritualists) and as further they required some type of group organization for the preservation of ritual beliefs and practices within the caste, a trend in the direction of clan or gotra exogamy began to manifest itself in their ranks. Since they admitted outsiders to their caste, as ancient records demonstrate, and even lived among the aborigines, occasionally marrying women from the non-Aryan population, there is every reason to believe that the inspiration leading to the formation of exogamous gotras came from the aborigines. The systematization of the Brahminic gotras and pravaras into a series of exogamous clans named after the seven Vedic rishis (saints or ancestors: Jamadagni, Gautama, Bharadvaja, Atri, Visvamitra, Kasyapa and Vasistha) a few centuries before the Christian era was the work of Baudhayana, whom tradition assigns to the south of India. Thereafter, the Kshatriyas adopted gotras in imitation of the Brahmins, but their gotras remained more ornamental than functional; and the lower castes, wishing to raise their status, followed in their footsteps.[4]

In concluding, therefore, that the Aryan gotras owed their origin to the clan organization of the aborigines, Niggemeyer notes that the Aryans took in the main only the principle of clan exogamy, but not the accompanying idea in totemism, the mystic bond with the totem (animal, plant or inanimate object). He finds this strange, but adds that the mystic bond also occurs frequently, as among the Shivalli Brahmins of Kanara for instance.[5] But the fact that in adopting the idea of clan organization from the aborigines the higher castes discarded the often accompanying totemism can be explained by the additional fact that totemism was foreign to the Aryans and was rejected as undignified or by the fact that a totemless clan organization is not exclusively a modern phenomenon arising as a later and attenuated form from the totemic clan organization (Risley, Russell, Niggemeyer), but that it has its roots in a distant past in the form of both localized and dispersed clans, and preceded the formation of a totemic clan organization, which is essentially a product of convergence. It is therefore possible that gotra exogamy owed its inspiration to tribes with a clan organization but without totemism.

The entry of totemism into the lower ranks of the caste system such as the Telugu castes, the Kanara castes, the Marathi-speaking castes and other castes in Central India in consequence of the racial and cultural interaction at the lower levels is another contribution of aboriginal society to Hindu civilization at those levels.

Other views seeking to show a possible connexion between totemism and certain phenomena in Hindu civilization are of a more speculative nature; and some of the facts with which they deal can be better explained in other terms. Thus, some have interpreted the names of a few Vedic rishis along totemic lines (see ch. x, n. 2). Others have seen traces of totemism in the vehicles of the Hindu gods—Brahma rides on a goose (hansa), Vishnu on a creature which is half an eagle and half a man (garuda), Siva on a bull (nandi), Yama on a buffalo, Karttikeya on a peacock, Kamadeva on a parrot, Agni on a ram, Varuna on a fish, Vayu on an antelope, Sani on a vulture, Durga on a tiger, and Ganesa is accompanied by a rat. Some of the incarnations of the Hindu gods have also been ascribed to totemic influences. Thus, Vishnu appears as a boar (varaha), tortoise (kurma), fish (matsya), man-lion (narasinha), and a white horse (kalki). Rudra and Indra also appear in the form of a boar. Legends of a seemingly totemic nature have likewise been recorded for persons in high positions. It is, for instance, said that Chandragupta, king of Ujjain, was the son of a scorpion, since his mother accidentally swallowed the emission of a scorpion and conceived by its means. The Jaitwas of Rajputana trace their descent to the monkey-god Hanuman, and allege that the spines of their princes are elongated like a tail. In the fortieth canto of the Ramayana one of the wives of King Sagara gave birth to a gourd or cane containing 60,000 sons; and the wolf has been traditionally connected with a settlement of Janwar Rajputs who believe that the animal will not harm their children.[6] Tree cults like those centring in the tulsi and the pipal, and animal cults relating to the tiger, the snake and the monkey have been likewise given a totemic basis; and so too have tree marriages, found among both the aborigines and the higher castes. In 1929 Rice advocated the view that the caste system took its rise from totemism and the taboos which commonly accompany it, and stressed the sacredness of the kitchen and the principle that food can easily convey harmful qualities in totemic and primitive belief. Earlier Guha also advanced ideas like those of Rice in his unpublished doctoral dissertation at Harvard University.[7] But, as Ghurye points out, theriomorphism (or therianthropism as he calls it) in the higher religions including Hinduism follows from the idea of consubstantiality or the belief that in reality a difference of substance between gods, men and other elements in the universe did not exist;[8] and, as Haekel tells us, we must guard against the superficial and formal use of the term ' totemism ', and must therefore examine apparently totemic phenomena more exactly and critically than was hitherto the practice. This necessitates tracing their interrelationships in the social and ideological structure and working out their historically-conditioned local relations and strata.[9]

Turning next to the effects of Hindu civilization on the totemic organization of the aborigines, we shall note first what Risley has had to say on the subject, since he was one of the earliest students of the phenomenon to attempt its systematic analysis. Risley points out that the gradual Brahminization of the aborigines does not maintain a uniform character throughout the country. In Bengal, however, he isolates four processes as follows: (i) Having become landed proprietors, the leading men of the tribe enroll themselves in one of the higher castes such as that of the Rajputs, employ Brahmin priests who supply them with a mythical ancestor and other necessary legends, and propagate the view that they belong to some hitherto unheard-of clan of the Rajput community. (ii) A number of aborigines become members of a Hindu sect and lose their tribal name in the process. (iii) A whole tribe, or a large part of one, assumes the status of a new caste by entering the ranks of Hinduism, and although the group claims a remote antiquity as a caste, their name distinguishes them from any of the standard or recognized castes. (iv) An entire tribe or a large part of one becomes slowly converted to Hinduism without giving up its tribal name.

Risley also lists four stages in exogamous organization represented by the following groups: (i) The Oraon and the Santal with their totemic organization. (ii) The Bhumij who still have totemic, exogamous divisions, but are gradually forgetting the totems denoted by the names of their subdivisions, and will soon give them up for more elevated designations. When this point is reached the tribe will have become a caste, and will continue to get rid of all customs which might betray its true origin. As a caste it will be more endogamous than as a tribe. The Bhumij, who are still in a state of transition, have borrowed the name Sandilya from the Brahmins, and what was formerly the name of a Vedic saint has now come to mean a bird. (iii) The Mahili, the Kora and the Kurmi, who all claim to be Hindus, but have recently broken away from their tribal con- nexions (the Mahili and the Kurmi from the Santal and the Kora from the Munda). (iv) The Kumhar of Orissa, who rank just below the Karan or writer caste, and have thus only two or three castes above them. They have two endogamous sub- castes: the Uria Kumhar and the Khattya Kumhar. The former have the following exogamous sections: Kaundinya (tiger), Sarpa (snake), Neul (weasel), Goru (cow), Mudir (frog), Bhadbhadaria (sparrow), and Kurmina (tortoise). Totem taboos and traces of totem worship still exist among them. The latter have only one section and are endogamous. Both subcastes, realizing that the totemic names are likely to betray their origins, state that they are in fact the names of saints who were present at Daksha's horse sacrifice and who transformed themselves into animals to escape the anger of Siva whom Daksha forgot to invite. The section of the Khattya Kumhar is known as Kasyapa and they venerate the tortoise (kachhap). They tell an odd story to explain the practice. There are many lower castes in Bengal which have begun to claim the status of pure Hindus, and have hence taken advantage of the resemblance between kachhap and kas- yap to convert their totemic names into eponymous ones. They have also begun to borrow other Brahminic gotras. Thus the Bhar of Manbhum, hereditary servants of a Rajput raja, have two sections named after the peacock and the bel fruit respec- tively and five others are eponymous. As the gotras were origi- nally Brahminic, the Kshatriyas and the Vaisyas had no gotras of their own to start with. But they were allowed to adopt the gotras of the family priest of their ancestors, and this practice spread by imitation to the other castes in Bengal.

Of the five types of exogamous units found in India—totemic, territorial, titular, eponymous, and local, communal or family sections—the eponymous gotras are confined to the Brahmins and the castes which imitate them; the local, communal or family sections (thar, kul, mul), says Risley, are small, have arisen re- cently, and trace their origin to ancestors who are much less remote than those of the Brahminic gotras or the Rajput clans;

the titular septs are found among castes in a state of transition, which have got rid of their totems, but have not yet adopted full-blown eponyms, most of these titles (Manjhi: village headman, Naiya or Laya: village priest, Manki: head of a group of villages) being selected at random and with no reference to a real ancestor who held the office in question; and the territorial septs are found among the Rajputs and trading castes allied to them, but also among tribal groups like the Khond of Orissa. There are finally castes with no sections, which therefore base their marriage restrictions on prohibited degrees. Such castes are more numerous in eastern and northern Bengal, and might have borrowed their marriage rules from the Muslims.[10]

A more searching investigation into the effects of Hindu civilization on the totemic organization of the aborigines is that of Niggemeyer. Broadly speaking these effects, says Niggemeyer, may be classified into (*a*) the emergence of new forms and secondary transformations, and (*b*) an all-round decline in the coastal areas and the more accessible areas of the inland regions.

Totem worship at marriages, the Oraon cult and probably also the Birhor cult, mourning for the dead totem through the destruction of earthen pots and other scattered traces of reverence and worship have developed through the intrusion of Hindu ideas.

The notion of endogamy has entered the tribal world through the influence of the caste system and the entry of several tribes into it, converting the formerly loosely organized tribes into endogamous units and the equality of the totem clans into an order based on hierarchy and hypergamy. Thus arose the widely distributed polytomous castes (or castes which are divided first into endogamous subcastes and then into totemic exogamous clans) and groups which occupy a certain middle position between tribes and castes.

There are tribes and castes which have exogamous clans named totemically and some named after localities, titles and the like. The latter variety is a new form which arose out of the totem clan exogamy of the aborigines, the totemism being discarded because it was foreign to the Brahmins who borrowed the idea of clan exogamy from the primitive population. The localization of the totem clans, now found only among the Palia Bhil and perhaps not so long ago among the Birhor and the Munda, was disrupted by the impact of Hindu civilization. Non-genuine totems like ocean, garden, island, white, darkness and inanimate objects like umbrella, gun, sovereign, garland and cake, which also serve as totems, are comparatively recent additions to the usual list of animal, plant and object totems.

The disintegration of totemism under the impact of Hindu civilization is illustrated by the following facts: (i) The sub-clans of some tribes and castes (the Pahira, the Aiyarakulu, the Maravar and the Komati) are non-totemic, and this is a secondary development. (ii) Some tribes or parts of them have taken to agriculture and have more or less adapted themselves to the caste system. They thus tend to replace totem clan exogamy by blood-relationship exogamy (the Kurmi) or by other forms of exogamy such as village exogamy (the Pahira, the Parja, the Kharia, the Bharia and the Baiswar), or family and kin-group exogamy (the Maratha). Among some (the Asur, the Gadaba) the wilder sections retain totemic clan exogamy with taboos, but the more settled sections have forgotten totemism altogether; among others other forms of exogamy (represented chiefly by a tendency towards the exogamy of family and kin groups) exist side by side with totem clan exogamy—the Sudha of Sambalpur have totemic gotras and non-totemic family groups or bargas, the Dumal in Sonpur have totemic gots, family names chiefly designated by occupations and mitti (earth) or groups with names of towns in Orissa (marriage being allowed when at least one of the three groups is different between bride and bridegroom), the Dhor and the Bhoi in Bombay and the Medare Burud in Hyderabad have a double system, totem clans and family names; and the Bhoi have furthermore begun to adopt Brahminic gotras quite recently. Among the Chasa clan exogamy has been entirely replaced by family group exogamy and among the Khadra by blood-relationship exogamy up to three generations. Blood-relationship exogamy among the tribes is derived from the high civilizations of India. (iii) The decline of totem taboos is represented by their circumvention or weakening as among the Oraon (the Salt clan is not allowed to eat salt from the hand, the Pig clan must not eat the head of a pig) or by their elimination as among the Kawar (among whom important animals like the deer and the goat are no longer tabooed) or among the Chauhan (among whom only one species of rice is forbidden). Among the more Hinduized sections of the Kharia there are no totem taboos, and among the Dewar to whom the meanings of their clan names are no longer clear there are likewise no totem taboos. Sometimes, when the totem is forgotten, other objects become tabooed (the Komati, the Gond, the Kuruba, the Korava). As only one-third of the tribes and castes have totem taboos, this may have been partly due to the disintegrative effects of Hindu civilization. (iv) Hindu civilization has been particularly destructive towards the inner relationship between man and totem, primarily because it lacks this relationship. Only traces of this relationship are left, as also of totem descent; whereas myths of encounters with the totem, which are very frequent, are of recent origin and arose after totemism had begun to disintegrate and to lose its original meaning. Thus totemism degenerated into mere externals with an emphasis on exogamy. (v) A peculiar result of the impact of Hindu civilization (which arose from the racial and cultural intermixture of the advanced populations and the aborigines) is that the gotra system which owed its origin to the clan exogamy of the aborigines is now sought after and imitated by these very aborigines with increasing fervour.

Niggemeyer's view that the conversion of totemism into a matter of externals is a consequence of the impact of Hindu civilization is shared by several interpreters of the phenomenon. It is, however, in need of a significant modification. What we have called 'formal social totemism' characterized by totem names, totem taboos, totem clan exogamy and a scattering of inner elements like a sense of kinship with the totem, belief in totem descent and various other forms of respect, follows after and from apical group totemism which is represented in India today by the Birhor (and perhaps also by the Asur). The central element in apical group totemism is a strong clan-and-totem identification which has been sanctified among the Birhor by being converted into a cult. The spread of the totemic organization to the neighbouring tribes from the group immediately ancestral to the Birhor of today implies the prior existence among these tribes of a system of localized or dispersed clans without totemism. The totemic idea was contagious and spread rapidly because of the possibility it offered of naming and identifying clans and in justifying, maintaining and vivifying clan exogamy. Perhaps the clan-and-totem identification with its roots in the unconscious urges towards complementarity and dependence ritualized among the Birhor did not spread together with the notion of totem exogamy among the neighbouring tribes because of their emotional attachment to localities as original homelands. Hence totem names, totem taboos (rule of avoidance) and totem clan exogamy became the main pillars of formal social totemism before the entry of the advanced populations into India. These elements grew into a more or less formal unity as is evidenced by the totemic organization of the Agaria, the Muria Gond, the Oraon, the Santal and other groups; and this perhaps gave rise in turn to more or less sporadic elements of an ideological nature—secondary justifications of a pre-existing structure. The contact with Hindu civilization intensified the formal character or externalized form of formal social totemism, produced new formations and other secondary transformations in an initial phase of compromise, and as a later phase speeded up the disintegration and disappearance of totemism.

The view that exogamous units other than totemic clans— clans named after localities, titles, nicknames and eponyms and family kinship groups—arose later in India as a result of the impact of Hindu civilization on the totemic organization of the aborigines (or for other reasons) is represented by Risley, Russell, Niggemeyer and others, but also requires an important modification in the light of the new orientations in ethnology and the new ethnographic material on Indian tribes. Two strongly established conclusions in recent ethnology are that kinship groups and clans can arise again and again from joint families when the corresponding conditions and necessities are present,[11] and that non-totemic clans are both an ancient and widely-spread phenomenon (Goldenweiser, Lowie, Murdock). The evidence from India and neighbouring areas also indicates that non-totemic clans both localized and dispersed are a relatively old phenomenon. The Seligmanns point out that there is considerable evidence to suggest that the non-totemic clans of the Vedda of Ceylon were once territorially fixed. The Chenchu have a non-totemic clan organization which was once probably locally oriented, but Fürer-Haimendorf opines that they might have borrowed it from some patrilineal neighbours. Most of the jungle tribes of South India like the Kanikar, the Mudavan, the Manne and the Urali have non-totemic clans, but like the Vedda descent is matrilineal. The matrilineal descent might suggest a late acquisition; but it is probable that matrilineal descent percolated downwards on a patrilineal clan organization developed or acquired earlier. Aiyappan, for instance, tells us that in the history of many castes in Malabar one notices a change from patriliny to matriliny.[12] The Hill Pantaram are patrilineal and have the elements of a clan system, but it is not a ' proper ' one, adds Fürer-Haimendorf. The Baiga have both territorial exogamy without totemism and clan exogamy with traces of totemism very likely borrowed from the Gond. The Gond in turn seem to have been originally organized into exogamous, territorial, non-totemic clans (Fuchs). The Bhil clans, too, are largely non-totemic; and so are the Reddi clans.[13] Hence it can be maintained that non-totemic clans of the localized and dispersed types are of great antiquity in India. On theoretical grounds one can presume that they existed before the emergence of clan totemism, which is essentially a product of convergence (diffusion, independent invention and development) in geographically limited areas. These non-totemic clans were probably named after localities or after common ancestors; and Hindu civiliza-

tion accentuated the process. The evidence for the actual localization of the totemic clans in India is meagre. Niggemeyer, basing
himself on Roy, mentions the Palia Bhil as having localized
totem clans, whereas the neighbouring Kalia Bhil have dispersed
totem clans. Roy's opinion that the Kalia Bhil represent an old
or special form has not been confirmed by Koppers' inquiries.
The existence of localized totem clans among the Palia Bhil,
therefore, requires confirmation. The Birhor and the Munda
have dispersed totemic clans, but also possess traditions which
point towards their former localization. The displacement of
localized clans by dispersed clans would follow from the facts of
population growth and the attendant migrations.

The processes and products of acculturation in India from
the limited standpoint of the contact between the advanced
civilizations and the totemic organization of the aborigines may
be conceptualized as follows:

(1) The contact of the later immigrants (Aryans, Dravidians)
with the aborigines represented an encounter between advanced
groups on the one side and backward groups on the other. Racial
and cultural differences served to underline the superiority of
the newcomers and the inferiority of the indigenous population.
This gives us the concept of *superiority*. It is a value-charged
term, but is of fundamental significance in acculturation, since
it suffuses the consciousness of the participants in the contact-
situation, and is the main cause of various types of reaction
within the acculturative framework.

(2) The superiority of the newcomers, however, did not entirely hinder the process of *interrelated stimuli and responses* between them and the aborigines, from which sprang the gotra
system of the Brahmins, Hinduism and the Indian civilization
on the one side, and on the other new formations and secondary
transformations like the worship of the totem image at marriages,
the totem cult of the Oraon and certain forms of mourning for
the dead totem. The interrelationship of stimuli and responses
between the two groups in the contact situation made for *causal
complexity* and merging of diffusion and creativity (of which
one form is Kroeber's stimulus diffusion). This renders analysis,
conceptualization and the tracing of origins difficult. That is
why, for instance, the problem of caste origins remains a controverted question.[14]

(3) The superior group responded by endeavouring to close
its ranks to outsiders—hence *endogamy* which with the encroachment of the caste idea into the tribal world tended to make
tribal groups formerly rather loosely organized somewhat endogamous, produced the phenomenon of polytomous tribes and

castes (that is, of tribes and castes with non-totemic, endogamous subdivisions which in turn break up into totemic, exogamous clans), and in one or two instances endogamous totemic units (the Dhunniya caste in Uttar Pradesh[15] and perhaps the Kachari; though, as we have seen, the endogamy of the Kachari clans has been called into question). In a few instances (the Pahira, the Parja, the Plains Bhuiya) the tendency towards clan endogamy has been ascribed to the reduction in population strength or to influences from Hindu civilization. A more recent study of the tribes in the neighbourhood of Ranchi indicates that among both converted and non-converted tribals [16] the clan system is still traceable, that clan exogamy is still prevalent among the converted Munda, Oraon, and Kharia in the city, but that in the tribal villages new sub-clans which are essentially endogamous are being formed and that they function as endogamous units within the main clan. The tribals are forgetting the origin of their totemic clans and the religious force of totemism is fast declining. Cases of marriage within the same clan have also been reported.[17]

(4) In broad terms the aborigines responded in the form of *reaction or contra-acculturation*, of *adaptation* or the combination of original and foreign traits, and of *acceptance or assimilation* to both behaviour patterns and inner values.[18] Contra-acculturation is illustrated in India by the retreat of some groups of aborigines (the Birhor, the Muria Gond, the Juang and many others) into the fastnesses of hills and jungles and other inaccessible areas, where they were able to retain their totemic organization relatively unimpaired. Adaptation is a halfway house to assimilation, and results first in compromise and then in phenomena of decline and disintegration.

(5) The effort at *compromise* is illustrated by the emergence of forms of totem worship through the infiltration of Hindu beliefs into the world of the aborigines (examples are the worship of the totem image at marriages, and more specifically the worship among the Chasa, a cultivating caste in Orissa, of the elephant-headed god, Ganesh, by the Elephant sept and of Pawan, god of the wind, by the Deer sept because the deer is regarded as being swift as the wind,[19] by the *co-existence* in tribes and castes of exogamous units named variously—totemically, titularly, territorially and eponymously (the Barai, the Basor, the Bhaina, the Dhimar and several other tribes and castes in Central India and further south), and by the acceptance of Sanskritic terms like gotra and kul as general designations for totemic clans.

(6) The *decline and disintegration* manifest themselves

through *dislocation, scatter, externalization* and *enfeeblement* and end in *total displacement*. Dislocation is illustrated by the fact that some groups have totems but not identical totem names (some instances among the Bhil, the Lodha of West Bengal, and all septs among the Gond of the Adilabad district),[20] by taboos on other objects when the totem is forgotten (the Gond, the Kuruba, the Komati) and by the augmentation of non-genuine totems. Scatter is illustrated by the uneven and sporadic distribution of certain totemic traits, either resulting from the disturbance of a former more uniform spread or from individual and sporadic reassertions of the totemic spirit in an anti-totemic climate. An instance of the former case is the fact that only one-third of the totemic tribes and castes still possess totemic taboos, and that within each tribe or caste itself the taboos have generally an uneven distribution; instances of the latter are perhaps some examples of totem descent. Externalization signifies the displacement of the inner bonds of totemism—clan-and-totem identification, the sense of kinship, a mystic or emotional attachment to the totem and the like. That the impact of Hindu civilization has added to the externalization of totemism in India is evidenced by the fact that it has in several instances degenerated into the 'merest peg' for exogamy to hang on (Hutton). Enfeeblement covers both weakening of individual totemic traits and the general enervation of the integrated character or formal unity of totemism. When a tribe is fully assimilated, the total or almost total displacement of totemism occurs. Instances of total displacement, however, are difficult to locate because of the complex interrelations between tribes and castes, both racially and culturally.

(7) The complex interrelations between tribes and castes which have been going on for several hundreds of years can well be interpreted by means of the concept of *continuum*. As Bailey points out, 'There is no single and accepted criterion by which to distinguish a tribe from a caste'. He therefore concludes: 'The only solution to this problem is to postulate a continuum, at one end of which is a society whose political system is entirely of the segmentary egalitarian type, and which contains no dependents whatsoever; and at the other end of which is a society in which segmentary political relations exist only between a very small proportion of the total society, and most people act in the system in the role of dependents.'[21] Totemically considered, the continuum would have at one end groups which break up immediately into totemic, exogamous, egalitarian clans, and at the other groups with prohibited degrees or blood-relationship exogamy located towards the higher reaches

of the prevailing hierarchical system. In between there are tribes which break up into two or more sections (sub-tribes), the more primitive of which still retain their totemic organization relatively unimpaired, and the more Hinduized having lost much of it (examples are the Kharia, the Kol, the Bhuiya). This is the process of *sectional acculturation*. Other tribes get converted into castes on the lower fringes of Hinduism, but reveal their tribal origins through the retention among other things of totemic elements—*partial acculturation*. Most of the lower castes, however, appear to be of mixed origins as the variety of their clan names suggest (Russell). This is *acculturation through ethnic or demographic intermixture*. The adoption of the clan idea by the Brahmins from the aborigines and the imitation of the gotra system by the lower castes and tribes because of its prestige value is an instance of *cross-acculturation*.

(8) *Acculturation by capillarity* is evidenced by the creeping of totemic elements upwards along the scale of caste hierarchy, but with diminishing vigour. This process unfolds a broad generalization: the higher the status of the caste, the less totemically oriented is its internal organization. There are, for example, few instances of totemic traces among the Brahmins and Kshatriyas, but more among the Vaisyas and Sudras.

(9) Areawise also the spread of totemism outwards from its primary centre, the northeastern areas of Central India, reveals broadly speaking a tendency towards greater externalization, enfeeblement, scatter and so on, the further away one moves from the radiating centre. This is the *process of increasing areal attrition from the centre of spread*. Its relevance to this part of the present work is that the bulk of the totemic groups outside the northeast area are castes on the lower fringes of Hinduism, and that fact has doubtless contributed to the areal attrition.

(10) *Convergent acculturation* on the totemic plane is best exemplified by the Maratha system. In this system an essentially non-totemic belief rooted in Hindu civilization (Abbott) has converged with totemic elements entering from other areas, and has engendered a semi-blended totemic system which remains stultified (*concept of stultification*) because of Brahminic and other Hinduistic influences and hindrances, or has yielded ground to them.

(11) The impact of western civilization on the totemic organization of the Indian aborigines is less evident. But from certain trends unleashed by that civilization in India—the transformation of caste into class,[22] of the joint family into the nuclear family, of group exogamy into prohibited degrees and so on—

it may be presumed that the anti-totemic forces have gained ground with the western impact *(westernization)*.

(12) The general effect in recent times of the acculturative influences, both Hindu and western, on the totemic organization of the Indian aborigines can, therefore, be said to be a growing trend towards its *total displacement or extinction*.

## NOTES AND REFERENCES

[1] Malinowski, 1951, 23; Beals, 1953, 626; Barnett, 1953.

[2] Winick, 1956, 3. See also Herskovits, 1938 and Beals, 1953.

[3] To mention but three names: Koppers, 1921-2; Roy in his articles on ' Caste, Race, and Religion in India ' in *Man in India*; and Hutton, 1961, 170-82, 223-62.

[4] Karve, 1953, 58-68, 115.

[5] 1933, 437, 594.

[6] Crooke, 1894, 239-40, 260, 262, 282, 285, 287-8. Ruben believes that Vishnu embodies the totemic animal-gods of the mesolithic hunters, and also the sun-god. The tortoise which is connected with Vishnu (kurma) appears among many tribes as a totem—the Bhumij, the Bhuinar, the Birhor, the Gond, the Oraon, the Kharia, the Turi, the Pan and others; and Kasyapa, the name of a Vedic rishi, has no Indo-Germanic etymology (1939, 2, 242).

[7] Hutton, 1961, 178, 255; A. Bhattacharyya, 1947.

[8] 1962, 1-4.

[9] 1946, 99, 121.

[10] 1891, I, i-lxxi.

[11] Haekel, 1936, 32.

[12] 1937, 30.

[13] See also Naik, 1949.

[14] Ghurye, 1932; Hutton, 1961; Zinkin, 1962.

[15] Crooke, 1896, II, 297; Niggemeyer, 1933, 438.

[16] Presumably converted to Christianity.

[17] A personal communication (23 June 1961) from L. P. Vidyarthi of the University of Ranchi, based on field research.

[18] Beals, 1953, 670.

[19] Russell & Hiralal, 1916, II, 425.

[20] Koppers, 1948, 118; Bhowmick, 1963, 53-8; Hassan, 1920, I, 221.

[21] 1960, 263-4.

[22] Ghurye, 1950.

# XII

## *CONCLUSION*

THE CONCLUSIONS to which we have arrived in the course of this study can be briefly summarized as follows:

(1) The most basic factor from which totemism took its psychological rise is the finitude of human nature and the partly conscious, partly unconscious urges or impulsions towards complementarity and dependence which spring from it. These urges express themselves in various ways. In the proto-totemic phase they find their fulfilment in various ritual or ideological relations to animals and plants; in the totemic phase proper they find their fulfilment largely in the clan, which comes to represent the sense of social solidarity very strongly. The clan totem is a symbol of clan solidarity.

(2) Group totemism grows chiefly through the process of convergence, which includes different types of diffusion and certain degrees of independent creation and development. The blending of the clan idea with proto-totemic elements is a fundamental instance of convergence in the process of totemization.

(3) The course of totemic development in general follows broadly speaking (that is, apart from local variations) the following phases:

(a) The proto-totemic phase, which begins with beliefs and practices connected with animals and plants of a loose and floating nature and ends in more integrated complexes such as those worked out for Africa by Baumann.

(b) Early forms of group totemism in families, lineages, local groups and clans. All but clan totemism are unstable forms. Clan totemism in its beginnings has been named quasi-totemism.

(c) Apical group totemism, which is characterized mainly by a strong clan-and-totem identification.

(d) Formal social totemism, in which the clan-and-totem identification has begun to wither away.

(e) Totemism in decline, which is characterized by a weakening of totemic attitudes and a scattering of totemic traits.

Thus in the main two totemic upsurges or peaks of development

can be said to manifest themselves on the totemic continuum—
the proto-totemic complex and apical clan totemism.

(4) Concretely, totemism expresses itself in relatively variable
complexes of characteristically totemic elements and in variable
systems of totemic and non-totemic elements which are more or
less integrated with one another. The variability of the complexes
and systems can be ascribed broadly to the complex nature of
the two terms in the polar relationship between man and environment and the complex interactions arising between them
necessitating the historical approach as fundamental in cultural
anthropology (or ethnology). It can more narrowly be ascribed
to the process of convergence through which these complexes
and systems emerge and the peculiar dynamics of totemic development and disintegration.

(5) Indian totemism appears in essentials to have arisen and
developed in India itself. Many indications of a general and
specific nature speak in favour of this proposition; but conclusive evidence is lacking. Therefore the alternative possibility
cannot be altogether shut out.

(6) Within the Indian subcontinent in its totality clan totemism has probably had two centres of emergence which were more
or less independent of each other: the extreme northeast (Assam)
and the northeastern areas of Central India. The quasi-totemism
of the extreme northeast is of the primary variety, that is to say,
it represents the independent emergence of an early phase of
clan totemism which has remained undeveloped at that level.
From the standpoint of inheritance it breaks up into two groups:
(a) the matrilineal quasi-totemism of the Khasi and the Garo,
and (b) the patrilineal quasi-totemism of the other tribes in the
area. The quasi-totemism of the Khasi and the Garo owes its
origin to stimuli or elements inherent in the area itself, and not
borrowed from beyond that area. The primary quasi-totemism of
the extreme northeast is not as old as the patrilineal totemism
elsewhere in India.

(7) The totemism of the rest of India can be regionally classified as follows: (a) the northeastern area, (b) the southeastern
area, and (c) the southwestern area. From the point of view of
age, intensity and affiliation the totemism of the northeastern
area breaks up into two parts: (i) the apical clan totemism of
the Birhor and perhaps of the Asur also, and (ii) the formal
social totemism of certain other tribes in the area. The apical
clan totemism of the area is characterized by a strong clan-and-
totem identification and reaches back perhaps into a somewhat
specialized hunting culture in the Palaeolithic. The formal social
totemism is characterized by totem names, totem taboos, clan

exogamy and other attenuated elements occurring sporadically. It represents the convergence of totemic stimuli and elements radiating outwards from a group immediately ancestral to the Birhor and the localized or dispersed clans of other groups without totemism. Therefore Hindu civilization was not the primary cause of the emergence of formal social totemism, but merely added to its formal or externalized character. Both groups are patrilineal. The totemism of the southeast is likewise patrilineal, but is characterized by the increase of inanimate objects as totems and by non-genuine totems. This fact indicates that it is much less old than the totemism of the northeast. The totemism of the southwest, again, falls mainly into two significant groups: into the matrilineal totemism of the Kanarese castes and the patrilineal totemism of the Marathi-speaking tribes and castes. Both these forms are also relatively young in age.

(8) The course of totemic development in India can be described as follows: (a) A proto-totemic phase with beliefs and practices relating to animals and plants of a loose and floating character. One finds them somewhat more concentrated among the Andaman Islanders; but sporadically and unorganizedly at all the levels of the primitive population in India. A proto-totemic complex as such does not, however, exist in India today. (b) A primary quasi-totemic phase which, however, occurs rarely in India. (c) The apical group totemism of the Birhor, which is the oldest strongly formed totemism in the country. (d) A phase of formal social totemism. It arose perhaps after the spread of a more settled existence among the tribes of the area. (e) From the northeastern areas of Central India totemism spread southwards, first into the Telugu-speaking area, and from there westwards into the ranks of the Kanarese castes, where it converged with matrilineal elements. From the Kanarese castes stimuli and elements spread northwards into the ranks of the Marathi-speaking tribes and castes, where the devak concept of the Marathas converged with these stimuli and elements, engendering the half-formed totemic system characteristic of that region.

(9) Multiplication rites and sex totemism, as among the Australian tribes, do not occur in India. The evidence for the ritual consumption of the totem and for totem tattooing is scanty and unconvincing. The existence of a full-fledged dual organization in India still remains to be proved.

(10) The solitary instance of individual totemism which occurs among the Asur and the extremely restricted spread of the inner aspect of totemism, that is, a strong clan-and-totem identification (the Birhor, the Asur), help in locating the area and group in

which clan totemism probably first arose. This area is the north-east, and the group consisted of the ancestors of the Birhor and the Asur, but not the entire population called in their totality Proto-Australoid or Weddid, or even Gondid.

(11) The older view that the non-totemic, exogamous units arose in India from the totemic clans through the elimination of their totemic contents is no longer tenable as an absolute generalization. Some evidence indicates that non-totemic localized and dispersed clans existed before the rise of clan totemism in India, and that the totemic complexes and systems arose as a result of convergence.

(12) Totemism in India is almost entirely of the clan variety and was originally associated with patriliny and clan exogamy. The evidence of totemism in smaller groups like families and lineages is of an indirect nature, that is to say, the former occurrence of totemism in such groups can be inferred from the nature of the myths in which an individual ancestor had encounters or experiences with the totem.

(13) The greater number of the totemic myths is of the type which describes parallel relations. Such myths are not necessarily or entirely a late development. If the totemic complex of the Birhor is taken as a criterion, a possibility which emerges is that totem descent myths and belief in totem descent are later occurrences which arose sporadically as the totemic stimuli radiated outwards from their original centre and made possible the emergence of formal social totemism.

(14) Totemic elements are widely distributed in India, but the extreme south and large areas in the north and northwest are non-totemic.

(15) Totem worship in almost all its forms in India, like the worship of the totem or its image at marriages, the totem cult of the Oraon, the destruction or casting away of earthen pots accompanied by baths and shaves as a sign of mourning for the dead totem, and the deification of certain former totems (the tiger, the cobra, the monkey) have risen relatively recently as a result of influences emanating from Hindu civilization.

(16) The collision of Hindu civilization with the totemic organization of the aborigines produced on the one hand certain compromise phenomena (like the worship of the totem at marriages and the cult of the Oraon), and on the other released forces of decline and disintegration. Western influences contributed also to the destruction of totemism in India.

(17) The new ethnographic material, that is, the monographs which were published after 1933, as well as the older monographs, are more reliable than the earlier compilations because

they are mostly the products of trained field-workers. They have
in great part served to show that the original bearers of totemism cannot be equated with large categories such as Proto-
Australoid or Weddid (Gondid). Most of the ethnographic works
published after 1933 deal with the primitive tribes, whereas most
of the lower castes have been neglected. Geographically considered, the tribes and castes of South India have been relatively
neglected by ethnographically trained field-workers.

# BIBLIOGRAPHY

ABBOTT, J. *The Keys of Power.* London, 1932.

AIYAPPAN, A. *Social and Physical Anthropology of the Nayadis of Malabar.* Madras, 1937.

— 'The Tribes of South and South-West India.' *The Adivasis.* Delhi, 1955.

BAILEY, F. G. *Tribe, Caste and Nation: A Study of Political Activity and Political Change in Highland Orissa.* Manchester, 1960.

BAINES, A. *Ethnography.* Strassburg, 1912.

BARNETT, H. G. *Innovation: The Basis of Cultural Change.* New York, 1953.

BASU, P. C. 'The Racial Affinities of the Oraons.' *Transactions of the Bose Research Institute,* IX. Calcutta, 1933-4.

BAUMANN, H. 'Afrikanische Wild- und Buschgeister.' *Zeitschrift für Ethnologie,* LXX, 208-39. 1938.

— 'Das Tier als Alter Ego in Afrika: Zur Frage des afrikanischen Individualtotemismus.' *Paideuma,* V, 167-88. 1952a.

— 'Individueller und Kollektiver Totemismus.' *Actes du XIV Congrès International,* IV, 134-52. Rome, 1952b.

BEALS, R. 'Acculturation.' A. L. Kroeber (Ed.), *Anthropology Today: An Encyclopaedic Inventory.* Chicago, 1953.

BERNHEIM, E. *Lehrbuch der historischen Methode und der Geschichtsphilosophie.* Leipzig, 1908.

BHATTACHARYYA, A. 'The Tiger-Cult and its Literature.' *Man in India,* XXVII, 44-56. 1947.

— 'An Account of the Birhor of Palamau.' *Bull. Dept. Anthro.,* II, 1-10. Calcutta, 1953.

BHOWMICK, P. K. 'Savars of Midnapore (West Bengal).' *Vanyajati,* III, 60-4. 1955.

— *The Lodhas of West Bengal.* Calcutta, 1963.

BIDNEY, D. *Theoretical Anthropology.* New York, 1953.

BISWAS, P. C. *Primitive Religion, Social Organisation, Law and Government amongst the Santals.* Calcutta, 1935.

— *Santals of the Santal Parganas.* Delhi, 1956.

BOMPAS, C. H. *Folklore of the Santal Parganas.* London, 1909.

BORNEMANN, F. 'P. W. Schmidt's Studien über den Totemismus in Asien und Ozeanien.' *Anthropos,* LI, 595-734. 1956.

BOSE, P. B. 'Chhattisgar, Notes on its Tribes, Sects and Castes.' *Journal of the Asiatic Society of Bengal,* LIX, 269-300. 1891.

BOSE, N. K. 'Juang Associations.' *Man in India,* IX, 47-53. 1929.

BOWLES, GORDON T. 'Linguistic and Racial Aspects of the Munda Problem.' *Studies in the Anthropology of Oceania and Asia: Papers of the Peabody Museum of America,* XX, 81-101. 1943.

BRIGGS, G. W. *The Chamars.* Bombay and Madras, 1920.

BROUGH, J. *The Early Brahmanical System of Gotra and Pravara: A Translation of the Gotra-Pravara-Manjari of Purusottama-Pandita with an Introduction.* Cambridge, 1953.

BULCK, G. 'Beiträge zur Methodik der Völkerkunde.' *Wiener Beiträge zur Kulturgeschichte und Linguistik,* II. 1931.

BURADKAR, M. P. ' Totemism among the Gonds.' *Man in India*, XX, 114-43, 268-88. 1940.

— ' Clan Organisation of the Gonds.' *Man in India*, XXVII, 127-36. 1947.

CHAPEKAR, L. N. *Thakurs of the Sahyadri*. Bombay, 1960.

CHATTERJEE, A. & DAS, T. *The Hos of Seraikella*. Calcutta, 1922.

CHILDE, V. G. *New Light on the Most Ancient East*. London, 1954.

CIPRIANI, L. ' Report on a Survey of the Little Andaman during 1952-1953.' *Bull. Dept. Anthro.*, II, 61-82. Calcutta, 1953.

— ' Altertümlichkeit und Bedeutung der Kultur der Andamaner.' *Festschrift: Paul Schebesta zum 75. Geburtstag*. Vienna-Mödling, 1963.

CROOKE, W. *An Introduction to the Popular Religion and Folklore of Northern India*. Allahabad, 1894.

— *The Tribes and Castes of the North-Western Provinces and Oudh*. 4 vols. Calcutta, 1896.

CULSHAW, W. J. *Tribal Heritage: A Study of the Santals*. London, 1949.

DALTON, E. T. *Descriptive Ethnology of Bengal*. Calcutta, 1872.

DANI, A. H. *Prehistory and Protohistory of Eastern India*. Calcutta, 1960.

DAS, A. K. & RAHA, M. N. *The Oraons of Sunderban*. Calcutta, 1963.

DAS, T. C. *The Bhumijas of Seraikella*. Calcutta, 1931a.

— *The Wild Kharias of Dhalbhum*. Calcutta, 1931b.

DATTA-MAJUMDAR, N. *The Santal: A Study in Culture Change*. Delhi, 1956.

DAVE, P. C. *The Grasias*. Delhi, 1960.

DEHON, P. *Religion and Customs of the Uraons*. Memoir of the Asiatic Society of Bengal, I, 121-81. 1906.

DITTMER, K. ' Zum Problem des Wesens, des Ursprungs und der Entwicklung des Clantotemismus.' *Zeitschrift für Ethnologie*, LXXVI, 189-200. 1951.

— *Allgemeine Völkerkunde*. Braunschweig, 1954.

DRISCOLL, J. T. ' Totemism.' *The Catholic Encyclopaedia*, XIV, 789-94. 1913.

DRIVER, W. H. ' The Korkus.' *Jour. Asiatic Soc. Beng.*, LXI, 128-32. 1893.

DUBE, S. C. *The Kamar*. Lucknow, 1951.

DUFF-SUTHERLAND-DUNBAR, G. *Abors and Galongs: Notes on Certain Hill Tribes of the Indo-Tibetan Border*. Memoir of the Asiatic Soc. Beng., V, 1-91. 1915.

DURKHEIM, E. *The Elementary Forms of the Religious Life*. London, 1915.

EHRENFELS, O. R. ' The Dual System and Motherright in India.' *Anthropos*, XXXV-XXXVI, 655-80. 1940-1.

— *Motherright in India*. Hyderabad, 1941.

— *Kadar of Cochin*. Madras, 1952.

EICKSTEDT, E. *Rassenkunde und Rassengeschichte der Menschheit*. Stuttgart, 1934.

— *Rassendynamik von Ostasien: China und Japan, Tai und Kmer von der Urzeit bis Heute*. Berlin, 1944.

ELKIN, A. P. ' Totemism in North-Western Australia: The Kimberley Division.' ' Studies in Australian Totemism: Subsection, Section and Moiety Totemism.' ' Studies in Australian Totemism: The Nature of Australian Totemism.' ' Cult Totemism and Mythology in Northern South Australia.' *Oceania*, III, 257-96, 438-81; IV, 65-90; IV, 113-31; V, 171-92. 1933-4.

ELWIN, V. *The Baiga*. London, 1939.

— *The Agaria*. Calcutta, 1942.

— *The Aboriginals*. Bombay, 1943.

— *The Muria and their Ghotul.* Bombay, 1947.

— 'Notes on the Juang.' *Man in India,* xxviii, 1-146. 1948.

— *Bondo Highlander.* Bombay, 1950.

— *The Religion of an Indian Tribe.* Bombay, 1955.

ENDLE, S. *The Kacharis.* London, 1911.

ENTHOVEN, R. E. 'The Study of Ethnography in the Bombay Presidency.' *Journal of the Bombay Anthropological Society,* viii, 433-45. 1909.

— 'Totem Theories.' *Silver Jubilee Memorial Number, Jour. Bom. Anthro. Soc.,* 63-6. 1911.

— *The Tribes and Castes of Bombay.* 3 vols. Bombay, 1920-2.

— 'The Devaks of the Deccan and Konkan.' *Jour. Bom. Anthro. Soc.,* xiii, 1-14. 1924a.

— 'Some Further Notes on the Devaks of the Bombay Presidency.' *Jour. Bom. Anthro. Soc.,* xiii, 649-57. 1924b.

— *The Folklore of Bombay.* Oxford, 1924c.

— *The Folklore of Gujarat.* Undated.

FAWCETT, F. 'The Kondayam Kottai Maravars, a Dravidian Tribe of Tinnevelly, Southern India.' *Jour. Anthro. Institute, Britain and Ireland,* xxxiii, 57-65. 1903.

— *Nayars of Malabar.* Madras, 1915.

FISCHER, E. *The Necessity of Art.* Harmondsworth, 1963.

FISCHER, J. L. 'Totemism on Truk and Ponape.' *American Anthropologist,* l, 250-65. 1957.

FORSYTH, J. *The Highlands of Central India.* London, 1872.

FRAZER, J. G. *Totemism and Exogamy.* 4 vols. London, 1910.

— *Totemica: A Supplement to Totemism and Exogamy.* London, 1937.

FREUD, S. *Totem and Taboo.* (First published in *Imago,* 1912-13.) London, 1960.

FRIEDRICH, A. 'Die Forschung über das frühzeitliche Jägertum.' *Paideuma,* iii, 20-43. 1941.

FRIEND-PEREIRA, J. E. 'Totemism among the Khonds.' *Jour. Asiatic Soc. Beng.,* lxxiii, 39-56. 1904.

FUCHS, S. *The Children of Hari: A Study of the Nimar Balahis in the Central Provinces of India.* Vienna, 1950.

— 'The Social Organisation of the Gond in Eastern Mandla.' *Kultur und Sprache,* ix, 204-17. 1952.

— *Social Origins.* Bombay, 1957.

— *The Gond und Bhumia of Eastern Mandla.* Bombay, 1960a.

— *Tales of Gondwana.* Bombay, 1960b.

FÜRER-HAIMENDORF, C. 'Gibt es in Hinterindien Totemistische Kultur?' *Mitteilungen der Anthropologischen Gesellschaft in Wien,* lxii, 328-37. 1932.

— 'Das Gemeinschaftsleben der Konyak-Naga von Assam.' *MAGW,* lxxi, 1-101. 1941.

— *The Chenchus.* London, 1943a.

— 'Megalithic Ritual among the Gadabas and Bondos of Orissa.' *Jour. Asiatic Soc. Beng.,* ix, 149-78. 1943b.

— 'The Problem of Megalithic Cultures in Middle India.' *Man in India,* xxv, 73-86. 1945a.

— *The Reddis of the Bison Hills: A Study in Acculturation.* London, 1945b.

— *The Raj Gonds of Adilabad.* London, 1948.

— 'Youth-Dormitories and Community Houses in India.' *Anthropos,* xlv, 119-44. 1950.

— ' The Pardhans: The Bards of the Raj Gonds.' *The Eastern Anthro-
pologist*, IV, 172-84. 1951.
— ' New Aspects of the Dravidian Problem.' *Actes du IVe Congrès
International des Sciences Anthropologiques et Ethnologiques*, 162-6.
Vienna, 1954.
GABRIEL, L. *Vom Brahma zur Existenz.* Vienna, 1954.
— *Mensch und Welt in der Entscheidung.* Vienna, 1961.
GAUSDAL, J. *The Santal Khuts.* Oslo, 1960.
GHOSH, H. N. ' The Bhumij of Chota Nagpur.' *Journal, Bihar and
Orissa Research Society*, II, 265-82. 1916.
GHURYE, G. S. ' Dual Organisation In India.' *Jour. Anthro. Institute,
Britain and Ireland*, LIII, 79-91. 1923.
— *Caste and Race in India.* London, 1932.
— *Caste and Class in India.* Bombay, 1950.
— *The Mahadev Kolis.* Bombay, 1957.
— *The Scheduled Tribes.* Bombay, 1959.
— *Family and Kin in Indo-European Culture.* Bombay, 1962a.
— *Gods and Men.* Bombay, 1962b.
GOLDENWEISER, A. A. ' Totemism: An Analytical Study.' *Journal of
American Folklore*, XXIII, 179-293. 1910.
— ' The Method of Investigating Totemism.' *Anthropos*, X-XI, 256-65.
1913-16.
— ' Form and Content in Totemism.' *American Anthropologist*, XX,
280-95. 1918.
— ' Totemism: An Essay on Religion and Society.' V. F. Calverton
(Ed.), *The Making of Man*, 363-92. New York, 1931.
— ' Totemism.' *Encyclopaedia of the Social Sciences*, XIII-XIV. 657-61.
1951.
GORDON, D. H. *The Prehistoric Background of Indian Culture.* Bombay,
1960.
GRAEBNER, F. *Die Methode der Ethnologie.* Heidelberg, 1911
— ' Ethnologie.' Hinneberg's *Kultur der Gegenwart*, V. 435-587.
Leipzig, 1923.
GRIERSON, G. A. ' Munda and Dravidian.' *Linguistic Survey of India*, IV.
Calcutta, 1906.
— *Linguistic Survey of India*, I, Part 1, Introductory. Calcutta, 1927.
GRIFFITHS, W. G. *The Kol Tribe of Central India.* Calcutta, 1946.
GRIGSON, W. V. *The Maria Gonds of Bastar.* London, 1938.
GUHA, B. S. ' Racial Affinities of the Peoples of India.' *Census of India,
1931*, I, India, Part 3, Ethnographical. Simla, 1935.
— ' Progress of Anthropology in India during the Past Twenty-Five
Years.' *Indian Science Congress Association*, 300-35. Calcutta, 1938.
— *Racial Elements in the Population.* Bombay, 1944.
GURDON, P. R. T. *The Khasis.* London, 1907.
HAEKEL, J. ' Pseudo-Totemismus.' *Mitteilungsblatt der Gesellschaft für
Völkerkunde*, Nr. 8, 31-42. 1938.
— ' Uber Wesen und Ursprung des Totemismus.' *MAGW*, LXIX, 243-60.
1939.
— ' Idolkult und Dualsystem bei den Ugriern: Zum Problem des
eurasiatischen Totemismus.' *Archiv für Völkerkunde*, I, 95-163.
1946.
— ' Zum Individual- und Geschlechtstotemismus in Australien.' *Acta
Ethnologica et Linguistica*, 1-75. Vienna, 1950.
— ' Zum Totemismus der afrikanischen Pygmäen.' *Zeitschrift für
Ethnologie*, LXXVI, 157-88. 1951.

— 'Der heutige Stand des Totemismusproblems.' *MAGW*, LXXXII, 33-49. 1952.

— 'Zum Problem des Mutterrechtes.' *Paideuma*, V, 298-322, 481-508. 1953-4.

— 'Zum heutigen Forschungsstand der historischen Ethnologie.' *Festschrift: Die Wiener Schule der Völkerkunde*, 17-90. Vienna, 1956.

— 'Religion.' L. Adam & H. Trimborn: *Lehrbuch der Völkerkunde*, 40-72. Stuttgart, 1958.

— 'Zur gegenwärtigen Forschungssituation der Wiener Schule der Ethnologie.' *Wartenstein Symposion*, 127-47. Horn, Niederösterreich, 1959a.

— 'Trends and Intellectual Interests in Current Austrian Ethnology.' *American Anthropologist*, LXI, 865-74. 1959b.

— 'Bemerkungen zu Rahmanns Besprechung von J. Hackel: Zum heutigen Forschungsstand der historischen Ethnologie.' *Anthropos*, LVI, 274-6. 1961.

— 'Totemismus.' *Die Religion in Geschichte und Gegenwart*, VI, 954-5. 1962.

HAHN, F. 'Some Notes on the Religion and Superstitions of the Oraos.' *Jour. Asiatic Soc. Beng.*, LXXII, Part 3, 12-19. 1904.

HASSAN, S. S. *The Castes and Tribes of H.E.H. the Nizam's Dominions.* Bombay, 1920.

HELD, G. J. *The Mahabharata: An Ethnological Study.* London, 1935.

HEINE-GELDERN, R. 'Gibt es eine austroasiatische Rasse?' *Archiv für Anthropologie*, 79-99. Braunschweig, 1920.

— 'Mutterrecht und Kopfjagd im westlichen Hinterindien.' *MAGW*, LI, 105-40. 1921.

— 'Die Megalithen Südostasiens und ihre Bedeutung für die Klärung der Megalithenfrage in Europa und Polynesien.' *Anthropos*, XXIII, 276-315. 1928a.

— 'Ein Beitrag zur Chronologie des Neolithikums in Südostasien.' *Festschrift: P. W. Schmidt*, 809-43. Vienna, 1928b.

— 'Orissa und die Mundavölker im Periplus des Erythräischen Meeres.' *Beiträge zur historischen Geographie, Kulturgeographie, Ethnologie, und Kartographie, vornehmlich des Orients*, 157-71. Leipzig and Vienna, 1929.

— 'Urheimat und Früheste Wanderungen der Austronesier.' *Anthropos*, XXVII, 543-619. 1932.

— 'Zur Rassen- und Urgeschichte Indiens.' *Zeitschrift für Ethnologie*, III, 248-52. 1936.

— 'Prehistoric Research in the Netherland Indies.' *Science and Scientists in the Netherland Indies*, 129-67. New York, 1945.

— 'The Coming of the Aryans and the End of the Harappa Civilisation.' *Man*, LVI, 136-40. 1956.

— 'A Special List of Tribes of Primitive Hunters and Food-Gatherers.' *Bulletin of the International Committee on Urgent Anthropological and Ethnological Research*, No. 1, 13-47. Vienna, 1958.

— 'Das Megalithproblem.' *Wartenstein Symposion*, 162-82. Horn, Niederösterreich, 1959.

HERAS, H. *Studies in Proto-Indo-Mediterranean Culture.* Bombay, 1953.

HERRMANN, F. *Symbolik in den Religionen der Naturvölker.* Stuttgart, 1961.

HERSKOVITS, M. J. *Acculturation: The Study of Culture Contact.* New York, 1938.

HEVESY, W. F. *Finnisch-Ugrisches aus Indien.* Vienna, 1932.

— 'A False Linguistic Family.' *Journal of the Bihar and Orissa Research Society*, xx, 251-3. 1934.

— 'Munda Tongues Finno-Ugrian.' *Journal, Bihar and Orissa Research Society*, xxi, 103-5. 1935.

HIVALE, S. *The Pardhans of the Upper Narbada Valley*. Bombay, 1946.

HODSON, T. C. *The Meitheis*. London, 1908.

— *The Naga Tribes of Manipur*. London, 1911.

— *The Primitive Culture of India*. London, 1922.

HOFFMANN, J. 'Principles of Succession and Inheritance among the Mundas.' *Journal, Bihar and Orissa Research Society*, i, 5-19. 1915.

HOFFMANN, J. & VAN EMELEN, A. *Encyclopaedia Mundarica*. 13 vols. Patna, 1930-1941.

HOPKINS, E. W. 'The Background of Totemism.' *The Smithsonian Report for 1918*, 573-84. 1920.

HUTTON, J. H. *The Angami Nagas*. London, 1921a.

— *The Sema Nagas*. London, 1921b.

— 'A Negrito Substratum in the Population of Assam.' *Man in India*, ii, 257-62. 1927.

— *Census of India, 1931, Volume I, Part 1, Report*. Delhi, 1933.

— *Caste in India*. Bombay, 1961.

IYER, ANANTHA KRISHNA L. K. *The Cochin Tribes and Castes*. 2 vols. Madras, 1909-12.

IYER, L. A. K. *The Travancore Tribes and Castes*. 3 vols. Trivandrum, 1937-41.

JACOBS, M. & STERN, B. J. *Outline of Anthropology*. New York, 1947.

JENSEN, A. E. *Mythos und Kult bei Naturvölkern*. Wiesbaden, 1960.

KARANDIKAR, S. V. *Hindu Exogamy*. Bombay, 1928.

KARVE, I. *Kinship Organisation in India*. Poona, 1953.

KHAN, G. A. 'The Chenchus.' *Census of India, 1931, I, India, Part 3, Ethnographical*. Simla, 1935.

KLUCKHOHN, C. 'Some Reflections on the Method and Theory of the Kulturkreislehre.' *American Anthropologist*, xxxviii, 157-96. 1936.

KONRAD, P. 'Zur Ethnographie der Bhils.' *Anthropos*, xxxiv, 23-117. 1939.

KOPPERS, W. 'Kulturkreislehre und Buddhismus.' *Anthropos*, xvi-xvii, 442-58. 1921-2.

— 'Der Totemismus als menschheitsgeschichtliches Problem.' *Anthropos*, xxxi, 159-76. 1936.

— 'The Kolis in North-West India.' *Ethnos*, i-ii, 1-18. 1943.

— 'India and Dual Organisation.' *Acta Tropica*, i, 72-119. 1944.

— *Die Bhil in Zentralindien*. Vienna, 1948.

— 'Zum Rassen- und Sprachenproblem in Indien.' *Die Sprache*, i, 217-34. 1949.

— *Primitive Man and his World Picture*. London, 1952.

— 'Der historische Grundcharakter der Völkerkunde.' *Studium Generale*, vii, 135-43. 1954.

— 'Diffusion: Transmission and Acceptance.' *Yearbook of Anthropology*. New York, 1955.

— 'Grundsätzliches und Geschichtliches zur ethnologischen Kulturkreislehre.' *Wartenstein Symposion*, 110-26. Horn, Niederösterreich, 1959.

KROEBER, A. L. 'Totem and Taboo: An Ethnologic Psycho-Analysis.' *American Anthropologist*, xxii, 48-55. 1920.

— 'Stimulus Diffusion.' *American Anthropologist*, xxxxii, 1-20. 1940.

LANG, A. *The Secret of the Totem*. London, 1905.

LEUVA, K. K. *The Asur: A Study of Primitive Iron-Smelters.* Delhi, 1963.

LEVI-STRAUSS, C. *Le Totémisme Aujourd'hui.* Paris, 1962.

LOWIE, R. H. *The History of Ethnological Theory.* London, 1938.
— *Primitive Religion.* New York, 1948.
— *Primitive Society.* London, 1949.
— *Social Organization.* New York, 1960.

LUARD, C. E. *The Jungle Tribes of Malwa.* Lucknow, 1909a.
— ' Miscellaneous Castes.' *The Ethnographical Survey of the Central Indian Agency,* IV. Lucknow, 1909b.

LUKACS, G. *Studies in European Realism.* London, 1950.

MACDONELL, A. A. *Vedic Mythology.* Strassburg, 1897.

MACIVER, R. M. *The Challenge of the Passing Years.* New York, 1963.

MACPHERSON, W. *Memorials of Service in India.* London, 1865.

MAJUMDAR, D. N. ' Totemism and Origin of Clans.' *Journal of the American Oriental Society,* L, 221-32.
— *A Tribe in Transition: A Study in Culture Pattern.* Calcutta, 1937.
— ' The Relationship of the Austric-speaking Tribes of India, with special reference to the Measurements of Hos and Saoras.' *Proceedings of the Indian Academy of Sciences,* VII, 1-21. 1938.
— ' Tribal Culture and Acculturation.' *Man in India,* XIX, Nos. 2-3. 1939.
— *The Fortunes of Primitive Tribes.* Lucknow, 1944.
— *The Affairs of a Tribe: A Study in Tribal Dynamics.* Lucknow, 1950a.
— *Race Realities in Cultural Gujarat.* Bombay, 1950b.
— *Races and Cultures of India.* Bombay, 1961.

MAJUMDAR, D. N. & MADAN, T. N. *An Introduction to Social Anthropology.* Bombay, 1956.

MALINOWSKI, B. *Die Dynamik des Kulturwandels.* Vienna and Stuttgart, 1951.

MANNDORFF, H. ' Notes on Some Primitive Hunting Tribes of Southern and Central India.' *Bulletin of the International Committee on Urgent Anthropological and Ethnological Research,* No. 3, 40-4. 1960.

MARINGER, J. *Vorgeschichtliche Religion.* Cologne, 1956.

MAZUMDAR, B. C. *The Aborigines of the Highlands of Central India.* Calcutta, 1927.

MENGHIN, O. *Weltgeschichte der Steinzeit.* Vienna, 1931.

MILKE, W. ' Totemzentren und Vermehrungsriten in Australien und Ozeanien.' *Zeitschrift für Ethnologie,* LXXXVI, 211-27. 1937.

MILLS, J. P. *The Lhota Nagas.* London, 1922.
— *The Ao Nagas.* London, 1926.
— ' Folk Tales in Lhota Naga.' *Journal and Proceedings, Asiatic Soc. Beng., New Series,* XXII, 239-318. 1928.
— *The Rengma Nagas.* London, 1937.

MONFRINI, P. S. *La Tribu dei Santal.* Milan, 1929.

MUKHERJEE, B. ' Socio-economic Organisation of the Kanikkar of Travancore.' *Bull. Dept. Anthro.,* II, 33-82. Calcutta, 1953.

MULLAN, C. S. *Census of India, 1931, III, Assam, Part 1, Report.* Shillong. 1932.

MURDOCK, J. P. *Social Structure.* New York, 1949.

NAG, D. S. *Tribal Economy.* Delhi, 1958.

NAIK, T. B. ' Territorial Exogamy.' *Man in India,* XXIX, 6-17. 1949.
— *The Bhils.* Delhi, 1956.

NANJUNDAYYA, H. V. & IYER, ANANTHA KRISHNA. *The Mysore Tribes and Castes.* 4 vols. Mysore, 1928-35.

20

NARR, K. J. ' Das höhere Jägertum: Jüngere Jagd- und Sammelstufe.' *Historia Mundi*, I, 502-22. Berne, 1952.
— *Urgeschichte der Kultur*. Stuttgart, 1961.

NATH, Y. V. S. *Bhils of Ratanmal*. Baroda, 1961.

NIGGEMEYER, H. ' Totemismus in Vorderindien.' *Anthropos*, XXVIII, 407-61, 579-619. 1933.
— *Kuttia Kond: Dschungelbauern in Orissa*. Munich, 1964.

PARRY, N. E. *The Lakhers*. London, 1932.

PENNIMAN, T. K. *A Hundred Years of Anthropology*. London, 1952.

PETRI, H. ' Kult-Totemismus in Australien.' *Paideuma*, IV, 44-58. 1950.

PIDDINGTON, R. *An Introduction to Social Anthropology*. London, 1950.

PIGGOTT, S. *Prehistoric India*. Harmondsworth, 1950.

PLAYFAIR, A. *The Garos*. London, 1909.

PRZYLUSKI, J. ' Totémisme et Végétalisme dans l'Inde.' *Revue de l'Histoire des Religions*, XLVI, 347-64. 1927.

PUNEKAR, B. V. *The Son Kolis of Bombay*. Bombay, 1959.

RADCLIFFE-BROWN, A. R. ' The Definition of Totemism.' *Anthropos*, IX, 622-30. 1914.
— *The Andaman Islanders*. Cambridge, 1933.
— *Structure and Function in Primitive Society*. London, 1952.

RAGHAVIAH, R. *The Yanadis*. Delhi, 1962.

RAHMANN, R. ' Gottheiten der Primitivstämme im Nordöstlichen Vorderindien.' *Anthropos*, XXXI, 37-96. 1936.

RANDA, A. *Handbuch der Weltgeschichte*, I. Olten, Switzerland, 1954.

RAO, C. H. ' The Kasubas: A Forest Tribe of the Nilgiris.' *Anthropos*, V, 178-81. 1909.
— ' The Gonds of the Eastern Ghauts, India.' *Anthropos*, V, 791-7. 1910.

RAO, P. S. *Among the Gonds of Adilabad*. Hyderabad, 1949.

RAY CHOWDHURY, T. C. ' The Bhumij of Mayurbhanj—Orissa.' *Man in India*, IX, 95-115. 1929.

RISLEY, H. ' Primitive Marriage in Bengal.' *The Asiatic Quarterly Review*, July, 71-96. 1886.
— *The Tribes and Castes of Bengal*. 2 vols. Calcutta, 1891-2.
— *The Peoples of India*. London, 1915.

RISLEY, H. & GAIT, E. *Census of India, 1901, I, India, Part 1, Report*. Calcutta, 1903.

RIVERS, W. H. R. *The Todas*. New York, 1906.

ROBERTSON, A. *The Mahar Folk*. Calcutta, 1938.

ROHEIM, G. *Australian Totemism: A Psycho-Analytic Study in Anthropology*. London, 1925.

ROSE, H. A. *A Glossary of the Tribes and Castes of the Punjab and North-West Frontier Province*. 3 vols. Lahore, 1911-19.

ROY, S. C. *The Mundas and their Country*. Calcutta, 1912.
— ' Probable Traces of Totem Worship among the Oraons.' *Journal, Bihar and Orissa Research Society*, I, 53-6. 1915a.
— *The Oraons of Chota Nagpur*. Ranchi, 1915b.
— ' A Note on Totemism amongst the Asurs.' *JBORS*, III, 567-71. 1917.
— ' The Pahiras of Chota Nagpur.' ' Kinship and Marriage Organisation of the Pahiras.' *JBORS*, VI, 527-39; VII, 25-32. 1920, 1921.
— ' The Black Bhils of Jaisamand Lake in Rajputana.' *JBORS*, X, 97-113. 1924.
— ' Totemism and Religion.' *JBORS*, XI, 162-76. 1925a.

— *The Birhors: A little-known jungle-tribe of Chota Nagpur.* Ranchi, 1925b.

— 'The Asurs—ancient and modern.' *JBORS*, xii, 147-52. 1926.

— *Oraon Religion and Customs.* Ranchi, 1928.

— 'Some Interesting Aspects of Orissan Ethnology.' *JBORS*, xxiv, 319-35. 1933.

— *The Hill Bhuiyas of Orissa.* Ranchi, 1935.

ROY, S. C. & ROY, R. C. *The Kharias.* Ranchi, 1937.

RUBEN, W. *Eisenschmiede und Dämonen in Indien.* Leiden, 1939.

RUSSELL, R. V. & HIRALAL. *The Tribes and Castes of the Central Provinces of India.* 4 vols. London, 1916.

SALDANHA, J. A. 'Balis and Totems in Kanara.' *Jour. Bom. Anthro. Soc.*, viii, 382-7. 1909.

— 'Balis and Totems in Kanara.' *Jour. Bom. Anthro. Soc.*, ix, 255-80. 1912.

SANKALIA, H. D. *Indian Archaeology Today.* London, 1962.

SARKAR, S. S. *The Malers of the Rajmahal Hills.* Calcutta, 1938.

— *The Aboriginal Races of India.* Calcutta, 1954.

SAVE, K. J. *The Warlis.* Bombay, 1945.

SCHMIDT, W. *Die Mon-Khmer Völker: Ein Bindeglied zwischen Völkern Zentralasiens und Austronesiens.* Braunschweig, 1906.

— 'Totemismus, viehzüchterischer Nomadismus und Mutterrecht.' *Anthropos*, x-xi, 593-610. 1915-16.

— 'Die Abwendung vom Evolutionismus und die Hinwendung zum Historizismus in der Amerikanistik.' *Anthropos*, xvi-xvii, 487-519. 1921-2.

— *The Origin and Growth of Religion.* London, 1931.

— 'Die Stellung der Munda Sprachen.' *Bulletin, School of Oriental Studies, London*, vii, 729-38. 1945.

— 'Rejoinder to Bowles.' *Anthropos*, xli-xliv, 924-9. 1946-9.

SCHMIDT, W. & KOPPERS, W. *Völker und Kulturen.* Regensburg, 1924.

— *Handbuch der Methode der kulturhistorischen Ethnologie.* Münster, 1937.

SCHNEIDER, D. M. & GOUGH, K. *Matrilineal Kinship.* Berkeley and Los Angeles, 1961.

SELIGMANN, C. G. & B. Z. *The Veddas.* Cambridge, 1911.

SHAFER, R. *Ethnography of Ancient India.* Wiesbaden, 1954.

SHAH, P. G. *The Dublas of Gujarat.* Delhi, 1958.

— *Naikas-Naikdas—A Gujarati Tribe.* Bombay, 1959.

SHAKESPEAR, J. *The Lushei Kuki Clans.* London, 1912.

SIEBER, S. A. & MUELLER, F. H. *The Social Life of Primitive Man.* Techny, Illinois, 1950.

SINGH, I. *The Gondwana and the Gonds.* Lucknow, 1944.

SMITH, W. C. *The Ao Naga Tribe of Assam: A Study in Ethnology and Sociology.* London, 1925.

SOMASUNDARAM, A. M. 'A Note on the Gadabas of Koraput District.' *Man in India*, xxix, 36-45. 1949.

STURROCK, J. *Madras District Manuals: South Canara.* 2 vols. Madras, 1894-5.

SUBBARAO, B. *The Personality of India.* Baroda, 1958.

TAMARIA, D. N. S. 'A Few Traditions Regarding the Origin of Tamaria Clans.' *Man in India*, ii, 176-82. 1922.

THURNWALD, R. 'Die Psychologie des Totemismus.' *Anthropos*, xii-xiii, 1094-113; xiv-xv, 496-531. 1917-20.

THURSTON, E. & RANGACHARI, K. *Castes and Tribes of Southern India.* 7 vols. Madras, 1909.

TOD, J. *Annals and Antiquities of Rajasthan or the Central and Western Rajput States of India.* London, 1920.

VENKATACHAR, C. S. ' Central India Agency.' *Census of India, 1931, XX, Part 1, Report.* Delhi, 1933.

VIDYARTHI, L. P. *The Maler.* Calcutta, 1963.

WARNER, W. LLOYD. *A Black Civilisation.* Chicago, 1958.

WEBSTER, H. *Taboo: A Sociological Study.* London, 1942.

WELING, A. N. *The Katkaris.* Bombay, 1934.

WENINGER, M. ' Physisch-Anthropologische Untersuchungen an einigen Stämmen Zentralindiens. '*Acta Ethnologica et Linguistica, 3.* Vienna, 1952.

WHEELER, R. E. M. ' Brahmagiri and Chandravalli 1947, Megalithic and other Cultures in Chitaldrug District, Mysore State.' *Ancient India, 4.* 1947-8.

— *The Indus Civilisation.* Cambridge, 1953.

WINFIELD, W. *A Grammar of the Kui Language.* Calcutta, 1928.

WINICK, C. *Dictionary of Anthropology.* New York, 1956.

ZERRIES O. *Wild- und Buschgeister in Südamerika.* Wiesbaden, 1954.

ZINKIN, T. *Caste Today.* London, 1962.

*Essays in Anthropology Presented to Rai Bahadur Sarat Chandra Roy.* Lucknow, undated.

*Census of India, Assam, I, Report, 1891.*

*Notes and Queries on Anthropology.* London, 1951.

# INDEX

In the following pages all the tribes and castes, both totemic and non-totemic, which have their habitat in the area to which this study pertains and which have been mentioned in it have been duly registered. In general Niggemeyer's list of totemic tribes and castes in India (*Anthropos*, XXVIII, 601-19, 1933) will also be found useful.

Teli, 187

Telugu-speaking population, 61, 84, 85, 92, 93, 168, 173-8, 224, 238, 239, 240, 241, 243, 268

Thakur, 194, 196, 198, 200, 244

theriomorphism, 269

Thomson, George, 49-50, 51, 59n

Thurnwald, R., 19-20, 52

Thurston, E., 119, 149, 171-86 *pass.*, 199, 229, 255, 256

Tibetans, 265n

time criteria, 21, 27

Tod, James, 203, 251

Toda, 67, 173

Togata, 176

Toreya, 184, 244-5

totem, ambivalent attitude towards, 48, 51; cross, 9, 137, 138; definition of, 8, 63; emblem, 15, 37, 38, 42, 46, 48, 54, 55, 88, 101, 102, 147, 166, 236; etymology of, 57n; identification, 37, 48, 112, 263n; indirect, 24; linked, 24, 38; mourning for, 37; multiplex, 9, 24, 38, 55, 77; myths, 18, 37, 38, 40, 48, 54, 74, 81, 103, 104-5, 111, 119, 123, 218-19, 228, 230, 235, 259, 273, 283; partial, 24; ritual consumption of, 71, 137, 142, 253, 282; split, 9, 24, 77, 137, 138, 146, 148; taboos, 10, 13, 16, 24, 37, 38, 48; tattoo, 15

totemism, age of, 11, 41; areas of, 25; assimilation of, 6, 13; clan, 33, 36, 38, 39, 41, 42, 51, 52, 53, 54, 55, 56; conception theory of, 9, 11, 71, 72; cult, 55, 233; definitions of, 1, 13, 18, 33, 36, 46, 47, 55-7; descent, 23, 37, 38, 45, 48, 65, 87, 165; disintegration (decline) of, 6, 10, 39, 54, 55, 57, 280; economic-magical theory of, 9, 11, 65, 71; external soul theory of, 9, 71; in Australia, 3, 9, 11, 15, 23-4, 33, 39, 40, 42, 53, 55, 100, 101, 103, 233; independent origins of, 6, 11-12, 35, 41, 44, 54; individual, 9, 13, 17, 25, 33-4, 39-41, 42, 44, 45, 47, 52, 53,

55, 56, 87; in families and lineages, 37, 39, 54, 283; integral approach to, 45-57; Marxist interpretation of, 50; proto-, 36, 43, 45, 47, 50-3, 55, 56, 87, 210, 226, 233, 280, 281; pseudo-, 9, 263n; pure, 10; religious side of, 9-10, 24, 35, 63, 69; sex, 9, 13, 17, 22, 25, 37, 39, 53, 55; single origin of, 6, 35, 41, 45, 226; social side of, 9-10, 35, 63, 69, 71; sociological theory of, 33-5; variability of, 12-15, 48-9, 54-5, 56, 226, 281

*Totemism and Exogamy*, 3, 8, 12, 262n

totemism in India, age of, 2, 67, 85, 225, 260, 281-2; and Hindu gods, 268-9; area of spread, 1, 82, 258, 283; avoidance rules (taboos), 2, 80-1, 123, 165, 199, 272, 277; conceptual, 62, 71; cult, 80, 101, 102, 103, 117, 147, 148, 234-6, 271, 273, 275, 283; descent, 81, 89, 100, 104, 105, 107, 108, 110, 112, 117, 123, 137, 142, 146, 157, 164, 166, 167n, 174, 215-20, 228, 235, 238, 259, 268, 273, 277, 283; disintegration (decline) of, 70, 75, 80, 81, 85, 86, 97, 106, 122, 123, 135, 147, 164, 165, 230, 238, 260, 271, 273-4, 276-7, 283; districts of, 2, 74, 83, 281-2; early works on, 3-4; individual, 2, 79, 97, 98-100, 124, 146, 165, 166, 210, 228, 282; inheritance of, 1, 78-9, 93, 98, 101, 138, 199-200, 242, 281, 283; in Vedic literature, 262n, 268; matrilineal-totemic regions, 1, 25, 26, 78-9, 82-3, 281, 282; mourning for the totem, 2, 80, 81, 89, 98, 114, 121, 134, 137, 138, 143, 152, 219, 238, 246, 258, 271, 275, 283; multiple origins of, 69, 253; non-genuine totems, 77, 83, 85, 177, 199, 240, 277, 282; original bearers of, 2, 4, 61, 67, 74, 83-5, 92, 125, 126, 129, 154, 166, 224-5, 232, 258, 284; place of origin, 86, 225-6, 281; primary centre of, 238, 239, 258-9,

3